Learning Disability Subtyping

Stephen R. Hooper   W. Grant Willis

Learning Disability Subtyping

Neuropsychological Foundations,
Conceptual Models, and Issues in
Clinical Differentiation

Springer-Verlag
New York Berlin Heidelberg
London Paris Tokyo

Stephen R. Hooper Ph.D.
The Clinical Center for the Study of Development and Learning
Department of Psychiatry
University of North Carolina School of Medicine
Chapel Hill, NC 27599-7255, USA

W. Grant Willis Ph.D.
Department of Psychology
University of Rhode Island
Kingston, RI 02881-0808, USA

Library of Congress Cataloging-in-Publication Data
Hooper, Stephen R.
    Learning disability subtyping : neuropsychological foundations,
conceptual models, and issues in clinical differentiation / Stephen
R. Hooper, W. Grant Willis.
        p. cm.
    Bibliography: p.
    Includes index.
    ISBN (invalid) 0-387-96803-3 (alk. paper)
    1. Learning disabilities.   I. Willis, W. Grant.   II. Title.
    [DNLM: 1. Learning Disorders—classification.   WS 15 H788L]
RJ506.L4H66   1989
G18.92'858—dc19
DNLM/DLC
for Library of Congress   88-39218

Printed on acid-free paper.

Typeset by Asco Trade Typesetting Ltd., North Point, Hong Kong.
Printed and bound by R.R. Donnelley & Sons, Harrisonburg, Virginia.
Printed in the United States of America.

9 8 7 6 5 4 3 2 1

ISBN 0-387-96808-3 Springer-Verlag New York Berlin Heidelberg
ISBN 3-540-96808-3 Springer-Verlag Berlin Heidelberg New York

To my family (S.R.H.)
To people with learning disabilities (W.G.W.)

Foreword

The publication of this very important volume comes at a timely juncture in the history of learning disabilities. The focus of this volume is on developing a multidisciplinary understanding of the complexities of the research on learning disabilities and its various subtypes. It also will serve as an important compendium of the subtyping literature, particularly with respect to pertinent issues of nosology, specific subtyping models, neuropsychological diagnosis, and treatment.

As the authors so correctly suggest, the differential diagnosis of learning disabilities subtypes is a critical first step in developing theoretically sound programs of psychoeducational intervention. Clearly, one must have some idea about the general abilities of a child before realistic expectations can be charted. Also, how can one plan a program of intervention without some knowledge of the deficient components of achievement within a domain? Does it not make both conceptual and practical sense to identify an individual's relative strengths and weaknesses so that abilities or strengths can be utilized to optimize functioning in areas of deficit? Although these all sound like reasonable precursors to assisting individuals in need of academic assistance, there are those who would argue otherwise. Importantly, however, the Director of the National Institutes of Health, in a recent report to Congress, advocates exactly what this volume proposes.

Indeed, there are important needs to be addressed, and the literature reviewed herein strongly supports the conclusions drawn by these authors. There is ample evidence of subtypes of learning disabilities, and a concurrent need exists for a standardized nosology. There is a need for more psychometrically refined neuropsychological and neurodiagnostic procedures, both for children currently in school and for those of preschool age. There also is an urgent need for standardized markers and variables that should be employed in all research efforts. There are studies currently underway that are investigating the very specific issue of whether subtype-by-treatment interactions occur and to what degree. Although there are few actual data about this important issue, within the next 5 years, some conclusions may indeed be warranted. This volume succeeds in outlining many of the issues with respect to treatment.

Thus, in my view, the authors of this volume have provided us all (e.g., psychologists, educators, physicians, and parents) with a comprehensive neuropsychological perspective as to what the presumed neurological basis is, how cognitive, academic, linguistic, and social-emotional systems are implicated, how the subtypes can be viewed as discretely different, and what the literature says about assessment and intervention. This book does far more than summarize the present state of affairs in a well written manner; it provides a solid conceptual perspective about where we have been, what we have done, and perhaps most important, what we need to do next to ensure that learning-disabled individuals will profit from our most productive research efforts.

University of Georgia   George W. Hynd
Athens, Georgia

Preface

The conceptualization of learning disabilities has a long history. Case descriptions of children with unusual learning profiles, for example, were presented in the 1800s. Although the actual term, *learning disability*, was not coined until the middle 1960s, the clinical and research legacy left a trail of findings supporting the existence of such a learning phenomenon. Many of the findings related to this phenomenon, however, were conflictual and, subsequently, provided little guidance to the clinician and researcher interested in working with these children. These concerns did not constrain researchers' efforts to investigate this disorder but, unfortunately, these efforts rarely occurred from a unified perspective.

From both research and clinical perspectives, the study of learning disabilities had become a burdensome and confusing quagmire. There were blatant problems in the clinical components of evaluation, diagnosis, and treatment. Problems also existed in even more fundamental aspects of this disorder, including such basics as definitional issues and conceptual foundations. Although clinicians and researchers continue to struggle with these difficulties when working with this population, there have been relatively recent advances in this field that may help to bring greater clarification and understanding to this clinical and research area.

Over the past three decades, there has been a steady proliferation of research investigating the neuropsychological factors contributing to learning disabilities. One of the major research trends that has emerged from these efforts is that a learning disability actually is a generic classification that represents a heterogeneous group of neurologically based disorders. The identification of reliable subtypes has the potential to lend assistance to the evaluation and diagnosis of learning disorders. It also has the potential to improve the specificity of treatment programs and intervention plans for these individuals. By attempting to classify learning problems according to more homogeneous groupings, researchers will be able to begin to bring some clarity to the confusing mass of learning disability research that has been conducted to date. Research efforts ultimately will become more theoretically sound and, thus, clinically useful if a reliable and valid classification model can be developed.

Given this evolving literature on learning disability subtyping, it becomes important for this information to be gathered from time to time in a single resource so that it can be evaluated efficiently and effectively. Rourke (1985) presented the first publication addressing this need, largely focusing on his landmark efforts in the subtyping area. In a complementary fashion, this volume also addresses this need by providing a comprehensive compendium of the subtyping models derived to date. As such, the volume is intended for students, practitioners, and researchers across a wide array of fields who are interested in learning disability subtyping.

The book is divided into four major sections. The first section is concerned with providing a historical and conceptual framework from which to view the subtyping efforts. Chapter 1 provides an overview of historical antecedents to learning disabilities, along with a discussion of definitional issues crucial to this field. Chapter 2 is concerned with the neurological foundations for the study of learning disability subtyping and its proposed classification models.

The second section is devoted exclusively to the various subtyping models. Chapter 3 deals with an overview of all of the clinical-inferential subtyping attempts completed to date, and Chapter 4 presents an overview of classification models employing empirical strategies and techniques. Specific issues directly related to subtype derivation are discussed in Chapter 5.

The third section deals with specific components of the subtyping process. Chapter 6 is concerned with the neuropsychological assessment of subtypes, and Chapter 7 deals with emergent concerns pertaining to important social-emotional features of learning disability subtypes. Chapter 8 provides an overview of treatment models and issues related to intervention programs with children showing particular learning profiles. A particular emphasis in this chapter is placed on the few studies that have been conducted to date exploring treatment interventions for specific subtypes.

Finally, the last section provides a summary of the literature published to date, emphasizing recent advances and future directions of the subtyping endeavor.

The classification of children with learning disabilities has extraordinary potential to bring greater clarity to clinical and experimental efforts in this field. We hope that our overview of the subtyping literature and related issues contributes to this important endeavor.

Chapel Hill, NC   Stephen R. Hooper
Kingston, RI   W. Grant Willis

Acknowledgments

Although the time spent drafting and redrafting this volume was great, our efforts would never have reached fruition without the help of several "significant others." We would like to extend our sincere appreciation to Teresa Buckner and Elizabeth Scott at the Clinical Center for the Study of Development and Learning for their efficient clerical assistance in preparing this volume. We also would like to thank Dr. Mary Gail Becker at The Pennsylvania State University for her input on several of the chapters. Finally, we would be remiss if a heart-felt "thank you" were not given to the editorial staff at Springer-Verlag. In particular, we would like to thank Dr. Robert Kidd for his unending patience with us during the process of completing this volume. Despite this excellent support, however, we remain responsible for any shortcomings of this volume.

Contents

Foreword vii
  George W. Hynd
Preface ix
Acknowledgments xi

SECTION I: FOUNDATIONS FOR SUBTYPE ANALYSIS

1 Historical Foundations and Definitional Issues 3
    Early Case Studies 4
    Single-Factor Conceptualizations 6
    Case Study Methodology Revisited 12
    Definitional Issues in Learning Disabilities 13
    Summary 18

2 Neuropsychological Foundations 20
    Nervous System Development 21
    Functional Brain Organization 23
    Functional Systems 29
    Conclusions 37

SECTION II: SUBTYPING MODELS AND CLASSIFICATION ISSUES

3 Clinical-Inferential Classification Models 41
    Achievement Classification Models 41
    Neurocognitive Classification Models 50
    Neurolinguistic Classification Models 56
    Combined Classification Models 58
    Conclusions 60

4 Empirical Classification Models 62
    Empirical Classification Methods 63

Achievement Classification Models 71
Neurocognitive Classification Models 73
Neurolinguistic Classification Models 81
Combined Classification Models 83
Behavioral Classification Models 90
Conclusions 91

5 Issues in Classification and Subtype Derivation 92
Definitional and Conceptual Issues 92
Sampling Issues 98
Variable Selection 101
Developmental Considerations 103
Empirical Versus Clinical-Inferential Classification Methods 104
Conclusions 105

SECTION III: CLINICAL ISSUES RELATED TO SUBTYPING

6 Neuropsychological Assessment 109
Neuropsychological Approaches 110
Issues in Neuropsychological Assessment of Subtypes 134
Conclusions 138

7 Social-Emotional Features 139
Research with Heterogeneous Groups 140
Research with Homogeneous Groups 147
Conclusions 162

8 Treatment 164
Unidimensional Treatment Approaches 165
Neuropsychologically Based Treatment Approaches 169
Subtype-to-Treatment Linkages 177
Issues in Subtype-to-Treatment Planning 189
Summary 192

SECTION IV: EPILOGUE

9 Summary and Future Directions 195
Advances in Learning Disability Subtyping 196
Future Directions 200

References 202
Author Index 237
Subject Index 247

Section I Foundations for Subtype Analysis

1
Historical Foundations and Definitional Issues

The conceptualization of learning disabilities has progressed from attempts to identify a single underlying cause to attempts to implicate multiple, perhaps interactive, factors. This trend, clearly evident in the ongoing development of its definitions, acknowledges the heterogeneous nature of learning disabilities. Research endeavors also have emerged to address this claim from theoretical and applied perspectives. The conceptualization of learning disabilities as a heterogeneous group of disorders has received support from the field of neuropsychology (e.g., Rourke, 1985), as well as from other related fields such as neurology and neuropathology. As is discussed in Chapter 2, contemporary neurodevelopmental theory implicates a variety of functional systems in the learning process and disturbances thereof.

Clearly, definitional issues pertaining to learning disabilities will continue to be debated, particularly those pertinent to operational criteria for the clinician (see, e.g., Bryan, Bay, & Donahue, 1988), and evidence will continue to be advanced to improve our understanding of neurodevelopment and functional brain organization in this population. It also is clear that the conceptualization of learning disabilities as a heterogeneous classification is rapidly gaining acceptance. In fact, Rourke (1983) has stated that "the determination of reliable subtypes of learning disabilities would appear to be the most pressing issue at this time" (p. 573) confronting the study of learning problems. Similarly, Adelman and Taylor (1986) called for research efforts to be directed toward the development of valid differential diagnostic procedures. They advocated the importance of using procedures that distinguish between various kinds of learning disabilities and those that differentiate learning disabilities from other kinds of handicaps that impede learning (e.g., Mental Retardation, Attention-deficit Hyperactivity Disorder). Essential to such efforts is the need for a theoretically based, clinically relevant classification scheme. Such a nosology would facilitate comparisons of research across studies and samples.

In contrast, other investigators might argue that because definitional issues are the foundation for developing a classification system for learning disabilities, these issues should be resolved first. For example, the lack of a guiding, accepted, and relatively adequate definition of learning disabilities has prompted some investigators to question even the existence of these disorders (Algozzine & Ysseldyke, 1986; Epps, Ysseldyke, & Algozzine, 1983, 1985). These arguments not withstanding, the evidence supporting the existence of learning disabilities is substantial (Childs & Finucci, 1983; Wilson, 1985) and there have been numerous attempts to investigate the heterogeneity of this group of learning problems.

Although these definitional difficulties and subsequent diagnostic criteria will continue to be debated, it is clear that individuals with learning disabilities represent an increasing number, with many having significant educational, social, and, perhaps, psychiatric needs. With the increased survival rate of many high-risk infants, estimates have been projected that the population of children with learning disabilities will exceed the combined population of children with seizure disorders, cerebral palsies, and severe mental retardation (Duane, 1979). Clinically, this figure translates into an expected incidence rate of about 20 to 30 children per 1,000 (Hynd, Obrzut, Hayes, & Becker, 1986). Further, figures from the U.S. Department of Education (1984) reveal that learning disabled children account for 38% of all special education recipients, making this the number one disability in terms of categorical funding (Doris, 1986). Consequently, the study of learning disabilities will continue to be an important area to the clinician and researcher.

This chapter addresses the study of learning disability subtyping from a historical perspective. Such a perspective is useful in forming the foundation for the study of learning disability subtyping and its proposed classification models. Early case study data are presented to illustrate the heterogeneity of this group of disorders. Some of the single-factor theories proposed to account for learning problems are then briefly discussed. The recent resurgence of case study methodology in studying learning disabilities also is presented. Finally, an overview of the development of contemporary definitions of learning disabilities is presented and some related diagnostic issues are identified.

Early Case Studies

Kirk (1963) is generally recognized as coining the term *learning disability*, but the study of children with specific learning difficulties has a clinical and research legacy dating back over 100 years. At that time several investigators presented case study data depicting learning problems of a specific nature. Kussmaul (1877) was among the first scientists to report a patient who, although having no visual impairment, was unable to read words. Kussmaul used the term *word blindness* to describe this condition.

Hinshelwood (1895) later described two adult cases who had been referred to him because of visual difficulties. The first patient, a middle-aged male with no previous medical history, was employed as a teacher of French and German languages. About 1 month prior to his evaluation, this man found himself unable to read a student's written work. Upon evaluation the man could identify numbers and, although he could see letters, he was unable to label them. Surprisingly, he showed no memory deficits or problems with writing fluently to dictation, but he could not read what he had written. A right homonymous hemianopsia (i.e., a right visual half-field loss in each eye) was present. Despite 6 months of intervention, little improvement was noted in this patient's reading skills.

Hinshelwood's second case was a 38-year-old female who apparently had experienced a seizure 1 year prior to evaluation. Although her main complaints were headaches and visual difficulties, she evidenced right-sided weakness and mild speech problems. Although this women showed adequate visual acuity, she had difficulty recognizing her surroundings, she could not read, and a right visual-field deficit was present. In comparing these two cases, Hinshelwood was perhaps the first investigator to recognize the heterogeneity of specific learning difficulties and to assert the importance of a thorough assessment in delineating differences between such cases.

Morgan (1896) was among the first to describe an adolescent case with specific learning problems. He reported that after 7 years of instruction, a 14-year-old male could read only letters and single syllables. The adolescent's writing to dictation also was poor. Morgan called this set of symptoms, "pure word blindness." In 1898 Bastian described another adolescent with similar symptoms. Despite adequate speech and language skills, athletic prowess, and good arithmetic skills, an 18-year-old male consistently manifested word reversals in reading and severe deficiencies in spelling.

Additional case reports of specific learning problems continued to appear at the beginning of the 1900s. Following his adult cases, Hinshelwood (1900, 1902) presented two child cases showing similar academic deficits (i.e., reading problems), but relatively different symptom profiles. Both cases were diagnosed as "congenital word blindness." The older patient (age 11 years) had an exceptional auditory memory and demonstrated this by learning his assignments without reading. He could recite the alphabet, verbally label pictures, and spell most monosyllabic words. He could recognize only a few letters and words by sight, however, even after 4 years of instruction. In contrast, the younger patient (age 10 years) maintained an adequate sight-word vocabulary, but evidenced difficulty reading uncommon monosyllabic words. Spelling skills also were relatively intact in this patient.

Other cases reported during this time further emphasized the heterogeneous nature of specific learning deficits. Several of these case reports postulated that a familial component might be contributing to learning difficulties. Stephenson (1905), for example, described a case of congenital word blindness affecting three generations. He reported that a 14-year-old female patient, despite significant reading problems, was able to perform mathematics and geometry adequately, demonstrate intact receptive capabilities and memory skills, and show slow but accurate graphomotor abilities. In addition, this case was significant for a positive family history of reading disorder, extending to her maternal aunts and maternal grandmother.

Fisher (1905) described the case of a 6-year-old female with reading problems that provided further support for a familial component to this specific learning impediment. This patient presented numerous letter reversals and juxtapositions in her reading, performed poorly on arithmetic tasks, and misnamed musical notes. The family history included an uncle with chronic reading and spelling problems. Hinshelwood (1909) further substantiated a possible familial component of reading problems by describing four such cases occurring within the same family.

Jackson (1906) was among the first from the United States to contribute to this evolving literature. He described two additional cases and noted a greater frequency of specific reading problems among males than females. In an attempt to refine the conceptualization of congenital word blindness, Jackson proposed the term *developmental alexia*. He defined this as a developmental problem related to the recognition of written symbols.

Other such terms also began to emerge. Clairborne (1906), for example, introduced the term *word amblyopia* (i.e., incomplete word blindness). *Bradylexia, congenital word blindness*, and *amnesia visualis verbalis*, to name but a few, were introduced by others (see Hynd & Cohen, 1983; Pirozzolo, 1979). As can be surmised, each term was derived on the basis of specific case observations and the orientation of the different investigators.

Given these early case reports, a knowledge base with respect to specific learning problems (i.e., reading) was beginning to be established by the early 1900s. By this time, accumulated data suggested that learning disabilities: (a) were present in children, adolescents, and adults with relatively intact cognitive functions; (b) occurred more frequently among males than females; (c) were heterogeneous in terms of symptom manifestation, differentially affecting reading, spelling, and higher order cognitive functioning; (d) were generally unresponsive to traditional learning opportunities and instructional settings; (e) appeared to have a familial component; and (f) required a comprehensive clinical assessment for accurate diagnosis.

Single-Factor Conceptualizations

Although most of these early case studies suggested that learning problems were heterogeneous in nature, nearly all of the research that followed focused primarily on single-factor conceptualizations. These conceptualizations, most of which stemmed from the work of Orton (1928, 1937), sought to identify a single deficient process that contributed to the learning problem. These studies contributed to a multitude of often disparate single-factor theories.

Although entire volumes have been devoted to single-factor explanations (e.g., Satz, Rardin, & Ross, 1971), five of the most prominent conceptualizations are discussed. These include: (a) delayed development in cerebral dominance (Orton, 1928, 1937; Satz et al., 1971); (b) visual-perceptual deficits (Frostig, 1964; Kephart, 1971; Lyle & Goyen, 1968, 1975); (c) auditory-perceptual deficits and associated language inefficiencies (de Hirsch, Jansky, & Langford, 1966); (d) deficits in intersensory integration (Birch & Belmont, 1964, 1965; Senf, 1969); and (e) attention/memory deficits (Lyle & Goyen, 1968, 1975; Thomson & Wilsher, 1978).

Delayed Cerebral Dominance

The case study approach provided support for the notion of learning disabilities, but it was not until 1928 that a theoretical basis for learning problems was advanced. Orton (1928, 1937), using a more objective approach to assessment, described children who exhibited difficulties with letter sequences, letter differentiation, and letter juxtapositions. Orton attributed these difficulties to a neurodevelopmental failure in establishing cerebral dominance. Based on his clinical observation that there was a higher incidence of reading problems in children with mixed handedness, Orton hypothesized a cerebral explanation. He proposed that the left cerebral hemisphere failed to achieve functional superiority in these children, and that this was directly related to deficiencies in information processing, ultimately leading to reading problems.

Hynd and Cohen (1983) attributed much of the popularity of this conceptualization to its underlying theme of development. The implicit assumption, of course, was that with proper instruction these children could attain normal levels of functioning. The concept of developmental delay or maturational lag subsequently received considerable support (Bakker, 1973; Satz et al., 1971), but more recent scrutiny from a neuropsychological perspective (e.g., Tramontana & Hooper, 1988) has questioned its general validity and clinical utility. As Hynd and Cohen noted, another reason for the popularity of this theory included its deceptive face validity in that many learning disabled children do show mixed lateral preferences for eyedness, handedness, and footedness along with written and visual-perceptual reversals. We now understand, of course, that many non-learning disabled children also show similar lateral preference patterns (Reynolds, 1981b).

The concept of incomplete or delayed cerebral dominance, however, has now been refuted (Benton, 1975; Kinsbourne & Hiscock, 1981). Instead, more complex conceptualizations of learning problems have emerged from hemispheric studies using dichotic listening and visual half-field paradigms (McKeever & Van Deventer, 1975; Witelson & Rabinovitch, 1972; Yeni-Komshian, Isenberg, & Goldstein, 1975). In fact, Thomson (1984) outlined five different research models that have emerged since Orton's original work. These are: (a) a lack of left-hemisphere specialization for language abilities, (b) the concept of maturational delays in cerebral specialization, (c) impairment in the left hemisphere, (d) interference of the right hemisphere with the development of the left, and (e) inefficient interhemispheric integration. Several of these lines of research have been seriously challenged, but Orton's theory was seminal in stimulating over 50 years of scientific investigations with learning problem children and adolescents.

Orton's contributions also influenced Witelson (1976) who proposed that at least two factors are important in the development of reading problems. One of these factors involves the left hemisphere with a disruption of language-based functions. The other factor involves bilateral representation of spatial processing, often considered to be primarily a right-hemisphere task, that interferes with the efficiency or development of linguistic abilities. Witelson's proposal illustrates that Orton's original theory was important to the emergence of subtype conceptualizations and their neurological foundations.

Visual-Perceptual Deficits

Closely related to Orton's delayed cerebral dominance model were several theories implicating deficits in visual-perceptual abilities (Bender, 1956, 1957; Frostig, 1964; Hermann, 1959; Kephart, 1971). Bender (1956, 1957) implicated poor figure-ground visual perception in reading deficits, and Kephart (1971) and Frostig (1964) proposed that faulty visual-motor integration was the underlying cause. Hermann (1959) believed higher order visual-spatial processing deficits primarily were responsible for the learning difficulties, but added an interesting speculation that these specific deficits were genetically based.

Initially, considerable support was generated for these visual-perceptual single-factor conceptualizations (Lyle, 1969; Lyle & Goyen, 1968, 1975). Additional support came from longitudinal investigations searching for precursors of learning disabilities (Satz, Taylor, Friel, & Fletcher, 1978). Data from the Florida Longitudinal Project (Satz et al., 1978) suggested that deficits in visual-perceptual and visual-motor functioning, particularly during the early primary grades, were the best predictors of later learning problems.

Other studies related to the visual-perceptual processing deficit model advanced the notion that disabled learners show faulty eye movements, particularly during reading. These studies showed that reading disabled children had eye movements that were erratic and brief (Bouma & Legein,

1977) with excessive fixations (Pavlidis, 1978; Pirozzolo & Rayner, 1978), regressions (Elterman, Abel, Daroff, Dell 'Osso, & Bornstein, 1980), and return-sweep inaccuracies (Pirozzolo, 1979). Of relevance to the subtyping literature is that Pirozzolo (1979) found that these eye-movement difficulties were associated primarily with a visual-spatial subtype of dyslexia. Faulty eye movements presented less in an auditory-linguistic subtype, particularly on nonreading tasks, and they were not present in a normal comparison sample.

Despite this support, however, other investigators suggested that visual-perceptual deficits were not the sole cause of learning problems (Benton, 1975; Nielsen & Ringe, 1969; Vellutino, 1978). In addition to significant methodological concerns for much of this research in general, Vellutino (1978) noted that many visual-perceptual problems in both younger and older poor readers were secondary to deficiencies in verbal-mediation strategies. Exclusive of Pirozzolo's (1979) work with eye-movement patterns, the visual-perceptual deficit model was unable to account for the multiple deficits found in many learning disabled individuals. Thus, the foundation for a multidimensional conceptualization continued to evolve.

Auditory-Perceptual Deficits

Wepman (1960) initially suggested that auditory discrimination difficulties evolved from developmental delays in speech perception and, in part, were due to auditory acuity. Generally, these difficulties have been associated with poor reading (Goldberg & Schiffman, 1972; Henry, 1975) and deficient spelling (Clark, 1970; Silver, 1968; Valtin, 1973), although other investigators have challenged these results (Hammill & Larsen, 1974; Richardson, Di Benedetton, & Bradley, 1977).

Other researchers have implicated a more complicated relationship between auditory perception and learning difficulties. Tallal (1980) suggested that reading disabled children have a poorer auditory perception that adversely affects the development of phonic skills and efficient auditory processing. Morency, Wepman, and Hass (1970) proposed that auditory discrimination deficits were not necessarily perceptual, but more related to misarticulations and oral-motor dysfunction. Matthews and Seymour (1981) noted a similar conditional relationship.

Extending from the simple auditory processing deficits model to understanding learning disabilities, other investigators began to discover deficits in the related domains of language abilities and linguistic competence. Vellutino (1979) and associates (Vellutino, Steger, DeSetto, & Phillips, 1975; Vellutino, Steger, Kaman, & DeSetto, 1975), for example, presented evidence using verbal and nonverbal learning tasks consistent with the idea that reading disabled children have primary difficulties in verbal learning, verbal abstraction, and generalization of verbal information. Blank and Bridger (1964, 1966) obtained similar findings in their work with disabled

readers and verbal classification. Phonological deficits also have been proposed as being responsible for learning/reading impediments (Denckla &
Rudel, 1976a, 1976b; Fox & Routh, 1980; Montgomery, 1981; Shankweiler
& Liberman, 1972), as well as other linguistic factors such as syntactic competence (Wiig, Semel, & Crouse, 1973), semantic knowledge (Waller,
1976), and the use of one's internal lexicon (Ellis, 1981; Ellis & Miles,
1981).

Similar to the visual-perceptual deficit models, however, the auditory-
perceptual deficit models lacked breadth in accounting for all of the
psychoeducational problems manifested by deficient learners. Further,
many of the language-based models implicated underlying general language disturbances and, in fact, some researchers (Wolfus, Moscovitch, &
Kinsbourne, 1980) have been unable to document a significant relationship
between auditory-perceptual deficits and language/learning impairment.
Finally, as Spreen (1978) cogently noted, if there is a disruption of language that is *general*, then the argument for a learning impediment that is
specific becomes less tenable. Although Spreen's position could be debated, it is clear that underlying language deficiencies, whether general or
specific in their presentation, do not account for all of the deficits that can
be exhibited by the disabled learner.

Intersensory Integration Deficits

Another single-factor model that evolved linked learning disabilities to
poor intersensory integration. Intersensory integration refers to the development of cortical, and perhaps subcortical, connections among the
sensory areas of the brain (e.g., Luria's tertiary regions; see Chapter 2)
that contribute to learning. As such, Birch and Belmont (1964, 1965) suggested that deficits in these connections may be one of the primary con-
tributors to learning impairment.

Birch (1962) noted that inferior learners could be distinguished from
normal learners on tasks demanding intersensory abilities and that these
distinctions were nonspecific with respect to modality. Birch and Belmont
(1964, 1965) provided initial support for this conceptualization, but it
quickly fell into disfavor because of methodological and procedural flaws
(Blank & Bridger, 1966; Blank, Weider, & Bridger, 1968; Sterritt & Rudnick, 1966). For example, data showed that the original studies of Birch
and Belmont measured intramodal integration (i.e., within modality processing such as visual-temporal to visual-spatial connections) rather than
intersensory integration (i.e., between modalities such as auditory to visual
connections). Further, disabled learners were observed to have significant
deficits on both kinds of processing. This led Blank et al. (1968) to suggest
that these deficits were a result of deficient symbolic mediation rather than
specific sensory integration impairment.

Some evidence to support this single-factor conceptualization has emerged from studies employing bisensory memory (Senf, 1969; Senf & Feshback, 1970) and temporal-order recall tasks (Bakker, 1967, 1972). Even using these tasks, however, mixed support has surfaced. Senf and Freundl (1971) speculated that other processes influenced the intersensory integration capabilities of the disabled learner (e.g., being stimulus bound; difficulties discriminating, encoding, and retrieving visual information separate from auditory information; organizational deficiencies) and that intersensory integration could not be solely responsible for the various presentations of learning disabilities. Further, Groenendaal and Bakker (1971) suggested that poor readers showed deficits only in processing the temporal order of verbal material in a meaningful context, and that these children did not differ from normals in the temporal processing of non-meaningful nonverbal stimuli.

Attention/Memory Deficits

Dissatisfied with the rapidly accumulating number of single-factor theories advanced to account for learning disabilities, some investigators attempted to identify a common link among the various perceptual processing deficiencies within this population. Chief among these links were attention-deficit and memory-deficit theories. In an early effort of this kind, for example, Dykman, Ackerman, Clements, and Peters (1971) advocated an attention-deficit explanation for learning disabilities. They suggested that specific visual, auditory, kinesthetic, and expressive impairments were surface manifestations of basic attentional problems. Support for this position accumulated during the 1970s (Hynd, Obrzut, Hynd, & Connor, 1978, Traver & Hallahan, 1974; Traver, Hallahan, Cohen, & Kauffman, 1977; Traver, Hallahan, Kauffman, & Ball, 1976) when Ross (1976) proposed that learning disabled individuals were delayed relative to nonlearning disabled cohorts in terms of selective attentional development. Relatively more recent research (Krupski, 1986; Willis, 1985a) suggested that some of this earlier work may have been influenced by uncontrolled behavioral variance associated with particular task materials and encoding requirements.

Memory deficits also have been implicated as a primary contributor to learning disabilities. Cohen and Netley (1978, 1981), for example, found that disabled readers exhibited limited short-term memory capacity and significant deficits in their use of verbal recall strategies. Similarly, Nelson and Warrington (1980) speculated that the short-term memory deficits in disabled learners were due to poor cognitive interrelationships between both graphemic-phonemic associations and graphemic-semantic associations. This speculation was supported by the work of Jorm (1979a, 1979b).

Although Nelson and Warrington also postulated long-term memory deficits to be present, their results were equivocal. Recent evidence has suggested, however, that apparent long-term memory deficits in learning disabled children are related more to the task of learning how to retrieve information from memory (i.e., strategies) than to specific deficiencies in memory capacity (Brainerd, Kingma, & Howe, 1986). Brainerd et al. (1986) postulated that the effects of this poor and/or inefficient implementation of retrieval strategies are cumulative and, during adolescence and adulthood, would begin to encroach upon memory capacity.

Attention/memory deficits alone, however, have not been able to account for the full range of deficits seen in the learning disabled population. For example, Lyle and Goyen (1968, 1975) contested the purported short-term memory deficits in this population in favor of slow information processing speed. Nonetheless, whether attention/memory deficits are causal or consequential, they frequently occur as specific information processing inefficiencies of the learning disabled individual.

Case Study Methodology Revisited

As the number of single-factor models and, more recently, subtyping models has increased, several investigators have proposed that the search for a specific underlying cause or subtyping model is too simplistic, given the complexities of the central nervous system (Hynd & Hynd, 1984; Hynd, Connor, & Nieves, 1988; Olson, Kliegl, & Davidson, 1983; Olson, Kliegl, Davidson, & Foltz, 1985). Olson et al. (1983, 1985), for instance, proposed that differences among learning disabled individuals are distributed continuously rather than distinctly as would be characteristic of subtypes.

Olson et al. (1985) found individual differences to be present both within and between groups of normal and disabled readers. They also noted, however, that the phonological skill level was related significantly to reading style in the disabled readers, a finding not characteristic of normal readers. Further, these investigators stated that specific reading problems were attributed to the specific situations at designated points of performance on multiple dimensions. This suggests that learning disabilities not only reflect continuous variability, but are dynamic, a finding also supported by Spreen and Haaf (1986). Although this case study approach requires further refinement, the concept of a continuum of cognitive processes is an interesting one because it suggests that subcategorization of variables may be artificial and equivocal.

From a similar perspective, Hynd et al. (1988) considered the neurolinguistic, neuroanatomical, and neurophysiological data on dyslexia and suggested that the number of learning disability subtypes may be limited only by current assessment sophistication. In considering the neuroanatomical correlates of reading disability alone (see Chapter 2), a high degree of psychometric variability would be expected. Thus, Hynd et al. reasoned that, conceptually, each individual case could display a qualitatively different profile of neurolinguistic abilities.

Case study methodology also has been advocated with respect to developing individualized treatment programs (Raim & Adams, 1982; Wilson & Baddeley, 1986). Raim stated that "A case study can help to clarify for the student the puzzling contradictions and the range of irregularities that characterize the learning disabled child" (p. 116). Case studies also support Salvia and Ysseldyke's (1981) "ecology of the child" in the development of appropriate treatment alternatives. Similarly, Wilson and Baddeley (1986) provided a series of case studies of patients with acquired dyslexia in which specific, individualized treatment plans were implemented and evaluated. Their results suggested that the single case study methodology in educational intervention is important within this population. Thus, single case study models for learning disabilities challenge both the theoretical basis as well as the clinical utility of many of the classification approaches currently proposed.

Definitional Issues in Learning Disabilities

Contemporary classification approaches also are challenged by a variety of definitional and diagnostic issues. Definitions of learning disabilities, for example, have been controversial since the introduction of the term. As early as 1972, Cruickshank published a list of 40 different terms used to describe these disorders, and Vaughan and Hodges (1973) subsequently compiled a collection of 38 different definitions. Definitions have continued to proliferate and, more recently, Epps et al. (1983, 1985) described no fewer than 14 different ways to define learning disabilities in an operational manner. Table 1.1 provides five of the official definitions adopted by the United States government and/or the major professional organizations concerned with the study of learning disabilities.

One of the first formal definitions of learning disabilities was proposed by the National Advisory Committee on the Handicapped (NACH) and later was incorporated into the Children with Specific Learning Disability Act of 1969 (P.L. 91-230, The Elementary and Secondary Amendments of 1969). The current federal definition of learning disabilities in the Education for All Handicapped Children Act of 1975 (P.L. 94-142), which was amended in 1986 to include the preschool population (P.L. 99-457), represents only a slight modification of the original NACH definition. These definitions are listed in Table 1.1. Although these definitions served as initial efforts to bring clarity to the field of learning disabilities, they were too general, lacked operational criteria, and treated learning disabilities as a single disorder.

Despite adoption of the P.L. 94-142 definition by nearly all state education departments, there never has been unanimous satisfaction with this definition. In an effort to generate a more acceptable definition of learning disability, representatives from six organizations formed the National Joint Committee for Learning Disabilities (NJCLD). The organizations com-

TABLE 1.1. Definitions of learning disabilities.

National Advisory Committee on the Handicapped (NACH)

Children with special learning disabilities exhibit a disorder in one or more of the basic psychological processes involved in understanding or using spoken or written languages. These may be manifested in disorders of listening, thinking, talking, reading, writing, spelling, or arithmetic. They include conditions which have been referred to as perceptual handicaps, brain injury, minimal brain dysfunction, dyslexia, developmental aphasia, etc. They do *not* include learning problems which are due primarily to visual, hearing or motor handicaps, to mental retardation, emotional disturbance or to environmental disadvantage. (U.S. Office of Education, 1968, p. 34)

Education for All Handicapped Children Act of 1975 (P.L. 94-142)

Specific learning disability means a disorder in one or more of the basic psychological processes involved in understanding or using language, spoken or written, in which the disorder may manifest itself in an imperfect ability to listen, think, speak, read, write, spell, or to do mathematical calculations. The term includes such conditions as perceptual handicaps, brain injury, minimal brain dysfunction, dyslexia, and developmental aphasia. The term does not include children who have learning problems which are primarily the result of visual, hearing, or motor handicaps, or mental retardation, or emotional disturbance, or of environmental cultural, or economic disadvantage. (U.S. Office of Education, 1977, p. 65083)

National Joint Committee for Learning Disabilities (NJCLD)

Learning disabilities is a generic term that refers to a heterogeneous group of disorders manifested by significant difficulties in the acquisition and use of listening, speaking, reading, writing, reasoning or mathematical abilities. These disorders are intrinsic to the individual and presumed to be due to central nervous system dysfunction. Even though a learning disability may occur concomitantly with other handicapping conditions (e.g., sensory impairment, mental retardation, social and emotional disturbance) or environmental influences (e.g., cultural differences, insufficient/inappropriate instruction, psychogenic factors), it is not the direct result of those conditions or influences. (Hammill et al., 1981, p. 336)

Association for Children and Adults with Learning Disabilities (ACLD)

Specific Learning Disabilities is a chronic condition of presumed neurological origin which selectively interferes with the development, integration, and/or demonstration of verbal and/ or non-verbal abilities. Specific Learning Disabilities exists as a distinct handicapping condition in the presence of average to superior intelligence, adequate sensory motor systems, and adequate learning opportunities. The condition varies in its manifestations and in degree of severity. Throughout life the condition can affect self-esteem, education, vocation, socialization, and/or daily living activities. (ACLD, 1985, pp. 1, 19)

Interagency Committee on Learning Disabilities (ICLD)

Learning disabilities is a generic term that refers to a heterogeneous group of disorders manifested by significant difficulties in the acquisition and use of listening, speaking, reading, writing, reasoning, or mathematical abilities, or of social skills. These disorders are intrinsic to the individual and presumed to be due to central nervous system dysfunction. Even though a learning disability may occur concomitantly with other handicapping conditions (e.g., sensory impairment, mental retardation, social and emotional disturbance), with socioenvironmental influences (e.g., cultural differences, insufficient or inappropriate instruction, psychogenic factors), and especially with attention deficit disorder, all of which may cause learning problems, a learning disability is not the direct result of those conditions or influences (ICLD, 1987, p. 222).

---

prised by the NJCLD were the Association for Children and Adults with Learning Disabilities, the American Speech-Language-Hearing Association, the Council for Learning Disabilities, the Division for Children with Communication Disorders, the International Reading Association, and the Orton Dyslexia Society (Hammill, Leigh, McNutt, & Larsen, 1981). The NJCLD definition is presented in Table 1.1. This definition is noteworthy in that it represented an improvement over its predecessors in at least three aspects.

First, the proposed definition specifically recognized the heterogeneous nature of learning disabilities and formally provided the conceptual foundation for subtype analysis for this group of disorders. Second, the definition acknowledged the neurobiological basis hypothesized to be related to these disorders of learning and, thus, formally recognized its historical development within a neurological framework. Finally, the definition allowed for a learning disability to exist concurrently with other handicapping conditions. Although the NJCLD definition represented an improvement over previous attempts, however, it also suffered from a lack of specificity and operational criteria.

Table 1.1 also lists a more recent definition proposed by the Association for Children and Adults with Learning Disabilities (ACLD). Although this definition also does not suggest operational criteria, it does introduce the chronic nature of learning disabilities. From a treatment perspective, this definition acknowledges that, although some learning disabilities may be circumvented by compensatory strategies, not all may be remediated. Further, the ACLD definition also mentions the pervasive impact that a learning disability potentially can have upon an individual's academic and nonacademic functioning.

The most recent definition of learning disabilities listed in Table 1.1 has been proposed by the Interagency Committee on Learning Disabilities (ICLD, 1987), a multidisciplinary group mandated by the Health Research Extension Act of 1985 (P.L. 99-158). Although this definition includes the core components of its predecessors, it also presents additional conceptual and practical concerns for the researcher and clinician. Specifically, this definition includes deficiencies in social skills within the parameters of learning disabilities. Similarly, the inclusion of sociocultural influences in the definition along with the impact of Attention-deficit Hyperactivity Disorder also provide for additional diagnostic dilemmas for those working with individuals with learning problems. In fact, the U.S. Department of Education has not endorsed this definition (ICLD, 1987).

Despite the apparent progress in the definition of learning disabilities, diagnosis of this group of disorders continues to be hindered by the blatant lack of guiding operational criteria. This lack of relatively accepted operational guidelines affects the clinical utility of the diagnosis of learning disabilities and, consequently, also affects any attempts to determine incidence and prevalence rates.

Clinical Utility

In general, the clinical utility of a diagnostic process is a reflection of the validity of that process (Cromwell, Blashfield, & Strauss, 1975). Diagnoses typically are considered to be valid if they specify the course that a disorder is likely to take or if they define treatment strategies that are likely to be effective. There are a variety of kinds of psychological diagnoses (Nathan, 1967), and these differ in terms of their clinical utility. For example, a diagnosis may be important from an etiological perspective if it serves to specify a cause for a group of symptoms. Alternatively, a diagnosis may be descriptive in the sense that its primary function is to delineate a group of symptoms. Finally, a diagnosis may be prognostic in the sense that its primary function is to predict the course of a particular disorder, with and without treatment. The clinical utility and, therefore, the validity of a diagnosis improve as definitions evolve from etiological to descriptive to prognostic levels.

This evolutionary process is far from complete with respect to learning disability diagnosis. The changes noted in the definitions of learning disabilities, however, do reflect this evolutionary process. For example, the current definitions of learning disabilities acknowledge the heterogeneous nature of this group of disorders. This conceptualization represents a refinement at the descriptive level and implicates the need for improved connections between diagnosis and specific treatment strategies. Additional advances also have been noted with respect to the prognosis of individuals with learning disabilities (Schonhaut & Satz, 1983), suggesting further progress in this evolutionary process. Despite these efforts, however, the etiology of learning disabilities remains speculative in the majority of cases. This has prompted some to question the concept of learning disability (e.g., Ysseldyke, Algozzine, Shinn, & McGue, 1982) and others to remain solely descriptive in their work with these individuals (e.g., Levine, 1987).

Despite the progress noted in the evolution of the diagnosis of learning disabilities, significant definitional and diagnostic issues remain. Reasons for this are linked directly to fundamental errors of diagnostic decision making, such as using inconsistent rules (McDermott, 1981; Perlmutter & Parus, 1983). In particular, there are at least two specific issues germane to learning disability diagnoses that warrant brief mention. These issues include the exclusionary nature of some definitions and the statistical nature of others.

Issues with Exclusionary Criteria

Despite apparent progress in terms of specificity, current definitions and diagnoses of learning disabilities are largely exclusionary. Essentially, a learning disability is described as an unexplained intraindividual discrepancy between academic aptitude and achievement. As Ross (1976) suggested, when stripped of those clauses that specify what learning disabilities are not, most definitions are little more than tautological suggestions that learning disabilities are inabilities to learn.

Exclusionary criteria also have been questioned in terms of pragmatic and clinical utility. Taylor, Satz, and Friel (1979), for example, examined children with learning problems and found no cognitive, academic, or affective differences between those who could and those who could not be classified as learning disabled according to typical exclusionary criteria. In addition, the use of exclusionary diagnostic criteria also leads to a multitude of problems with clinical decision making.

For example, Ysseldyke and Algozzine (1983) noted that the school multidisciplinary team, a school/community-based group of individuals charged with determining eligibility for special education services, tends to be arbitrary, subjective, and, consequently, inconsistent in its placement decisions. To illustrate this, these investigators found a learning disability class placement rate that was no better than chance, with decisions typically based on assessment tools that were technically inadequate. Further, Ysseldyke and Algozzine found that although the bulk of time at multidisciplinary meetings is spent reviewing test results, these psychoeducational results often are viewed as useless by the teacher other than serving to confirm the obvious (i.e., that the child has learning problems). Lastly, when classification decisions are based on exclusionary criteria it seems that little time actually is spent discussing the specific curriculum and behavioral changes that would lead to a more successful educational experience for the individual.

Based on these and other data, Fletcher and Morris (1986) criticized current taxonomies for identifying learning disabilities and suggested an alternative theoretical framework for classification research. This framework, which espouses improvement in the diagnostic process, is particularly germane to the issue of learning disability subtyping and is discussed in greater detail in Chapter 5.

Issues with Statistical Criteria

Inherent in nearly all definitions of learning disabilities is the concept of an intraindividual difference, or discrepancy, between academic achievement and academic aptitude, in favor of the latter. The concept of discrepancy was proposed in an effort to operationalize the diagnosis of learning disabilities (Bateman, 1966; McCarthy, 1975) and, consequently, numerous discrepancy formulas have been proposed to define a discrepancy. There is no consensus of protocol, however, and major diagnostic problems have been associated with the use of specific discrepancy formulas.

For example, Epps et al. (1983, 1985) identified six different ability—achievement discrepancy formulas, as well as four additional grade-placement–achievement discrepancy formulas, for learning disability identification. These formulas differed to the extent that reliance on their use potentially would have resulted in diverse diagnostic and educational placement decisions (Farnham-Diggory, 1986). In fact, Ysseldyke et al. (1983) reported that 85% of the school-aged population could be classified as learning disabled using one or more of the current discrepancy formulas.

Shepard (1983) argued that the various formulas developed to date are seriously flawed, both logistically and methodologically, in that they typically assume that all children should be functioning at or above grade/age level expectancies. Further, various factors can exert a significant effect on the discrepancy formulas, such as a high correlation between the ability and achievement tests selected, statistical regression, test reliability, and developmental variables. Even the regression method of discrepancy determination, which has been cited as perhaps least subject to error and misinterpretation among the various approaches, has been noted to have serious methodological, statistical, and psychometric deficiencies when used as the sole criterion for learning disability identification (Shepard, 1980).

Generally, quantification efforts designed to operationalize definitions of learning disabilities have not met with much success. One of the major reasons for this is the significant variability that can be demonstrated by learning disabled individuals. Consequently, the parameters of quantification are less than clear and a simple discrepancy formula cannot account for the extensive variability noted within or among such individuals.

For these and other reasons, the Board of Trustees of the Council for Learning Disabilities (1987) voiced strong opposition to the use of discrepancy formulas in the identification of learning disabilities, and further suggested that these formula should be phased out. Alternatively, when mandated by state or local agencies, it was warned that these formulas should be used only with extreme caution and should be viewed as only one source of information. Thus, the lack of a standard, methodologically adequate procedure for determining this central characteristic of any learning disability (i.e., the ability—achievement discrepancy) also has been, and continues to be, a serious hindrance to clinical and theoretical progress in understanding this heterogeneous group of disorders. Efforts to improve this aspect of the various definitions continue to be explored (Boyan, 1985; Tittemore, Lawson, & Inglis, 1985), although the recent emphasis of the field on subtyping ultimately may have a greater impact.

Summary

The early case studies, the single-factor models, the resurgence of case study approaches to learning disabilities, and progress in refining definitions together provide a foundation for conceptualizing learning disabilities in a multidimensional manner. Each of the single-factor models gained some limited support during its existence, but none could explain the full range of problems presented by children with learning impediments in a satisfactory manner. It is likely that each of these single-factor models addressed a specific dysfunctional component or neurological substrate in the learning process and, from that perspective, contributed to an improved understanding of that functional system and its interactive complexities. Although none of the single-factor models has been able to account for all behavioral variance within the learning disabled population, the clinical presentation of many of the early case studies and the prevalence of single-factor models together provide a good foundation for investigations of the multidimensional nature of learning disabilities. This foundation began to be forged with the emergence, through case studies, of syndromes directly related to specific learning problems, and continues to be acknowledged in the most recent definitions of learning disabilities.

2
Neuropsychological Foundations

The approach to learning disabilities adopted here is one that recognizes the presumptive role of the central nervous system (CNS) in this heterogeneous group of disorders. Clearly, there are relationships between overt and covert forms of human behavior (e.g., speech, language, learning, problem solving) and CNS functioning. Therefore, learning disabilities are assumed to be associated with particular patterns of CNS dysfunction. Given this assumption, it seems reasonable to speculate that various subtypes of learning disabilities might be associated differentially with specific patterns of CNS dysfunction. Currently, both of these ideas probably are better considered as hypotheses rather than conclusions, but evidence is accruing in favor of their support.

For example, dyslexics have been differentiated from normals and, less frequently, from other clinical populations in terms of electroencephalography (Byring & Jarvilehto, 1985; Cohen & Breslin, 1982), cortical cytoarchitecture (Galaburda, Sherman, Rosen, Aboitiz, & Geschwind, 1985), magnetic resonance imaging of the brain (Jernigan, Tallal, & Bellugi, 1988), positron emission tomography of cerebral metabolic rates (Gross-Glenn et al., 1988), regional cerebral blood flow (Rumsey, Berman, Horwitz, Denckla, & Weinberger, 1988), and, inconsistently, computed tomography of the brain (Denckla, LeMay, & Chapman, 1985; Haslam, Dalby, Johns, & Rademaker, 1981; Hier, LeMay, Rosenberger, & Perlo, 1978; Rosenberger & Hier, 1980). Moreover, other exploratory studies have noted differences in electroencephalography (Fried, Tanguay, Boder, Doubleday, & Greensite, 1981) and regional cerebral blood flow (Hynd, Hynd, Sullivan, & Kingsbury, 1987) among specific subtypes of developmental dyslexics. Thus, in addition to well-documented behavioral findings, there is growing support from anatomical and physiological data for a direct link between learning disability subtypes and anomalous neurological functioning.

The focus in this chapter is on the neuropsychological foundations for learning disability subtyping. Neuropsychology is the study of brain–behavior relationships, and behaviors of particular interest in the context of learning disabilities, of course, include cognitive/academic ones. Given the finding that most learning disability subtypes are developmental rather than acquired, an appreciation of developmental neuropsychology is particularly useful in conceptualizing these disorders. A major theme of this perspective on developmental neuropsychology concerns the marked discontinuities characteristic of human development. Thus, it is likely that brain-behavior relationships change throughout the life span and that functional brain organization covaries with ontogeny.

This chapter presents basic principles of developmental neuropsychology that are germane to an understanding of learning disability subtypes. Introductions to the structural development of the nervous system and to functional brain organization are presented. The fundamental concept of a functional system then is illustrated through a discussion of arithmetic and reading, two processes especially relevant to particular subtypes of learning disabilities.

Nervous System Development

The human nervous system begins to develop approximately 2 weeks after conception. This early differentiation of embryonic tissue is called neurulation. During this critical stage of development, a closed cylinder of cells, called the neural tube, is formed. By 4 weeks after conception all precursors of the nervous system already have been formed either normally or in a teratogenic fashion.

Neurodevelopment continues to progress by way of proliferation, migration, differentiation, and death of nerve cells and glia. Cells proliferate through mitosis and, for neurons, this process is essentially completed by 6 months after conception. Cell proliferation occurs in particular germinal zones throughout the neural tube. Many more neurons are formed than are necessary during cellular proliferation, however, and a significant proportion of these cells normally die throughout development. Cells migrate to other locations in the brain and spinal cord, and they undergo further differentiation that extends to postnatal as well as prenatal periods of development. Neurodevelopmental errors during these processes (e.g., neural dysplasias and ectopias) have been linked to learning disabilities (Galaburda et al., 1985).

As a result of these neurodevelopmental processes, by the time the process of neurulation has been completed, three dilations or primary brain vesicles have been formed at the anterior end of the neural tube. This is illustrated in Diagram A of Figure 2.1, which shows the progressive differentiation of the brain at three levels of development. These three major subdivisions of the human embryonic brain (i.e., the rhombencephalon, mesencephalon, and prosencephalon) further differentiate into five secondary brain vesicles throughout the course of prenatal development. This is

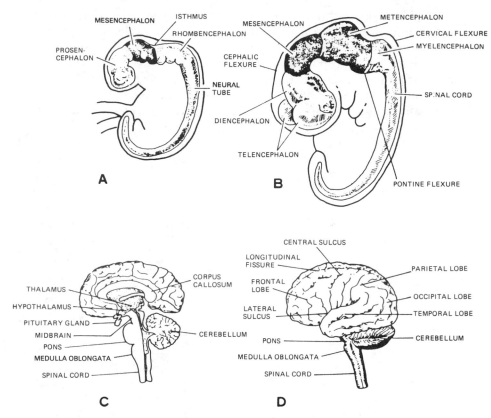

FIGURE 2.1. Differentiation of the brain at three levels of development. A, lateral view of primary brain vesicles; B, lateral view of secondary brain vesicles; C, mid-sagittal section of mature brain; D, lateral view of mature brain. (From Hynd, G.W., & Willis, W.G. (1988). *Pediatric neuropsychology* (p. 29). Orlando, FL: Grune & Stratton. With permission).

shown Diagram B of Figure 2.1. First, the prosencephalon (i.e., the most anterior vesicle) subdivides into the more posterior diencephalon and the more anterior telencephalon. Second, the rhombencephalon (i.e., the most posterior vesicle) subdivides into the more posterior myelencephalon and the more anterior metencephalon. Although the mesencephalon, or midbrain, becomes more differentiated with development, it does not subdivide any further.

Each of the secondary brain vesicles continues to develop and differentiate. It is from these vesicles that the major structures of the mature human brain are derived. These may be seen in Diagrams C and D of Figure 2.1. For example, the most posterior region of the mature brain, the medulla oblongata, is derived from the myelencephalon. The pons and cerebellum are derived from the metencephalon. The thalamus, hypothalamus, and epithalamus are derived from the diencephalon. The basal ganglia and cerebral cortex are derived from the telencephalon.

When parturition occurs at approximately 280 days postconception, the gross anatomy of the average neonatal brain is similar to the adult brain. Brain weight, however, continues to increase rapidly, from about 300 to 350 grams at birth to about 80% of its adult weight of 1,250 to 1,500 grams after 4 years. This postnatal increase in brain weight is principally associated with an increase in the size and complexity of existing neurons and with progressive myelination, a process that improves the efficiency of neural conduction.

Various sensory and motor functions of the major neuroanatomical structures have been studied extensively at gross anatomical levels as well as fine cellular levels, but the relationships between all structures and functions are far from completely understood. It is clear that by birth all sense modalities are functional and that the postnatal development of reflexes and motility follows an orderly sequence (Willis & Widerstrom, 1986). The neurobiological substrates for these sensory and motor functions are fairly precisely documented when compared to hypothesized substrates for higher order cognitive functions, largely because higher order functions are inherently less precise in their organization. These functions, however, are particularly relevant to a complete understanding of learning disability subtypes. These functions are discussed in the context of functional systems, a fundamental concept that is based on some familiarity with functional brain organization.

Functional Brain Organization

From a neuropsychological perspective, it is useful to conceptualize the brain in a manner consistent with Luria's (1970) organization. He proposed that there are three basic functional units of the brain: the subcortical, posterior cortical, and anterior cortical. Each of these units incorporates distinctive functions that are mutually interdependent. Thus, there are extensive interconnections within and among these units. All three units are involved in the performance of any given behavior, covert as well as overt, and each unit influences and is influenced by the other units. Figure 2.2 shows the regions of the brain included in each of these units as well as the hierarchical nature of zones within the cortical units.

Subcortical Unit

The subcortical unit of the brain is associated with the brainstem reticular formation and is illustrated in Diagram A of Figure 2.2. The reticular formation is a concept based on brain morphology that includes groups of

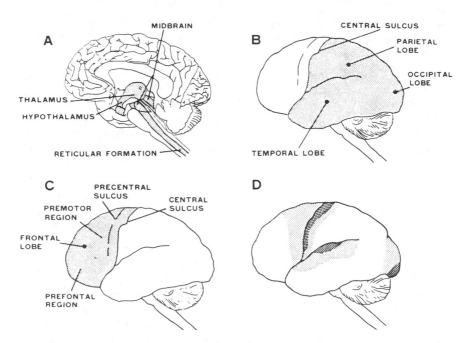

FIGURE 2.2. Luria's three functional units of the brain. A, subcortical unit; B, posterior cortical unit; C, anterior cortical unit; D, hierarchical organization within the cortical units; primary zones are shaded heavily; secondary zones are shaded lightly; tertiary zones are unshaded cortical regions. (From Hynd, G.W., & Willis, W.G. (1988). *Pediatric neuropsychology* (p. 107). Orlando, FL: Grune & Stratton. With permission.)

neurons from the regions of the medulla oblongata, pons, and midbrain. Through a system of projection fibers, the reticular formation influences and is influenced by neuroanatomical structures located more anteriorally and posteriorally along the craniocaudal axis. Luria (1973) suggested that conscious activity always involves this unit, as well as the other two units, of the brain. Brodal (1981) emphasized the role of this unit in autonomic activity as well. The morphological features of the reticular formation support the notion that this group of neurons is involved in the activation, inhibition, and regulation of CNS activities.

Brodal (1981) proposed the functional concept of the "activating system" to correspond to the structural concept of the reticular formation. This is descriptive of the characteristic electrophysiological response of the brainstem reticular formation to stimulation that signals attention or alertness. Similarly, Luria (1973) described the functional significance of this unit of the brain for the "maintenance of . . . [an] *optimal level of cortical tone* . . . essential for the organized course of mental activity" (p. 45).

Sources of activation to the subcortical unit of the brain may be metabolic, environmental, or cortical regulatory. The latter influence, in particular, emphasizes the interdependent relationship of the three units of the brain. Although the subcortical unit normally mediates a degree of cortical activation that is proportional to the intensity of the source of stimulation, that relationship can become distorted in the presence of dysfunction of the subcortical unit. This is consistent, for example, with the notion advanced by some theorists that the attention deficits and hyperactivity that accompany some learning disability subtypes may be associated with dysfunctions affecting this unit of the brain or those regions with which it has extensive interconnections (Zametkin & Rapoport, 1986).

Cortical Units

The cerebral cortex occupies the surfaces of the cerebral hemispheres. It is a highly differentiated structure that comprises six layers of cells of varying morphology. Particular cell layers may be well developed or indistinct, depending on the region in which they are located. These cytoarchitectonic differences provide the structural basis for the differentiation and hierarchical organization within the two cortical functional units of the brain. At about 2 weeks following conception, a major sulcus, the lateral fissure, develops that divides the telencephalon into two hemispheres. Between 14 and 20 weeks after conception, other major sulci develop (Dooling, Chi, & Gilles, 1983) that divide each cerebral hemisphere into four lobes. These lobes are the frontal, temporal, parietal, and occipital.

HEMISPHERIC LATERALIZATION

Functional asymmetries associated with the cortex of the cerebral hemispheres have been a major source of interest to neuropsychologists for many years. These asymmetries, or cerebral hemispheric lateralizations, refer to the relative (as opposed to exclusive) specialization of one cerebral hemisphere for a particular function. It was once thought that only higher order cognitive functions were subject to lateralization (Luria, 1973; Moscovitch, 1979). Data have emerged to suggest, however, that it seems equally likely that some sensory functions also may be lateralized, albeit perhaps less strongly (Davidoff, 1982).

Through the clinical and scientific interests in cerebral lateralization, several well-documented findings have emerged that are relevant to a developmental perspective on this topic. For example, it was once believed that the cerebral hemispheres were equipotential for function at birth and became progressively more lateralized for function with postnatal development (Lenneberg, 1967). There now is evidence to refute this hypothesis. Research conducted at anatomical, physiological, and behavioral levels of analysis strongly supports the notion that the cerebral hemispheres are specialized, at least for some functions, at a very early age (Hynd & Willis,

1988). Speech-related cognitive functions, in particular, appear to be functionally lateralized to the left cerebral hemisphere by birth or shortly thereafter. This does not suggest that interactions among various cerebral regions are constant throughout development, but it does indicate that particular aspects of cerebral hemispheric lateralization appear independent of developmental influences.

POSTERIOR CORTICAL UNIT

According to Luria's (1973) functional organization of the brain, the cortical units are not considered in terms of the sagittal axis of cerebral hemispheric lateralization (i.e., left versus right) but, instead, they are considered in terms of the coronal axis that demarcates posterior from anterior divisions. The cortex of the parietal, occipital, and temporal lobes comprises the posterior cortical unit as shown in Diagram B of Figure 2.2. Within this unit there is a hierarchical arrangement of primary, secondary, and tertiary zones. These zones are depicted in Diagram D of Figure 2.2. There is one primary zone within each of the three lobes, and each primary zone is essentially surrounded by a secondary zone. A major tertiary zone of the posterior cortical unit is demarcated by the parieto-occipito-temporal region of overlap, which roughly corresponds to a neuroanatomical structure known as the angular gyrus.

The common function of the posterior cortical unit is for the reception, analysis, and storage of information. The primary and secondary zones within this unit are modality specific for function. Thus, primary and secondary zones within the parietal, occipital, and temporal lobes are functionally specialized for the processing of kinesthetic/somatosensory, visual, and auditory stimuli, respectively. Olfactory and gustatory sense modalities also are represented in this functional unit of the brain, but they assume relatively minor emphasis in humans.

The primary (i.e., projection) zones essentially function in an afferent fashion to discriminate among various stimuli in a highly specific manner. Additionally, they function in an efferent fashion, influencing sensory receptors (e.g., retina, cochlea) to ensure optimal perceptual capabilities. In contrast, the secondary (i.e., association or gnostic) zones are adapted especially for relaying afferent impulses to the tertiary zones for further analysis. Although also modality specific, the functions of the secondary zones are more integrative than the primary zones. Thus, although lesions to the primary zones usually are associated with sensory deficits of the corresponding modality, lesions to the secondary zones are likely to disrupt higher order cognitive processes because of a disorganization in the perception of complex groups of stimuli and the relationship among them (Luria, 1970). In addition, disruption of the primary and/or secondary zones also may have an influence on the subsequent development of other associated regions and, consequently, upon behavior.

The tertiary zones of the posterior cortical unit are functionally specialized for the multimodal integration of stimuli. Luria (1973) suggested that this integrative function may be associated with the process of abstract thinking and memorization (i.e., storage) of organized experience, involving the conversion of successive stimuli into simultaneously processed groups. In this sense, lesions to this zone are likely to impair the simultaneous synthesis of information (Luria, 1980), a cognitive process clearly related to a variety of higher order academic functions such as arithmetic and reading (Das, Kirby, & Jarman, 1979; Kaufman & Kaufman, 1983).

ANTERIOR CORTICAL UNIT

Within the anterior cortical unit, presented in Diagram C of Figure 2.2, there is also a hierarchical arrangement and development of primary, secondary, and tertiary zones. The primary zones are concerned with the most basic elements of motor movement, whereas the secondary zones are functionally specialized for the preparation of motor programs and organized movement. These motor programs are executed by neurons of the primary zones of the anterior cortical division. In contrast to the progression of function from primary to secondary to tertiary zones in the posterior cortical unit, the process is reversed in the anterior unit. The functions associated with the secondary and primary zones of the cortical division are guided by tertiary influences.

The tertiary zones, located in the prefrontal regions of the frontal lobes, receive significant afferent input from the posterior cortical unit and are believed to be essential for the performance of goal-directed, selective behavior. Luria (1973) suggested that these zones "play a decisive role in the formation of intentions and programmes, and in the regulation and verification of the most complex forms of human behaviour" (p. 84). Such behavior, for example, includes motor, speech, and intellectual (e.g., problem solving) acts. The tertiary zones also have been implicated in the mediating of consciousness, affective states, and memory functions (Luria, 1980). There are extensive interconnections between this unit and the subcortical unit of the brain and, further, the regulatory role of the anterior cortical unit has been implicated in the attention deficits and hyperactivity that often accompany some learning disability subtypes (Lou, Henriksen, & Bruhn, 1984). Many of these behaviors may be characterized by the successive synthesis of information, a cognitive process that has been shown to differentiate reading disabled children from normal children (Hooper & Hynd, 1985).

DEVELOPMENTAL ISSUES

Even though its experiential basis was primarily established with adult patients, Luria's (1970) theory of functional organization provides a useful framework for conceptualizing potential brain-behavior relationships throughout the life span. Given the marked discontinuities in human development, however, a complete understanding of child and adolescent brain–behavior relationships, especially those that concern higher order cognitive functions, is not a simple mater of generalization from research with adult samples. Instead, additional research is required that evaluates established theories in consideration of these developmental discontinuities.

For example, the development of primary, secondary, and tertiary cortical zones follows an ontogenetic course. Based on morphological evidence, Luria (1980) suggested that primary cortical zones appear mature by birth, secondary zones by the first few months postnatally, and tertiary zones by the first few years postnatally. Within child and adolescent populations, however, specific functions subserved by the major units of the brain, especially the tertiary zones, presently are ill defined.

Some preliminary findings have begun to surface, however, linking specific cognitive functions to selected aspects of neurodevelopment. Passler, Isaac, and Hynd (1985) and Becker, Isaac, and Hynd (1987) found evidence suggesting a developmental progression of behaviors associated with frontal lobe development in children from about ages 5 to 12. Using a similar methodology, Heverly, Isaac, and Hynd (1986) found a developmental progression with respect to tactile-visual discrimination functions and associated parietal lobe development.

Although these efforts are noteworthy, more research delineating specific structure–function linkages clearly is needed, particularly with respect to its application to learning disability subtypes. Indeed, Rourke (1987) proposed a theory to help guide this kind of research. This theory is based on selected aspects of a model of differential hemispheric functioning advanced by Goldberg and Costa (1981). Based primarily on data and speculative evidence derived from adult samples, Goldberg and Costa asserted that the right hemisphere is relatively more specialized for intermodal integration whereas the left hemisphere is more specialized for intramodal integration. Neuroanatomically, these investigators postulated that intramodal integration may be related to the higher ratio of grey matter (i.e., neuronal mass and short nonmyelinated fibers) to white matter (i.e., long myelinated fibers) characteristic of the left hemisphere, whereas intermodal integration may be related to the lower ratio characteristic of the right hemisphere.

Rourke modified this model from a developmental perspective and extended it to account for nonverbal learning disabilities. Rourke hypothesized that an increased grey-to-white matter ratio (i.e., lesioned, excised, or dysfunctional white matter) interacts with developmental parameters to result in nonverbal learning disabilities. He reasoned that although a significant lesion in the right hemisphere may be *sufficient* to produce a nonverbal learning disability, it is the destruction of white matter (i.e., matter associated with intermodal functions) that is *necessary* to produce these learning disabilities. Rourke proposed this component as a first approximation of a developmental neuropsychological theory for nonverbal learning disabilities. Given this neuroanatomical basis, Rourke's theory is noteworthy, particularly as it may contribute to conceptualizations of differential diagnosis and, perhaps, issues of severity related to nonverbal learning disabilities; however, this theory awaits empirical evaluation.

Functional Systems

Clearly, the human central nervous system is highly specialized for function. This fact, however, often is misconstrued to suggest that particular regions of the brain operate independently. Currently, for example, there is an abundance of popular press literature that dichotomously characterizes the two cerebral hemispheres and suggests that individuals primarily may be "left-brained" or "right-brained." Such literature renders a disservice to the discipline of neuropsychology by its oversimplification, and it is especially problematic when applied to treatments for learning disabled children. In addition to impeding progress in understanding brain-behavior relationships, this kind of misconstruction is inconsistent with the concept of a neurological functional system that provides the substrates for behavior, a fundamental concept elaborated in detail by Luria (1980).

Thus, although even the neonatal brain is highly differentiated for function, the neural substrates for these functions correspond to systems of components rather than to discrete regions. These components operate interdependently toward a unified result. One approach to neuropsychological evaluation is to investigate the integrity of functional systems by examining their component parts. In order to use this approach effectively, clinicians must be able to qualitatively analyze complex systems of behavior according to these individual components. Additionally, it often is useful to know the neuroanatomical bases for those components. This is a difficult task because there is less than an optimal research base. This is particularly true for child and adolescent populations. Moreover, especially for higher order cognitive processes such as spelling, arithmetic, and reading, relationships among components of functional systems may change developmentally.

For example, during early stages of postnatal development, relatively direct and associative processes are dominant. During later stages, however, more complex integration related to speech and higher order cognitive processes becomes more pronounced. On the basis of this cognitive developmental progression, Vygotsky (1960) was among the first to speculate that cerebral lesions that are associated with relatively basic sensory processes and that occur during early childhood adversely affect higher order cognitive functioning. This is because the foundation for the higher order cognitive functioning is disrupted. Similar lesions that occur during adulthood, however, are expected to have a much more limited effect because the functional systems that subserve the higher order cognitive functions already are formed. Consequently, Vygotsky proposed that during early stages of development, cerebral lesions primarily disrupt hierarchically higher components of functional systems subserved by the affected region, whereas during later stages of development, cerebral lesions primarily disrupt hierarchically lower components that may be regulated by the affected region. Vygotsky's hypothesis is a reasonable one, but there currently is limited empirical evidence to support it (Rutter, 1981).

On the basis of electrophysiological data, Valsiner (1983) also argued that relationships among components of functional systems may change developmentally. Supporting evidence was provided by Merola and Liederman (1985) who found that the degree to which conflicting portions of simultaneous tasks were processed separately by the cerebral hemispheres increased with age. Thus, although additional validating research is required, evidence is accumulating that suggests a dependent relationship between development and interactions among components of functional systems. To illustrate, potential neurobiological substrates associated with arithmetic and reading are discussed as two examples of functional systems because they are paricularly germane to an understanding of learning disability subtyping.

Arithmetic

There currently is no conclusive evidence about the relationship between arithmetical ability and brain functioning. In fact, although there are a number of case reports of the arithmetical errors made by patients with localizable brain lesions (e.g., Deloche & Seron, 1982; Grafman, Passafiume, Faglioni, & Boller, 1982; Warrington, 1982), there is little research that integrates current understanding of mathematical cognition with contemporary principles of neuropsychology. As an initial effort, Deloche and Seron (1987) attempted to advance the understanding of calculation and number processing deficits through a focus on the neuropsychological features of these broad forms of learning disabilities and recent research in mathematical cognition. Well-considered approaches such as these suggest that the understanding of mathematical learning disability subtypes has the potential for great improvement within the next decade.

EFFECTS OF LESIONS

Although the neuropsychology of mathematical cognition is a relatively recent area of investigation, it is clear that the notion of a localized brain region associated with arithmetical functioning is untenable. Luria (1980), for example, analyzed disturbances of arithmetical operations and the syndrome of acalculia, particularly in terms of various forms of complex spatial analysis and synthesis problems. On the basis of clinical investigations primarily conducted with traumatically injured adult males, Luria suggested that disturbances of arithmetical operations may be associated with circumscribed lesions of many different parts of the brain as well as more generalized forms of depressed cerebral activity.

Luria (1960) observed, for example, that lesions of the left inferoparietal (i.e., parieto-occipital) regions often produced acalculia through a disintegration of visual-spatial synthesis, a cognitive function that he believed provided the foundation for the concept of number and arithmetical operations. Luria described his observations of the differential effects of lesions in various regions of the left inferoparietal cortex that did and did not extend to the visual region of the cortex. As would be expected, occipital lesions primarily involving the visual system were associated with visual-perceptual disturbances such as confusion of graphically similar numerals (e.g., 6 and 9; 69 and 96). Lesions that did not extend to visual regions of the cortex were more associated with a disintegration of the number concept, which was manifested in particular problems with reading and writing numbers, and calculating (Luria, 1970, 1980).

Patients with lesions of left temporal and posterior frontal regions also presented mathematical dysfunctions, perhaps secondary to aphasias affecting Wernicke's (i.e., aspects of the left temporal superior and middle gyri) and Broca's (i.e., base of the third frontal gyrus) areas, respectively. In contrast to lesions of the left inferoparietal regions, these lesions selectively affected complex arithmetical operations. These operations required individual stages to be completed in a serial fashion, relying on overt and covert speech processes, but spatially oriented functions remained intact. Dahmen, Hartje, Büssing, and Sturm (1982) found that different kinds of mathematical errors differentiated aphasics with posterior versus anterior lesions. In contrast to Luria, however, these investigators found that aphasics with posterior lesions did make a number of spatially oriented errors.

For prefrontal lesions, Luria (1980) suggested that although spatially oriented functions remained intact, the dysfunctional regulatory role of the verbal association system impaired arithmetical competence as manifested through irrelevant associations and perseveration. Finally, Luria suggested that arithmetical operations also can be disrupted through general cerebral disturbances, such as those that might be associated with attention and arousal (Luria, 1970).

A FUNCTIONAL SYSTEM FOR ARITHMETIC

Relatively few other investigations have been conducted to examine potential components of a functional system for arithmetic. Benton (1987) and Spiers (1987) have provided reviews of most of the work that has been conducted in this area. As Luria (1980) suggested, the cortical aspects of a functional system for arithmetic essentially seem lateralized to posterior temporo-parieto-occipital regions of the left, or language-dominant, hemisphere. Early case reports that suggested that acalculia, especially spatial subtypes, was primarily associated with lesions of the posterior right cerebral hemisphere (Hécaen, Angelergues, & Houillier, 1961) generally have not been supported in more recent empirical studies (Grafman, Passafiume, Faglioni, & Boller, 1982).

Several relatively more localized regions have been implicated as components of a functional system for arithmetic. For example, consistent with Luria's (1980) description, lesions of the occipital association regions may impair the visual imagery or schemata that are believed to be necessary to perform nonautomatic calculations (Benton, 1987). Additionally, Deloche and Seron (1982) described differential patterns of errors that were characteristic of Wernicke's and Broca's aphasics who were required to transcode numeral forms of numbers (e.g., five hundred and twenty-one) to digit sequences (e.g., 521). Results of their investigation suggested that Wernicke's area may be involved in the sequential organization of numerals, whereas Broca's area may be more related to grammatical aspects of the transcoding task.

The linguistic nature of the errors made by these aphasics led Spiers (1987) to suggest that the lesioned cortical regions responsible for these characteristic errors may subserve particular aspects of a variety of cognitive tasks that incidentally include both language and calculation. This is an important possibility to consider, especially in terms of the functional system that has been postulated to subserve reading. Components of both functional systems appear to be remarkably similar.

Independent of language function, however, Grafman et al. (1982) found that the left angular gyrus may have special significance for calculation. Moreover, again independent of language function, Warrington (1982) found that the accurate retrieval of specific computational values may depend on direct semantic entry access for number facts, perhaps subserved by the parieto-occipital region of the left cerebral hemisphere.

Based on this research, Spiers (1987) proposed that regions of the left temporal lobe may contribute to: (a) decoding sounds into digits, (b) sequencing digits to form numbers, and (c) sequencing numbers for accurate calculation. Further, the angular gyrus may contribute to the spatial algorithms required for performing calculations. Other aspects of this functional system may be related to the retrieval of specific computational values. Additional research suggests that other components probably are involved, such as Broca's area and the occipital regions of the visual system. It also is reasonable to assume that the arousal and attention regulation functions of both the brainstem and prefrontal lobes are involved in a functional system for arithmetic.

SUMMARY

There presently is broad consensus that arithmetical functioning is not localized but, instead, is subserved by a functional system that comprises a number of components. Several possible components of this functional system have been postulated and studied. There are different viewpoints concerning the independence of functional systems for arithmetic and language functioning, but particular subtypes of arithmetical disability can present independently of language disturbance. Similarly, circumscribed lesions can affect arithmetic selectively, but leave language functions intact.

The limited research to date suggests that although disturbances in arithmetical operations can result from a variety of brain lesions, the cortical substrates of a functional system for arithmetic may be lateralized relatively more to the left than to the right cerebral hemisphere. Structures that have been implicated as components of such a functional system include the visual association areas of the occipital lobes, angular gyrus, Wernicke's area, Broca's area, and other overlapping zones of the temporo-parieto-occipital regions of the left cerebral hemisphere. With the mounting evidence that particular kinds of mathematical errors may contribute to differentiation among various lesion sites and, subsequently, to distinct mathematical subtypes, more refined methods of error analysis have the potential to contribute to understanding the neuropsychology of mathematical learning disabilities.

Clinically, this kind of understanding would be useful in guiding the assessment process for an individual with a mathematical learning disability. Moreover, such an understanding would help to generate hypotheses about particular subtypes of mathematical learning disabilities that could be subjected to empirical confirmation. Other questions also must be addressed. For example, how might the type of arithmetic task affect brain functioning for a particular individual? Would the degree of lateralization of function be dependent upon the kind of task (e.g., geometry, calculation, word problems) and/or its complexity? The interaction among type of arithmetic task, chronological age, and hemispheric functioning remains to be explored for normally functioning individuals, for disabled learners, and for learning disability subtypes.

Reading

At one time it was believed that reading was localized to the left angular gyrus. Similar to the hypothesized functional system of arithmetic, however, it is unlikely that a complex function such as reading is subserved adequately by such a discrete cortical area. Instead, like arithmetic, the neural substrate for reading generally is considered as a functional system, relatively lateralized to the left cerebral hemisphere, and composed of a number of interconnected components. Given its clear relationship to language function, the process of reading has been subject to more detailed neuropsychological study than arithmetic. Even so, functional systems proposed for reading are still largely theoretical, incompletely validated, and, consequently, constantly evolving (Hynd & Semrud-Clikeman, 1988).

A Functional System for Reading

Luria (1980) considered reading as well as writing to be special forms of speech activity. According to this conception, the reading process begins with the visual perception and analysis of a grapheme. The gapheme is recoded to its phonemic structure that is subsequently comprehended. The automaticity of this process varies as a function of development. Thus, during initial stages of reading, all of the operations noted are incorporated in a clear serial fashion. However, during later stages, graphemes may come to elicit direct comprehension of written words or even entire phrases, essentially eliminating intermediate phonemic analysis and synthesis.

When the process of reading is considered in this fashion, a number of components of a substrate functional system are implicated. For example, Hynd and Hynd (1984) suggested that graphemes are registered in the occipital lobes where they are associated with known letters or words. This information then is shared with input from other sensory modalities in the region of the left angular gyrus. Linguistic semantic comprehension of this multimodal integration of information may be subserved in the region of the planum temporale (i.e., a region on the floor of the lateral sulcus) and Wernicke's area of the temporal lobe. Finally, the comprehended information potentially is communicated to Broca's area by way of the arcuate fasciculus, an intrahemispheric band of connecting fibers. This putative functional system for reading is sometimes referred to as the Wernicke-Geschwind model (Mayeux & Kandel, 1985).

Based on this putative functional system for reading, Hynd and Hynd (1984) hypothesized that particular subtypes of dyslexia, based on a neurolinguistic subtype model proposed by Marshall (1984; see Chapter 3), may follow from dysfunction involving particular components and interconnections. For example, developmental surface dyslexia, which is characterized by an overreliance on phonological rules such that reading of irregular words is affected, may be due to an impaired process in semantic access to what is read. Neuroanatomically, this may be related to a disruption of pathways associated with Wernicke's area. Developmental phonological dyslexia, which is characterized by an inability to apply phonological rules, may be due to an impaired process in grapheme-phoneme conversions. Neuroanatomically, this may be related to a disruption of pathways associated with the angular gyrus. Other subtypes also have been proposed based on this functional system, and specific treatment interventions have been suggested (Hynd, 1986).

Supporting Evidence

Similar to the proposed functional system for arithmetic, the functional system for reading is hypothetical and there currently is limited empirical validation for this putative neural substrate (Hynd et al., 1987). Essentially, there have been three lines of investigation that provide some support for a neural substrate for reading, and these include electrophysiological, neuroimaging, and autopsy studies.

Of these three kinds of studies, the autopsy studies perhaps provide the strongest support for a neural substrate, but even results of these relatively few investigations are compromised by a number of methodological problems. Among the most serious is that although gross and fine brain morphology of dyslexics have been compared with normals, comparisons generally have not been made with other clinical subgroups. Particularly in view of the accumulating evidence previously discussed that postulates a functional system for arithmetic that is quite similar to a putative functional system for reading, and perhaps language as well, such comparisons are necessary. For example, it is possible that these putative functional systems subserve a general cognitive-academic function (e.g., crystallized intelligence) and are not specific to particular academic processes. Such a hypothesis is supported by the relatively robust finding that general cognitive abilities (e.g., Wechsler Intelligence Scale for Children–Revised Full Scale IQ) are among the strongest predictors of specific neuropsychological test performance (Hynd & Willis, 1988).

A number of studies have identified differences in the brain electrical activity of dyslexics as compared to normals (Duffy, Burchfiel, & Lombroso, 1979; Duffy, Denckla, Bartels, & Sandini, 1980; Duffy, Denckla, Bartels, Sandini, & Kiessling, 1980; Fried et al., 1981; Languis & Wittrock, 1986; Rosenthal, 1980). For example, Duffy and his colleagues found that although the brain electrical activity of normals and dyslexics did not differ during baseline conditions, brain electrical activity appeared to differ during reading and listening tasks, particularly in Broca's area, the left temporal region, Wernicke's area, and the angular gyrus. As noted earlier, all of these regions are thought to be important components of a functional system for reading. These efforts have been criticized on methodological grounds, however, because associated conclusions about the underlying neurological substrate structures are primarily inferential rather than direct (Hynd & Semrud-Clikeman, 1988; Taylor, 1987; Taylor & Fletcher, 1983).

Similar criticisms have been directed at studies that have relied on neuroimaging techniques, such as computerized tomography and magnetic resonance imaging of the brain. Hynd and Semrud-Clikeman (1988) critically reviewed eight of the most recent neuroimaging studies of dyslexics (Denckla et al., 1985; Haslam et al., 1981; Hier et al., 1978; Leisman & Ashkenazi, 1980; LeMay, 1981; Parkins, Roberts, Reinarz, & Varney, 1987; Rosenberger & Hier, 1980; Rumsey et al., 1986). Despite the great clinical and methodological heterogeneity of these studies, they proffered three tentative conclusions. First, computerized tomography and magnetic resonance imaging techniques may reveal very few abnormalities in the gross brain morphology of developmental dyslexics. Second, these neuroimaging techniques may reveal significant deviations in normal patterns of brain symmetry and asymmetry for developmental dyslexics. Finally, these deviant patterns of brain asymmetry may be related to deficient expressive language functions in developmental dyslexics.

Neuropathological evidence linking a neural functional system substrate to reading comes from the limited autopsy studies conducted on the brains of developmental dyslexics (Drake, 1968; Galaburda & Kemper, 1979; Galaburda et al., 1985). For example, Galaburda et al. (1985) found cortical abnormalities in all cases studied. Neuronal ectopias and cytoarchitectonic dysplasias (i.e., abnormalities in the location and growth of nerve cells) were found predominantly in the left cerebral hemisphere near the perisylvian region (i.e., around the lateral sulcus) in the brains of the developmental dyslexics. The plana temporale, normally showing asymmetry favoring the left hemisphere, were symmetric. Other abnormalities also were found in particular thalamic nuclei (e.g., medial geniculate body) and the supplementary motor area. Although challenged on methodological grounds (Satz & Soper, 1986), these data support a hypothesis advanced by Geschwind and Behan (1982) concerning a potential relationship between effects of immune development, testosterone production, and errors in prenatal neurodevelopmental processes important to corticogenesis (e.g., proliferation, migration, differentiation, and neuronal necrosis).

Although this model for a functional system for reading has received support, it has not gone unchallenged. Hynd and Semrud-Clikeman (1988) recently noted that there are obvious inconsistencies between this neurolinguisitically based functional system and neuropathological data. In their review, these investigators noted that although neurolinguistic theory stresses the involvement of the bilateral posterior and left perisylvian cortex, evidence from postmortem and neurometabolic studies implicate bilateral frontal and left perisylvian cortical regions. In addition, the neurolinguistic model does not involve supplementary motor cortex or subcortical areas, whereas data from the postmortem studies suggest that these regions may be part of the reading functional system. Further research is needed to address these inconsistencies in the literature.

SUMMARY

Similar to mathematical functioning, there is broad consensus that reading is not localized but, rather, is subserved by a functional system that comprises a number of components. These components seem relatively lateralized to the left cerebral hemisphere and most likely include aspects of the occipital lobes bilaterally, the angular gyrus, Wernicke's area, the planum temporale, and Broca's area. It is reasonable to speculate that other components and interconnections also may be involved, such as particular thalamic and reticular formation nuclei, and that reading may be more of a bihemispheric task than once believed. Nonetheless, empirical evidence is accruing that supports a distinct neurobiological substrate for reading, and hypotheses have been proposed that implicate errors in prenatal corticogenesis in developmental dyslexia. Although the functional system that traditionally has been postulated to subserve reading is remarkably similar to that which may subserve mathematical functions, it is clear that reading and mathematical learning disability subtypes can present independently. Further research is needed to address not only the specific components of reading and mathematical functional systems, respectively, but to determine their degree of interdependence.

Conclusions

Presently, evidence is accruing that supports the hypothesis that learning disabilities are linked to anomalous neurological functioning. Given this evidence and the fact that most learning disabilities are developmental rather than acquired, a number of basic principles of developmental neuropsychology are germane to an understanding of the subtyping of these disorders. Such principles include those that relate to development of the nervous system, functional organization of the brain, and functional systems. How these developmental principles interact with learning tasks and their complexity also is of importance.

Luria's (1970) theory of functional brain organization provides a useful framework for conceptualizing brain-behavior relationships throughout the life span. Some evidence suggests, however, that these relationships may change as a function of development. Thus, we cannot generalize research conducted with adults to children and adolescents. Basically, research is needed to document brain-behavior relationships at different times during the life span, particularly as it may describe these relationships in individuals with disorders such as learning disabilities.

It is clear that overt and covert behaviors and functions cannot be localized to discrete cerebral regions. Further, their neurobiological substrates comprise functional systems of a variety of neural components and interconnections. Putative functional systems associated with arithmetic and reading are illustrative. Clearly, continued research within the discipline of developmental neuropsychology is important to a progressive understanding of learning disabilities and its respective subtypes.

Section II   Subtyping Models and Classification Issues

3
Clinical-Inferential Classification Models

Many subtype models for learning disabilities have been proposed. Given the high frequency of reading problems as compared to other learning difficulties, many of these models have focused on identifying reading disability subtypes. More recent studies, however, have begun to address other academic areas as well. The search for homogeneous subtypes of learning disabilities is well illustrated by the appearance of nearly 100 classification studies in the literature since 1963. Even more studies have used subtyping models in related research endeavors. Approximately half of these studies have used clinical-inferential models in attempting to provide an acceptable classification system.

Clinical-inferential models of subtype derivation represent attempts to group individuals into homogeneous clusters by identifying similarities in their performance profiles. These are largely post hoc models in which the investigator typically uses measures of achievement and cognition as the basis for group separation. Table 3.1 provides an overview of most of the clinical-inferential models that have been advanced to date.

Prior to the emergence of high-speed technological assistance, these clinical-inferential models were the prototypes for subtype derivation studies. As can be seen from Table 3.1, however, clinical-inferential models for subtyping have waned during the 1980s in favor of empirical computerized counterparts. Even so, these models are seminal in the subtyping literature. Studies using clinical-inferential models can be grouped into achievement models, neurocognitive models (e.g., using intellectual, neuropsychological variables), neurolinguistic models, and combined models that attempted to derive subtypes based on several different variables (e.g., achievement, language, intellectual).

Achievement Classification Models

For achievement subtype models, the basis of the classification is determined by academic levels and patterns. Thus, much of the importance of

TABLE 3.1. Clinical-inferential learning disability subtyping models.

Classification models	Subtypes
Achievement models	
Boder (1970)	Dysphonetic dyslexia
	Dyseidetic dyslexia
	Alexic dyslexia (mixed)
Ingram, Mason, & Blackburn (1970)	Audio-phonic
	Visuo-spatial
	Combined
Rourke & Finlayson (1978)	Reading/spelling deficits
	Arithmetic deficits
	Reading/spelling/arithmetic deficits
Sweeney & Rourke (1978)	Phonetic spelling deficits
	Dysphonetic spelling deficits
Mitterer (1982)	Recoding readers
	Whole-word readers
Thomson (1982)	Auditory-linguistic deficits
	Visual-spatial deficits
	Mixed deficits
Badian (1983)	Spatial dyscalculia
	Anarithmetic
	Attentional-sequential dyscalculia
	Alexia and agraphia for numbers
Frith (1983)	Phonological spelling deficits
	Lexical spelling deficits
Lovett (1984)	Reading accuracy disabled
	Reading rate disabled
Lennox & Siegel (1988)	Reading disabled
	Arithmetic disabled
Siegel & Ryan (1988)	Reading deficits
	Writing-arithmetic deficits
	Attention deficits
Neurocognitive models	
Kinsbourne & Warrington (1963)	Language retarded
	Gerstmann
Quiros (1964)	Central auditory processing dyslexia
	Visual-perceptual dyslexia
Bannatyne (1966)	Minimal neurological dyslexia
	Genetic dyslexia
Johnson & Myklebust (1967)	Audiophonic dyslexia
	Visuospatial dyslexia
Bateman (1968)	Auditory memory deficits
	Visual memory deficits
	Combined
Smith (1970)	Symbol manipulation and auditory sequencing deficits
	Spatial-perceptual deficits
	Mixed
Rourke, Young, & Flewelling (1971)	PIQ > VIQ
	PIQ < VIQ
	PIQ = VIQ

TABLE 3.1. Continued.

Classification models	Subtypes
Denckla (1972)	Specific language disturbance
	Specific visuo-spatial disability
	Motor dyscontrol
	Mixed
Mattis, French, & Rapin (1975)	Language disordered
	Articulatory and graphomotor dyscoordination
	Visual-perceptual
Smith, Coleman, Dokecki, &	High IQ
Davis (1977)	Low IQ
Mattis, Erenberg, & French	Language deficits
(1978)	Articulatory-graphomotor deficits
	Visual-perceptual deficits
	Phonemic sequencing deficits
	Subtype with two of the above
Myklebust (1978)	Auditory processing deficits
	Visual processing deficits
	Language impaired
	Intersensory integration
Bakker (1979a)	P-type dyslexia
	L-type dyslexia
Pirozzolo (1979)	Auditory-linguistic subtype
	Visual-spatial subtype
Wilson & Risucci (1986)	Expressive deficits
	Receptive deficits
	Memory and retrieval deficits
	Global deficits
	No deficits
Neurolinguistic models	
de Ajuriaguerra (1966)	Poor language comprehension and production
	Comprehension > production
Marshall & Newcombe (1973)	Visual dyslexia
	Surface dyslexia
	Deep dyslexia
Beauvois & Derouesne (1979)	Phonological dyslexia
Wolfus, Moscovitch, &	Expressive
Kinsbourne (1980)	Expressive-receptive
Denckla (1981)	Anomic disorder
	Anomic disorder with repetition deficits
	Dysphonemic sequencing disorder
	Verbal memory disorder
	Mixed language disorder
	Right hemisyndrome with mixed language disorder
Warrington (1981)	Concrete word dyslexia
Deloche, Andreewsky, & Desi	Surface dyslexia
(1982)	
Rapin & Allen (1983)	Phonological, morphological, and syntactic deficits
	Severe expressive syndrome with intact comprehension
	Verbal auditory agnosia

TABLE 3.1. Continued.

Classification models	Subtypes
	Mute autistic syndrome
	Autistic syndrome with echolalia
	Semantic-pragmatic syndrome without autism
	Syntactic-pragmatic syndrome
Sevush (1983)	Surface dyslexia
	Deep dyslexia
	Phonological dyslexia
Marshall (1984)	Surface dyslexia
	Direct dyslexia
	Phonological dyslexia
	Deep dyslexia
Curtiss & Tallal (1988)	Expressive language deficits
	Receptive language deficits
	Mixed language deficits
Combined models	
Nelson & Warrington (1974)	Reading-spelling deficits
	Spelling deficits
Vernon (1977)	Deficits in analyzing visual shapes
	Deficits in analyzing whole words into phonemes
	Deficits in the acquisition of grapheme-phoneme associations
	Deficits in grasping irregularities in grapheme-to-phoneme association and complex orthography
	Deficits in grouping single words into phrases and sentences
Omenn & Weber (1978)	Auditory deficits
	Visual deficits
	Mixed deficits
Decker & DeFries (1981)	Spatial reasoning and reading deficits
	Coding speed and reading deficits
	Mixed deficits
	Normal pattern with low reading achievement
Weller & Strawser (1987)	Nonlearning disabled
	Production deficits
	Verbal organization disorders
	Nonverbal organization disorders
	Global dysfunction

these models lies in their potential ecological validity. For these models, individuals are grouped or subtyped according to their learning profiles.

Boder's Reading Subtype Model

This particular kind of clinical-inferential classification model is well illustrated by the early subtyping efforts of Boder (1970, 1971, 1973). Her subtype model was based on an individual's performance on simple word recognition and spelling tasks. Boder predicted that because the processes involved in reading and spelling likely are interrelated, these performance tasks would discriminate effectively among normal, retarded, and dyslexic readers. These tasks also were predicted to discriminate among subtypes of dyslexics. Boder reasoned that if dyslexia were due to neurological factors, then these factors would manifest specific and differential reading-spelling patterns.

Using a screening tool designed to detect qualitative as well as quantitative reading and spelling errors, Boder proposed five distinct reading patterns. These were a normal pattern, a retarded reading pattern, and three different dyslexic patterns. The three dyslexic patterns were: (a) dysphonetic dyslexia, (b) dyseidetic dyslexia, and (c) alexia. Boder noted that none of these dyslexic patterns was characteristic of normal readers and that specific reading-spelling patterns were stable over time, even when overall reading level improved.

Dysphonetic readers were characterized by deficient phonetic decoding strategies, poor letter-sound integration, and weak auditory memory. These children tended to be global, gestalt readers who were unable to decipher unfamiliar words. These children showed frequent misspellings in their written work with specific errors characterized by nonphonetic attempts, semantic substitutions (e.g., "car" for "automobile"), and unintelligible letter strings. Boder estimated the prevalence rate of this subtype to be about 62%, making it the largest single group of dyslexics within her sample.

In contrast, *dyseidetic* readers were characterized by poor visual-perceptual abilities and weak visual memory skills. These children employed phonetic decoding strategies almost exclusively and had limited sight-word vocabularies. Their overreliance on phonetic decoding strategies tended to interfere with the flow and rate of the reading task and, consequently, also tended to interfere with reading comprehension. Although general spelling skills were less appropriate than expected for age, errors tended to be phonetically accurate (e.g., "biznes" for "business"). Boder estimated the prevalence rate of this subtype to be about 9%, making it the smallest single group of dyslexics within her sample.

The *alexic* readers, Boder's third subtype, were characterized by a combination of deficits. These children demonstrated primary processing deficiencies in both visual-perceptual and phonetic decoding strategies. Boder contended that this subtype was the most severely impaired of the three subtypes and that without aggressive intervention these children would probably not learn to read. Boder estimated the prevalence rate of the alexic subtype to be about 22% of her disabled reader sample.

The distinctions among these dyslexic subtypes often can become blurred. For example, it is difficult to distinguish dyseidetic from alexic children at young ages because of their general lack of exposure to phonics skills at that level. In fact, Hynd and Cohen (1983) noted that this may have been responsible for the relatively higher prevalence of alexics in the

Boder sample. Similarly, using only spelling patterns can contribute to difficulty in distinguishing alexic from dysphonetic children. The clinician, however, is assisted here by the fact that alexic children typically have a lower level of general reading skills and, that without remediation, alexic children usually remain at a primer reading level.

In addition to her classification model for reading disabilities, Boder provided a screening instrument to classify children in a systematic manner (Boder & Jarrico, 1982). The Boder Test of Reading-Spelling Patterns requires an individual to perform reading recognition and spelling tasks. Both tasks are based on graded lists of words. This screening instrument is discussed more fully in Chapter 6. Although Boder is commended for providing a systematic screening instrument to complement her subtyping model, the Boder Test of Reading-Spelling Patterns has received mixed reviews (Alexander, 1984; Bing, 1985; Hynd, 1984; Reynolds, 1984).

RESEARCH ON BODER'S MODEL

Evidence has surfaced to provide mixed support for Boder's clinical classification model. Neurophysiologically, Fried (1979), Fried et al. (1981), and Rosenthal (1982) provided evidence demonstrating that Boder's subtypes showed distinctive EEG and evoked potential patterns. Generally, these data implicated left cerebral hemispheric involvement for the dysphonetic subtype and right cerebral hemispheric involvement for the dyseidetic subtype. Leisman and Ashkenazi (1980), however, were unable to replicate these results.

Flynn and Deering (in press) obtained somewhat different results using Boder's subtypes and electrophysiological measures. The investigators divided 44 children (mean age = 7 years, 10 months) into Boder's dyslexic subtypes and performed spectral analysis of theta and alpha brain waves during cognitive tasks. Although differences were noted among the three subtypes, Flynn and Deering found the children with the dyseidetic pattern to show significant increases from baseline in left temporal-parietal (i.e., in the area of the angular gyrus) theta during cognitive tasks. These findings are not inconsistent with speculations asserted by Fried (1979), Fried et al. (1981), and Rosenthal (1982), but Flynn and Deering added that the dyseidetic pattern also could be attributable to overutilization of early developing linguistic skills rather than deficient visual-perceptual abilities.

Neuropsychologically, data also have presented mixed results in support of Boder's model and variants thereof. Studies of bisensory and visual memory (Bayliss & Liversey, 1985; Obrzut, 1979), simultaneous-sequential processing (Aaron, 1978; Nockleby & Galbraith, 1984), and intrasensory integration (Bauserman & Obrzut, 1981), as well as procedures such as time-sharing (Dalby & Gibson, 1981; Menken, 1981) and dichotic listening (Malatesha & Dougan, 1982; Obrzut, 1979; Town, Buff, & Cohen, 1988), have provided support for interhemispheric and behavioral differences among Boder's subtypes, particularly between the dysphonetic and dyseidetic subtypes. Support also has accrued for the initial prevalence estimates for each of the three subtypes (Ginn, 1979; Sporn, 1981).

In contrast, however, Hooper and Hynd (1985) were unable to differentiate among Boder's subtypes in terms of psychometric performance on cognitive subtests of the Kaufman Assessment Battery for Children (Kaufman & Kaufman, 1983). Although a pooled dyslexic group differed significantly from a retarded-reader group and a normal control group, no differences were noted among specific dyslexic subtypes on the K-ABC Simultaneous and Sequential Processing Scales. Similarly, Holmes and Peper (1977) were unable to differentiate among dyslexic subtypes in terms of a variety of cognitive and educational tasks, with the exception for the number of spelling errors made. These investigators did note, however, that the number of spelling errors successfully discriminated among groups. Aylward (1984), using a modification of Boder's screening instrument (i.e., the Denver Reading and Spelling Test; Camp & McCabe, 1977), also found no differences among dyslexic subtypes on a dichotic listening task, a hemiretinal task with linguistic stimuli, or a hemiretinal task with spatial stimuli.

These equivocal findings raise questions about the utility of this subtyping model. In fact, Roeltgen (1985) suggested that symptoms associated with disorders of writing or spelling may not implicate, parallel, or even correlate with disorders and deficits found in reading. Boder's model appears intuitively appealing, particularly given its clinical manageability (e.g., the use of only three basic diagnostic variables). Given the complexities of the reading process, however, this model will continue to require refinement if it is to prove truly useful in classification.

Other Reading and Spelling Subtype Models

In addition to Boder's subtyping model, other clinical-inferential models also emerged based on reading and spelling achievement. Occurring concurrently with Boder's work, for example, Ingram, Mason, and Blackburn (1970) provided support for a similar clinical conceptualization. In a sample of 62 children who met the criteria for developmental dyslexia, three subtypes of reading problems emerged. *Audio-phonic* dyslexics exhibited primary deficits in sound discrimination, sound blending, phonic analysis, and speech-to-sound abilities. *Visuo-spatial* dyslexics showed primary deficits in recognizing simple words and orthographic problems, such as letter reversals and letter and syllable transpositions. The third subtype comprised children who showed a combination of these deficits. A similar system was devised by Thomson (1982) who classified children as *auditory-linguistic*, *visual-spatial*, and *mixed* subtypes based on reading and spelling errors.

Other studies also have specifically addressed reading from a subtype perspective. Lovett (1984), for example, described a classification model for specific reading dysfunction based on accuracy and rate dimensions. Although these dimensions are not novel to the reading literature, they do represent relatively new concepts in the subtyping literature, particularly the rate dimension. *Accuracy* disabled readers, of course, evidenced significant difficulties in reading accuracy, whereas *rate* disabled readers evidenced significant difficulties in reading rate despite relatively intact reading accuracy. Although no reading comprehension differences were noted between these subtypes, the accuracy disabled readers showed poorer spelling achievement and greater difficulty with manipulation of language structures as well as possible reading-acquisition deviancies. Although rate disabled readers showed relatively intact language comprehension skills, these children may account for a significant number of special education referrals. One reason for this phenomenon is because their cognitive skill deficits may not be manifested until learning materials increase in length and complexity.

Mitterer (1982) described two reading disabled subtypes that were characterized by the quality of their reading errors. Similar to Boder's dyseidetic subtype, the *recoding* readers appeared to use phonetic strategies continuously in the reading process. In contrast, the *whole-word* subtype was similar to Boder's dysphonetic pattern in that these children exclusively employed whole-word strategies in their reading. Mitterer's subtype model is noteworthy in that it is one of the few clinical-inferential achievement classification models to use both reading recognition and reading comprehension measures in identifying subtypes.

Just as Lovett (1984) and Mitterer (1982) described subtypes unique to reading, Sweeney and Rourke (1978) and Frith (1983) described subtypes unique to spelling. In a cross-sectional study, Sweeney and Rourke (1978) analyzed the Wide Range Achievement Test (WRAT) Spelling Subtest for disabled learners according to phonetic accuracy. These investigators divided their sample into a younger age group (i.e., children ages 8 to 10 years) and an older age group (i.e., children ages 12 to 14 years). Within each age group children were further subdivided into good spellers (i.e., phonetically accurate) and poor spellers (i.e., phonetically inaccurate). They found that poor spellers were discriminated more effectively from good spellers across a variety of neuropsychological tasks, especially at the older age levels. Sweeney and Rourke noted that those spellers who evidenced the use of phonetic principles, even in their spelling errors, seemed to have a better academic prognosis than their dysphonetic counterparts.

Similarly, Frith (1983) also described two subtypes of spelling disabilities. One of the subtypes involved phonological spelling deficits, and the other involved lexical spelling deficits. Phonological, or nonlexical, skills involve accurate phoneme-to-grapheme translations. Deficits in these skills contribute to spelling errors characterized by a high frequency of dysphonetic spellings that may omit consonant clusters. According to

Frith, these deficits always seem to be related to reading deficits. In contrast, lexical skills involve the ability to store letter strings in their correct sequence and to access these letter strings in an efficient manner. Children with lexical deficits can become adequate readers because they have developed partial cue strategies in the reading process. It is precisely these strategies, however, that hinder efficient and accurate development of spelling skills.

General Achievement Subtype Models

To date, there is only one clinical-inferential model that has been offered exclusively to address subtypes of arithmetic learning disabilities. Badian (1983) proposed four subtypes of developmental dyscalculia, *spatial* dyscalculia, *anarithmetic*, *attentional-sequential* dyscalculia, and *alexia and agraphia for numbers*, but little data have been generated with respect to their validity. Other clinical-inferential models have focused more generally on academic skills to include arithmetic along with reading and spelling.

Using rigorous diagnostic criteria, for example, Rourke and Finlayson (1978) clinically grouped 45 children with Average intelligence, ages 9 to 14, who were referred for neuropsychological evaluation. Three subtypes were identified based on predetermined performance criteria on the WRAT. *Subtype 1* consisted of 15 children who scored at least 2 years below expected grade-level placement on the WRAT Reading, Spelling, and Arithmetic subtests. All of the scores were below the 19th percentile and the grade-level equivalent discrepancy between any two of the three WRAT subtests was less than 1 year. *Subtype 2* consisted of 15 children who scored below the 15th percentile on WRAT Reading and Spelling, where both of these scores were at least 1.8 years below the WRAT Arithmetic score. *Subtype 3* consisted of 15 children who demonstrated the opposite pattern from Subtype 2 (i.e., WRAT Reading and Spelling grade-level equivalents exceeded WRAT Arithmetic by at least 2 years). These groups were compared across the Halstead-Reitan Battery and ancillary neuropsychological tests. The 16 tests included measures of auditory- and visual-perceptual abilities. Findings indicated that Subtypes 1 and 2 were superior to Subtype 3 on visual-perceptual and visual-spatial tasks, whereas Subtype 3 was superior to Subtypes 1 and 2 on auditory-perceptual tasks.

Rourke and Strang (1978) demonstrated further validity for these subtypes by comparing their performances on a battery of motor, psychomotor, and tactile-perceptual tasks. Although no differences were noted on simple motor tasks, Subtype 2 showed average psychomotor abilities and poor right-handed tactile-perceptual abilities. Subtype 3, however, showed bilateral impairment in psychomotor and tactile-perceptual abilities. Thus, it appeared that Subtype 2 (i.e., reading and spelling deficits) performed more poorly on tasks typically associated with left hemispheric functioning, whereas Subtype 3 (i.e., arithmetic deficits) performed more poorly on tasks typically associated with right hemispheric functioning. Subsequent studies have shown differences between these two clinical subtypes on tasks measuring concept formation, nonverbal reasoning abilities, and the ability to profit from feedback, in favor of Subtype 2 (Strang & Rourke, 1983). Siegel and Linder (1984) also demonstrated differences between these subtypes on phonemic memory tasks, in favor of Subtype 3.

Extensions of this methodology also have surfaced that have provided additional support for this subtyping conceputalization (Breen, 1986; Fletcher, 1985; Nolan, Hammeke, & Barkley, 1983). Fletcher (1985), using the WRAT and predetermined achievement criteria, separated learning disabled children into four subtypes that comprised Rourke's three subtypes plus a *spelling-arithmetic-deficient* subtype. Fletcher demonstrated that these clinical subtypes manifested significantly different memory patterns. For example, the arithmetic-deficient and spelling-arithmetic-deficient subtypes showed low nonverbal storage and retrieval abilities, the reading-spelling-deficient subtype showed verbal-retrieval problems, and the reading-spelling-arithmetic-deficient subtype showed verbal and nonverbal retrieval problems in addition to nonverbal storage deficits.

Breen (1986) replicated Rourke's clinical learning disability subtypes using the Woodcock-Johnson Psycho-Educational Battery and found similar results. Nolan et al. (1983) also documented partial support for these achievement-based subtypes. Specific profiles on the Luria-Nebraska Neuropsychological Battery were identified for three learning disabled subtypes. This methodology also has been used to explore working memory deficits (Siegel & Ryan, 1988) and specific spelling patterns (Lennox & Siegel, 1988) in various achievement subtypes.

Neurocognitive Classification Models

Neurocognitive models for grouping learning disabled children have provided an impetus for much of the subtyping literature. These models have attempted to group children homogeneously by using measures of various cognitive functions such as memory, attention, and visual-spatial abilities.

Dual-Subtype Models

Although Myklebust and Johnson (1962) initially discussed the heterogeneity of learning disabilities by approaching this multidimensional conceptualization from a "psychoneurological" perspective, Kinsbourne and Warrington (1963) are typically credited with making the first attempt to group children with learning disabilities in a homogeneous fashion.

Working with a small sample ($n = 13$) of 8- to 14-year-old children referred because of reading disabilities, these investigators established two distinct clinical subtypes based on discrepancies between Verbal IQ (VIQ) and Performance IQ (PIQ) on the Wechsler Intelligence Scale for Children (WISC) (the Wechsler Adult Intelligence Scale [WAIS] was administered to one 31-year-old patient). All Subtype 1 members ($n = 6$) demonstrated a VIQ-PIQ discrepancy of at least 20 points, in favor of the PIQ. These members also manifested speech acquisition delays and deficits in receptive and expressive language. Kinsbourne and Warrington called this subtype, *language retarded*, and speculated about possible relationships with adult aphasia. Subtype 2 members ($n = 7$) demonstrated the opposite IQ discrepancy (PIQ < VIQ) in addition to finger agnosia, left-right confusion, constructional difficulties, and arithmetic deficits. They called this subtype the *Gerstmann group*. Despite a small sample size, Kinsbourne and Warrington had begun to establish a foundation for the subtyping literature.

The efforts of Kinsbourne and Warrington quickly were followed by a number of clinical-inferential studies using neurocognitive variables, typically the WISC, to identify homogeneous subtypes of learning disabled children (Bannatyne, 1966; Bateman, 1968; Johnson & Myklebust, 1967; Quiros, 1964; Smith, 1970). After presenting a multifactorial model of dyslexia, for example, Johnson and Myklebust (1967) described two learning disability subtypes. *Audiophonic* dyslexia was characterized by auditory processing weaknesses including deficits in discrimination, memory, and sequencing. *Visuospatial* dyslexia was characterized by visual processing weaknesses such as discrimination, spatial visualization, and memory. Quiros (1964) also provided a two-subtype delineation of learning disabilities in describing *central auditory processing* dyslexia and *visual perceptual* dyslexia.

In contrast, Bannatyne (1966) presented a different subtype conceptualization. Although two basic subtype patterns also were identified, this conceptualization was based on neurological functioning and genetics. The first subtype, *genetic dyslexia*, showed deficits in auditory processing skills (e.g., discrimination, sound-symbol relationships), but this subtype was characterized by relatively low verbal ability. The second subtype, *minimal neurological dyslexia*, showed deficits in all processing domains that contributed to the learning impediments. Smith, Coleman, Dokecki, and Davis (1977) also presented two subtypes of learning disabilities, using IQ as the discriminator. These included a *low IQ* subtype and a *high IQ* subtype.

Still other dual subtype models were presented by Pirozzolo (1979) and Bakker (1979a). Pirozzolo (1979) proposed two subtypes of developmental dyslexia, one having distinct *auditory-linguistic* deficits relative to visual-perceptual strengths, and the other having *visual-spatial* deficits relative to intact verbal abilities. Using a comprehensive neuropsychological battery that included the WISC-R, Raven's Progressive Matrices, and neurolinguistic analyses of reading and writing errors, Pirozzolo was able to describe these two subtypes in an semioperational fashion. These criteria are listed

TABLE 3.2. Neuropsychological diagnostic criteria for the subtypes in the Pirozzolo (1979) model.

Auditory-linguistic subtype	Visual-spatial subtype
Average to Above Average PIQ	Average to Above Average VIQ
Low VIQ relative to PIQ	Low PIQ relative to VIQ
Delayed language onset	Right-left disorientation
Expressive speech deficits	Finger agnosia
Anomia, object or color naming deficits	Early evidence for mirror or inverted writing
Agrammatism	Spatial dysgraphia
Phonological reading errors	Visual reading errors
Poor phoneme-to-grapheme correspondence in spelling	Letter and word reversals in spelling
Letter-by-letter decoding	Phonetic decoding
Normal eye movements	Faulty eye movements
Intact visual-spatial skills	Intact oral language skills

Adapted from Pirozzolo, F.J. (1981) Language and brain: Neuropsychological aspects of developmental reading disability. *School Psychology Review*, *10*, 350–355. With permission.

in Table 3.2 (Pirozzolo, 1981). Specifically, the auditory-linguistic dyslexic subtype showed deficits in language processing characterized by expressive and receptive language difficulties, and grapheme-to-morpheme problems. The visual-spatial dyslexic subtype showed processing deficiencies in the visual-perceptual domain. These processing problems included right-left discrimination problems, finger agnosia, visual-spatial deficits, and visual encoding problems.

Case study evidence recently has emerged to provide ecological validity for the auditory-linguistic subtype (Obrzut, 1982) and the visual-spatial subtype (Hooper, Hynd, & Tramontana, 1988). Cases illustrating the neuropsychological parameters of these two subtypes also were presented by Hynd and Cohen (1983). Pirozzolo is one of the first investigators to hypothesize the existence of many learning disability subtypes, but he believed that these auditory-linguistic and visual-spatial subtypes probably represented the most common forms of learning disabilities.

Bakker (1979a) also proposed a clinical-inferential model with two subtypes of learning disabilities. This particular conceptualization is noteworthy because of its developmental perspective. Concentrating largely on reading disabled children, Bakker reviewed evidence suggesting that the right cerebral hemisphere is the primary mediator in the beginning stages of learning to read. This was based largely on the assumption that reading appears to be more visual-perceptual and less linguistic during these early stages of the reading process. As the demands of learning to read begin to become more linguistically complex, however, the reading process begins to be mediated more by left cerebral hemisphere strategies. Consequently, as the reading process develops from single letters, to monosyllabic and multisyllabic words, to simple and more complex sentences, there should be a normal shift from right to left hemisphere-mediated reading strategies, although a developmental increase in hemispheric asymmetry may not be seen. This has been called the *balance model*.

When learning to read, some children may show an overuse of right hemisphere strategies (i.e., perceptual) and poor emergence of left hemisphere strategies. Bakker labeled these children *P-type dyslexics* (perceptual deficits) because they learn to read using visual-perceptual strategies, and continue to show an overreliance on these strategies as reading progresses. Conversely, *L-type dyslexics* (linguistic deficits) show an overreliance on left hemisphere strategies and poor emergence of right hemisphere functioning. These children demonstrate an overreliance on linguistic-semantic strategies throughout the development of reading.

Subsequent hemispheric dominance studies have begun to provide support for Bakker's conceptualization (Bakker, 1979b, 1981; Bakker, Licht, Kok, & Bouma, 1980; Bakker, Moerland, & Goekoop-Hoefkens, 1981; Keefe & Swinney, 1979). Tomlinson-Keasey and Kelly (1979a, 1979b) also have demonstrated this conceptualization with respect to spelling and arithmetic. Further, Van Strien, Bakker, Bouma, and Koops (1988) have begun to show familial antecedents of these two kinds of dyslexia. Although Pirozzolo and Bakker's models began to show empirical linkages of learning problems to assumed brain functions, Bakker's model also provided support for viewing learning problems from a developmental perspective.

Multiple-Subtype Models

In addition to the dual-subtype models, models using neurocognitive variables also produced other multiple-subtype conceptualizations. Using the WISC, for example, Smith (1970) clinically separated the profiles of retarded readers into three subtypes. These subtypes were distinct from each other and none of the subtypes reportedly were found in a comparison group of normal readers. *Subtype 1* was characterized by poor auditory sequential skills and symbol manipulation, but intact visual-spatial skills. *Subtype 2* was characterized by the reverse profile, whereas *Subtype 3* showed a mixed profile of deficits.

Rourke, Young, and Flewelling (1971) demonstrated a similar tripartite breakdown of disabled learners using the WISC in a sample of children, ages 9 to 14 ($n = 90$). These subtypes were a $VIQ > PIQ$ subtype, a $VIQ < PIQ$ subtype, and a $VIQ = PIQ$ subtype. Rourke et al. were able to demonstate external validity for these subtypes based on an extensive battery of neuropsychological tests (i.e., Halstead-Reitan Battery).

Bateman (1968) also provided evidence to show the existence of three learning disability subtypes using the Illinois Test of Psycholinguistic Abilities (ITPA). Consistent with many of the other studies described, Bateman classified children into three subtypes representing auditory deficits with relative visual strengths, visual deficits with relative auditory strengths, and combined deficits. Bateman's conceputalization, however, is somewhat different in that she found that deficits tended to be almost exclusively related to short-term memory in a specific modality.

Wilson and Risucci (1986) offered a well-developed conceptualization for the classification of language disabled preschool children. Drawing largely on neuropsychological assessment methods, Wilson and Risucci (1986) clinically identified five subtypes. These were an *expressive language* subtype, a *receptive language* subtype, and a *globally deficient language* subtype. Two additional subtypes included children who exhibited *memory and retrieval* problems and *no deficits*.

This classification model is important because of its use of quantified rules for subtype membership and its reliance on a neuropsychological assessment battery. Moreover, Wilson and Risucci (1986) have begun to establish internal and external validity for this classification model. For example, good comparative results were obtained when the clinical subtypes were evaluated against a stringently applied cluster analysis. Clearly, this study provides an excellent example of carefully considered research in learning disability subtyping and classification.

Mattis, French, and Rapin (1975) reported the existence of at least three independent learning disability subtypes. Employing neuropsychological techniques, Mattis et al. grouped children ($n = 113$), ranging in age from 11 to 12, into a brain-damaged reader group, a brain-damaged dyslexic group, and a non-brain-damaged dyslexic group. All of the children had an IQ score of 80 or greater, and none showed evidence of severe psychopathology. The reading disabled children scored at least 2 years below grade level on WRAT Reading (i.e., recognition).

After the three groups were formed, a comprehensive neuropsychological battery was administered that included the WISC or WAIS, the Benton Test of Visual Retention, Raven's Coloured or Standard Progressive Matrices, Illinois Test of Psycholinguistic Abilities (ITPA) Sound Blending Subtest, Purdue Pegboard, and other related measures of language and motor abilities. The results of these tests were used to identify three relatively homogeneous subtypes. These subtypes were a *language disorder* syndrome, an *articulatory and graphomotor dyscoordination* syndrome, and a *visual-perceptual disorder* syndrome. These three subtypes accounted for approximately 39%, 37%, and 16% of the sample, respectively. Taken together, these three syndromes accounted for over 93% of the total reading disabled sample. Based on these findings, Mattis et al. provided quantitative guidelines for determining each of the subtypes based on the neuropsychological battery. These guidelines are discussed further in Chapter 6.

Similar to the Mattis et al. model, Denckla (1972) also described three learning disability subtypes based on neuropsychological data. These in-

:luded a *specific language disturbance* subtype, a *visuo-spatial disability* subtype, and a *motor dyscontrol* subtype. Denckla noted, however, that about 70% of the sample of disabled learners showed either a mixed deficit pattern or did not align with any of the three subtypes. This latter finding suggested that, although broad-band learning disability subtypes may exist, the clinical manifestations of learning disabilities are extremely variable and, consequently, classification efforts will be a formidable task.

Denckla's work received further support from a replication attempt by Mattis, Erenberg, and French (1978). Using 8- to 10-year-old black and Hispanic children, these investigators replicated the three dyslexic patterns and found evidence for two additional subtypes. These were a *phonemic sequencing deficits* subtype, which accounted for about 10% of the sample, and a *mixed* subtype that exhibited characteristics of two of the subtypes. This latter group also accounted for about 10% of the sample. The language disordered subtype still comprised the largest percentage of children (i.e., 63%), but the sizes of the articulatory and graphomotor dyscoordination subtype and the visual-perceptual disordered subtype diminished to about 10% and 5%, respectively.

Of all the neurocognitive models, the Mattis et al. studies are significant from several vantage points. First, these investigators were instrumental in emphasizing the importance of multiple comparison groups. This is important so that rival interpretive hypotheses can be minimized in establishing legitimate subtypes. Second, and perhaps more important to the subtyping literature, these investigators were among the first to attempt to replicate their subtyping model, thereby addressing the issue of validity.

Despite the success of Mattis et al. (1975), more recent studies have not been able to replicate these findings (Pennington, Smith, McCabe, Kimberling, & Lubs, 1984; Smith, Pennington, Kimberling, & Lubs, 1983). Even so, in support of the general issue of subtyping, Mattis et al. (1978, p. 52) stated that "regardless of the number of syndromes to be eventually determined, there appears to be sufficient evidence to date to submit that a dyslexia syndromes model which presumes several independent causal defects is a tenable working hypothesis to guide future research."

Finally, following up earlier work with Johnson (Johnson & Myklebust, 1967; Myklebust & Johnson, 1962), Myklebust (1978) proposed the existence of at least four major learning disability subtypes. One of the subtypes was predicted to show primary deficits in auditory processing, particularly in the phoneme-to-grapheme formation of words. A second subtype was predicted to exhibit visual processing deficits and be unable to gain symbolic meaning from letters and words in an efficient manner. The other two subtypes were predicted to show integrative deficits, one having deficiencies primarily in the language domain and the other primarily in intermodal processing. Myklebust believed that the deficits inherent to these subtypes represented a conceptual framework from which to view learning disabilities.

Neurolinguistic Classification Models

Closely related to the neurocognitive models are subtyping models based on neurolinguistic variables. One of the primary differences between the two models is that neurolinguistic models tend to focus on language processing variables as well as selective, qualitative aspects of an individual's learning dysfunction.

Language-Based Subtype Models

These models exclusively used language variables in determining specific learning disability subtypes. For example, Curtiss and Tallal (1988) classified 100 language impaired preschool children into three subtypes. One subtype showed expressive language deficits, the second showed receptive language deficits, and the third showed deficits in both processing domains. Similar classifications identifying two subtypes also have been offered by de Ajuriaguerra (1966) and Wolfus et al. (1980). In the Curtiss and Tallal study, however, the performance differences among each clinical subtype were evidenced only in linguistic processing skills and not in linguistic competence (e.g., grammatical skills). These data document the importance of task, as opposed to modality, parameters in language impaired preschoolers. They also illustrate the qualitative nature of this particular clinical-inferential model.

Using a battery of language tests encompassing skills in vocabulary, memory, and naming, Denckla (1981) identified six subtypes of language impairment in a sample of learning disabled children. *Anomic* disorders were characterized by subnormal naming with normal comprehension and repetition. Another subtype exhibited anomic disorder with repetition deficits. *Dysphonemic sequencing* disorders were characterized by poor repetition with phonemic substitutions and missequencing, but with normal naming, comprehension, and speech production. A fourth subtype had *verbal memory* disorder. This subtype experienced poor sentence repetition and verbal-paired-associate learning, but showed relatively intact naming, comprehension, and speech production. Denckla also found evidence for two mixed subtypes, a *right hemisyndrome with mixed language* disorder and a *mixed* subtype manifesting subnormal repetition, and impaired comprehension, phonemic memory, and sequencing.

Similarly, Rapin and Allen (1983) identified seven different subtypes of learning disabled children using measures of expressive language, comprehension, and interactive behaviors. These included three subtypes that exhibited significant expressive disorders. One of these three subtypes was a *phonologic-syntactic* subtype with or without oral-motor apraxia. The second subtype showed severe expressive difficulties with good comprehension, and the third subtype, *syntactic-pragmatic* subtype, showed grossly impaired syntax and limited pragmatic language.

Two additional subtypes were autistic in nature. One of these was *severe autism with mutism* that was impaired in every feature of oral language and symbolic functioning. The second, *autistic syndrome with echolalia*, exhibited limited spontaneous production, with the majority of speech being echolalic. Children within these subtypes also had communication difficulties encompassing other modalities besides the acoustic-oral one and typically showed associated deficits in affective responsiveness and overall cognition.

A sixth subtype, *verbal auditory agnosia*, was characterized by no comprehension of speech and limited expressive skills. These deficits tended to evolve from an early stage of linguistic development, thus contributing to the severe auditory agnosia. Visual processing abilities were relatively preserved. The final subtype offered by Rapin and Allen was the *semantic-pragmatic* subtype. This subtype was characterized by impaired syntax, limited functional use of language, echolalia, and poor semantic processing.

Reading-Based Subtype Models

Along with the more traditional model for grouping language disorders in a homogeneous fashion, neurolinguists also have made progress in subtyping reading disabilities. Marshall (1984) provided a classification model based largely on the adult literature on acquired alexia. This classification model encompassed four basic subtypes of reading disabilities. These included surface dyslexia, deep dyslexia, phonological dyslexia, and direct dyslexia.

Surface dyslexia was characterized by difficulty with the visual aspects of word recognition. Despite good phonological capabilities for regular and irregular words, whole-word recognition and reading comprehension were impaired. Individuals with surface dyslexia also showed an inability to use context clues in deciphering written text. Given these deficits in accessing the visual modality in the reading process, individuals showing surface dyslexia usually read better aloud than silently. Deloche, Andreewsky, and Desi (1982) described these same characteristics in their surface dyslexia subtype.

The second subtype described by Marshall (1984) was *deep dyslexia*. This subtype was characterized by adequate reading of familiar words, but frequent semantic paralexias when reading aloud (e.g., substituting "car" for "automobile"). Reading errors also were characterized by visual confusion and a dependence on concrete problem-solving strategies. Despite these inherent deficits, these individuals are able to employ context clues adequately and, consequently, tend to show satisfactory reading comprehension. Some investigators have speculated that deep dyslexia is related to anomia. Specifically, it appears that these individuals can access the correct semantic category, but an incorrect visual-semantic association occurs resulting in the paralexic response. Other researchers have suggested that the deep dyslexic reading pattern of these individuals is mediated primarily by the right cerebral hemisphere (Coltheart, 1980; Saffran, Bogyo, Schwartz, & Martin, 1980) as opposed to the neurolinguistic processes associated with the left cerebral hemisphere (Hynd & Hynd, 1984). Siegel (1985) provided case study data to support the existence of this subtype of dyslexia in childhood.

The third neurolinguistic subtype that Marshall (1984) described was *phonological dyslexia*. This subtype was characterized by severe deficiencies in efficiently accessing the phoneme-to-grapheme system. These individuals typically add or delete prefixes and suffixes in their reading, although this finding is equivocal (Funnell, 1983). In contrast to deep dyslexia, phonological dyslexia is characterized by an average oral vocabulary. In a case study of developmental phonological dyslexia, Temple and Marshall (1983) noted that oral reading errors tended to be orthographically similar to the target word or derivational forms of the target word. Beauvois and Derouesne (1979) similarly described this neurolinguistic subtype.

Finally, Marshall (1984) described *direct dyslexia*. This subtype was characterized by adequate or accelerated oral reading capabilities for regular and irregular words. Comprehension skills, however, typically were poorly developed and dysfunctional. Direct dyslexia also has been called hyperlexia (McClure & Hynd, 1983).

Other neurolinguistic classification models also have been presented that identify subtypes similar to those reported by Marshall (Marshall & Newcombe, 1973; Sevush, 1983). In addition, Marshall and Newcombe (1973) identified *visual dyslexia* and Warrington (1981) proposed *concrete word dyslexia*. Similar to most other neurolinguistic subtypes, research on these subtypes is sparse. To date, many of these data have been collected from work with brain-injured adults, but few studies describing these specific subtypes have been conducted with samples of individuals exhibiting developmental learning disabilities. Nonetheless, the neurolinguistic models of subtyping show much promise because they demand detailed descriptions of *how* a child performs. Moreover, as discussed in Chapter 2, these models have begun to be linked to putative neuroanatomical substrates of the learning process (Hynd & Hynd, 1984).

Combined Classification Models

Efforts to combine neurocognitive, achievement, and neurolinguistic variables in the search for clinical subtypes have been limited. This has been due largely to difficulty in controlling the number of variables and potential interactions involved without the aid of high-speed computer technology. Nonetheless, there have been five attempts to combine variables in an effort to describe learning disability subtypes (Decker & DeFries, 1981;

Nelson & Warrington, 1974; Omenn & Weber, 1978; Vernon, 1979, Weller & Strawser, 1987).

In a quasi-combination of variables, Nelson and Warrington (1974) undertook two investigations of reading and spelling disabled children. In their first study, these investigators demonstrated that WISC VIQ decrements were much more associated with severity of reading disabilities than with spelling disabilities. In their second investigation, they classified spelling disabled children ($n = 87$) into two subtypes. *Subtype 1* had only spelling problems, whereas *Subtype 2* exhibited reading and spelling problems. Nelson and Warrington found that Subtype 2 had a significantly lower WISC VIQ than Subtype 1, although the two subtypes did not differ in terms of nonverbal abilities. Further, Subtype 1 evidenced a greater tendency to make phonetically accurate errors than Subtype 2. They hypothesized that Subtype 2 maintained a more generalized language dysfunction, whereas Subtype 1 demonstrated a more specific language dysfunction (i.e., spelling).

Omenn and Weber (1978) used cognitive and achievement measures to classify individuals in their sample as *auditory* dyslexics, *visual* dyslexics, and dyslexics showing mixed deficits. Although few behavioral and no electrophysiological differences were noted among these subtypes, these investigators did document family histories consistent with each respective subtype (e.g., the auditory dyslexics demonstrated family histories consistent with this specific subtype).

In 1981, Decker and DeFries postulated that the reason for the lack of evidence showing a genetic transmission of reading disabilities was related directly to the heterogeneous nature of those disabilities. They reasoned that this heterogeneity could mask relationships that actually may exist. Using a large sample of 125 reading disabled children, 250 parents of the probands, and 250 comparison parents, Decker and DeFries evaluated all participants on a battery of tests measuring achievement, intelligence, and perceptual speed. Score profiles were plotted for each child and all scores were identified as normal or impaired. This procedure resulted in four different subtypes for the proband sample. These were a subtype with reading deficits due largely to spatial reasoning, a subtype with visual-perceptual speed deficits, a *mixed pattern* subtype, and a *normal pattern with low reading achievement* subtype. Despite the ambitiousness of this study and the subtype model proposed, results did not show evidence for the familial transmission hypothesis.

Finally, Vernon (1977, 1979) reviewed the literature on dyslexia and postulated the existence of at lest five different subtypes. These subtypes were described as having deficits in: (a) analyzing visual shapes, (b) analyzing whole words into phonemes, (c) acquiring grapheme-to-phoneme associations, (d) grasping irregularities in grapheme and phoneme associations and in processing complex orthography, and (e) grouping single words into phrases and sentences. This subtyping model has not yet been validated;

however, it appears similar to the other clinical-inferential models presented. A comparable subtyping model also has been presented recently by Weller and Strawser (1987) based on their integration of the learning disability literature.

Conclusions

Clinical-inferential models have provided a great deal of evidence to support the multidimensional nature of learning disabilities. Many studies have provided clinical classification schemes based on achievement, neurocognitive, neurolinguistic, and combined variables. Although these models fall short of establishing a definitive classification methodology, they do exemplify the complexities of learning disorders and serve to underscore the need for a valid differential nosology.

From the clinical-inferential models proposed to date, there appears to be at least three broad-band subtypes documented in terms of achievement, neurocognitive, and combined classification variables. The most commonly reported subtype is characterized by auditory-linguistic deficits. The other two comprise a subtype showing visual-perceptual deficits and another one showing a combination of deficits. Other clinical-inferential subtypes have been proposed, such as those with motor deficiencies, but most of these clinically derived subtypes represent modifications of the three broad-band descriptions.

Subtype models derived from neurolinguistic approaches classify learning disabled children in a more refined manner based on selective linguistic deficits. Indeed, Vellutino (1978) suggested that language deficits represented the primary impediment in disabled learners. Although the neurolinguistic models have the potential to provide links to neuroanatomical models of learning, by their very nature they are overly dependent on linguistic measures and verbal language conceptualizations. Van der Vlugt and Satz (1985) cautioned that despite the utility of a neurolinguistic model for qualitatively describing learning disabilities, other subtypes of learning disability should not be overlooked, particularly as the quest for relevant intervention techniques continues. Such a limited perspective potentially could preclude applications to other kinds of learning disabilities that result from nonlanguage deficits. Even though neurolinguistic models have limited their foci primarily to reading, from a qualitative perspective they have been productive to the subtyping literature more generally. These models are noteworthy for their attention to linguistic detail and their focus on processes by which children learn.

The clinical-inferential subtyping models have provided a foundation for the acceptance of the concept of heterogeneity of learning disabilities. Noteworthy among these attempts at classification have been models proposed by Mattis et al. (1975), Boder (1970), Pirozzolo (1979), Rourke

(Rourke & Finlayson, 1978), and Wilson and Risucci (1986). Not only has each of these investigators provided a clinical classification model, but each has assisted the clinician and researcher by also suggesting an assessment model that includes specific guidelines for subtype membership. In addition, Bakker (1979a) has provided a developmental paradigm from which to understand the neurodevelopmental parameters of learning disability subtyping.

Individual case study models noted in Chapter 1 also have contributed to clinical-inferential models by highlighting the importance of intervention strategies based on specific quantitative and qualitative assessment data. Clearly, this is consistent with the underlying mission of nearly all classification studies.

4
Empirical Classification Models

Although many of the clinical-inferential classification models make intuitive sense and, in fact, may represent broad-band descriptions for a learning disability nosology, there also are inherent problems with these models. Generally, the clinical-inferential models suffer from methodological weaknesses, limited data reduction strategies, and questionable validity. Consequently, the clinical utility of these methods is limited, especially when used to build classification systems that comprise numerous interacting variables.

Currently, with the ready availability of advanced computer technologies, many of the problems manifested by clinical-inferential models can be addressed effectively by empirical classification techniques (e.g., Q-type factor analysis, cluster analysis). Generally, the methods used to develop these models are designed to group *subjects* on the basis of profile similarities. One major advantage is that these methods can be used to generate classifications schemes and, consequently, contribute to the validation of the classification model. These complex methods are not new to the biological sciences, but they only recently have been applied to the behavioral sciences.

Given the complexities involved in using these grouping methods, they require rapid data management capabilities afforded by computerized technology. It is important to note, however, that these methods are not truly statistical in nature because they are not based on probabilistic models. Further, they serve to organize any data set, even random numbers, into relatively homogeneous groupings. Consequently, the number of clusters derived and their interpretive significance require sound clinical judgment on the part of the investigator.

This chapter reviews the literature associated with the various empirical classification models derived in the search for learning disability subtypes. Initially, given the recency of these classification methods to the behavioral science domain, a brief description of these techniques is provided. Empirical classification models of learning disability subtypes are then described. As with the clinical-inferential models, this chapter is divided into models using achievement variables, neurocognitive variables, neurolinguistic variables, and a combination of variables. Studies with empirically derived models are presented in Table 4.1.

Empirical Classification Methods

Empirical classification methods are used for subgroup delineation. Unless these delineated subgroups have been properly validated, however, results of these methods should not be used for individual diagnosis (see Morris, Blashfield, & Satz, 1981). Basically, the term *cluster analysis* is used to describe this group of classification methods.

Morris et al. (1981) presented six fundamental steps that should be followed in any empirical classification attempt. The first two steps are related to preparation for performing the clustering. First, it is important to select the sample to be classified in a careful manner. In this regard, Morris et al. noted that "without standard randomized sampling techniques, it is clearly possible to generate 'unnatural' subgroups due to a biased sample," (pp. 84–85). Second, the selection of variables or attributes to be included in the multivariate matrix is crucial to maximizing potential subtype differences. Here, investigators must select variables that reflect theoretically relevant dimensions for the population being studied (e.g., neurocognitive and academic functions for the learning disabled population).

The next three steps are related directly to the cluster analysis. The first step here is to determine an appropriate *similarity* or *distance* measure. This process, or "ordination," occurs when each subject is classified, simultaneously, according to the preselected measurement dimensions as defined by the test variables (Adams, 1985).

Different kinds of ordination measures focus on selective aspects of individual test-score profiles. Similarity measures, such as correlation, describe profile congruence (i.e., shape and scatter), but they do not describe levels of performance. Typically, correlation coefficients are similarity measures for Q-type factor analysis. In contrast, distance measures, such as squared Euclidean distance, can address profile pattern as well as level of performance, even if this is not a significant variable under consideration (Adams, 1985). This may lead to a masking of profile similarity, particularly if profile elevations are large (Fletcher & Satz, 1985). The Cattell Profile Pattern Coefficient also has been proposed to address both similarity and distance in classification research (Cattell, Coulter, & Tsujioka, 1966), but no subtyping studies have employed this method to date. There are no clearly established rules for selecting a measure of similarity or difference, and investigators need to determine the importance of various components of the data (e.g., profile shape, variability, elevation) in selecting the most useful measure.

The fourth step in using empirical classification methods is the selection

TABLE 4.1. Empirical learning disability subtyping models.

Classification models	Technique	Subtypes
Achievement models		
Satz & Moris (1981)	Cluster analysis	2 Learning problem groups (undescribed) 7 Normal groups
Van der Vlugt & Satz (1985)	Cluster analysis	5 Learning problem groups (undescribed) 4 Normal groups
DeLuca, Del Dotto, & Rourke (1987)	Cluster analysis	Mild deficits in tactile perception and aspects of expressive language, short-term memory, attention Deficits in tactile problem solving, visual-motor speed, language Mild deficits in psychomotor skills, finger localization, conceptual flexibility Deficits in retrieval, organization, visual manipulation, conceptual flexibility, finger graphesthesias, spelling, math
Johnston, Fennell, & Satz (1987)	Cluster analysis	Learning disabled-nonspecific Specific reading disability 4 Normal groups
Neurocognitive models		
Vance, Wallbrown, & Blaha (1978)	Q-type factor analysis	Distractibility deficits Perceptual-organization deficits Language disorder–automatic Language disorder–pervasive Behavioral comprehension, labeling deficits
Fisk & Rourke (1979)	Q-type factor analysis	Auditory-verbal deficits, impaired tactile perception Motor, auditory-verbal processing deficits Auditory-verbal, memory, tactile perception deficits (not seen in 9- to 10-year-olds)
Petrauskas & Rourke (1979)	Cluster analysis	Language deficits Linguistic, sequencing, finger localization deficits Normals
Lyon & Watson (1981)	Cluster analysis	Language comprehension, memory, sound blending, visual-spatial deficits Language comprehension, auditory memory, visual-motor deficits Aphasic Expressive, receptive language deficits Visuoperceptive deficits Normal pattern with low reading skills
Satz & Morris (1981)	Cluster analysis	Global language deficits Specific language deficits Visual perceptual deficits Mixed deficits Unexpected (normal profile with low reading skills)
Lyon, Stewart, & Freedman (1982)	Cluster analysis	Normal pattern Linguistic deficits Visual-spatial, visual-motor deficits Auditory comprehension, selected visual-perceptual deficits Mixed deficits

TABLE 4.1. Continued.

Classification models	Technique	Subtypes
Hale & Saxe (1983)	Q-type factor analysis	High spatial, low sequential abilities VIQ > PIQ Attention deficits Visual-spatial deficits
Del Dotto & Rourke (1985)	Q-type factor analysis Cluster analysis	Poor linguistic, sequential, haptic abilities; low achievement Auditory-verbal deficits, low achievement Mild auditory-verbal deficits, severe haptic deficits, low achievement Deficits in fine eye-hand coordination and speed, spelling and math Inconsistent linguistic abilities, mild deficits in bilateral motor speed and control, reading > spelling, math PIQ > VIQ, normal cognitive abilities Deficits in verbal labeling, low math

Joschko & Rourke (1985)	5 Clustering procedures	Younger group (ages 6 to 8)
		  Poor general perception, motor; academic deficits
		  Poor auditory perception, sequencing, academics
		Older group (ages 9 to 14)
		  Poor auditory perception
		  Poor tactile and auditory perception; motor and academic deficits

McKinney, Short, & Feagans (1985)	Cluster analysis	Linguistic deficits Mixed—severe visual-perceptual, mild linguistic deficits Mixed—mild visual, linguistic deficits Normal pattern, low coding 2 Normal patterns
Korhonen (1985)	Cluster analysis	Normal pattern General language deficits Visuomotor deficits General deficiency Naming deficits Mixed deficits
Snow, Cohen, & Holliman (1985)	Cluster analysis	Global deficits Attention deficits Language deficits Mild language deficits 2 Normal groups
Van der Vlugt & Satz (1985)	Cluster analysis	Severe global language deficits Selective language, perceptual deficits Mild global language deficits Severe global language, selective perceptual-motor deficits Severe global language, perceptual deficits Global visual-perceptual-motor deficits Normal

TABLE 4.1. Continued.

Classification models	Technique	Subtypes
Morris, Blashfield, & Satz (1986)	Cluster analysis	Deficient verbal skills with poor achievement, more active, emotionally reactive, increasing strengths in visual-perceptual-motor skills with age Increasing deficits in verbal-conceptual skills, below-average achievement Below-average achievement, familial component Normal, above-average achievement Normal
Shinn-Strieker (1986)	Cluster analysis	Dysphonetic Dyseidetic Mixed
Johnston et al. (1987)	Cluster analysis	2 Specific nonverbal deficits Global visual-perceptual deficit Unexpected Mild mixed deficits Normal
Leton, Miyamoto, & Ryckman (1987)	Cluster analysis	Attention deficits Verbal-association deficits Visual-spatial, motor deficits
Snow, Koller, & Roberts (1987)	Cluster analysis	Low verbal comprehension, attention Deficient verbal comprehension Low perceptual organization, attention No deficit group, high attention 3 Generally low subgroups
Hooper & Hynd (1988)	Q-type factor analysis	Sequential < simultaneous processing Sequential > simultaneous processing Mixed processing deficits Normal
Lyytinen & Ahonen (1988)	Cluster analysis	General developmental delay Specific motor problems Motor control problems Spatial constructive problems Mild spatial constructive problems Kinesthetic problems
Neurolinguistic models Aram & Nation (1975)	Q-type factor analysis	Repetition strengths Nonspecific formulation-repetition deficits Generalized low performance Phonological comprehension-formulation-repetition deficit Comprehension deficits Formulation deficits
Feagans & Appelbaum (1986)	Cluster analysis	Intact syntax Intact semantic Hyperverbal Intact narrative Superior narrative Superior syntax and semantic

TABLE 4.1. Continued.

Classification models	Technique	Subtypes
Combined models		
Smith & Carrigan (1959)	Cluster analysis	Cognitive, perceptual-metabolic association deficits
		Low cognitive-perceptual abilities
		Undifferentiated
		2 Physically superior groups
Naidoo (1972)	Cluster analysis	Speech and language
		Visual-spatial
		Genetic
Doehring & Hoshko (1977)	Q-type factor analysis	Linguistic deficits
		Phonological deficits
		Intersensory integration deficits
		Visual-perceptual deficits
Doehring, Hoshko, & Bryans (1979)	Q-type factor analysis	Linguistic deficits
		Phonological deficits
		Intersensory integration deficits
Thomson, Hicks, & Wilsher (1980)	Q-type factor analysis	Auditory-perceptual deficits
		Sequencing deficits
		General written language deficits
		Specific verbal deficits
		Coding deficits
		Visual-spatial deficits
		Labeling deficits
Doehring, Trites, Patel, & Fiedorowicz (1981)	Q-type factor analysis	Type O reading disability
		Type A reading disability
		Type S reading disability
Watson, Goldgar, & Ryschon (1983)	Cluster analysis	Language disabled
		Visual processing deficit
		Minimal deficits
Meacham & Fisher (1984)	Q-type factor analysis	Reading disabled
		Language disabled
Snow & Hynd (1985b)	Q-type factor analysis	Expressive and receptive language deficits with impaired academics
		Reading and spelling deficits
		Expressive and receptive language deficits, tactile perception problems
		Borderline to low-average IQ, variable adaptive behavior, no achievement or processing discrepancy
Nussbaum & Bigler (1986)	Cluster analysis	VIQ > PIQ
		VIQ < PIQ
		Mixed
Short, Feagans, McKinney, & Appelbaum (1986)	Regression of IQ-achievement, age-achievement discrepancies	Overachievers
		Target achievers
		Underachievers
		Slow learners
		Disabled achievers
Smith, Goldgar, Pennington, Kimberling, & Lubs (1986)	Cluster analysis	Low auditory discrimination, sound blending, oral expression
		Global deficits

TABLE 4.1. Continued.

Classification models	Technique	Subtypes
Spreen & Haaf (1986)	Cluster analysis	Specific reading disorder, low WISC-R freedom from distractibility factor
		Group 1 (IQ > 69)
		Minimally impaired
		Severe pervasive deficits
		Arithmetic deficits
		Specific reading deficits
		Global-achievement and visual-perceptual deficits
		Global-achievement and linguistic deficits
		Group 2 (IQ > 79)
		Global-achievement and deficits, visual-perceptual deficits
		Global-achievement and linguistic deficits
		Mixed global deficits, poor left-right orientation
		Minimally impaired
		Severe pervasive deficits
		Specific arithmetic deficits
		Specific reading and visual-perceptual deficits
		Specific reading and graphomotor deficits
		Group 3 (at adulthood)
		Specific arithmetic deficits
		Specific reading deficits
		Global impairment, adequate sentence repetition and left-right orientation
		Visual-motor coordination and reading comprehension deficits
		Visual-motor coordination and deficits, adequate achievement
		Severe global achievement deficits
		Normal profiles, poor arithmetic
		2 Normal profiles
Speece (1987)	Cluster analysis	Short-term memory deficit
		Speed of recoding deficit
		Mild recoding/attention deficit
		Mild encoding/severe recoding deficit
		Marginal performance
		Mild memory/recoding deficit
Snow & Desch (1988)	Cluster analysis	Congenital anomalies
		Developmental delays
		Neurological dysfunction
		Neurological dysfunction-encephalitic subgroup
		Normal profile
Watson & Goldgar (1988)	Cluster analysis	Auditory processing deficits
		Auditory short-term memory, auditory and visual processing deficits
		Language deficits
		Auditory short-term memory and visual processing deficits

of an appropriate clustering technique. This typically includes a cluster analysis or Q-type factor analysis. The most popular techniques and their accompanying computer programs have been reviewed by Rourke and Adams (1984). Several of these are summarized here.

The next step involves the determination of the number of clusters. Although there are no explicit rules for determining the number of clusters, an examination of different results, perhaps in a successive fashion, is essential. Hierarchical trees allow for a visual inspection of the clusters derived, whereas clustering coefficients provide information related to the amount of variance accounted for by each cluster. Differences among cluster profile means also can be examined.

The final step necessary for using one of the clustering techniques is particularly important. Here, estimates of internal and external validity of the subtypes are generated. Internal validity procedures address the adequacy and stability of a particular subtyping solution and they help to minimize the subjective nature of many of the decisions required in clustering techniques. In fact, Everitt (1980) recommended that investigators apply several procedures (e.g., repeated runs with different subsets of the diagnostic variables) in determining the validities of final subtype groupings. External validity procedures typically address how the derived subtypes differ on criteria not included in the original design.

As can be surmised, clustering techniques are relatively complex and require statistical sophistication for proper use. More detailed information about these strategies can be found in other resources (e.g., Everitt, 1980; Skinner, 1978). Although there are numerous cluster analytic techniques (e.g., Rourke & Adams, 1984), this chapter only discusses several of the most widely used procedures for classifying homogeneous subtypes of learning disabilities. These are cluster analysis and factor-analytic variants.

Cluster Analysis

These classification techniques provide strategies for assigning subjects to relatively homogeneous groups. These techniques offer the investigator flexibility in the search for homogeneous subtypes of learning disabilities and they assess both profile pattern and elevation in identifying groupings of subjects. These techniques neither limit the number of clusters that can be generated nor rigidly adhere to models of linearity in classifying subjects into groups. Generally, these techniques attempt to minimize profile differences within a subtype and maximize profile differences among subtypes (Adams, 1985). As mentioned previously, the application of these techniques is quite complex, and the investigator needs to guard against "naive empiricism" (Morris et al. 1981) when using them. Swanson (1987, 1988) also noted similar concerns.

To date there have been numerous cluster analytic techniques proposed to be used in learning disability classification research. Indeed, these specific classification methods have been used the most frequently in subtyping studies. Among the most popular groups of clustering techniques is *hierarchical agglomerative*. Agglomerative techniques initiate the clustering process by combining the most similar pairs of observations and building the subtypes from that point in a multistage format.

Primary differences among variants of this group of clustering techniques are related to how similarity and difference coefficients are defined (e.g., single linkage methods, average linkage methods, minimum variance method). A primary problem with this group of techniques is that it is unable to correct for poor pairings at an early stage of the clustering process; thus, final clustering solutions may be based on less than optimal subject pairings.

Another popular group of cluster analytic techniques is *iterative partitioning*. These techniques are based on estimates of the number of clusters in a data set (k = number of clusters). For any given number of clusters, each cluster's centroid is estimated. The various iterative partitioning methods differ according to how k is chosen. For example, some are based on choosing centroids randomly, others are based on the distance between centroids, and still others permit the investigator to establish estimates. Subjects are then assigned to the clusters with the most similar centroids, and this process is replicated until a stable subgrouping of subjects is found.

In comparison to their hierarchical counterparts, the iterative techniques correct for subjects who are not optimally matched to a cluster by reassigning them to more appropriate groups. As Morris et al. (1981) noted, however, these techniques can become expensive, particularly if the initial partition was less than optimal, thus lengthening the time required to obtain an optimal solution.

Q-Type Factor Analysis

Factor-analytic techniques can be used to assign variables to homogeneous groups, or factors, based on the matrix of correlations for pairs of target variables. These techniques can be used to investigate relationships among selected variables (i.e., R-type factor analysis) or subjects (i.e., Q-type factor analysis). Rourke and Adams (1984) noted that these are only two of the six nonredundant pairs of interrelationships involving tests, people, and observation intervals that could be examined.

The primary utility of Q-type factor analysis lies in its ability to calculate the degree of similarity in the profile patterns of a target population. Initial, or principal, factors are extracted from a correlation matrix. These factors can then be rotated, using a variety of strategies (e.g., varimax) to obtain the best classification solution. Although there are no clear guiding principles for including subjects in particular clusters, factor loadings of greater than .49 tend to be the one generally accepted convention for clas- sification studies using Q-type factor analysis.

Although Q-type factor analysis has been used in about one third of the empirical classification studies conducted to date, it has been criticized. In addition to focusing solely on profile pattern to the exclusion of profile elevation, this technique has been criticized because of the conceptual dilemma of using a linear model across subjects and the issue of how to classify subjects who obtain multiple factor loadings (Everitt, 1980; Fleiss, Lawlor, Platman, & Fieve, 1971). Further, the number of subtypes derived using Q-type factor analysis always is one less than the number of depen- dent variables, potentially limiting the number of subtypes that are de- rived. Finally, although Sneath and Sokal (1973) provided descriptions of variants of this classification method, it is not clear if these variants are comparable to Q-type factor analysis, thus limiting the number of ways internal validity of a subtype model can be explored (Everitt, 1980). Inter- nal validity of subtypes derived from this classification technique, however, can be explored through a series of Q-type factor analyses on different target populations. Here, profile patterns of resultant subtypes typically are correlated between samples, and the subtypes with the highest correla- tions are retained as the final subtype solution. All of the subjects subse- quently are reclassified according to these retained subtypes.

Summary

Empirical classification methods clearly are useful for developing a nosolo- gy of learning disability subtypes, but their applications must be based on sound clinical thinking. Clustering techniques are limited by the quality of data input, and it is important for investigators to plan sample and variable selections wisely. Presently, few data suggest an advantage of one type of clustering technique over another. In fact, some equivocal evidence sug- gests that, given appropriate decisions at particular steps in these tech- niques (e.g., similarity and distance coefficient), derived subtype classifi- cation schemes may be similar (Del Dotto & Rourke, 1985), although evidence to the contrary also has been presented (Doehring, Hoshko, & Bryans, 1979; Morris & Blashfield, 1983). Although this issue will con- tinue to be debated, it appears that there is great potential in using the empirical methods to generate subtyping models for learning disabilities.

Achievement Classification Models

In contrast to the large number of studies using achievement variables in clinical-inferential models of subtyping, only four studies have used empir- ical classification methods with achievement data (DeLuca, Del Dotto, &

Rourke, 1987; Johnston, Fennell, & Satz, 1987; Satz & Morris, 1981; Van der Vlugt & Satz, 1985). The work of Satz and Morris (1981), Van der Vlugt and Satz (1985), and Johnston et al. (1987) is important because these investigators did not define the population a priori; instead, they used clustering techniques with large numbers of subjects to establish learning disabled and comparison groups. This strategy allowed for a more objective classification of probands and avoided the use of exclusionary criteria in the selection of learning disabled subjects (Satz & Morris, 1981).

Using hierarchical agglomerative cluster analysis of Wide Range Achievement Test (WRAT) data, Satz and Morris identified nine viable achievement clusters in a sample of 236 white males (mean age = 11 years). Seven of these clusters represented variants of a normal learning profile. Two of the clusters, however, showed significantly low achievement (i.e., reading deficit > 2 years) and warranted the designation of learning problem groups. External validation of the groups was demonstrated using Peabody Picture Vocabulary Test (PPVT) standard scores, neuropsychological performance, socioeconomic status, and neurological soft signs.

Two replication attempts also have emerged for this classification model. Using a Dutch sample, Van der Vlugt and Satz (1985) were able to replicate these procedures and subtypes with relative accuracy cross-culturally. Johnston et al. (1987) also replicated the Satz and Morris (1981) procedures and, although results were similar, this study showed some variation in the number of subtypes identified. Specifically, using 150 fifth-grade males, Johnston et al. applied a hierarchical agglomerative clustering technique to WRAT Reading, Spelling, and Arithmetic scores. This allowed for the development of an achievement-based classification model in which a learning disabled subsample could be identified. Examination of the achievement-based model revealed the presence of six stable subtypes, three less than the number identified by Satz and Morris (1981) and Van der Vlugt and Satz (1985) in their studies. Similar to the Van der Vlugt and Satz (1985) study, four of these subtypes were characterized by a normal learning profile. The other two reflected distinct achievement deficits. One of these subtypes, labeled a *nonspecific learning disability* subtype, showed generalized deficiencies across all achievement areas. This was similar to the original Satz and Morris findings. Although the second subtype reflected a specific achievement deficit, Johnston et al. found this deficiency in reading, whereas Satz and Morris found it in arithmetic. The incidence of learning problems roughly was equivalent in both studies. In all three of these studies, a second-order clustering was performed on neurocognitive variables for the combined two groups of learning problem children. This second-order clustering subsequently is described more completely when neurocognitive subtyping models are discussed.

Finally, DeLuca et al. (1987) also used clustering techniques to group children with arithmetic deficiencies into homogeneous subtypes. DeLuca et al. used 156 children, ages 9 to 14, with WRAT Arithmetic percentile scores less than 27 and Reading percentile scores greater than 40. All children were referred for evaluation of suspected neuropsychological impairment. Intellectual functioning for the sample was within an average range (i.e., Wechsler Intelligence Scale for Children [WISC] Full-Scale IQ = 85 to 115). Hierarchical cluster analytic techniques were used on WRAT Reading, Spelling, and Arithmetic standard scores. Four stable subtypes of arithmetic disabled children were identified.

The first subtype was characterized by mild deficits in tactile-perception, conceptual flexibility, and some aspects of expressive language. This group also showed inconsistent performance on tasks measuring attention, short-term auditory memory, and visual-spatial output. These children evidenced intact functioning, however, in nonverbal problem solving, motor skills, visual-perceptual organization, and selected aspects of language. The second subtype was characterized by significant deficiencies in higher order tactile perception, visual-motor speed and coordination, verbal fluency, verbal memory, and conceptual flexibility. This subtype also experienced difficulties in the efficient use of verbal mediation strategies.

The third subtype showed deficiencies in nonverbal problem solving and processing. Basic language abilities were relatively intact, but there were selective deficits in psychomotor skills, conceptual flexibility, and finger localization. This subtype evidenced average to above-average reading skills in the presence of poor arithmetic calculation skills. The final subtype manifested mild difficulties in verbal expression, conceptual flexibility, finger graphesthesia, and manipulation of visual-symbolic materials. This subtype experienced intact reading abilities despite significant deficits in spelling and arithmetic. Organizational deficiencies and poor work-study habits also were characteristic of this subtype.

The DeLuca et al. (1987) study is unique because the sample selected for study evidenced a specific area of deficit, thus allowing for examination of different profile patterns within the area of arithmetic achievement. This kind of investigation has potential to facilitate the development of more detailed intervention approaches and to provide prognostic information about particular subtypes. This study also is noteworthy because it highlights the heterogeneous nature of learning problems within as well as among specific achievement domains.

Neurocognitive Classification Models

Empirical classification studies using neurocognitive variables have included standard intellectual measures as well as an array of neuropsychological tasks in identifying learning disability subtypes. Several studies have used the Wechsler Intelligence Scales in deriving subtyping models (Hale & Saxe, 1983; Snow, Cohen, & Holliman, 1985; Snow, Koller, & Roberts, 1987; Vance, Wallbrown, & Blaha, 1978).

Intelligence Scale Models

Vance et al. (1978) reported one of the first studies to use the WISC-R exclusively in a classification venture with learning disabled children. Using Q-type factor analytic techniques on data derived from 128 elementary school children diagnosed as having a specific reading disability, Vance et al. identified five meaningful subtypes that accounted for about 75% of the sample. These were a subtype showing a high degree of distractibility, another subtype showing a disruption of visual-perceptual abilities, and three subtypes showing impediments in some aspect of language functioning.

Similarly, Hale and Saxe (1983) used Q-type factor analysis on WISC-R scores to develop a classification for a heterogeneous group of disabled learners. The sample comprised children with diagnoses of learning disabilities, emotional disturbance, and mental retardation. Children demonstrating average and low-average functioning also were included in the analysis. This study included an initial sample of 77 children and a validation sample of 192 children in the analyses.

Hale and Saxe used a variant of Q-type factor analysis, modal profile analysis, to identify subtypes. This technique applies Q-type factor analysis to two separate samples to determine the number of profiles within each sample. These within-sample profiles then are compared, and those profiles that are similar across the samples are retained as final modal profiles. Finally, all subjects are reclassified according to the final modal profiles. In contrast to traditional Q-type factor analysis, this technique results in profiles based on elevation, shape, and scatter. Using this technique, Hale and Saxe identified four subtypes of problem learners.

One subtype was characterized by relatively intact visual-spatial abilities, but impaired sequential processing skills. This subtype had significant reading deficits, despite average overall cognitive functioning, and nearly age-appropriate arithmetic skills. Another subtype was characterized by higher verbal than nonverbal abilities (i.e., VIQ > PIQ). The other two subtypes were more difficult to describe, but one tended to show attentional inefficiencies, and the other, visual-spatial weaknesses.

Snow et al. (1985, 1987) performed similar classification studies with the WISC-R and WAIS-R (Wechster Adult Intelligence Scale–Revised), but used hierarchical cluster analysis to identify groups of subjects. Using the WISC-R with identified learning disabled students (n = 106), Snow et al. (1985) found six subtypes. Three of these subtypes represented a continuum of intellectual functioning, with one subtype showing borderline abilities, one showing low-average abilities, and the other showing average abilities. The other three subtypes were consistent with specific learning disabilities. Two of these subtypes demonstrated specific language disturbance, whereas the third showed attentional inefficiencies as the primary contributor to the learning problems. Conspicuously absent from this classification model is a subtype showing primarily visual-perceptual deficits.

Snow et al. (1987) replicated these procedures with the WAIS-R with a sample of learning disabled adolescents and adults and found evidence for seven subtypes. Similar to the previous study with the WISC-R, Snow et al. found two subtypes characterized by various language disorders. Consistent with their previous subtype study with the WISC-R, no subtype showed specific visual-perceptual deficits, although one of the subtypes did manifest relative weaknesses in this processing domain. The other four subtypes showed few, if any, specific deficits and, curiously, one of the subtypes exhibited a relative strength in attentional abilities.

Hooper and Hynd (1988) presented a classification model based on the simultaneous and sequential cognitive processing subtests of a different intelligence scale, the Kaufman Assessment Battery for Children (K-ABC). Subjects in this study were reading disabled and normal functioning children ranging in age from 8 to 12 ($n = 117$). Results of Q-type factor analysis revealed the presence of four reliable subtypes accounting for over 91% of the sample. One subtype showed low sequential processing abilities, the second subtype evidenced low simultaneous processing, and the third demonstrated deficits in both information processing domains. The fourth subtype did not reflect any cognitive deficiencies as measured by the K-ABC. Although these subtypes made conceptual sense, external validity efforts provided only minimal support for these subtypes across measures of intelligence and achievement.

Summary

All of these studies identified specific subtypes based on intellectual measures. They are important because they attempted to classify learning problem students on the basis of instrumentation used in traditional clinical practice. Identified subtypes, however, clearly are consistent with the scales upon which they are based. Thus, models derived from the Wechsler scales identified basic subtypes characterized by deficits in visual-perceptual, verbal, and attentional skills, whereas the model derived from the K-ABC identified subtypes consistent with the simultaneous-sequential information processing dichotomy. All of these subtypes essentially reflect the factor structures of the measurement techniques, begging the question of their external validities. Even so, it is quite clear that learning disabled samples are heterogeneous with respect to traditional intellectual measures.

Neuropsychological Battery Models

Other neurocognitive approaches have used psychoeducational and neuropsychological variables in identifying learning disability subtypes. Empirical subtyping models developed by Rourke (Del Dotto & Rourke, 1985; Fisk & Rourke, 1979; Joschko & Rourke, 1985; Petrauskas & Rourke, 1979), Satz (Johnston et al., 1987; Morris, Blashfield, & Satz,

1986; Satz & Morris, 1981: Van der Vlugt & Satz, 1985), and Lyon (Lyon, Stewart, & Freedman, 1982; Lyon & Watson, 1981) have contributed significantly to neurocognitive subtyping efforts. The impact of these studies has created a theoretical basis for the subtyping models. In this sense, they have suggested putative brain-behavior relationships and have linked multidimensional conceptualizations of learning disabilities to neuropsychological theory. Some of these studies also have begun to elucidate the developmental courses of particular learning disability subtypes.

ROURKE AND COLLEAGUES

Petrauskas and Rourke (1979) identified four subtype patterns of performance on a neuropsychological battery. This battery comprised 44 measures classified into six categories as outlined by Reitan (1974). These were tactile-perceptual, sequencing, motoric, visual-spatial, auditory-verbal, and abstract-conceptual domains. The sample included 160 children, ages 7 and 8, of which 133 were retarded readers (i.e., WRAT Reading percentile < 26) and 27 normal readers (i.e., WRAT Reading percentile > 44). The overall sample initially was divided into two equal subsamples and Q-type factor analysis was performed on each subsample. Profiles that correlated significantly across samples were retained in the final subtype solution, and the Q-type factor analysis then was performed on the entire sample of 160 children.

The first subtype derived contained the largest grouping of subjects. It was characterized by auditory-verbal and language-related deficits. Reading and spelling achievement were lower than arithmetic functioning. The second subtype demonstrated deficits in visual sequencing, bilateral finger agnosia, and global achievement problems. This subtype also evidenced ipsative weaknesses on WISC Arithmetic, Coding, Information, and Digit Span subtests (i.e., the ACID pattern). The third reliable subtype showed right unilateral sensory and motor deficits. Specific impairment was observed in expressive speech and visual-motor coordination. The fourth subtype was not a reliable one, but generally reflected a normal neuropsychological profile. Petrauskas and Rourke speculated that, respectively, these subtypes were consistent with dysfunction involving (a) the temporal lobe of the left hemisphere, (b) the temporo-parieto-occipital regions of the left hemisphere, and (c) the frontal regions of the left hemisphere.

Fisk and Rourke (1979) used Q-type factor analysis in a cross-sectional fashion in their investigation of potential subtypes at three different ages, 9 to 10 years, 11 to 12 years, and 13 to 14 years (n = 264). In contrast to the Petrauskas and Rourke (1979) study, this investigation used children deficient in all achievement domains (i.e., WRAT Reading, Spelling, and Arithmetic percentiles < 31).

Results of Q-type factor analysis revealed two basic subtype patterns that emerged for all three age levels. A third subtype appeared only at the youngest and oldest age levels. *Subtype 1* was characterized by poor auditory-verbal processing with marked impairment in tactile perception. *Subtype 2* also was characterized by auditory-verbal deficiencies, but in addition showed motor deficits and impaired shifting of attentional sets. *Subtype 3* demonstrated auditory-verbal, memory, and tactile-perceptual problems. Given this cross-sectional design, developmental interpretations are tenuous, but these findings do suggest the importance of considering age-related factors in learning disability subtyping efforts. The results of this study also underscored the importance of psycholinguistic processes in generic learning problems.

More recent studies by Rourke and colleagues have continued to rely on empirical classification methodology to explore subtyping patterns in specific groups of children. Using five different clustering techniques, for example, Joschko and Rourke (1985) demonstrated the presence of four subtypes of the WISC ACID profile. Two of the subtypes occurred at the younger age level (i.e., ages 6 to 8) and were characterized by sensory-perceptual-motor deficits and by auditory processing deficits, respectively. Two subtypes also were found for the older age level (i.e., ages 9 to 14), with one subtype showing poor auditory perceptual abilities and the other manifesting deficient tactile and auditory perception accompanied by motor impairment.

Using similar methodology, Del Dotto and Rourke (1985) demonstrated specific subtype patterns for a large sample of left- and right-handed children (*n* = 322). The analysis identified three reliable subtypes. *Subtype 1* was characterized by poor auditory-linguistic skills, poor sequential processing, impaired haptic perception, and uniformly low achievement. *Subtype 2* was characterized by exclusive auditory-verbal deficits accompanied by global achievement problems. *Subtype 3* showed mild auditory-verbal deficits, but had severe tactile-perceptual impairment and global achievement deficiencies. In addition, four other less stable subtypes were identified. This study is especially significant because it is one of the few subtyping efforts that used a combination of clustering techniques (e.g., Q-type factor analysis versus cluster analysis) in a comparative manner and identified the same subtypes.

SATZ AND COLLEAGUES

Satz and his colleagues (Johnston et al., 1987; Morris et al., 1986; Satz & Morris, 1981; Van der Vlugt & Satz, 1985) also have made important contributions to the subtyping literature. These investigators were the first to identify learning disabled samples in an empirical manner from a larger group of children. In an initial clustering study, briefly described earlier, Satz and Morris (1981) identified two subtypes of children that demonstrated overall deficient achievement (i.e., at least a 2-year deficit). These subtypes, characterized by a greater proportion of soft neurological signs and poorer performances on neuropsychological testing, were designated as learning disabled.

These two subtypes were combined $(n = 89)$ and a second clustering technique was performed on four neuropsychological measures administered at the end of the fifth grade. This clustering technique identified five reliable subtypes: global and specific language impaired, visual-perceptual deficit, mixed deficit, and neuropsychologically intact with low achievement. These subtypes were validated across neurological variables, socioeconomic status, and parental reading levels. Additionally, they were replicated across samples (Johnston et al., 1987; Van der Vlugt & Satz, 1985) as well as across cultures with Dutch children (Van der Vlugt & Satz, 1985).

In an innovative study using longitudinal clustering techniques, Morris et al. (1986) presented a developmental classification model based on a sample of reading disabled children. Morris et al. classified 200 nonclinical normal and reading disordered males based on patterns of performance on eight neuropsychological measures. Four of these measures tapped verbal-conceptual abilities (e.g., verbal fluency) and four tested sensorimotor-perceptual skills (e.g., Embedded Figures Test). All 200 children were tested with all measures at the start of kindergarten, and again at the end of the second and fifth grades. Clustering techniques and subsequent internal and external validation procedures identified two reliable broad-band subtypes: good readers and poor readers.

This two-group classification was further differentiated into five subtypes. These included two good reader subtypes and three poor reader subtypes. *Subtype A* evidenced deficient verbal abilities and poor achievement. These children, however, showed a trend toward improving their visual-perceptual abilities over time. Teacher ratings also suggested that this group of boys was more physically active than their peers. *Subtype B* demonstrated increasingly poorer performance with age, particularly in verbal-conceptual abilities. This subtype was characterized by parental history of learning problems and a greater frequency of significant neurological findings and birth history events. *Subtype C* members and their families manifested below-average performance on all neuropsychological measures over time. *Subtypes D* and *E* showed average to above-average performance, and a lower incidence of significant neurological anomalies and birth difficulties. The performances of these subtypes were relatively stable over time. Although the results were obfuscated somewhat by limitations in the sample (i.e., all white males) and the use of an unvalidated clustering technique (i.e., longitudinal cluster analysis), this study was the first to address the issue of continuity of subtype topography.

Lyon and Colleagues

Lyon and his associates (Lyon, 1985b; Lyon, Rietta, Watson, Porch, & Rhodes, 1981; Lyon et al., 1982; Lyon & Watson, 1981) also have made a significant contribution to the subtyping literature. Using the Mattis et al. (1975) clinical-inferential subtyping model and clustering techniques, Lyon and Watson (1981) empirically identified six independent subtypes from a population of 11- to 12-year-old learning disabled youngsters (*n* = 100) and a matched group of normal achievers (*n* = 50). In addition to a *normal learner* subtype, Lyon and Watson found five disabled-reader subtypes.

Subtype 1 was characterized by mixed deficits in auditory processing, receptive language, visual memory, and visual-perceptual abilities. This subtype performed the poorest on academic tasks. *Subtype 2* demonstrated a similar, but less impaired, neuropsychological profile. *Subtype 3* was characterized by expressive and receptive language deficits, whereas *Subtype 5* appeared to be more severely impaired with respect to overall language functioning. Subtype 5 also manifested global achievement deficits. *Subtype 4* exhibited significant visual-perceptual impairment and, surprisingly, given the reported low prevalence of this kind of subtype (Boder, 1970; Mattis et al., 1975), comprised the largest number of children.

This subtyping model subsequently was replicated by Lyon et al. (1982) with 6- to 9-year-old disabled readers. The replication of these subtypes with a younger population suggested some degree of age-related stability for subtypes, albeit not necessarily for individuals. Evidence for external validity of these subtypes also has accrued. Specifically, both qualitative and quantitative differences among the subtypes have been noted on tasks of reading recognition, reading comprehension, oral reading, and spelling (Lyon et al., 1981, 1982). In contrast to the findings of Morris et al. (1986), however, these subtypes did not differ on measures of family history, major developmental milestones, or school history. Lyon (1983, 1985b) has begun to report data that link this subtyping model to treatment paradigms. This is a crucial endeavor that has not been addressed critically by other subtyping models (Lyon, Moats, & Flynn, in press).

In a quasi-replication of the Lyon et al. (1981) study, Shinn-Strieker (1986) reported a three-subtype classification model. Using a heterogeneous group of 92 children (i.e., emotionally disturbed, learning disabled, mildly retarded, normal), ranging in age from about 6 to 15, Shinn-Strieker identified three subtypes, the characteristics of which were similar to the clinical-inferential subtyping model proffered by Boder (1970). The deficit patterns also were consistent with subtypes proffered by Hooper and Hynd (1988) based on a study that used a simultaneous-sequential information processing model. One of the most important contributions of the Shinn-Strieker study, however, was that these profile patterns appeared to be independent of level of functioning. On the basis of these data, Shinn-Strieker argued that differential learning profiles can occur at all levels along the intellectual continuum. This argument clearly is consistent with currently accepted definitions of learning disabilities (see Chapter 1), but somewhat inconsistent with subtyping models based on intelligence scales (e.g., Snow et al., 1985).

OTHER INVESTIGATORS

Another empirical classification model based on 102 severely learning disabled children and neurocognitive variables has been reported (Leton, Miyamoto, & Ryckman, 1987). Similar to the Rourke empirical classification models, Leton et al. identified three reliable subtypes using cluster analytic techniques. These subtypes were characterized by deficits in: (a) attention and concentration, (b) verbal-associative intelligence, and (c) visual-spatial and motor functioning. Interestingly, the latter subtype comprised the largest number of subjects, but the predominance of this kind of learning disability is not consistent with findings from most other subtyping studies.

Another empirical classification model based on neuropsychological data was developed by Korhonen (1985), who identified six learning disability subtypes in a sample of 9- to 10-year-old mild learning disabled children ($n = 82$) and normal children ($n = 84$). Using several clustering techniques, Korhonen presented internal validity for five subtypes including: (a) *normal*, (b) *general language deficient*, (c) *visuo-motor deficits*, (d) *general deficiency*, and (e) *naming deficits*. A sixth subtype, *mixed deficits*, was derived but deemed to be minimally reliable. Some external validity also was obtained from measures of reading, writing, frequency of neurological soft signs, and behavioral ratings. Generally, the naming-deficit subtype contained the children with the most severe reading deficits.

In a 3-year follow-up study, Korhonen (1986, 1987, 1988) found that 64% of the learning disabled children continued to show severe reading and/or writing problems. The naming-deficit subtype showed the poorest prognosis in reading and the general-deficiency subtype in writing. In contrast to reports of other longitudinal studies (e.g., Schonhaut & Satz, 1983), Korhonen reported a decrease in the degree of neuropsychological impairment for the learning disabled relative to the normal children.

Korhonen's work is important because it was conducted with Finnish children speaking the Finnish language which is thought to be a phonologically regular language. Korhonen's learning disability subtypes mimic those obtained from other subtype models (e.g., Satz & Morris, 1981), and this finding suggests that subtype conceptualizations probably are not artifacts of specific language irregularities but, instead, represent viable entities.

Another longitudinal study conducted in Finland addressed the derivation of subtypes from a sample of motorically impaired ($n = 106$) and normal ($n = 40$) 7-year-old children. Lyytinen and Ahonen (1988) used cluster analysis on scores from a battery of motor tasks to identify six motorically impaired subtypes. These included subtypes with (a) general developmental delay, (b) specific motor problems, (c) motor control problems, (d) spatial constructive problems, (e) mild spatial constructive problems, and (f) kinesthetic problems. Follow-up of these children at age 11 revealed that nearly half of the motorically impaired subjects continued to show significant motor difficulties. In addition, many of the children in the motorically impaired subtypes manifested significant lags in their basic academic skills.

A final study in the neurocognitive domain was reported by McKinney, Short, and Feagans (1985) who provided evidence for a learning disability taxonomy from the Carolina Longitudinal Learning Disabilities Project (McKinney & Feagans, 1984). Using a cognitive battery designed to assess a wide range of linguistic and perceptual abilities, McKinney et al. classified 55 first- and second-grade, school-identified, learning disabled children into six subtypes. Three of the subtypes manifested normal cognitive profiles, with one of these subtypes showing marginally normal performance levels. The other three subtypes showed significant learning disabilities. One of these latter subtypes showed a specific language disturbance and the other two evidenced mixed perceptual-linguistic deficits.

McKinney et al. provided internal as well as external validity evidence for their subtyping model. They further demonstrated that the three learning disabled subtyes had poorer academic outcomes over a 3-year period than the three normal cognitive profile subtypes. These latter three subtypes, in turn, manifested fewer scholastic gains than randomly selected, normal learning peers. Additionally, this study suggested that, at least for younger learning disabled children, over a 3-year period there may be a high degree of subtype stability. The finding of subtype stability, of course, is consistent with the results of some studies (e.g., Lyon et al., 1982), but inconsistent with the results of others (e.g., Morris et al., 1986).

SUMMARY

Rourke, Satz, Lyon, and other investigators have proffered a variety of empirically derived learning disability subtyping models based on neuropsychological test battery performance profiles. These models each comprise from two to five different subtypes that describe various degrees, specificities, and combinations of linguistic impairment, sensory-perceptual deficit, and academic dysfunction. Important features of this work involve efforts to establish external validity as well as recent foci on developmental and cross-sectional parameters associated with learning disability subtypes. Although presently equivocal, these parameters address the stability of subtype topography across age levels, the prognosis for particular subtypes, and age related changes in subtype classification for individuals.

Neurolinguistic Classification Models

In comparison to the large number of studies that have used neurolinguistic and language variables to develop clinical-inferential learning disability classification models, only two studies have used these specific variables to develop empirical models (Aram & Nation, 1975; Feagans & Appelbaum, 1986). One of the major reasons for this is that, given the technological sophistication needed to perform clustering techniques, many lingusitic variables have been included in broader neurocognitive testing. Alternatively, these variables have been included in a combined fashion with a number of other variables.

The classification study completed by Aram and Nation (1975) actually represented one of the first studies to search for homogeneous subtypes of language impaired preschool children. Using Q-type factor analysis of measures of comprehension, formulation, and repetition of certain aspects of language (e.g., phonological, syntactic, and semantic), Aram and Nation identified six different subtypes.

Subtype 1 was characterized by repetition strengths and inconsistent speech comprehension and generation. *Subtype 2* exhibited nonspecific formulation-repetition deficits and generally impaired language skills. *Subtype 3* manifested a generalized low level of performance across all of the language measures. *Subtype 4* was characterized by phonological and comprehension-formulation deficiencies. *Subtypes 5* and *6* manifested comprehension and formulation deficits, respectively. Although this model requires replication, it is consistent with the previously noted clinical-inferential models based on neurolinguistic variables.

A second study specifically using neurolinguistic variables was conducted by Feagans and Appelbaum (1986). These investigators used a battery of six linguistic tasks designed to assess syntax, semantics, narrative discourse (i.e., comprehension and paraphrasing), number of words used in paraphrasing, and complexity of language used to paraphrase. The sample comprised fifty-five 6- and 7-year-old disabled learners. Cluster analytic techniques identified six reliable subtypes. In contrast to emphasizing deficits, an approach typically used in neuropsychological descriptions, these investigators chose to describe subtypes by emphasizing more positive strengths. *Subtype 1* was characterized by normal syntactic abilities despite below-average competence in all other linguistic skills. *Subtype 2* exhibited superior semantic skills, but an inability to paraphrase or understand narrative information. *Subtype 3* was characterized by excessive talking, but members of this subtype typically were able to use complex speech. This subtype, however, tended to show expressive semantic deficiencies. *Subtype 4* was characterized by relatively poorer syntax and semantic skills than narrative skills, whereas *Subtype 5* showed superior narrative abilities and relatively normal language patterns. *Subtype 6* also exhibited relatively normal language skills characterized by superior syntax and semantic skills. Internal and external validity efforts supported this classification model.

This study is noteworthy because it provided refined descriptions of the different language patterns that can be manifested in the learning disabled population. This is important given the relatively high incidence (i.e., approximately 50%) of language-related difficulties in this population

(Marge, 1972). Although this classification model, like most others, is non-definitive, Feagans and Appelbaum did employ clustering techniques in conjunction with a priori hypotheses. Thus, this investigation is more than simply exploratory. Children within this study were followed over several years in order to document achievement. Achievement deficits, both within and among subtypes, were relatively consistent with a priori hypotheses.

Combined Classification Models

The empirical classification models reviewed thus far are impressive in their scope. This is due largely to the classification methods used and their abilities to manage large data sets from multiple domains. These methods frequently have been used to identify learning disability subtypes since approximately the late 1970s; however, they first appeared in this literature as early as 1959.

Early Models

Smith and Carrigan (1959) were among the first to report an empirical classification model of homogeneous subtypes of learning disabled children. These investigators used a comprehensive battery of tests that assessed selective aspects of seven major domains: cognition, cognitive-perception, perception, perceptual-metabolic (i.e., Critical Flicker Fusion Task), sensory, personality, and achievement. With a small sample of 40 reading disabled elementary school children (i.e., the lowest 10% of retarded readers), cluster analysis was used to identify more homogeneous subtypes. These subtypes then were compared in terms of a number of medical (e.g., bone age) and physical (e.g., height) variables.

These procedures resulted in the identification of five subtypes. *Subtype 1* manifested cognitive-association and perceptual-metabolic deficits. *Subtype 2* showed low cognitive-perceptual abilities. *Subtype 3* was characterized by an undifferentiated pattern of deficits. The other two subtypes evidenced a general superiority to the other three groups. Although this study can be criticized from a number of perspectives (e.g., small sample size), it represents an early, ambitious, and relatively sophisticated attempt to subtype learning disabilities.

The next empirical classification study with this population was not reported for 13 years. Naidoo (1972) used cluster analysis to classify reading disabled children into a speech and language deficient subtype, a visuospatial deficit subtype, and a genetic subtype. Clearly, the empirical classification models proposed by Naidoo (1972) and by Smith and Carrigan (1959) were ahead of their time with respect to conceptualization and methodology.

Doehring and Colleagues

The work of Doehring and Hoshko (1977) extended the efforts of Naidoo (1972) and Smith and Carrigan (1959). Doehring and Hoshko used achievement-based tasks that required higher order cognitive abilities (e.g., visual perception, intersensory integration) in their classification model. Consequently, their model included a combination of variables to determine homogeneous subtypes.

Doehring and Hoshko administered 31 reading-related tasks measuring visual matching, auditory-visual matching, visual scanning, and oral reading to two separate groups of children. The first group, Group R, primarily comprised children with reading problems ($n = 34$). The second group, Group M, consisted of 31 children with diagnoses of learning disabilities, language disorders, and mental retardation.

Within Group R, a Q-type factor analysis identified three subtypes and classified 31 of the 34 children. *Subtype 1* was characterized by adequate performance on nearly all of the visual matching and auditory-visual matching tests, but deficient performance on oral reading of words and syllables. Generally, this combination of deficits suggested the presence of linguistic impairment. *Subtype 2* was characterized by difficulty in efficiently associating printed with spoken letters, poor performance on auditory-visual matching tasks, and deficits in oral reading. This subtype comprised children with phonological deficiencies. *Subtype 3* had a basic difficulty involving the rapid perception of grapheme and phoneme sequences. This was evidenced by poor performance on visual and auditory-visual matching tasks. Considered collectively, these deficits suggested possible impairment in intersensory integration.

These investigators also attempted to use external criteria to validate the subtypes. Using independent teacher recommendations for each child, it was suggested that Subtype 1 members receive comprehension training only, Subtype 2 remediation of comprehension, oral expression, and visual-auditory association, and Subtype 3 assistance for the development of phonetic analysis, written sequencing, oral expression, and sound-letter blending.

Group M was included primarily for comparative purposes. Empirical classification procedures also identified three subtypes within this group. Two of these subtypes resembled Group R Subtypes 2 and 3. The third subtype, however, was characterized by poor auditory-visual and visual scanning deficits, suggesting primary involvement of the visual-perceptual system. When Group R and Group M were combined, only the linguistic deficient subtype of Group R (i.e., Subtype 1) emerged independently. The visual-perceptual subtype of Group M was no longer distinct.

The study by Doehring and Hoshko (1977) was seminal in establishing a foundation for further attempts to classify disabled learners empirically. This study was seriously flawed, however, by the exclusion of a comparative group of normal learners. Subsequently, Doehring, Hoshko, and Bryans (1979) replicated the work of Doehring and Hoshko using the same sample of reading disabled children (i.e., Group R), in addition to a matched group of normal readers. Doehring et al. replicated the three learning disabled subtypes found in the previous study and homogeneously classified the normal readers as well.

In a third study, Doehring, Trites, Patel, and Fiedorowicz (1981) increased the number of assessment variables to include a wider variety of neuropsychological measures. Three subtypes were identified that were highly similar to those obtained by Doehring and Hoshko (1977) and Doehring et al. (1979). The specific subtypes were an oral reading disability (*Type O*), a subtype characterized by deficiencies in spoken and written word associations (*Type A*), and a subtype with sequencing problems (*Type S*). Doehring (1985) noted that these same subtypes were identified at three different age levels, when more stringent criteria of reading disability were used, and with retesting of a small subsample of children. Further, these subtypes were identified even when other reading-related variables were added and when cluster analytic techniques were used.

With the large number of neuropsychological variables, Doehring et al. (1981) initially postulated that a single profile pattern may be directly related to specific reading disability. When these variables were evaluated, however, this connection was elusive and it appeared that any specific reading pattern actually may have multiple underlying causes or correlates.

For example, Type O children could be classified into at least three additional subtypes. These subtypes reflected deficits in naming, auditory-verbal short-term memory, and motor planning and coordination. Type A children were the most likely to have global neuropsychological impairment, suggesting generalized cerebral dysfunction. A subtype of these children, however, tended to show excessive difficulties with verbal materials, implicating left hemisphere involvement. No intermodal deficiencies were found with Type A children; however, the measures included in the testing may not have assessed cross-modal abilities in an adequate manner. Children included in Type S did not show firm indications of sequential deficits, but a small subsample did manifest visual-perceptual deficiencies and conceptual impairment. These deficits suggested bilateral posterior cerebral dysfunction. Thus, this study provided further support for the empirical classification of learning disabled youngsters into homogeneous groups. It also supported the hypothesis of multiple causes for specific broad-band subtypes of reading disabled children.

Other Models

In contrast to the Q-type factor analysis techniques used in Doehring's work, Watson, Goldgar, and Ryschon (1983) used a hierarchical clustering technique. They classified 65 reading disabled children on the basis of a psychoeducational battery. Three stable and replicable subtypes were identified. *Subtype 1*, comprising about 31% of the sample, was characterized by poor visual processing abilities, deficient auditory short-term memory, but relatively intact language functions. *Subtype 2*, comprising about 26% of the sample, evidenced a global language impairment and deficient memory ability. This subtype, however, showed average visual processing skills. *Subtype 3*, comprising about 43% of the sample, was characterized by minimal reading deficiencies, although oral reading typically was impaired. Watson et al. attempted to validate this model against internal and external criteria. The subtypes did not satisfy mathematical standards for homogeneity, but this work was one of the first rigorous attempts to validate an empirical classification model for learning disabilities. Recently, Watson and Goldgar (1988) improved upon this methodology in the identification of four reliable reading disability subtypes.

Similar to studies using neuropsychological and achievement variables, Nussbaum and Bigler (1986) classified 75 learning disabled children into three subtypes based on the WISC-R, WRAT, and selected measures from the Halstead-Reitan Neuropsychological Battery. *Subtype 1* comprised about 31% of the sample and evidenced generalized low functioning on all tasks. The investigators hypothesized that this subtype showed generalized cerebral dysfunction. *Subtype 2*, comprising about 47% of the sample, was characterized by a moderate level of impairment. This subtype showed deficient language abilities, but relatively intact arithmetic and visual constructional skills.

Subtype 3, comprising about 22% of the sample, was characterized by a higher level of performance than the other two subtypes, but the opposite pattern of abilities from Subtype 2. Generally, these investigators identified three profiles of learning disabled children that roughly approximated deficits in left or right hemisphere functioning, or a generalized cerebral dysfunction. An attempt to differentiate these subtypes based on personality and behavioral dimensions was largely unsuccessful (see Chapter 7).

Alternative Perspectives

Empirical subtyping models based on a combination of variables also have explored the classification of disabled learners from other perspectives. Short, Feagans, McKinney, and Appelbaum (1986), for example, addressed the identification of learning disabled subtypes from a discrepancy formula perspective. Using a sample of 58 normal and 52 learning disabled children, these investigators created a unique classification model using regression techniques. A priori rules for classifying children into one of five reading subtypes were derived via simultaneous statistical consideration of age and IQ-achievement discrepancies. *Target achievers* obtained reading recognition scores within 5 months of predictions based on age and IQ. *Slow learners* obtained reading scores at least 6 months below predictions based on age, but consistent with predictions based on IQ. *Underachievers* obtained scores consistent with predictions based on age, but at least 6 months below predictions based on IQ. *Disabled achievers* obtained scores that were significantly below predictions based on both age and IQ, whereas overachievers obtained scores significantly above both of these predictions.

Short et al. noted that this combination of variables tended to reduce the rate of classification error in both learning disabled and normal samples. These investigators followed these samples longitudinally and found that, despite remedial services, the learning disabled sample became more impaired over 3 years. In addition to suggesting an innovative, educationally relevant classification model, this work supports Ysseldyke's notion that low achievement is the best descriptor of these children.

From a different perspective, Smith, Goldgar, Pennington, Kimberling, and Lubs (1986) examined possible genetic components of specific learning disabilities by attempting to identify phenotypically distinct subtypes. The sample comprised 47 individuals (46 reading disabled and 1 undiagnosed) ranging in age from about 9 to 69 years. Subjects were administered a comprehensive battery of neuropsychological tests and results were cluster analyzed. Three stable subtypes were identified.

Subtypes 1 ($n = 17$) and *3* ($n = 18$) were characterized by weak auditory discrimination, poor sound blending, and deficient oral expression. *Subtype 2* manifested global deficits across all neuropsychological measures. Despite the apparent homogeneity within these subtypes, however, these investigators were unable to document significant differences among the subtypes on achievement variables or a reading quotient. In fact, aside from elevation, profile shapes for the subtypes were remarkably similar.

This lack of distinction among subtypes suggested that the genetic hypothesis was only tenable, at best. Smith et al., however, argued that these findings implicated a poor relationship between the neuropsychological measures used and the history (i.e., past or present) of a reading disability rather than a flaw in the genetic hypothesis. Smith et al. suggested that investigators interested in studying learning disability subtypes should attempt to include genetic variables (e.g., positive family histories of learning problems, parental reading levels) in their construction of subtyping models.

In another study, Snow and Desch (1988) provided initial evidence for a classification model for learning problem children based solely on medical (e.g., history of encephalitis), developmental (e.g., speech and language milestones), and physical growth (e.g., height) parameters. With a large sample of children referred to a pediatric clinic ($n = 1,598$) because of learning and behavioral problems, Snow and Desch used cluster analysis to identify a reliable five-subtype solution.

Subtype 1 comprised 38 subjects and was characterized by a high frequency of congenital anomalies. Minor developmental delays were present in this subtype and its members were not as tall as the children in the other subtypes. *Subtype 2* comprised 110 subjects and was characterized by a history of general developmental delays. Motor and speech delays were most common in this subtype, but significant medical factors were not a characteristic of this subtype. *Subtype 3* was the largest group, having 1,249 members, and essentially was characterized by a normal profile. *Subtypes 4 and 5* manifested significant neurological dysfunction. Subtype 4 had the highest percentage of individuals who had received some kind of head trauma as well as the highest frequency of seizure disordered children. Subtype 5 was characterized primarily by a history significant for encephalitis or meningitis. External validity was established for this tentative model based on social status, social/adaptive functions, activity level, visual-motor abilities, achievement, and intelligence. Although this study requires replication, results support neurodevelopmental models of learning dysfunction.

From still another perspective, Spreen and Haaf (1986) presented an eloquent study that addressed many reliability and validity issues in empirical classification models. The initial phase of this study examined the classification patterns derived from an extensive battery measuring a wide array of cognitive abilities in two groups of learning disabled children. In the second phase of this study, a subgroup of these children and a matched comparison group were followed into adulthood and reevaluated in an effort to investigate the continuity of particular learning disability patterns. This study is important because of its focus on long-term outcome of particular subtypes. Similar to other research (e.g., Morris et al., 1986; Rourke & Orr, 1977; Satz et al., 1978), this study used a longitudinal design, but it is the only study to date that has followed specific subtype patterns into adulthood.

Children included in this study were referred to the University of Victoria Neuropsychology Clinic because of learning problems. The subjects ($n = 63$) were between the ages of 8 and 12 (mean age = 10.14 years), had a VIQ or PIQ greater than 69, showed no acquired brain damage, and evidenced no primary psychopathology. A second group of referred subjects ($n = 96$) was selected directly from clinic files according to similar criteria, except that the IQ cutoff was more stringent (i.e., VIQ or PIQ > 79). This group was included to assess the possible effects of intelligence on the learning disabled profiles. Approximately 92% of the first sample and 84% of the second sample performed significantly below expected levels (i.e., one standard deviation below age and grade) on reading, arithmetic, or both.

Cluster analysis identified six subtypes for the first sample (i.e., project referral group) and eight subtypes for the second sample (e.g., restricted IQ referral group) accounting for about 86% and 92% of the subjects, respectively. Subtypes in the first sample were two severity specific subtypes (i.e., *minimal* and *pervasive*), two specific learning disability subtypes (i.e., *arithmetic* and *reading*), and two subtypes showing global impairments in achievement and specific cognitive functions (i.e., *linguistic* and *visual-perceptual*). The eight subtypes generated in the second sample were similar. There were two severity subtypes, three specific achievement deficit subtypes (i.e., one arithmetic and two reading), two global achievement deficit subtypes, again implicating cognitive and linguistic deficiencies, respectively, and a mildly impaired global achievement subtype with specific problems in right-left orientation. None of these subtypes, however, was noted to differ in terms of degree of neurological impairment.

During a second phase of this study, 170 subjects were retested at age 24. This sample included 86% of the initial referred subjects and 46 normal subjects. Clustering techniques classified 100% of the subjects. Nine subtypes were identified (probably reflecting the larger sample size and the inclusion of normal subjects) as compared to six and eight subtypes at younger age levels.

Specifically, there appeared to be three groups of normal learners, with one perhaps having greater difficulty with arithmetic, three specific achievement subtypes, two globally impaired subtypes, and one visual-motor coordination subtype.

Although these subtypes appeared to resemble the child subtypes in terms of topography, subtype membership at the two age levels showed little correspondence. Only about 36% of the subjects were classified into similar clusters at both age levels, perhaps because of treatment or neurodevelopmental effects that occurred over the years. Subjects who, at childhood, were classified on the basis of visual-perceptual deficits, specific reading or arithmetic impairment, or severity continued to show these problems into adulthood. The linguistic deficient subtype found during middle childhood, however, was curiously absent during adulthood, with most of these subjects moving into adult clusters reflecting more global deficits. This may suggest a poor long-term prognosis for this subtype. These findings challenge the continuity of specific subtypes (Lyon et al., 1982; Morris et al., 1986; Rourke & Orr, 1977) and the primary ascendant-skill hypothesis postulated by Satz et al. (1978); however, they do underscore the importance of developmental parameters in learning disability subtypes.

Finally, several other empirical classification attempts based on combinations of variables have emerged with the learning disabled population. For example, Thomson, Hicks, and Wilsher (1980) provided support for the five subtype clinical-inferential classification model proposed by Vernon (1977); Snow and Hynd (1985b) identified three homogeneous subtypes of learning disabled children based on Q-type factor analysis of the Luria-Nebraska Neuropsychological Battery: Children's Revision; Meacham and Fisher (1984) identified four subtypes of learning patterns in kindergarten children (although these were not stable into the second grade); and Speece (1987) identified six clusters of learning disabilities based on experimental measures of information processing. It is likely that other subtyping models will be proposed based on different combinations of variables.

Summary

Empirical classification models for learning disability subtypes that are based on combinations of variables first appeared as early as 1959. The prevalence of these kinds of models rapidly increased during the latter 1970s. Currently, these models frequently are encountered in the literature on learning disability subtypes. The early models proffered by Smith and Carrigan (1959) and, later, by Naidoo (1972) were seminal to conceptual and methodological developments in this area.

During the late 1970s and extending into the 1980s, Doehring and colleagues advanced these earlier efforts. Several classification models were proposed that variously suggested three different subtypes. The neuropsychological concomitants of these subtypes implicated differential neural substrates and multicausal explanations for these disorders. More recently reported models are consistent with these ideas.

Still other perspectives also have characterized these combined variable, empirical classification models. For example, some models have emphasized age-achievement and IQ-achievement discrepancies, whereas others have emphasized genetic and physical concomitants of learning disabilities. Important contributions of some of these studies include well-defined efforts to assess internal and external validities of subtypes. Age-related parameters associated with the identification, stability, and membership of learning disability subtypes also have been addressed. Consequently, in addition to more reliable and valid subtype identification, implications for prognosis and treatment are beginning to emerge.

Behavioral Classification Models

The behavioral classification models are unique because they attempt to classify learning disabled children according to homogeneous subtypes based on observed or rated behaviors. These models are reviewed in Chapter 7 (see Table 7.1), but are mentioned briefly here because many are based on empirical classification methods.

For example, studies by Speece, McKinney, and Appelbaum (1985) and Porter and Rourke (1985) have grouped learning problem children into homogeneous subtypes based on structured behavioral ratings. Other investigations have begun to explore the behavioral adjustment, adaptive behavior, and social-emotional functioning of specific learning disability subtypes (e.g., Del Dotto, Fisk, & Rourke, 1988; Goldstein, Paul, &

Sanfilippo-Cohn, 1985; Nussbaum & Bigler, 1986; Ozols & Rourke, 1985; Satz & Morris, 1981; Strang & Rourke, 1985; Strawser & Weller, 1985; Weintraub & Mesulam, 1983). In addition to improving the sophistication of learning disability subtyping attempts, these models suggest that specific social-emotional features may be related to specific subtype patterns.

Conclusions

There are numerous pertinent issues related to empirical classification methods and numerous studies have used these methods to derive empirical models for learning disability subtypes. Clearly, the review of these empirical classification models suggests that the identification of two, three, or even four broad-band learning disability subtypes is not as simple as it appeared with the clinical-inferential models. The sophistication of the empirical classification methodology has enabled researchers to explore the complexities associated with degree of severity and specificity of impairment across, as well as within, a wide array of functional domains. The importance of including all conceptually relevant variables, as illustrated by the first clustering study attempted (Smith & Carrigan, 1959), in exploring the heterogeneity of learning problems cannot be overstated.

A number of methodological improvements have characterized the empirical classification literature (e.g., Morris et al., 1986). These improvements have provided a basis for understanding learning disability subtypes from a longitudinal perspective. Studies by Morris et al. (1986) and Spreen and Haaf (1986) represent important attempts to begin examining these issues.

Finally, given the homogeneous subtypes that now have been identified by various clustering techniques, initial attempts to describe and validate relationships among etiological factors, assessment, and treatment have been established. These kinds of relationships may be among the most important reasons to develop an adequate subtyping nosology. Even so, despite the rapid advancement in learning disability subtyping illustrated by the models reviewed in this chapter, a universally accepted clinical classification model has not yet been adopted. Perhaps this is because, as Satz and Morris (1981) noted, present classification models are probably best considered to be preliminary. As such, they require further refinement, especially in terms of validity and clinical applicability.

5
Issues in Classification and Subtype Derivation

The historical and neuropsychological foundations for conceptualizing learning disabilities in a multidimensional fashion and the many clinically and empirically based studies addressing the heterogeneous nature of this group of disorders attest to the remarkable progress made in the field of learning disability subtyping in a relatively brief amount of time. This progress has been impeded, however, by a number of fundamental issues related to these classification efforts. Rourke (1983), for example, presented issues that face the learning disability field in general. These included: (a) definitional concerns, (b) methodological issues, (c) the determination of reliable subtypes, (d) learning disability prediction, and (e) treatment issues. Clearly, all of these issues are directly related to the need for nosological clarification.

In this chapter, fundamental classification issues are discussed with specific reference to their implications for learning disability subtyping. Reasons for developing a learning disability nosology are presented, followed by a theoretical framework for researching these disorders. Several specific issues are addressed, such as those related to subject sampling, variable selection and assessment, and subtype continuity. The chapter concludes by addressing the classification methods used to derive specific subtype models.

Definitional and Conceptual Issues

A major obstacle that impedes progress in learning disability research is the lack of a universally accepted, operational definition. As described in Chapter 1, many definitions have been advanced but, to date, none has been universally embraced by researchers and clinicians. This has led to confusion even about what issues and factors are comprised by the domain of learning disabilities as well as a variety of assessment and identification problems.

Definitional problems have led some investigators to question the existence of learning disabilities (Algozzine & Ysseldyke, 1986; Ysseldyke & Algozzine, 1983). These problems have led others to believe that a poor conceptual understanding of generic learning problems obfuscates any meaningful attempt to develop a nosology of specific learning disability subtypes (Adelman, 1979a, 1979b; Senf, 1986; Swanson, 1987, 1988). Here, investigators have attempted to classify learning disabled individuals into more homogeneous subtypes when, in fact, specific learning disabilities may not be clearly differentiated from other learning problems (e.g., language disorders, attention deficit disorders).

Alternatively, some researchers (Adelman & Taylor, 1986) have argued a learning disability actually may represent one point on a continuum of learning problems. In this sense, a learning disability is conceptualized as only one of many different kinds of learning problems. This conceptualization serves to establish a learning disability as a diagnostic entity that is part of a broader scheme, yet separate from other learning problems. As such, explorations of distinct subtypes of a variety of learning problems is not precluded. Learning disabilities research, therefore, can focus on different levels, such as on the continuum of learning level, on the discrete subtype level, or on the continuum of severity level. Such a conceptualization is consistent with Skinner's (1981, 1986) model for psychiatric research. This conceptualization is illustrated in Figure 5.1.

With respect to Figure 5.1, readers should note, of course, that where disorders fall on a continuum of learning (i.e., Level 1) currently is unclear. Likewise, the exact number and kind of learning disability subtypes (Level 2) remain elusive. This conceptualization also has been adopted by the Task Force on Nosology (David, 1988), a multidisciplinary project in the beginning stages of development, which was designed to create a classification model for preschool children with disorders of higher order

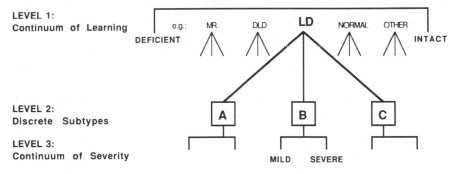

FIGURE 5.1. A conceptualization of levels of differentiation of learning disability subtypes. *Note.* MR = Mental Retardation; DLD = Developmental Language Disorder; LD = Learning Disability.

cognitive functioning. Preliminary results from this project suggest that children with prevasive developmental disorders can be distinguished from those with developmental language disorders (Morris, 1988). Within each of these groups of disorders, specific subtypes also have begun to be identified (Fein, Allen, & Waterhouse, 1988; Wilson, Aram, Rapin, & Allen, 1988).

Thus far, research efforts have succeeded somewhat at the continuum of learning, discrete subtype, and continuum of severity levels, but not in an orchestrated fashion. Further, even though the Task Force on Nosology has performed in such a manner, it has yet to address specific learning disabilities. Consequently, research results have contributed to confusion about various potential causes, correlates, and subtypes of learning disabilities. In the language of biological classification, it is unclear if learning disabilities are a "genus" (i.e., a heterogeneous group sharing some basic similarities) or a "species" (i.e., a homogeneous group within a larger heterogeneous group). Clearly, the subtype literature reported to date suggests that learning disabilities are a group of heterogeneous disorders; whether they are a genus or a species, however, remains to be clarified (Adelman & Taylor, 1986). Such clarification is crucial to the conceptual development of the field.

Implications for Subtype Classification

Given these definitional and conceptual problems, it is not surprising that currently there is no generally accepted learning disability classification model. The growing body of literature addressing the subtyping question, however, indicates that the field is moving, albeit slowly, toward that goal. Keogh (1983) advanced three reasons why such a classification model should be developed: advocacy, research, and intervention. A clearly delineated homogeneous group of disorders provides a basis for advocacy on behalf of individuals with differential risk factors and prognoses. Advocacy is important in order to obtain the support and resources needed to study particular problems. Such research leads to understanding, and understanding is prerequisite to intervention and treatment progress. Thus, a generally accepted classification model clearly is fundamental to efforts designed to improve service delivery.

Toward this goal, Adelman and Taylor (1986) identified four broad-band dimensions important to all learning disability subtyping models. These dimensions are shown in Figure 5.2 and include: cause, severity of problem manifestion, chronicity, and prevasiveness of problem manifestation. Thus, in terms of this framework, learning disability subtyping models should endeavor to address etiology, both in terms of personal and environmental factors. Morever, they should address the severity and the onset of the learning disability, two issues particularly germane to longitudinal research efforts. Finally, they should address the expansiveness of the

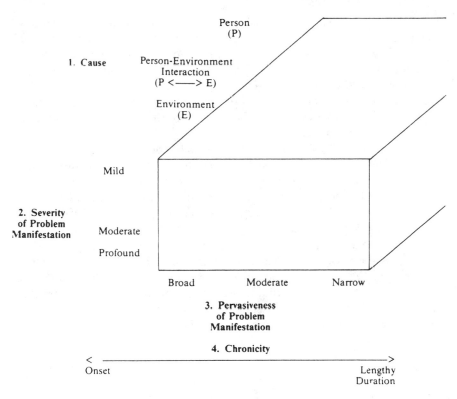

FIGURE 5.2. Four key dimensions of concern in classifying learning disability subtypes. (From Adelman, H.S., & Taylor, L. (1986) The problems of definition and differentiation and the need for a classification schema. *Journal of Learning Disabilities, 19*, 514–520. With permission.)

learning disability. For example, is the learning disability limited to reading recognition deficits or does it include other academic deficits as well?

Clearly, the field is moving toward the development of an appropriate classification model for learning disabilities and, perhaps more generally, learning problems. Related definitional issues, however, must be addressed from theoretical and applied perspectives. One result will be to facilitate comparisons among studies and ultimately to develop an acceptable and usable classification model. Toward this goal, investigators should continue to explore the conceptual issues in learning disabilities. It is there that the foundation for establishing a solid nosological framework begins (Adelman & Taylor, 1986).

A Conceptual Framework for Subtyping Research

It is clear from Chapters 3 and 4 that many different learning disability classification models have been proposed based on achievement, neurocognitive, and neurolinguistic variables using clinical and empirical methods. Much of this apparent progress, however, has been hampered by definitional issues and a poorly articulated conceptual framework for subtype development (see also Swanson, 1987, 1988). With several notable exceptions (e.g., Lyon et al., 1981; Mattis et al., 1975; Satz and Morris, 1981; Speece et al., 1985), most of the proposed classification models lack the conceptual frameworks from which to evaluate their respective subtyping schemes (Lyon & Risucci, 1988).

Skinner (1981, 1986) advanced one such conceptual framework to formulate and evaluate proposed classification models. This framework, shown in Figure 5.3, comprises three fundamental components that, according to Skinner, should characterize any classification model. These include: theory formulation, internal validation, and external validation. This framework has particular relevance to learning disability subtypes.

The first component, theory formulation, involves decisions regarding the theory upon which the classification model is based. These decisions include selecting a set of measures that coincide with the theoretical orientation of the model. Additionally, a priori hypotheses are proposed to assess the clinical and theoretical validities of identified subtypes (e.g., response to treatment, differences on variables, and tasks not included in

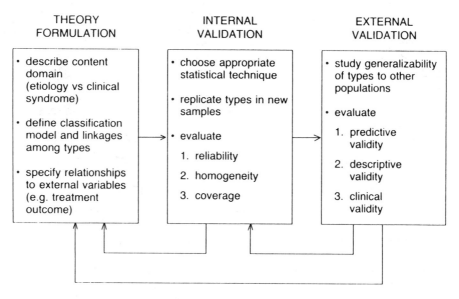

FIGURE 5.3. Conceptual framework for classification research. (From Skinner, H.A. (1986). Construct validation approach to psychiatric classification. In T. Millon & G.L. Klerman (Eds.), *Contemporary directions in psychopathology* (pp. 307–330). New York: Guilford Press. Adapted with permission.)

the subtype derivation). Other hypotheses address the relationships among the subtypes, and the relationship of the overall model to other learning parameters.

The second component, internal validation, refers to the reliability and validity of the identified subtypes. These psychometric issues involve selecting an appropriate classification technique to identify homogeneous subtypes of disabled learners (e.g., hierarchical cluster analysis). Currently, given the status of many classification techniques, there are few explicit rules for determining the reliability of a classification model (Blashfield, 1980; Morris et al., 1981). Fletcher and Morris (1986), however, suggested that internally valid typologies should (a) result in the classification of the majority of the sample into the identified subtypes, (b) result in homogeneous subtypes, (c) be replicable across samples and techniques (e.g., clinical groupings versus Q-type factor analysis), and (d) be based on reliable variables that are appropriate to a variety of samples. In particular, most subtyping models proffered to date fail to address the latter two points in a substantive manner.

Finally, the third component, external validation, is important independent of internal reliability and validity. Here, the obtained model is evaluated against external criteria (e.g., achievement) not used in the original derivation of the subtypes. Fletcher and Morris (1986) suggested that simple comparisons on external variables only partially addressed this component; moreover, results should be hypothesized a priori so that the utility of the subtyping model can be properly assessed in terms of specific parameters.

It is common to evaluate the validity of a typology via clinical comparisons of the subtypes with previously identified subtypes. For example, Lyon and Watson's specific language impaired subtypes are remarkably similar to Boder's dysphonetic subtype, Mattis et al.'s language subtype, and Satz and Morris' naming deficit subtype. Satz and Morris (1981), however, cautioned that, although many of the independently derived subtypes appear similar, these similarities do not truly provide valid evidence for a specific subtype. The validities of specific subtypes and subtyping models are more appropriately evaluted with other methods such as those outlined by Skinner.

Skinner's framework for developing and evaluating learning disability subtyping models emphasizes the conceptual or theoretical basis absent from many current models. Moreover, successive refinements of specific subtype models can be achieved through the interactive aspects of the three components of this framework. In fact, Adams (1985) suggested that internal validation should be evaluated during theory formulation, prior to any actual statistical analyses. He argued that this would tend to maximize benefits from subsequent empirical analyses. Skinner's framework provides a promising heuristic for guiding learning disability classification research.

The subtyping models proposed by Mattis et al. (1975), Speece et al. (1985), Satz and Morris (1981), and Lyon and Watson (1981) are good examples of research conducted withing a framework such as Skinner's. All of these models were based on neuropsychological theory and the measures upon which the models were based were carefully selected from that frame of reference. Further, each model was subjected to multiple reliability and validity examinations to evaluate the respective typology. The subtyping model proposed by Lyon and Watson (1981) is noteworthy in particular because a series of treatment studies have been initiated to determine its utility (Lyon, 1985a).

Sampling Issues

In addition to these definitional and conceptual issues, it is clear that if classification efforts are to advance, investigators must begin to select samples in a standardized fashion. At the very least, it is imperative that researchers completely describe samples and sample-selection procedures. Sampling difficulties have contributed to interpretive problems in generic learning disabilities research and now they have begun to obfuscate the subtyping research.

A common way of dealing with this problem is to select subjects from school-identified learning disabled populations. As MacMillan, Meyers, and Morrison (1980) noted, however, this does not address the problem satisfactorily. This is due primarily to the lack of a universally accepted definition for learning disabilities. For example, Epps, Ysseldyke, and Algozzine (1983, 1985) showed that a learning disability diagnosis depended on which of 14 different definitions was used. As many as 65% of a putative non-learning disabled group and as few as 7% of a putative learning disabled group were classified as learning disabled depending on the definition used. A similar problem of false-positive and false-negative classification was observed by Short, Feagans, McKinney, and Appelbaum (1986) who evaluated several discrepancy formulas for learning disability diagnosis.

In the widely cited "Colorado LD study," Shepard, Smith, and Vojir (1983) carefully selected a representative probability sample of 800 children who were identified and served as learning disabled in that state. Fewer than half of these children were found to exhibit characteristics consistent with definitions of learning disabilities in federal regulations or professional literature. Shepard et al. cautioned, therefore, that the learning disabilities label applied for the purpose of providing educational services cannot be assumed as valid. They further warned that if this label is used as a dependable sign of the disorder, then research on learning disabilities will be confounded. Thus, in one instance, research has shown that nearly any child can be diagnosed as learning disabled, given the multiple and widely variant definitions of the disorder (Epps et al., 1983, 1985). Research also has shown that the majority of children actually identified and served in school-based learning disability placements may not be truly learning disabled (Shepard et al. 1983).

Obviously, these issues are crucial to the study of learning disabilities and their subtypes. They also pose issues relevant to selecting comparison groups (Keogh, 1986). If the child is classified as learning diabled for one sample, it is unlikely that any meaningful results will be provided. With the exception of several cross-validation efforts (e.g., Lyon et al., 1982), research in this the field currently is unable to assure that a child classified as learning disabled for one study has the same characteristics as a child classified as learning disabled for another study.

Attempted Solutions

Several studies in the subtyping literature have attempted to address these sampling problems. For example, the subtyping studies conducted by Satz and colleagues (Johnston et al., 1987; Satz & Morris, 1981; Van der Vlugt & Satz, 1985) avoided sampling problems that are related to the exclusionary criteria of many definitions. These investigators used large, undifferentiated groups of children and empirically determined the subgroups to be designated as learning disabled. Subsequent analyses were based on this subsample of children. Similarly, the clinical subtyping studies conducted by Rourke and colleagues (Petrauskas & Rourke, 1979; Rourke & Finlayson, 1978) and Mattis et al. (1975) used a priori subject selection procedures prior to developing subtyping models.

Other strategies include selecting samples from children already placed in a variety of special education classrooms. These children then are combined cross-categorically prior to performing the subtyping analyses (e.g., Hale & Saxe, 1983). In these studies, children identified as learning disabled, emotionally disturbed, and mentally retarded all have been included in the pool of subjects to be subtyped. Although these strategies do not address all issues, such as how these children initially were placed into special education classrooms, they do broaden the pool of subjects to be classified and address some sampling concerns.

Finally, a system has been proposed to address these issues. The goal of the UCLA Marker Variable System (Keogh, Major-Kingsley, Omori-Gordon, & Reid, 1982) was to develop a comprehensive system for subject description (i.e., markers) in learning disability research. Essentially, the developers of this system conducted an extensive review of literature (i.e., over 4,600 citations for the years 1970–1977) and found that learning disability sample descriptions were fragmented, limited, and incomplete. Based on this review and a series of field studies, the marker system was proposed. This can be seen in Table 5.1.

As can be seen from the table, this system comprises four groups of

TABLE 5.1. The UCLA Marker Variable System.

Markers according to category
Descriptive Markers
Number of subjects by gender
Chronological age
Grade level
Race/ethnicity
Source of subjects
Socioeconomic status
Language background
Educational history
Educational placement
Physical and health status
Substantive Markers
Intellectual ability
Reading achievement
Arithmetic achievement
Behavior and emotional adjustment
Background Markers
Month/year of study
Geographic location
Locale
Exclusionary criteria
Control/comparison group(s)
Topical Markers
Activity level
Attention
Auditory perception
Fine-motor coordination
Gross-motor coordination
Memory
Oral language
Visual perception

Adapted from Keogh, B. K., Major-Kingsley, S., Omori-Gordon, H., & Reid, H. P. (1982). *A system of marker variables for the field of learning disabilities*. Syracuse, NY: Syracuse University Press. With permission.

markers. *Descriptive markers* refer to subject variables that describe basic demographic and background information. This kind of information, of course, is not unique to the learning disability field; rather, it characterizes all properly described research with human subjects. In contrast, *substantive markers* are unique to the learning disability field. This information describes the classification (e.g, learning disability, mental retardation, emotional disturbance) from which the subjects were selected and the definitions of learning disability that were used in subject selection (e.g., a particular discrepancy formula). Related to these descriptions are *background markers* that describe information useful in interpreting the data.

Finally, the system proposed specific *topical markers*. It typically is not feasible for investigators to have information on all of the topical markers listed because these markers are specific to a particular study (e.g., if attention were the primary focus of a study). Of course, a comprehensive neuropsychological evaluation has the advantage of addressing each of the topical markers via the assessment. Moreover, the specific topical markers may change as we learn more about what variables are important to various subtypes of learning disabilities. For example, some evidence suggests that genetic variables (Kimberling, Pennington, & Lubs, 1983; Kinsbourne, 1986) and autoimmune functions (Geschwind, 1986) may be useful in studying learning disabilities and their potential subtypes.

The UCLA Marker System represents an attempt to ameliorate many of the sampling difficulties that have characterized learning disabilities research. Further, this system has the potential to contribute to subtyping efforts by improving the validity of comparisons among studies and facilitating the integration of data sets.

Variable Selection

The issue of variable selection is directly related to sampling issues and the efforts advanced by the authors of the UCLA Marker System. Again, definitional problems contribute to an unrestricted range of variables that are of potential importance in learning disabilities and the subtypes thereof. Eysenck (1952) asserted that . . . "Qualitative or taxonomic discovery must precede quantitative measurement. Before we can measure, we must know what it is we want to measure" (p.34). This caution is particularly cogent for the study of learning disability subtyping.

As can be seen in Table 5.1, however, topical markers in particular have provided a conceptual foundation for studying learning disabilities in a more standardized fashion. Nonetheless, subtyping efforts to date have used a wide range of variables in developing subtyping models. Even within the cognitive domain, for example, different functions can be measured. Equally as important, similar functions can be measured by widely different assessment strategies. The relationships between variables to the phenomenon being studied are especially important when empirical clustering techniques are used because results are a function of input variables. Thus, in subtyping studies, it is crucial to select input variables on the basis of theoretical orientation, reliability, and validity.

From a neuropsychological perspective on learning disability subtyping, Adams (1985) suggested several criteria against which to evaluate potential variables prior to statistical analyses. These are listed in Table 5.2. Neuropsychologically, it is important for potential variables to show relationships to brain functions. This is relevant especially given the conceived neurological basis for learning disabilities. As noted previously, however,

TABLE 5.2. Proposed parameters for evaluating potential variables for inclusion in a learning disability subtyping model.

Evaluation parameters
Relationship of the variable to known effects of syndromes of brain damage or injury
Relationship of the variable to known paths of development or theoretical developmental frameworks
Relationship of the variable to more general experimental psychology concepts of the construct being measured
Evidence for the reliability of the variable in the widest sense
Evidence for the validity of the variable in the widest sense
Prospects that the variable might be adequate from the standpoint of Points 1 through 5 above, but would obscure or elucidate some other relevant attribute

Adapted from Adams, K. M. (1985). Theoretical, methodological, and statistical issues. In B. P. Rourke (Ed.), *Neuropsychology of learning disabilities. Essentials of subtype analysis* (p. 27). New York: Guilford Press. With permission.

these disorders are not typically characterized by classical hard signs of neurological dysfunction; therefore, variable selection should be judged accordingly.

It also is necessary to consider the variables selected in terms of neurodevelopmental issues. This criterion is illustrated well by the Florida Longitudinal Project (Satz et al., 1978) and by the subtyping study conducted by Rourke and Orr (1977). In these instances, neurodevelopmental theory formed the basis for variable selection and also for the subsequent assessment of relevant domains.

The next three criteria to be considered in variable selection are consistent with basic guidelines of psychometric theory. These include concerns about the reliabilities and validities of the variables. Finally, it is important for the investigator to consider how the selected variable might interact (or interfere) with other variables in the process of subtype identification. Not all relevant variables necessarily are founded on neuropsychological conceptualizations (e.g., socioeconomic status) and it is important for the investigator to explore how one variable might obfuscate the effects of other variables. Both the qualitative *and* quantitative aspects of these potential effects should be examined prior to including a variable in the classification study.

In addition, the kinds of variables selected often determine assessment methods. Assessment methods, of course, should be reliable across the age ranges of subjects studied. They also should reflect the construct they represent in an accurate manner across that age range. Further, selected variables should be considered within a developmental context in order to help create a dynamic assessment model (Rourke, Fisk, & Strang 1986). Finally, as Rourke et al. (1986) suggested, treatment recommendations should be linked directly to assessment procedures.

Developmental Considerations

The review of neurodevelopmental theory in Chapter 2 suggests that brain-behavior relationships are dynamic and that developmental changes in those relationships are characterized by both continuities and discontinuities. These developmental changes, however, are only beginning to be investigated. Effects of childhood central nervous system trauma and neurodevelopmental anomalies presently also are ill understood. It does seem reasonable, however, that neurodevelopmental issues should be considered in learning disability subtyping models. Further, it is reasonable to expect these models to be characterized by dynamic neurodevelopmental continuities and discontinuities.

In contrast to these expectations, the models presented in Chapters 3 and 4 suggest that variables are considered equally important at all age levels. As Adams (1985) noted, however, the actual "neurological weighting" of a particular variable may be greater at one time in a child's development than at another time. For example, in the Boder (1970) model, based on reading and spelling skills, the same kinds of tasks are used to determine the various subtypes at all age levels, despite evidence that the neurodevelopmental parameters associated with reading (e.g., Satz et al., 1978) and spelling (e.g., Frith, 1983) change with age.

Another example comes from the Florida Longitudinal Project. Here, Satz et al. (1978) asserted that visual-perceptual abilities were in primary ascendancy during the preschool and early elementary school years. Thus, they hypothesized that at that particular time in development, tasks assessing these skills would be better predictors of later learning problems than other tasks. Although this has been debated (Vellutino, 1978), this series of studies does emphasize the importance of developmental considerations in establishing learning disability typologies.

Related to these neurodevelopmental considerations are concerns about subtype continuity. To date, there have been only a few studies that have addressed these concerns longitudinally (Morris et al., 1986; Spreen & Haaf, 1986). Several others have addressed these concerns cross-sectionally (Lyon et al., 1982; Mattis et al., 1978; Rourke & Orr, 1977). Generally, data have provided relative support for the existence of particular subtypes over time, but not overwhelming support for continuity of subtype membership. For example, in their longitudinal investigation, Spreen and Haaf (1986) noted that many subjects changed classifications over time. A similar observation was reported by Morris et al. (1986). These findings suggest that children manifest different learning symptoms over time, even into adulthood (Spreen & Haaf, 1986). This is not unexpected given the plethora of variables that can impinge on a child's learning efficiency (e.g., social-emotional factors, remediation efforts), but how these variables interact over time (e.g., student-teacher-environment-materials interaction) and the issue of subtype continuity require further examination.

Finally, it is important for investigators to examine factors potentially related to the early identification of specific subtypes of learning disabled children. A great deal of research has been conducted on the early identification of generic learning disabilities, but none of these studies has addressed the subtype issue. For example, a recent review (Tramontana, Hooper, & Selzer, 1988) suggested a multitude of variables that are related to the early prediction of learning disabilities. Similar to the literature on unifactor theories of learning disabilities noted in Chapter 1, this suggests that learning disabilities should be conceived multidimensionally even during the preschool years. Two studies have attempted to address this concern with language disordered preschool children (Aram & Nation, 1975; Wilson & Risucci, 1986), but other investigations also should be pursued, particularly given the subtyping concerns outlined in this chapter as well as in other sources (e.g., Rourke, 1985).

Empirical Versus Clinical-Inferential Classification Methods

One final issue pertinent to developing subtyping models for learning disabilities concerns the selection of a classification method to identify subtypes. Should investigators use clinical-inferential methods in order to discern clinical rules for classification or should multivariate statistics be used instead? Clearly, a number of factors should be considered.

Clinical-inferential methods have provided the foundation for the subtyping literature and, indeed, several studies have made significant clinical contributions (Boder, 1970; Mattis et al., 1975). These methods, however, are limited by their inability to simultaneously manage a large array of information (e.g., the UCLA Marker System) in an objective fashion. This is especially problematic because correlations and interactions among variables inevitably are present. Further, these subjective methods are easily influenced by bias in clinical decision making at a variety of stages, such as during subtype development and subject classification. Given these concerns, Fletcher and Satz (1985) suggested that clinical-inferential methods are inconsistent with a primary goal of classification research: to identify naturally occurring subtypes.

Empirical methods do address these concerns, but they are not without their own potential problems. All of the issues discussed in this chapter, for example, influence the results of empirical classification methods. The ease with which multivariate classification techniques manage data is seductive in that it leaves the door open for investigators to fall prey to "naive empiricism." Clearly, the adequacy and strength of models derived by empirical classification methods are influenced by many a priori clinical decisions, including those regarding theoretical orientation, sample selection, and variable selection. The development of any empirically based classification model also should strictly adhere to standards of reliability and validity (e.g., Del Dotto & Rourke, 1985). These concerns typically are overlooked or marginally addressed by investigators using these classification techniques.

Obviously these are advantages and disadvantages to both clinical-inferential and empirical methods. Although these methods classically have been polarized in the literature, the learning disability subtype studies conducted to date would suggest that an integration of both methods perhaps is in order (see also Willis, 1988). Although subject to criticism (see, e.g., Meehl, 1973), an integration in which empirical methods are carefully evaluated in terms of well-considered, objective clinical judgments may facilitate the development of a truly reliable, valid, and, perhaps most important, clinically useful nosology for learning disability subtypes.

Conclusions

There are several pertinent issues related to learning disability subtyping. These include the need for a conceptual basis for a subtyping system, subject sampling and variable selection issues, and developmental concerns with respect to any subtyping model. Further, there are relative merits and limitations of all classification methods for identifying subtypes. Treatment issues, only briefly mentioned here, also are particularly important to the development of any learning disability subtyping model, and these are discussed in Chapter 8.

It is clear that a major obstacle in the subtyping literature thus far concerns definitional and conceptual issues. These issues obfuscate nearly every aspect of learning disability subtyping efforts. Despite the lack of a guiding definition or an adequate conceptual framework, efforts are proceeding and there presently is no universally accepted classification model, clinical-inferential or empirical, that captures the multiple and fragmented directions in which the field is progressing (see also Swanson, 1988). Although results are forthcoming, the efforts of the Task Force on Nosology (David, 1988) represent ambitious attempts to address issues in the classification of learning disorders.

In conclusion, as Lyon (1985b) cogently stated:

What is known is that such diversity in theoretical backgrounds, assessment task batteries, and statistical methodologies does not bode favorably for the development of a concise and coherent framework for learning disabilities. Unless we begin to combine our talents and resources in a search for a common conceptual and measurement base, subtyping is prone to failure even as a heuristic. (p. 33)

Clearly, progress in the area of learning disability subtyping depends on careful consideration of the issues that have been outlined here and that others also have articulated. It is important for investigators to consider these methodological and conceptual issues thoroughly if Lyon's concerns for this clinical and research domain are to be addressed.

Section III   Clinical Issues
Related to Subtyping

6
Neuropsychological Assessment

There has been a tremendous growth of interest in clinical neuropsychological assessment, particularly as it pertains to children and adolescents (Gaddes, 1985; Hynd & Obrzut, 1981; Obrzut & Hynd, 1986a, 1986b; Tramontana & Hooper, 1988). Hynd, Snow, and Becker (1986) cited two major reasons for this increased interest. One reason extends from the implementation of the Education for All Handicapped Children Act (P.L. 94-142; U.S. Office of Education, 1977) that provides services for a variety of children including those suffering from neurodevelopmental disorders and learning handicaps. Public Law 94-142 served to accentuate an important role for neuropsychological assessment, both in the identification of specific neurodevelopmental disorders and in helping to devise appropriate treatment plans. The second major reason cited by Hynd et al. concerns the increased prevalence of children surviving neurological illness/trauma, particularly during perinatal and neonatal periods of development. This has created a greater need for careful assessment of the extent, pattern, and developmental significance of possible neuropsychological sequelae in these survivors of serious childhood illness/trauma.

A particularly important component of the development of child neuropsychological assessment has involved the study of children with learning disabilities. In fact, the study of learning disabilities has been one of the most intensive areas of investigation in child neuropsychology. The explicit presumption of central nervous system dysfunction in current definitions of learning disability has served to underscore the important role of neuropsychological assessment in this field. Neuropsychological assessment has provided a means by which individuals can be grouped homogeneously, or subtyped, based on neuropsychological profiles. These assessment techniques have aided in describing these disabled learners in a more detailed fashion, have assisted in the development of specific treatment plans, and have provided a theoretical foundation for conceptualizing learning dysfunction. Generally, rationale for performing a neuropsychological assessment should include: (a) differentiation of functional versus organic disorders, (b) differential diagnosis (e.g., subtypes), (c) identification of strengths and weakness in cognitive functioning, (d) assistance in the development of intervention/management plans, (e) documentation of the rate of improvement or deterioration of function, and (f) research examining particular brain-behavior relationships and other related questions (Hynd & Willis, 1988). Thus, the application of neuropsychological principles and techniques to learning disabilities is consistent with current efforts to identify specific subtypes.

In the previous chapters of this volume, historical antecedents and neuropsychological foundations for learning disability subtypes have been presented. Specific models and issues in classification research have been discussed, but assessment strategies and conceptualizations only have been mentioned. This chapter addresses assessment issues from a neuropsychological perspective, with particular emphasis on the application of neuropsychological assessment to learning disability subtype identification. Various neuropsychological assessment approaches are described and relevant literature from the learning disability domain is presented. The chapter concludes with a discussion of issues pertinent to the neuropsychological diagnosis of learning disability subtypes.

Neuropsychological Approaches

Neuropsychological assessment strategies can be divided into several different approaches. These are: (a) the fixed battery approach, (b) eclectic test batteries, and (c) special purpose measures (Tramontana & Hooper, 1988).

Fixed Battery Approach

A fixed battery approach in neuropsychological assessment is one that attempts to provide a comprehensive assessment of brain function using an invariant set of validated test procedures. The composition of the battery is neither tailored to the presenting characteristics of an individual patient nor to specific clinical hypotheses. Rather, the emphasis is on administering as many of the designated procedures as the individual's condition will permit. Individual variability is assumed to be measured reasonably well when the battery is designed to assess a broad array of human capabilities. Moreover, the use of a fixed battery across individuals provides a standard data base on which different clinical groups can be compared.

Fixed batteries, such as the Halstead-Reitan Neuropsychological Battery (HRNB) and Luria-Nebraska Neuropsychological Battery (LNNB), currently represent the most commonly used approaches in neuropsychological assessment (Hynd et al., 1986). The frequency of their application to learning disability populations, however, is less clear. Information on these batteries relevant to learning disabilities is presented here, but the interested reader is referred to Hynd et al. (1986) for a more detailed review of these measures. Table 6.1 presents descriptions of these batteries in addition to a description of a newly developed neuropsychological battery for preschool children that appears to have promise for application to learning disabilities. A brief discussion of the use of standardized intellectual measures with learning disabilities also is provided.

HALSTEAD-REITAN NEUROPSYCHOLOGICAL BATTERY (HRNB)

Based on the pioneering work of Halstead (1947), who was attempting to isolate tasks that could measure what he termed, "biological intelligence," Reitan and his colleagues developed two versions of the HRNB for use with children: the Reitan-Indiana Neuropsychological Test Battery for Children (ages 5 to 8) and the Halstead-Reitan Neuropsychological Test Battery for Children (ages 9 to 14). In the process of developing these batteries, Reitan and Wolfson (1985) proposed that neuropsychological batteries should adhere to several criteria. First, batteries should be comprehensive across a wide range of human abilities. Second, they should be sensitive to focal as well as global neurological impairment, a feature particularly relevant for the neuropsychological assessment of learning disabled individuals. Finally, they should be psychometrically sound in order to provide clinically useful information about individuals.

The HRNB for older children is a downward extension of the adult version of the battery and comprises the following procedures: Lateral Dominance Examination, Aphasia Screening Test, Category Test (168 items), Tactual Performance Test (six blocks), Sensory Perceptual Examination (including Tactile Finger Recognition, Tactile Form Recognition, and Fingertip Number Writing), Grip Strength Test, Finger Oscillation Test, Trail-Making Test, Speech-Sounds Perception Test (three choice format), and Seashore Rhythm Test. The HRNB for younger children comprises modified versions of the tests in the older children's battery, but the Trail-Making Test, Speech-Sounds Perception Test, and Seashore Rhythm Test are excluded. Six additional tests are included that are suited specifically for use with younger children: Marching Test, Color Form Test, Progressive Figures Test, Matching Pictures Test, Target Test, and Individual Performance Test. Usually each version of the battery is supplemented by the appropriate Wechsler intelligence scale (i.e., Wechsler Preschool and Primary Scale of Intelligence [WPPSI] and Weshsler Intelligence Scale for Children–Revised [WISC-R]) and by a standardized test of academic achievement (e.g., Wide Range Achievement Test [WRAT]).

Performance on the HRNB is evaluated in terms of four methods of inference. These are: level of performance, pattern of performance, right-left differences, and pathognomonic signs. For the older children's battery, these four methods of inference have been operationalized in an actuarial

TABLE 6.1. Fixed neuropsychological test batteries.

Test battery	Age range	Subtests/Scales	Abilities assessed
Reitan-Indiana Neuropsychological Test Battery for Children	5–8 years	Category Test	Complex concept formation, basic reasoning abilities, intelligence
		Tactile Performance Test	Right–left-sided sensory perception, sensory recognition, spatial memory
		Finger Oscillation Test (finger tapping)	Right–left-sided motor speed
		Sensory-perceptual Measures	Sensory localization, sensory perception, sensory recognition
		Aphasia Screening Test	Letter identification, follow directions regarding right–left hands, copy simple geometric shapes, compute simple arithmetic problems
		Grip Strength Test (dynamometer)	Right–left-sided muscle strength
		Lateral Dominance Examination	Right–left-sided preferences
		Color Form Test	Cognitive flexibility, sequential reasoning
		Progressive Figures Test	Visual-spatial reasoning, congitive flexibility, sequential reasoning
		Matching Pictures Test	Perceptual generalization, ability to categorize
		Target Test	Pattern perception, ability to attend to and copy visual–spatial configurations
		Individual Performance Test	Visual perception, visual–motor integration
		Marching Test	Visual–motor integration, coordination
Halstead-Reitan Neuropsychological Test Battery for Children; and	9–14 years	Category Test	Complex concept formation, basic reasoning abilities, intelligence
		Tactual Performance Test	Right–left-sided sensory perception, sensory recognition, spatial memory, manual dexterity
		Seashore Rhythm Test	Sustained auditory attention, perception, and ability to match different auditory rhythmic sequences
Halstead-Reitan Neuropsychological Test Battery	15–adult	Speech-sounds Perception Test	Sustained attention, auditory perception, auditory visual integration
		Finger Oscillation (finger tapping)	Right–left-sided motor speed
		Tactile, Auditory, and Visual Imperception Test	Perception of unilateral and bilateral simultaneous sensory stimulation
		Tactile Finger-Recognition Test	Perception and localization of sensory stimulation
		Fingertip Number Writing Perception Test	Report numbers written on the finger tips
		Tactile Form Recognition Test	Sensory recognition, tactile–visual integration

Test	Age	Subtest	Description
Aphasia Screening Test			Letter identification, follow directions regarding right–left hands, copy simple geometric shapes, compute simple arithmetic problems
Grip Strength Test (dynamometer)			Right–left-sided muscle strength
Trail Making Test			Conceptual set shifting, memory attention (Part A & Part B)
Lateral Dominance Examination			Right–left-sided preference
Luria-Nebraska Neuropsychological Battery: Children's Revision; and	8–12 years	Motor Skills	Motor speed, coordination, ability to imitate motor movements
		Rhythm	Perceive and repeat rhythmic patterns, sing a song from memory
		Tactile	Finger localization, arm localization, two-point discrimination, movement discrimination, shape discrimination, stereognosis
		Visual	Visual recognition, visual discrimination
		Receptive Speech	Follow simple commands, comprehend visual–verbal directions, decode phonemes
Luria-Nebraska Neuropsychological Battery	13–adult	Expressive Language	Read and repeat words and simple sentences, name objects from description, use automated speech
		Writing	Analyze letter sequences, spell, write from dictation
		Reading	Letter and word recognition, sentence and paragraph reading, nonsense syllable reading
		Arithmetic	Simple arithmetical abilities, number writing, number recognition
		Memory	Verbal and nonverbal memory
		Intelligence	Vocabulary development, verbal reasoning, picture comprehension, social reasoning, deductive processes
Neuropsychological Investigation for Children–Revised Version	4–8 years	Orientation, Attention, Strategy	General orientation, strategy generation, inhibition and control, selective and sustained attention, distractibility
		Language	Auditory closure, receptive language, oral praxis (dynamic and kinesthetic), concept formation, naming, verbal fluency, reading readiness
		Motor and Sensory	Handedness, motor praxis (dynamic and kinesthetic), tactile perception, kinesthetic feedback
		Visual and Spatial	Visual discrimination, visual–spatial, left–right discrimination, neglect
		Memory	Immediate memory for numbers, words, faces, names, and story delayed recall for faces, names, and story

Adapted from Hynd, G. W., & Willis, W. G. (1988). *Pediatric neuropsychology* (pp. 148–149). Orlando, FL: Grune & Stratton. With permission.

system of rules for neuropsychological diagnosis (Selz & Reitan, 1979). Based on norms for 9- to 14-year-old children, each rule converts raw scores on the various HRNB measures to scaled scores ranging from 0 to 3. The system is based on only a single set of norms, however, and may subsequently contribute to higher expectations for younger children and lower expectations for older children. Additional normative data for the tasks of the HRNB have been provided by Knights (1966) as well as by Spreen and Gaddes (1969).

The HRNB has been found to discriminate effectively between normal children and those with documented brain damage. This has been demonstrated both with 5- to 8-year-olds (Klonoff, Robinson, & Thompson, 1969; Reitan, 1974) and 9- to 14-year-olds (Boll, 1974; Reed, Reitan, & Klove, 1965). In each of these studies, brain damaged children performed more poorly on most of the test variables comprised by the HRNB. Generally, deficits spanned both verbal-conceptual and perceptual-performance abilities. Interestingly, test variables from the WISC consistently were among the most discriminating measures.

Application to Learning Disabilities

The neuropsychological assessment of learning disabilities presents an assessment challenge because these disorders involve presumed rather than documented brain dysfunction. Consequently, learning disabled individuals are expected to show less overall impairment than individuals with known brain damage.

Using the HRNB, Selz and Reitan (1979) achieved an overall accuracy rate of about 73% in classifying 9- to 14-year-old children as normal, learning disabled, or brain damaged. Misclassifications were almost entirely in the direction of false negatives (i.e., classifying abnormal as normal), because their system of diagnostic rules tended to underestimate dysfunction in both the learning disabled and brain damaged groups. As expected, the learning disabled children showed an intermediate level of impairment in comparison to the other two groups. The accuracy rate improved to 87% when the learning disabled group was excluded and the remaining subjects were classified as either brain damaged or normal.

More recently, D'Armato, Gray, and Dean (in press) explored the relationship between HRNB and WISC-R results. In contrast to several reports citing significant relationships between HRNB findings and IQ (e.g, Seidenberg, Giordani, Berent, & Boll, 1983; Tramontana, Klee, & Boyd, 1984), D'Amato et al. found the HRNB results to be relatively independent of WISC-R scores (i.e., 10% overlap of the shared variance). In a related study, Strom, Gray, Dean, and Fischer (1987) examined the incremental validity of the HRNB for a large sample of school children referred for learning difficulties ($n = 989$; mean age = 11.4 years). Results indicated that adding HRNB results to WISC-R scores improved the accuracy of predicting WRAT scores by 16% to 30%, with particular improvement noted for the WRAT Reading and Spelling subtests. Thus, the HRNB appeared to account for a significant proportion of variance in academic achievement within this population.

Using a test battery based largely on the HRNB, Rourke and his colleagues also have shown that learning disabled children can be distinguished reliably on the basis of their neuropsychological assessment data. Perhaps more important, however, different subtypes of learning disabilities have been distinguished on the basis of different patterns of neuropsychological performance. Using clinical-inferential (Rourke & Finlayson, 1978; Rourke & Telegdy, 1971) and empirical (DeLuca, Del Dotto, & Rourke, 1987) classification methods, Rourke and colleagues demonstrated significant differences between achievement-based learning disability subtypes on HRNB measures. Sweeney and Rourke (1978) found similar results when two subtypes of spelling disordered children were compared on the HRNB. Empirical classification of individuals' performances on the HRNB tasks also have produced reliable and valid subtypes (Del Dotto & Rourke, 1985; Fisk & Rourke, 1979; Joschko & Rourke, 1985; Petrauskas & Rourke, 1979).

Generally, the performance of learning disabled individuals on the HRNB is distinctly different from that of normal and brain damaged individuals. In addition, these children can be distinguished from one another on the basis of their HRNB profiles. Although these data are relatively sparse, they do implicate clinical utility for the HRNB and its respective tasks in the diagnosis of learning disability subtypes.

LURIA-NEBRASKA NEUROPSYCHOLOGICAL BATTERY:
CHILDREN'S REVISION (LNNB-C)

Golden (1981) introduced a downward extension of the LNNB for children ranging from 8 to 12 years of age. The selection of test items was determined by administering the standard adult version of the battery (Golden, Hammeke, & Purisch, 1980) to normal children of above-average ability. Items that proved to be too difficult were eliminated, some new items were added, and other modifications in administration and scoring were made to adapt the battery for use with children. This resulted in a battery consisting of 149 test items (versus 269 in the adult version) on which normative data then were obtained from a sample of 125 normal children (i.e., 25 for each age level from 8 through 12).

The LNNB-C is organized in terms of 11 summary scales similar to those in the adult version: Motor, Rhythm, Tactile, Visual, Receptive Speech, Expressive Speech, Writing, Reading, Arithmetic, Memory, and Intellectual Processes. Also, like the adult version, these are supplemented by three second-order scales: Pathognomonic, consisting of 13 items in the battery that provide the best discrimination of brain damage, and Left and

Right Sensorimotor Scales (based on items from the Motor and Tactile Scales performed with the contralateral hand). Each item in the battery is scored on a 3-point scale (i.e., 0 to 2), with higher scores indicating impairment. Item scores are summed within each scale, and each scale sum is then converted to a T-score (mean = 50, standard deviation = 10). The usual rule for classifying a child as impaired is based on the presence of elevations on at least two of the summary scales that exceed a critical level cutoff adjusted, via a specific regression formula, for the child's age (Gustavson et al., 1984). Modified criterion rules have been recommended for maximizing the discrimination of neuropsychological impairment in special populations, including children with learning disabilities (Geary, Jennings, Schultz, & Alper, 1984) and psychiatric disorders (Tramontana & Boyd, 1986).

In addition to examining the level and pattern of scale elevations on the LNNB-C, interpretation is based on a careful analysis of performance on the individual items comprised by the battery. In comparison to the HRNB, test items on the LNNB-C are relatively simple and are geared more toward assessing the component skills underlying broader dimensions of function. It is this feature of the battery that is thought to incorporate Luria's (1966, 1973) emphasis on the qualitative analysis of component skill deficits. The reliability of this level of analysis is questionable, however, because the assessment of specific component skills generally rests on very few items. This is more of a problem on the LNNB-C than on the adult version of the battery because of the reduction of nearly half of the total item pool.

The LNNB-C has been found to discriminate effectively between brain damaged children and normal controls (Gustavson et al., 1984; Sawicki, Leark, Golden, & Karras, 1984; Wilkening, Golden, MacInnes, Plaisted, & Hermann, 1981). In the Gustavson et al. study, the presence of two or more scales above a critical level cutoff yielded classification accuracy rates of 79% for brain damaged children and 89% for normals, with an overall accuracy rate of 85%. When compared to the HRNB, the overall results of the two batteries have been found to correspond very highly, with a 91% rate of agreement in identifying neuropsychological impairment in brain damaged children (Berg et al., 1984). To date, however, there is little evidence about the validity of the LNNB-C in distinguishing different lesion characteristics in brain damaged children.

Application to Learning Disabilities

In contrast to the HRNB, there has been considerable research examining the LNNB-C with learning disabled children. Using a learning disabled sample, Snyder, Leark, Golden, Allison, and Grove (1983) found the LNNB-C Motor and Intellectual Processes Scales to correlate significantly with all Kaufman Assessment Battery for Children (K-ABC) cognitive processing scores, but not with K-ABC achievement. All of the LNNB-C scales, except Motor, Rhythm, Visual, and Intellectual Processes, however, correlated significantly with K-ABC achievement. In contrast, Snow, Hartlage, Hynd, and Grant (1983) did not find any significant relationships between the LNNB-C and the Minnesota Percepto-Diagnostic Test with a group of learning disabled children. A factor analysis of the summary scales of the LNNB-C for a learning disabled population revealed three factors accounting for approximately 64% of the variance (Snow & Hynd, 1985a). The factors were interpreted as assessing in a general academic achievement (i.e., Writing, Reading), sensory-motor functions (i.e., Motor, Rhythm, Tactile), and language-general intelligence (Visual, Receptive, Expressive, Arithmetic, Memory, and Intellectual).

The LNNB-C does appear to be useful in discriminating between heterogeneous groups of learning disabled children and normals (Geary & Gilger, 1984, 1985; Geary, Jennings, Schultz, & Alper, 1984; Hyman, 1983; Teeter, Boliek, Obrzut, & Malsch, 1986). For example, Geary and Gilger (1984) compared learning disabled with normal children who had been matched on Full-Scale IQ. They found the groups to differ significantly on the Rhythm, Expressive Speech, Writing, and Reading scales. Similarly, Geary et al. (1984) obtained about a 93% classification accuracy rate, including a successful classification of all learning disabled children, using the LNNB-C. In this study, Geary et al. considered a normal profile as less than two standard deviations above the regression formula criterion; a borderline profile as two standard deviations above the regression value, with one of those scales being either Writing or Arithmetic; and an abnormal profile as three or more scales two standard deviations above the regression value, or two scales above the value, excluding Writing and Arithmetic. As such, these investigators provided data for the clinical validity of these classification rules for identifying a learning disability. Hyman (1983) also found support for the discriminant validity of the LNNB-C. All 11 of the summary scales significantly differentiated normals from learning disabled children, with basic sensory-motor skills being relatively intact in the learning disabled sample. The LNNB-C also has been used to discriminate between learning disabled and slow-learner children; albeit, differences may be negated when IQ is covaried (Oehler-Stinnett, Stinnett, Wesley, & Anderson, 1988). Finally, it is noted that the adult version of the LNNB has been used to discriminate between heterogeneous groups of learning-disabled and nonlearning disabled adolescents as well (Lewis & Lorion, 1988).

Additionally, the LNNB-C has been used to validate and to identify learning disability subtypes. Nolan et al. (1983) compared 36 children who were assigned, in a clinical-inferential manner, to one of three subtypes depending on their performance on the WRAT: normal learners, reading and spelling disabled, and arithmetic disabled. The subtypes were compared on both the LNNB-C and the WISC-R. Using Full-Scale IQ and age as covariates, results for the LNNB-C indicated that there was a significant difference among the groups on the Expressive Speech, Writing, and Reading scales. Although the normal learners and the arithmetic disabled subtype performed significantly better on these three scales than the reading and spelling disabled subtype, there were no significant differences between the normals and arithmetic subtype. These data suggest that the LNNB-C may be more sensitive to language-based deficits than to visual-perceptual dysfunction. This is consistent with the findings of Snow et al. (1983) and of Gilger and Geary (1985).

Using a cognitive clinical-inferential subtype model, Morgan and Brown (1988) investigated the ability of the LNNB-C to discriminate among three learning disability subtypes. Based on WISC-R Verbal and Performance IQ differences, these investigators divided 82 learning disabled children into linguistic (i.e., VIQ<PIQ), visual-spatial (i.e., VIQ>PIQ), and mixed (i.e., VIQ = PIQ) subtypes. All three subtypes were comparable in terms of chronological age and WISC-R Full-Scale IQ. Morgan and Brown found none of the LNNB-C summary scales to discriminate among the subtypes.

Snow, Hynd, and Hartlage (1984) investigated LNNB-C performance differences of two subtypes of learning disabled children identified on the basis of severity (i.e., mild subtype, severe subtype) as determined by the amount of time in a learning disability classroom. Initial analysis indicated that the two groups differed significantly on 4 of the 11 scales (i.e., Receptive Speech, Writing, Reading, Arithmetic), in favor of the less impaired subtype. When WISC-R Full-Scale IQ and WRAT achievement scores were used as covariates, however, all group differences were eliminated. This indicates a strong relationship between IQ and the LNNB-C in this sample of children.

Finally, the LNNB-C also has been used to identify learning disability subtypes via empirical classification methods. Using Q-type factor analysis, Snow and Hynd (1985b) clustered the score profiles on the 11 LNNB-C summary scales for a group of learning disabled children. Three subtypes emerged. The subtypes reflected similar neuropsychological patterns; however, they were not found to differ on WISC-R or WRAT scores.

The LNNB-C does seem to discriminate effectively between learning disabled children and normals but, in covarying IQ, its discriminative power tends to be limited to selected scales (i.e., Expressive Speech, Writing, and Reading). It appears to be less sensitive to factors underlying math deficits than reading or spelling deficits in learning disabled children and, similarly, it appears more sensitive to language-based deficits than to visual-perceptual deficits. Furthermore, its capacity to discriminate among learning disability subtypes based on cognitive or severity variables may be compromised, especially when IQ and overall academic achievement are covaried. Thus, the LNNB-C may have limited applicability to learning disability subtyping.

NEUROPSYCHOLOGICAL INVESTIGATION FOR CHILDREN (NEPSY)

The NEPSY is a new battery that recently has been developed for the analysis of developmental disabilities in children ages 4 to 8 (Korkman, 1988). It is based largely on Luria's (1966) neuropsychological investigation and, as such, was designed to measure specific components of complex functions. In addition to the specific tasks proposed in Luria's investigation, Korkman included other tasks measuring functions not addressed by Luria's investigation. Some of these additional tasks were facial recognition, speeded naming, handedness, visual-motor precision, and block construction. Further, the short version of the Token Test, the Motor-Free Visual Perception Test, and the Developmental Test of Visual-Motor Integration were included in their original forms. Along with specific task additions, Korkman deleted several of Luria's original tasks because they lacked reliability or were too complex for young children. Although the final tasks of the NEPSY appear to have a vague resemblance to Luria's investigation, Korkman believed that the general outline of Luria's investigation was preserved by the task structure of the NEPSY.

The final battery consisted of 34 subtests measuring a wide array of functions. General functions assessed by the NEPSY are: (a) orientation, attention, and strategy; (b) language; (c) motor and sensory functions; (d) visual and spatial functions; and (e) memory. Subtests were constructed to be scaled tasks and to yield quantitative scores. Consistent with Luria's conceptualization of cognitive function, Korkman included numerous subcomponents of major functional domains (e.g., attention, speech) in an effort to preserve the qualitative features of Luria's investigation. In order to maintain the unique nature of each of these subcomponents, a factor analysis of the subcomponents was not deemed useful for the construction of this battery. The NEPSY was normed on a sample of 144 normal Finnish children and a standardization of the NEPSY is planned for a similar population in the United States (Korkman, 1988).

Application to Learning Disabilities

In contrast to the HRNB and the LNNB-C, the NEPSY was immediately used to discriminate different profiles of learning disabilities. One reason for this may be that the NEPSY was designed primarily to investigate neurodevelopmental dysfunction in children, whereas the HRNB and LNNB-C were designed primarily to investigate brain damage. This particularly may be cogent given the often subtle manifestations of many kinds of learning disabilities in contrast to the more frank behavioral manifestations of brain damage. Although still awaiting empirical confirmation, the NEPSY may have the potential to be more sensitive to neurodevelopmental learning dysfunction than its other fixed battery counterparts.

In the original validation of the NEPSY, Korkman devised a series of studies to identify specific learning disability subtypes in three relatively homogeneous groups of developmentally disabled children. These included 46 children at risk for learning and attentional disabilities, 40 children with language disorders, and 48 children with perceptual-motor disorders. Using Q-type factor analysis on the subjects' profiles on tests related to attention, Korkman identified five subtypes of attention disorders in her first group of at-risk children. These subtypes were characterized by: (a) language impairment, (b) attention deficits with impulsivity, (c) attention deficits with poor concentration, (d) learning problems, and (e) "normal" functioning. These five subtypes accounted for 87% of the variance in the sample. Using the same group of subjects, Korkman also identified four subtypes of learning disabled children. Applying Q-type factor analysis to individuals' performance profiles on tests related to reading and spelling acquisition, Korkman identified a global conceptual subtype, an auditory-phonemic subtype, a global auditory-phonemic subtype, and a normal profile subtype. These subtypes accounted for approximately 74% of the variance in the sample.

In addition to subtyping the at-risk children, Korkman applied Q-type factor analysis to the language disorder group and, separately to the perceptual-motor disorder group. On NEPSY tests related to language functioning, the clustering procedure identified five subtypes and accounted for 67% of the variance. These subtypes were characterized by global dysnomia, verbal dyspraxia, global receptive deficits, and auditory-phonemic receptive deficits. The five subtypes identified in children with perceptual-motor disorders accounted for approximately the same amount of variance (i.e., 65%). These subtypes were characterized by spatial impairment, mild visual-perceptual disturbance, and deficits in fine-motor precision. Two of the subtypes, showing global perceptual-motor deficits and mild kinesthetic dyspraxia, were significantly associated with neurological diagnoses.

The NEPSY is a new instrument that potentially can provide useful information to child neuropsychologists. Although its ultimate efficacy remains to be determined, it is clear that the NEPSY does present several advantages. It does seem well founded in neuropsychological theory and, consequently, assesses a wide range of cognitive functions. Initial validation studies with the NEPSY also suggest that this instrument maintains respectable psychometric standards. Moreover, the NEPSY was designed to be used primarily with children manifesting neurodevelopmental disorders and, as such, particularly may be applicable to children with learning disabilities. Its contributions to the subtype literature already have begun to emerge.

INTELLECTUAL BATTERIES

As can be surmised from Chapters 3 and 4, many intellectual batteries have been used in the study of learning disabilities. Although it is beyond the scope of this chapter to review these batteries in detail (see Sattler [1988] for a detailed review of intellectual assessment of children), they do deserve brief comment with respect to their application to subtyping.

Numerous assessment batteries designed to measure cognitive or intellectual abilities have been used alone or in tandem with other tasks from a neuropsychological perspective. Craig (1979) noted that the Wechsler intelligence scales traditionally have been included in the most popular batteries to assess neuropsychological problems for all age levels. To date, the Wechsler scales, particularly the WISC-R, have been the most widely used intellectual measures in the learning disability and subtyping literature. For example, the WISC-R has been used alone to identify subtypes of learning disabled individuals via clinical-inferential (Rourke, Young, & Flewelling, 1971; Smith et al., 1977) and empirical (Hale & Saxe, 1983; Vance et al., 1978) classification studies. It also has been used in tandem with a host of other measures (e.g., Raven's Progressive Matrices, HRNB, Peabody Picture Vocabulary Test–Revised as well as in part (e.g., Similarities subtest) for subtype identification.

Another cognitive assessment battery, the Kaufman Assessment Battery for Children (K-ABC) also holds promise for contributing to the neuropsychological assessment of learning disability subtypes. The K-ABC is unique in that it attempts to assess simultaneous and sequential processing in children, ages $2\frac{1}{2}$ to $12\frac{1}{2}$. It also provides achievement tests designed to screen basic academic skills. Further, the K-ABC was partially based on neuropsychological theory and, as such, the battery appears to hold promise for the identification of learning disability subtypes.

Although Hooper and Hynd (1986) found the K-ABC useful in distinguishing normal from learning disabled children, based largely on the poor performance of the learning disabled children on the sequential subtests, Kamphaus and Reynolds (1987) cautioned that learning disabled children's performance on the K-ABC typically is below the mean of normal children anyway. Further, the K-ABC has neither been successful in distinguishing among subtypes (Hooper & Hynd, 1985) nor in identifying them via empirical classification methods (Hooper & Hynd, 1988). Despite these preliminary findings and cautions, the clinical utility of the K-ABC for learning disability subtypes remains an important empirical question.

Other intellectual and cognitive batteries exist, such as the McCarthy Scales of Children's Abilities, the Woodcock-Johnson Tests of Cognitive Ability, and the Stanford-Binet Intelligence Scale, Fourth Edition, which may have potential application to neuropsychological assessment of learning disability subtypes. To date, however, there have been few studies that have used these batteries in such a manner. One of the primary reasons for this is that, although these tests are adequate measures of general intelligence and relatively good predictors of academic achievement, they are limited with respect to the repertoire of cognitive abilities assessed. Most of these measures were not designed to assess the broad array of functions and component functions typically measured by more comprehensive neuropsychological batteries. For example, the K-ABC was not designed to include tests of specific language functions, tactual perception, or visual-motor speed and, thus, can serve only as a complement to a comprehensive neuropsychological assessment.

SUMMARY

The HRNB, LNNB-C, and NEPSY are three major neuropsychological batteries that have relevance to the assessment of learning disability sub-types. The HRNB and the LNNB-C both have been used successfully in identifying learning disability subtypes, although both batteries have short-comings with respect to their ultimate clinical utility for subtyping. Generally, the HRNB appears to be less sensitive to language disabilities, where-as the LNNB-C may not be sensitive to visual-perceptual deficits. Given these findings, the ability of these batteries to identify subtypes based on an adequate sampling of cognitive tasks appears limited at this time.

Intellectual batteries also have contributed to subtype identification. In general, despite the development of learning disability classification models that have been based on intellectual measures, the scope of these models is limited by the breadth of abilities assessed by the battery. Thus, their applicability to the study of learning disability subtypes is limited in terms of scope and, consequently, in terms of the validity of the subtyping model. Although the intellectual batteries are useful, they should be used in tandem with other measures in order to assess a wider range of cognitive functions.

Eclectic Test Batteries

This approach attempts to preserve the quantitative nature of neuro-psychological assessment by selecting standardized tests that, when consid-ered collectively, measure a broad range of neuropsychological functions. There generally is at least an implicit outline of the relevant functions and abilities that should be assessed routinely. Any of a variety of available tests, however, may be selected to quantify the extent of deficit in each of the functional areas of interest. The psychometric properties of individual tests (e.g., reliability, validity, normative standards), as well as their abili-ties to complement the overall battery are factors that guide test selection. Professionals constructing eclectic batteries, however, should be aware that these collections of instruments, although designed around broad-band neuropsychological constructs, may not accurately reflect true profile differences. This is because data are compared across different normative samples, and the empirical relationships among measures only can be estimated.

Despite these concerns, eclectic batteries probably have been used most frequently in the study of learning disabilities as well as to identify specific subtypes. One of the main reasons for their popularity is that they allow for flexibility in test selection, thus minimizing the time required to conduct assessments. Another reason is that these batteries generally have shown remarkable similarity to the factor structure of traditional, or fixed, neuropsychological test batteries (Sutter & Battin, 1983; Sutter, Bishop, & Battin, 1986). Hooper, Hynd, and Tramontana (1988), for example, used this kind of approach in the neuropsychological assessment of a 13-year-old male with visual-spatial dyslexia. The resultant neuropsychological and academic profiles are illustrated in Figures 6.1 and 6.2, respectively. The

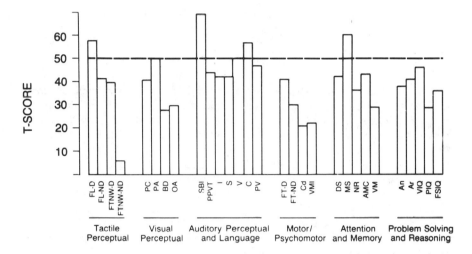

NEUROPSYCHOLOGICAL MEASURES

Figure 6.1. An example of an eclectic neuropsychological battery showing the performance of a 13-year-old male with visual-spatial dyslexia. FL–D = Finger Localization–Dominant Hand; FL–ND = Finger Localization–Nondominant Hand; FTNW–D = Fingertip Number Writing–Dominant Hand; FTNW–ND = Fingertip Number Writing–Nondominant Hand; PC = WISC-R Picture Completion Subtest; PA = WISC-R Picture Arrangement Subtest; BD = WISC-R Block Design Subtest; OA = WISC-R Object Assembly Subtest; SBI = WJ Sound Blending Subtest; PPVT = Peabody Picture Vocabulary Test–Revised; I = WISC-R Information Subtest; S = WISC-R Similarities Subtest; V = WISC-R Vocabulary Subtest; C = WISC-R Comprehension Subtest; PV = WJ Picture Vocabulary Subtest; FT–D = Finger Tapping–Dominant Hand; FT–ND = Finger Tapping–Nondominant Hand; Cd = WISC-R Coding Subtest; VMI = Developmental Test of Visual-Motor Integration; DS = WISC-R Digit Span Subtest; MS = WJ Memory for Sentences Subtest; NR = WJ Numbers Reversed Subtest; AMC = WJ Auditory Memory Cluster; VM = Benton Visual Retention Test; An = WJ Analogies Subtest; Ar = WISC-R Arithmetic Subtest; VIQ = WISC-R Verbal Scale IQ; PIQ = WISC-R Performance Scale IQ; FSIQ = WISC-R Full Scale IQ. (From Hooper, S.R., Hynd, G.W., & Tramontana, M.G. (1988). *Visual-spatial dyslexia: A neuropsychological case report.* Manuscript submitted for publication. With permission.)

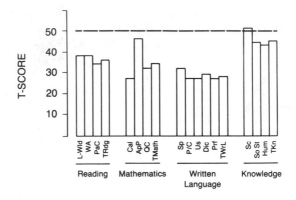

ACADEMIC ACHIEVEMENT MEASURES

FIGURE 6.2. The academic achievement of the eclectic neuropsychological battery showing the performance of a 13-year-old male with visual-spatial dyslexia. All measures are from the Woodcock-Johnson Psychoeducational Battery. L-WId = Letter-Word Identification Subtest; WA = Word Attack Subtest; PaC = Passage Comprehension Subtest; TRdg = Reading Cluster; Cal = Calculations Subtest; ApP = Applied Problems Subtest; QC = Quantitative Concepts; TMath = Mathematics Cluster; Sp = Spelling; P/C = Punctuation and Capitalization; Us = Usage; Dic = Dictation Subtest; Prf = Proofing Subtest; TWrL = Written Language Cluster; Sc = Science Subtest; SoSt = Social Studies Subtest; Hum = Humanities Subtest; TKn = Knowledge Cluster. (From Hooper, S.R., Hynd, G.W., & Tramontana, M.G. (1988). *Visual-spatial dyslexia: A neuropsychological case report.* Manuscript submitted for publication. With permission.)

battery was based on broad-band domains of functioning proposed by Reitan (1974). Specific instruments included the WISC-R, portions of the Woodcock-Johnson Psychoeducational Battery and HRNB, and other related tasks (e.g., Developmental Test of Visual-Motor Integration).

Although an eclectic neuropsychological battery can assume many forms, several eclectic batteries have been proposed to date to assess learning disability subtypes. In particular, the eclectic neuropsychological assessment batteries proposed by Mattis et al. (1975), Obrzut (1981), Aaron (1981), and Wilson and Risucci (1986) are reviewed here.

MATTIS ET AL. (1975) ASSESSMENT MODEL

Mattis et al. (1975) provided a neuropsychological assessment model designed to differentiate specific subtypes of dyslexia. Included in this battery were the Wechsler Adult Intelligence Scale (WAIS) or WISC, Benton Test of Visual Retention, Raven Coloured or Standard Progressive Matrices, ITPA Sound Blending, Purdue Pegboard, Spreen-Benton Token Test

TABLE 6.2. Neuropsychological procedures and diagnostic criteria for subtypes in the Mattis et al. (1975) model.

I. Language Disorder
    A. Anomia: 20% or greater proportion of errors on the Naming Test *and* one of the following:
        1. Disorder of comprehension: Performance on Token Test at least 1 *SD* below the mean; *or*
        2. Disorder of imitative speech: Performance *greater than* 1 *SD* below the mean on the Sentence Repetition Test; *or*
        3. Disorder of speech sound discrimination: 10% or greater proportion of errors on discrimination of "e" rhyming letters

II. Articulatory and Graphomotor Dyscoordination
    A. Performance on ITPA Sound Blending subtest *greater than* 1 *SD* below the mean; *and*
    B. Performance on graphomotor test *greater than* 1 *SD* below the mean; *and*
    C. Acousto-sensory and receptive language processes within normal limits

III. Visuospatial Perceptual Disorder
    A. Verbal IQ *more than* 10 points above Performance IQ; *and*
    B. Raven's Coloured Progressive Matrices percentile *less than* equivalent Performance IQ; *and*
    C. Benton Test of Visual Retention (10-sec exposure, immediate reproduction) score *at or below* the Borderline level

Adapted from Mattis, S., French, J. H., & Rapin, I. (1975). Dyslexia in children and young adults: Three independent neuropsychological syndromes. *Developmental Medicine and Child Neurology, 17*, 150–163. Adapted with permission.

and Sentence Repetition Subtests, and WRAT. Graphomotor coordination, speech-sound discrimination, and verbal labeling also were assessed. Using clinical-inferential classification methods, Mattis et al. provided assessment-based rules for identifying three specific dyslexic subtypes (see Chapter 3). These criteria are presented in Table 6.2. Many aspects of these diagnostic rules were adopted by the Child Neurology Society in the development of a proposed Nosology on Disorders of Cortical Function in Children (1981). Mattis et al. were one of the first groups of investigators to provide clinicians and researchers with clinical classification rules for the identification of learning disability subtypes.

The learning disability subtyping studies described by Lyon (e.g., Lyon & Watson, 1981) also used the Mattis et al. procedures. In lieu of the classification criteria provided by Mattis et al., however, Lyon applied empirical classification methods to identify homogeneous subtypes of learning disabilities. The studies conducted by Lyon and colleagues are noteworthy not only because they have developed a classification system based largely on the Mattis et al. procedures, but also because they have proffered treatment programs based on this subtyping model (see Chapter 8).

OBRZUT (1981) ASSESSMENT MODEL

Obrzut (1981) proposed a conceptual framework for the neuropsychological assessment of children. Generally, this framework considers broad-band domains of functioning, derived largely from Johnson and Myklebust's (1967) hierarchy of information processing. Obrzut believed that this conceptual hierarchy had the potential to lead to a more organized and systematic appraisal of children, particularly those manifesting neurodevelopmental learning disorders. This hierarchy consisted of the broad-band neuropsychological domains of sensation, perception, memory, symbolization, and conceptualization.

Obrzut noted that tasks within each of these domains should be sensitive to a variety of functions. Thus, his objective of the neuropsychological assessment was to devise comprehensive tests spanning (a) a wide range of higher (e.g., language) and lower (e.g., motor) level cerebral functions and (b) Reitan's four methods of inference (e.g., pattern of performance). Generally, all tests included in eclectic batteries should conform to accepted psychometric standards. Hynd and colleagues (Hynd & Cohen, 1983; Hynd, Connor, & Nieves, 1988) slightly modified this conceptual hierarchy, particularly with respect to its application to learning disability subtypes. This conceptual hierarchy and selected instruments that assess particular domains are presented in Table 6.3.

TABLE 6.3. Conceptual hierarchy and selected evaluation procedures for neuropsychological assessment of subtypes.

I. Sensation & sensory recognition

   Acuity
      Visual
      Auditory

   Recognition
      Finger agnosia
      Finger-tip number writing
      Tactile form recognition

II. Perception

   Auditory
      Speech Sounds Perception Test
      Seashore Rhythm Test

   Visual
      Bender Gestalt Test
      Developmental Test of Visual-Motor Integration
      Benton Visual Retention Test

   Tactile-Kinesthetic
      Tactual Performance Test

III. Motor

   Cerebellar screening

TABLE 6.3. Continued.

    Tandem walking
    Tests for dysarthria
    Fine-motor coordination
    Tests for nystagmus

  Lateral Dominance-Motor
    Grip strength
    Edinburgh Inventory
    Finger tapping

IV. Psycholinguistic
  Screening measures
    Aphasia Screening Test
    Fluency Test
    Peabody Picture Vocabulary Test–Revised

  Formal assessment
    Illinois Test of Psycholinguistic Abilities
    Boston Aphasia Screening Test

  Language asymmetries
    Dichotic listening
    Visual half-field tasks
    Time-sharing tasks

V. Academic
  Comprehensive battery
    Peabody Individual Achievement Test–Revised
    Woodcock-Johnson Psychoeducational Battery

  Reading Tests
    Durrell Analysis of Reading Difficulties
    Gates-McKillop Reading Mastery Tests
    Woodcock Reading Mastery Test–Revised

  Clinical measures
    Test for phonetic sounds (nonsense words)
    Test for vowel principles (nonsense words)
    Syllabication (nonsense words)
    Oral reading passages (graded)
    Try-Outs-Diagnostic teaching
    Phonemic segmentation
    Flash vocabulary

VI. Cognitive-Intellectual
    Category Test
    Raven's Coloured Progressive Matrices
    Kaufman Assessment Battery for Children
    Wechsler Intelligence Scale for Children–Revised
    Stanford-Binet Intelligence Scale (4th ed.)

Adapted from Hynd, G. W., Connor, R. T., & Nieves, N. (1988). Learning disabilities sub-
types: Perspectives and methodological issues in clinical assessment. In M. G. Tramontana &
S. R. Hooper (Eds.), *Assessment issues in child neuropsychology* (pp. 281–312). New York:
Plenum Publishing Corp. With permission.

This hierarchy represents a framework in which assessment procedures efficiently may be related to information processing systems important to adequate functioning in learning disabled children. It also suggests that by carefully selecting measures, one can assess efficiently information processing domains that are directly related to specific referral questions. Similar to most other eclectic approaches, however, this approach requires that examiners be familiar with a large number of assessment procedures.

NEUROPSYCHOLOGICAL KEY APPROACH

Aaron (1981) proposed the Neuropsychological Key Approach to the study of learning disabilities. This model represents a logical approach to decision-making rules and is based on four major premises: (a) learning disabilities are a heterogeneous group of disorders, (b) learning disabilities result from an imbalance in information-processing abilities rather than a generalized deficit, (c) learning disabilities are due to anomalies in neurological development and should be distinguished from organic brain damage, and (d) attempts at remediation (e.g., perceptual-motor training) with this heterogeneous group of children have been unsuccessful. Aaron's Key consists of 11 tests that include an intelligence measure, Durrell Analysis of Reading Difficulty, Durrell Oral Reading and oral description of two pictures, sight vocabulary from various reading inventories, Northwestern Syntax Screening Test, Token Test for Children, Memory for Faces Test, Sequential Memory Test, Manual-Dexterity Test, WISC-R Digit Span Subtest, and Matching Familiar Figures Test.

Based on the subject's performance on these 11 tasks, the Key Approach requires that the examiner engage in a series of decisions in order to derive a specific diagnosis. The first two decisions are: (a) identifying the child as possibly learning disabled by examining the level of intellectual performance (i.e., IQ > 90) and (b) examining the pattern of neuropsychological performance for inconsistencies. If inconsistencies are present, then it becomes important to determine if the disability is related to language or to visual-gestalt dysfunctions. The next three decisions provide a more refined investigation of specific tasks reflecting the area of dyfunction. Finally, the subject's neuropsychological profile is examined for evidence of attentional inefficiencies and hyperactivity that may interfere with learning. Aaron (1981) reported that few children clearly fall within the parameters outlined by the Key (i.e., language subtypes or visual gestalt subtypes), but this approach does offer a unique and systematic strategy for deriving subtype diagnosis. The ultimate validity of this approach remains to be accrued.

WILSON AND RISUCCI (1986) ASSESSMENT MODEL

These investigators derived an eclectic battery consistent with frameworks provided by Obrzut (1981) and by Mattis et al. (1975). This battery was proposed for the subtyping of language disordered preschool children and was described further by Wilson (1986). It assesses broad-band domains such as auditory perception, auditory discrimination, auditory cognition, auditory memory, retrieval, visual discrimination, visual spatialization, visual cognition, and visual memory. Specific psychometric tasks are used to assess each of these broad-band domains. This battery has been useful in developing inclusion rules to identify clinical-inferential subtypes (e.g., auditory cognition lower than visual cognition) in a sample of language disordered preschool children.

SUMMARY

Eclectic neuropsychological battery approaches have been successful in providing a basis for thorough assessments of the cognitive functioning of learning disabled individuals. These approaches typically are based on conceptualized frameworks of neuropsychological functions. They have the advantage of allowing the examiner to select from a wide variety of normed tasks to assess particular domains. Moreover, they also have the potential to contribute to the development of classification criteria for subtype identification.

Special-Purpose Measures

In addition to fixed and eclectic battery approaches to neuropsychological assessment of children with learning disabilities, there are many individual measures and specialized test batteries available to assess more specific aspects of neuropsychological functioning. Examples include Benton's Motor Impersistence Battery and other special-purpose tests (Benton, Hamsher, Varney, & Spreen, 1983), the Goldman-Fristoe-Woodcock (1974) Auditory Skills Battery, the children's version of the Califorina Verbal Learning Test (Delis, Kramer, Kaplan, & Ober, 1986), and the Wisconsin Card Sorting Test (Heaton, 1981), to name only a few. Some measures have been validated on the basis of their ability to predict specific childhood outcomes, such as the Florida Kindergarten Screening Battery, which appears to provide an effective way to identify children at risk for reading disabilities (Satz & Fletcher, 1982). This latter battery also contributed to one of the most methodologically sound subtyping studies conducted to date (Satz & Morris, 1981). There also are procedures for assessing specific aspects of learning disability subtypes, such as dichotic listening paradigms (Bakker, 1979b) and metacognitive techniques (Wiener, 1986; Wong, Wong, Perry & Sawatsky, 1986). Among all of these specialized measures, however, the Boder Test of Reading-Spelling Patterns (Boder & Jarrico, 1982) probably has the most significant history with respect to the subtyping literature.

KNOWN WORDS		UNKNOWN WORDS	
RESPONSE		RESPONSE	
Actual	Correct	Actual	Correct
awake	**awake**	_kimit_	**climate**
child	**child**	_kicited_	**excited**
Blocked	**block**	_budge_	**badge**
hunper	**hunger**	_intermend_	**entertainment**
north	**north**	_attbetec athletic_	**athletic**
grite	**great**	_wrist_	**wrist**
knife	**knife**	_flute_	**freight**
Luiaf	**laugh**	_coff_	**cough**
Lisiten	**listen**	_karten_	**character**
shourd	**should**	_bisness_	**business**

FIGURE 6.3. An example of a list of known and unknown spelling words from the Boder Test of Reading-Spelling Patterns for a 13-year-old male with visual-spatial dyslexia. (From Hooper, S.R., Hynd, G.W., & Tramontana, M.G. (1988). *Visual-spatial dyslexia: A neuropsychological case report.* Manuscript submitted for publication. With permission.)

BODER TEST OF READING-SPELLING PATTERNS

Based on her model of reading disability subtypes discussed in Chapter 3, Boder provided a screening instrument to classify children in a systematic manner (Boder & Jarrico, 1982). The Boder Test of Reading-Spelling Patterns (BTRSP) requires a child to perform a reading recognition task with graded lists of 20 single words. There are an equal number of phonetic and nonphonetic words in each list. A reading grade level and reading quotient are obtained from this task. Based on the child's reading performance, an individualized list of spelling words is selected to reflect words that are in the child's sight-word vocabulary (i.e., Known Words) and those that are not (i.e., Unknown Words). A sample list of spelling words provided for a child with visual-spatial dyslexia is presented in Figure 6.3. These words are divided equally between phonetically regular and irregular words. The variables of reading quotient, percentage of known words spelled correctly, and percentage of unknown words with good phonetic equivalents, as determined by a priori rules, are combined to identify a specific subtype. This process is illustrated in Figure 6.4.

Although Boder is commended for providing a systematic procedure to complement her subtyping model, recent reviews of the BTRSP have been mixed. Several authors reported the BTRSP test to be useful as a clinical

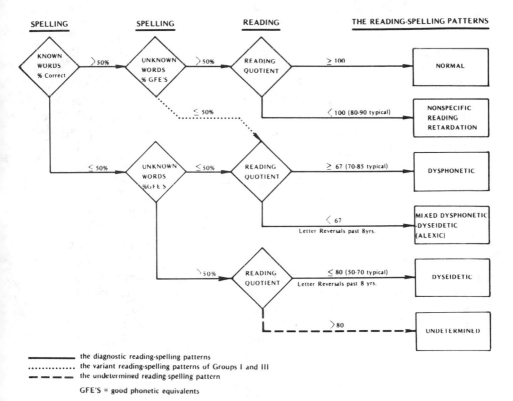

SPELLING   SPELLING   READING   THE READING-SPELLING PATTERNS

─────── the diagnostic reading-spelling patterns
.... the variant reading-spelling patterns of Groups I and III
▬ ▬ ▬ the undetermined reading spelling pattern

GFE'S = good phonetic equivalents

FIGURE 6.4. Diagnostic flowchart from the Boder Test of Reading-Spelling Patterns. From Boder, E., & Jarrico, S. (1982). *The Boder Test of Reading-Spelling Patterns* (p. 39). New York: Grune & Stratton. With permission.

Note. Boder and Jarrico (personal communication, July 11, 1988) have noted that this schematic does not fully reflect BTRSP diagnostic procedures. First, the "Undetermined" dyslexic pattern should be labeled "Remediated" because it typically is shown by remediated dysphonetics and, more rarely, by remediated dyseidetic or mixed dyslexics. Second, as stated in the BTRSP manual, normals and nonspecifics with secondary reading retardation typically correctly spell 70 to 100% of Known Words. These subtypes and the dyseidetic subtypes can write as GFEs 70 to 100% of Unknown Words. In fact, for normal, nonspecific, and dyseidetic readers GFE scores of at least 80% in the Unknown Words list can be expected. Scores of 60% in either spelling list should be regarded as borderline and calling for further evaluation. Future editions of the BTRSP should address these criteria empirically. Finally, examiners should not overlook the qualitative aspects of the reading pattern, notably the reading errors, in differentiating the remediated dysphonetic from dyseidetic dyslexics. There are no formal rules for scoring reading errors, but the BTRSP manual does describe characteristic reading errors of each subtype. Plans for a revised second edition of the BTRSP should recognize the increasing prevalence of the remediated dyslexic pattern.

screening tool (Bing, 1985; Hynd, 1984; Telzrow, Century, Redmond, Whitaker, & Zimmerman, 1983), but others identified serious concerns. Alexander (1984), for example, noted that the BTRSP completely excludes comprehension and general interactive aspects of the reading process. Reynolds (1984) further criticized the BTRSP from a psychometric perspective. Similarly, Bing (1985) cited concerns about the reading quotient, a variant of the Myklebust (1968) Learning Quotient. Although the manual of the BTRSP (Boder & Jarrico, 1982) does provide for mental-age adjustments in the reading quotient, Bing (1985) cautioned that identical congnitive levels neither can be inferred by the same mental age at different chronological ages, nor necessarily can be interpreted as similar in children of the same chronological age. This is due largely to the fact that BTRSP reading quotient does not have a constant standard deviation across age and, consequently, does not represent a true standard score.

Other major diagnostic components of the BTRSP also are problematic. For example, although the spelling scores have not been scrutinized as closely as their reading-component counterparts, an absence of difficulty-level standardization presents an interpretive dilemma. Here, different spelling lists are generated for each child assessed, and there are no data about list comparabilities. This creates potential diagnostic problems because children can be classified as impaired or nonimpaired based on word lists of different relative difficulties. This contributes to assessment bias in favor of lists comprising particular collections of words (Reynolds, 1984).

The reliability and validity of the BTRSP also require further examination if it is to be used to differentiate among various dyslexic subtypes. Moreover, the validation of the various components of the diagnostic model becomes especially important when it is recognized that the internal validity of the model cannot be determined statistically. The model, for example, is based on dichotomous decision making (i.e., scores above or below a predetermined cutoff) with only three variables in the decision-making matrix. Consequently, validating the subtyping model through an empirical clustering technique becomes a moot point because the number of subtypes derived can be no more than two (i.e., the number of variables $-1 =$ the number of subtypes possible). Thus, external validation of this model is extraordinarily important.

Nockleby and Galbraith (1984) demonstrated partial support for the BTRSP by comparing its results to an eclectic battery of gestalt and analytic-sequential tasks. Although these investigators posited some support for the components of the BTRSP, particularly as they contributed to the dysphonetic and nonspecific subtypes, a large proportion of cases were identified as false negatives. Other researchers have found a high percentage of severely delayed readers to be misclassified by the BTRSP as nonspecifics as well (Lund, Yingling, Galin, Marcus & Simons, 1984).

This validity concern has been addressed further by comparing the diagnostic components of the BTRSP to reading and spelling subtests of the

Stanford Achievement Test in a reading disabled sample (Hooper, 1988). Although reading components of the BTRSP correlated with tasks of reading recognition, word analysis, word knowledge, and, somewhat surprisingly, reading comprehension on the Stanford Achievement Test, the BTRSP tended to estimate the reading skills of the sample as more impaired than indicated by the Stanford. Further, there was no relationship between the BTRSP spelling measures and the Spelling subtest of the Stanford. The percent of unknown words with good phonetic equivalents, however, did correlate with selected aspects of reading achievement such as word analysis, word knowledge, and overall reading.

Clearly, further investigations examining the utility of the BTRSP are needed, and Reynolds' (1984) concerns should be considered by those using this tool in clinical settings. Modifications of classification rules have been offered by Pennington et al. (1983) and by Campe and McCabe (1977), but few data are reported regarding the clinical and psychometric aspects of these changes. Indeed, plans for revision of the BTRSP are in progress (E. Boder, personal communication, June 21, 1988). Although the Boder Test of Reading-Spelling Patterns represents an attempt to identify learning disability subtypes within a preconceived clinical-inferential model, at this time it clearly should be used as only one part of a more comprehensive assessment battery.

SUMMARY

Special-purpose neuropsychological measures typically are designed to assess selected aspects of an individual's functioning. As such, they should be used as only part of a more comprehensive neuropsychological battery or as screening devices to determine the likelihood of the presence of learning disabilities. Although there are many different kinds of special-purpose measures, the BTRSP was emphasized here largely because of its intended application to learning disability subtypes. The BTRSP has provided clinicians and researchers with a quick, convenient screening task to subtype learning disabled individuals, but the efficacy of this test and the subtyping model from which it was derived awaits further clarification.

Summary

Various approaches to neuropsychological assessment have been used to identify and evaluate learning disabilities and particular subtypes thereof. These include both fixed and eclectic neuropsychological batteries. Other neuropsychological approaches, such as qualitative (Christensen, 1975; Luria, 1966, 1973) and process-oriented (Milberg, Hebben, & Kaplan, 1986; Wilson, 1986) approaches, also exist and have potential for application to learning disability subtyping, but they have not yet been documented for this purpose.

To date, the eclectic batteries appear to have been used the most frequently for learning disabilities and subtype identification. This probably is related to their flexibility, potential for hypothesis testing, utility across settings, and shorter administration time. Selected measures, such as the BTRSP, also appear to hold promise for application to subtyping, but such measures are used most appropriately in conjunction with a more comprehensive neuropsychological battery.

Issues in Neuropsychological Assessment of Subtypes

Clearly, the neuropsychological assessment of learning disability subtypes is a complex task. The neuropsychological foundations of cognitive functioning and associated interactive social-emotional features contribute to this complexity. Consequently, the neuropsychological assessment of learning disability subtypes should attempt to maintain multiple frames of reference in evaluating potential learning problems. Toward this end there are several important issues to consider.

Elements of Neuropsychological Assessment

Consideration of the multifaceted nature of learning disorders requires a comprehensive approach to assessment. Hynd et al. (1988) advocated that a neuropsychological assessment battery should reflect tasks constructed around a wide array of functions. Moreover, a battery should include tasks on which these children perform poorly (e.g., linguistic). Hynd et al. also suggested that a battery should be flexible in order to address referral questions efficiently and to relate directly to the subtyping literature.

Further, Lyon et al. (1988) noted that it is important to the ecological validity of the assessment that the testing strategies relate to specific suggestions for intervention. In contrast, however, Stanovich (1988) cogently argued that methods used for learning disability diagnosis appropriately may be quite different from educationally relevant interventions. Further, in emphasizing the importance of basic (as opposed to applied) research in the field of learning disabilities, Swanson (1988) asserted that it is not necessarily the case that investigations that lack ecological validity cannot contribute to ecologically valid theories of learning disabilities, including those that address treatment intervention (see also Kavale, 1988).

Finally, it is important to recognize that the evaluation of individuals with specific learning needs should never occur in isolation. Individuals performing neuropsychological assessments should be open to the possibility of interactive effects of other variables (e.g., social-emotional features) with the cognitive evaluation. Here, it is important for assessment to include thorough descriptions of learning problems, the circumstances during which they occur, and the concerns and expectations of all involved (e.g., parents, teachers, child). It is perhaps best that these kinds of evaluations occur within multidisciplinary frameworks.

Other Neurodiagnostic Measures

Although it is beyond the scope of this volume to review other neurodiagnostic measures used with the learning disability population (the interested reader is referred to Hynd & Willis [1988] and Morris, Levy, & Pirozzolo [1988] for a more complete review of these measures), the relationship of neuropsychological assessment to these other measures along the structure-function continuum does deserve mention. The literature reviewed in Chapters 1 and 2 suggests a strong neurological basis for learning disabilities, and the relationship between cognitive-behavioral measures and substrate neurological processes is important to understanding learning problems.

As noted in Chapter 2, the lateralized asymmetry of brain structure (i.e., left cerebral hemisphere planum temporale larger than homologous region of the right cerebral hemisphere) may be a normal anatomical marker for functional lateral dominance. Perhaps depatures from this asymmetry may be markers for structural anomalies associated with learning disorders. Several autopsy reports of learning disabled patients have described deviations from this normal asymmetry as well as other cytoarchitectonic anomalies (Drake, 1968; Galaburda & Kemper, 1979; Galaburda et al., 1985). Hier et al. (1978) examined the computerized tomography (CT) images from 24 developmental dyslexics and found that 42% had a reversal of the expected anatomical asymmetry. This finding also correlated with a lower mean verbal IQ of these patients. In contrast, however, Denckla et al. (1985) found only 20% of CT scans to be abnormal for a group of learning disabled children showing neurobehavioral evidence of lateralized dysfunction. Further, in reviewing the literature on neuroimaging techniques and postmortem findings, Hynd and Semrud-Clikeman (1988) concluded that, just as neurobehavioral measures suffer from inferential linkages to structure, these data also suffer from inferential linkages to neurobehavioral function. Clearly, the relationship between neuroanatomical structure and neurobehavioral function needs continued investigation with the learning disability population, particularly as it may be applied to subtypes.

More research has been conducted on the neurophysiological functioning of learning disabled individuals, and several studies have used subtype models in exploring electrophysiological differences among subtypes. Electroencephalography (EEG) is a technique for amplifying and recording the variations in the electrical potentials, assumed to originate within the brain, detectable on the scalp. EEG methodology has been refined in recent years by the use of computer-based analytic techniques that have contributed to rapid analyses of these data (e.g., brain electrical activity mapping, evoked potentials). As noted in Chapter 2, most of the research conducted to date with these techniques suggests that there are significant EEG differences between normal achievers and learning disabled children (Fein et al., 1983; Sklar, Hanley, & Simmons, 1973). In fact, Lubar et al. (1985) correctly identified about 79% of normals and 76% of learning disabled children using EEG techniques. Moreover, Cohen and Breslin (1984) concluded from their work that significant differences between the evoked potentials of normals and dyslexics were related to the way that the two hemispheres processed visual information. In addition, some data have begun to emerge that suggest that there are specific EEG patterns that may be associated with specific learning disability subtypes (Fried et al., 1981; Holcomb, Ackerman, & Dykman, 1985).

Other neurodiagnostic procedures have been used with learning disabled individuals, such as regional cerebral blow flow (Hynd et al., 1987), to explore relationships between brain metabolism of a radioactive isotope (i.e., ^{133}xenon) and cognitive function. Although all of these neurodiagnostic techniques hold promise for the assessment and identification of learning disability subtypes, and indeed some advances have been asserted (e.g., EEGs and their electrophysiological variants), their relationships to actual behavior and cognitive functioning in this population remain inconclusive to date.

Developmental Considerations

In addition to constructing a comprehensive neuropsychological battery and attempting to make inferences to brain structure, the neuropsychological assessment of learning disabled individuals also should be sensitive to developmental variables. For example, it now is clear that, from a neurodevelopmental perspective, children cannot be assessed as if they were "little adults." The discontinuous processes of brain maturation that may extend into adolescence, young adulthood and, indeed, throughout the life span, require that assessment methods be developed that can adequately and accurately assess neuro-behavior functioning in individuals at all age levels. This is particularly important for investigators working with young children because of the remarkably rapid and dynamic neuropsychological maturation characteristic of this developmental period. Developmental normative data are important to the construction of a neuropsychological assessment battery and, as such, should be a major criterion for determining the inclusion of a particular task. These data also are important for interpreting specific pathognomonic signs that may be associated with specific developmental expectations for an individual of a given age.

Related to developmental issues is the concept of learning disability continuity. Schonhaut and Satz (1983) concluded from their review of follow-up outcome studies of learning disabled children that prognosis tends to be guarded, at best. The subtyping of learning disabilities may provide a clearer picture about the prognoses of these disorders, particularly as they emerge into adulthood. For example, as noted in Chapter 5, Spreen and Haaf (1986) observed in their longitudinal study that, although general subtypes remained the same, there was significant movement of individuals among the subtypes, suggesting that there may be inconsistencies in the manifestation of learning disabilities over time. From the few studies conducted to date exploring subtype continuity, it is clear that assessment strategies should address potential prognoses that may be associated with particular subtype patterns.

Assessment-Treatment Linkages

A primary reason for conducting neuropsychological assessment is to apply this information to the development of an individual treatment plan. Indeed, these assessment-treatment linkages are a fundamental reason for the avid interest in the homogeneous classification of learning disability subtypes. Consequently, it is important for assessment tasks to be capable of guiding specific treatment options, an issue that may be independent of ecological validity (cf. Lyon et al., 1988; Stanovich, 1988). Thus, assessment tasks should include both formative (i.e., process oriented) and summative (i.e., product oriented) measures.

Based on the need for neuropsychological assessment to include both formative and summative measures, other assessment perspectives need to be adapted for learning disabilities. For example, Szekeres, Ylvisaker, and Cohen (1987) noted numerous variables to consider in their work with patients undergoing closed head injury rehabilitation. These investigators observed their patient's responses to real-life situations and established training of appropriate compensatory strategies based on these daily performances. As such, their approach acknowledges the complex interactions between variables inherent with a head injury population. This technology is available to contribute to the neuropsychological assessment and identification of learning disability subtypes, but it awaits valid application to this group of disorders. Additional assessment-treatment linkages are discussed in Chapter 8, particularly as they relate to learning disability subtypes.

Conclusions

There are numerous fixed and eclectic approaches to the neuropsychological assessment of learning disabilities, but it does not appear that one is more viable than another for the further delineation of subtypes. The eclectic approaches, however, do appear to have the most flexibilty with respect to breadth of coverage, hypothesis testing, and, depending on the tasks selected, treatment linkages. Clearly, neuropsychological assessment should not stand alone for learning disabled individuals but, rather, should be complemented by other kinds of assessments. In particular, it is important for continued efforts to be directed toward improving our understanding of how various factors, such as social-emotional ones, mitigate neuropsychological assessment results, and how neurological structures relate to functions and behaviors. Finally, issues to be considered in constructing an assessment battery to identify and evaluate learning disabled individuals should include developmental concerns and the relationship between the assessment process and treatment. Although there has been a multitude of research presented that has addressed these concerns, at the present time there is no one best approach to the neuropsychological assessment of subtypes.

The ability to assess all of the parameters of the learning disabled individual and to distinguish among subtypes are formidable goals. Neuropsychological theory and its associated assessment approaches appear to have the potential to advance thinking in these domains, but, as Gaddes (1985, p.90) commented, "This attempt to relate neurological, psychosocial, and educational knowledge is a radical one and is still in its infancy."

7
Social-Emotional Features

Clearly, much has been learned about the neurocognitive, neurolinguistic, and academic characteristics of learning disabilities over the past two decades. For instance, the term *learning disability* is a generic one, and truly productive research must focus on clearly defined subtypes of the disorder. A body of knowledge has now accumulated that has progressed from a preoccupation with single-factor models for heterogeneous samples of learning disabled individuals to a more fruitful approach focusing on neurocognitive, neurolinguistic, and academic features of relatively homogeneous samples.

Despite the importance of these foci, they have tended to overshadow important social-emotional (i.e., psychosocial and affective) features of the disorder. Currently, researchers are beginning to examine these social-emotional features. The study of these features has paralleled the broader field from which it was derived, but has progressed much more rapidly. Thus, even though this literature is still in an early stage of development, efforts that initially focused on heterogeneously defined samples and etiological concerns already have begun to shift to a more extensive focus on subtyping issues.

The focus of this chapter is directed at the social-emotional features of learning disabilities. Initially, selected hypotheses that have been proposed to account for these features are critically reviewed. These hypotheses and the studies that have been conducted to evaluate them have involved primarily undifferentiated groups of learning disabled individuals. This research clearly documents the importance of subtyping in learning disabilities with reference to social-emotional variables and provides a rich source of new hypotheses as well. The chapter then describes in detail the limited subtyping research that has been conducted to date. The preliminary results of these studies militate against firm conclusions, but they do suggest potentially productive avenues for further study and some tentative implications for clinical practice.

Research with Heterogeneous Groups

The majority of research on the social-emotional features of learning disabilities has been conducted with heterogeneous samples. Moreover, most of this research has been guided by etiological hypotheses for the disorder. For example, social-emotional problems have been considered as both antecedents and consequences of learning disabilities as well as manifestations of a general impairment that underlies the disorder. Examples of these hypotheses are critically discussed as illustrations.

Social-Emotional Antecedents and Consequences

A number of etiological hypotheses of learning disabilities have been proposed in which the social-emotional features of the disorder are considered as antecedents. In these instances, these features are viewed as causing the neurocognitive, neurolinguistic, and academic characteristics of learning disabilities. Alternatively, these features have been considered as consequences of learning disabilities, caused, for example, by academic failure and associated ostracism within the school milieu. Research on classification and labeling and affective antecedents of learning disabilities are discussed in order to illustrate these hypotheses.

CLASSIFICATION AND LABELING

For many years diagnosticians have been concerned with social-emotional issues assoicated with classifying and labeling an individual as handicapped. From a psychosocial perspective for example, Guskin (1978) proposed a sequential casual formulation of the label-validation process that leads from teacher expectation to student achievement. In this sense, the label of "learning disability" potentially leads to a stereotypical teacher expectancy manifested as a particular stimulus to which the student responds. This stimulus is different than usual, perhaps because it is more direct, clearer, and easier, and it tends to elicit a different response. Different responses lead to different levels of progress, and different progress provides a convenient validation of the original diagnostic label.

Indeed, empirical evidence confirms that teacher interactions with learning disabled students differ both quantitatively and qualitatively from interactions with non-learning disabled students (Bryan, 1974a; Chapman, Larsen, & Parker, 1979; Dorval, McKinney, & Feagans, 1982), lending support to psychosocial explanations for the disorder and its concomitants. Learning disabled students, for example, are more likely to be criticized and ignored in academic interactions and to be excluded from nonacademic interactions by their teachers than students who are not learning disabled. Further, based on data showing correlations between teacher ratings of students and student ratings of classmates, Bruck (1986) suggested that negative teacher perceptions of learning disabled students may be communicated to the classmates of those students.

From a neuropsychological perspective, a learning disability is typically perceived as inherent to the individual rather than as a socially constructed phenomenon. This does not preclude, however, the susceptibility of the afflicted individual's behavior to environmental influences. When analyzed from a social learning theoretical perspective, the factors of person, environment, and behavior function as determinants of each other, and their relative influences vary as a function of particular personal and environmental factors (Bandura, 1977).

Bartel and Guskin (1980) described an alternative psychosocial paradigm for understanding learning disabilities. They suggested that handicapped individuals are more distinctive in terms of the characteristic response of others to them than in terms of their intrinsic characteristics. In this somewhat controversial paradigm, the society selects particular norms, usually perceived as relevant by that society, to be desirable or undesirable (e.g., academic competence). In this sense, Bartel and Guskin's notion of a learning disability requires one to acknowledge some initial differentiating characteristic (i.e., the normative standard) that sets in motion the social categorization inherent in the process. Those who fail to conform to these selected norms are subsequently labeled as deviant (e.g., learning disabled), grouped accordingly, and treated differentially.

When an individual moves from one group to another, role expectations change. Thus, Bartel and Guskin (1980) proposed that many behaviors typically considered to be intrinsic to the labeled individual may actually be due to a desire to match externally imposed role expectations associated with satisfactory outcomes. The learning disability, in effect, is created through a social process in which a distinctive mode of treatment is prescribed for those who fail to meet normative expectations established by society. Individuals with recognizable learning disabilities are expected to behave in a particular fashion and, moreover, to internalize a negative self-evaluation for challenging the norm selected by the society.

Regardless of the degree to which we might be willing to accept these psychosocial explanations for learning disabilities as truth, they do illustrate potential influences of social-extrinsic (as opposed to individual-intrinsic) factors on the course of this group of disorders.

AFFECTIVE ANTECEDENTS

A related etiological hypothesis contends that affective factors, as opposed to psychosocial factors, lead to learning disabilities. This viewpoint frequently is omitted from discussions of the etiology of learning disabilities because it is disparate from traditional, more accepted definitions of the disorder (Goldstein & Dundon, 1987), For example, as discussed in Chapter 1, the definition of a child with a learning disability proffered in P.L.

94–142 ". . . does not include children who have learning problems which are primarily the result of . . . emotional disturbance . . ." (U.S. Office of Education, 1977). Similarly, the National Joint Committee for Learning Disabilities proposed that "Even though a learning disability may occur concomitantly with other handicapping conditions (e.g., . . . emotional disturbance) . . . it is not the direct result of those conditions . . ." (Hammill et al., 1981, p. 336). Thus, although these definitions do not exclude the possibility of a coincident occurrence of a learning disability with an emotional disturbance, the latter is clearly auxiliary to the former.

Very little research has posited a presumptive role of psychological adjustment problems or emotional disturbance in the etiology of learning disabilities. Instead, these two groups are typically classified and treated differentially, even though emotionally disturbed individuals frequently present cognitive-academic psychometric profiles that are characteristic of learning disabilities (Cawley & Webster, 1981; Glavin & Annesley, 1971; Hallahan & Kauffman, 1977; Kauffman, 1981). There have been essentially two noninteractive lines of study, however, that have addressed the issue of psychological adjustment problems as antecedents of learning disabilities. The work of Goldstein and colleagues (Goldstein & Dundon, 1987; Goldstein et al., 1985) and of Kinsbourne and Caplan (1979) is illustrative.

Affective Explanation

Goldstein and Dundon (1987) posited the affective dimension as clearly antecedent to learning disabilities, at least for one subtype of the disorder. The dependent relationship between cognition and affect provides the foundation for this unconventional hypothesis.

Central to their thesis, Goldstein and Dundon (1987) invoked the concept of limited capacity that refers to the resources (or mental energy) available to individuals for the performance of mental or cognitive activities (Kahneman, 1973). Capacity is believed to vary intraindividually as a function of task variables such as task difficulty and number of tasks being performed concurrently, as well as a function of subject variables such as arousal, motivation, and affect. In terms of a learning disability, affective variables (e.g., depression) are predicted to diminish the amount of capacity available for the performance of tasks requiring effort (Hasher & Zacks, 1979). Indeed, a number of investigators have found that depression may lead to diminished capacity for learning, resulting in failure on effortful tasks such as reading and arithmetic (Henderson, 1983; Weingartner, Cohen, Murphy, Martello, & Gerdt, 1981). In this sense, the affective dimension is seen as presumptive in the etiology of a learning disability. Goldstein et al. (1985) provided limited empirical support for this hypothesis with reference to one subtype of a learning disability. That study is discussed in detail in a subsequent section of this chapter.

Failure Explanation

In contrast to the position in which psychological adjustment problems are viewed as presumptive, Kinsbourne and Caplan (1979) described a "cycle of failure" in which psychological adjustment problems can be viewed as intermediary; that is, as a consequence as well as an antecedent in relation to learning problems. In this paradigm, learning difficulties or academic failure elicit secondary psychosocial adjustment problems such as feelings of inferiority, hopelessness, and anxiety. The adjustment problems escalate to a magnitude to which they interfere with cognitive-academic functions and, consequently, result in further learning difficulties and academic failure. The events within this cycle become exacerbated and the initial learning difficulties become aggravated, resulting in a learning disability. Psychological effects associated with the subsequent diagnostic, placement, and treatment processes may further compound these problems. Moreover, a variety of personality problems related to self-concept, locus of control, and temperament variables also often are assumed to be secondary to these processes, although the assumption of their secondary nature probably is not warranted by the available data (Bender, 1987).

This paradigm and the inherent assumption of extrinsic (as opposed to intrinsic) factors leading to the learning disability have been criticized by Bruck (1986) on empirical grounds for lack of direct research support. In fact, in one of the few longitudinal studies conducted to date, Kistner and Osborne (1987) found learning disabled children to be more negative in their self-perceptions of academic and nonacademic abilities, but these perceptions did not deteriorate over a 2-year period. Moreover, perceptions of physical competence improved over this time period. More studies of a longitudinal nature will be necessary to address these questions. At present, most supporting evidence is correlational and logical causality is, therefore, difficult to demonstrate in the absence of more extensive analyses.

Social-Emotional Manifestations

An alternative hypothesis to those in which social-emotional features are considered as antecedents or consequences of learning disabilities has been termed "the social cognition hypothesis" (Pearl, 1987). This hypothesis posits that the same underlying disorder that causes the neurocognitive, linguistic, and academic deficits characteristic of learning disabilities also causes the social-emotional features of the disorder.

In her review of the research bearing on this hypothesis, Bruck (1986) suggested that although data do not conclusively support this position, some data do reject the notion that the social-emotional features of learning disabilities are primary differentiating characteristics of the disorder.

For example, those social-emotional characteristics that differentiate learning disabled from non-learning disabled children are similar to those associated with other kinds of handicapping conditions such as mental retardation, emotional disturbance, and neurological impairment (Campbell, 1974; Cullinan, Epstein, & Dembinski, 1979; Gajar, 1979; Maheady, Maitland, & Sainato, 1984; Waterman, Sobesky, Silvern, Aoki, & McCaufay, 1981). Bruck suggested that these data militate against the position that social-emotional characteristics of learning disabilities are manifestations of the same cognitive deficit that underlies its academic features. Rather, given the commonality of these characteristics with other forms of child psychopathology, they more likely represent a general reaction to (i.e., consequence of) the condition.

Although this argument is a reasonable one, most contemporary diagnostic taxonomies involve simultaneous consideration of a number of symptoms that reliably coincide in the form of a syndrome (cf. empirical classification methods). Thus, a particular symptom within a syndrome need not be pathognomonic in order to be central or primary to the disorder in terms of clinical differentiation. This is certainly the case for the generic syndome that is labeled a learning disability. For example, few would argue that a primary feature of learning disabilities is academic dysfunction. Yet, academic dysfunction does not differentiate learning disabilities from other problems such as poor motivation for academic tasks or mental retardation. Instead, it the coincidence of academic dysfunction with other, nonpathognomonic symptoms that defines a learning disability and differentiates it from these other kinds of problems.

INTERPERSONAL ADJUSTMENT PROBLEMS

Interpersonal adjustment problems frequently are assumed to be a major social-emotional manifestation of learning disabilities. The hypothesis that learning disabled individuals are at high risk for developing interpersonal relationship and adjustment problems has been studied extensively. As a heterogeneous group, for example, learning disabled individuals typically are not well liked by non-learning disabled peers (Bryan, 1974b, 1976; Garrett & Crump, 1980; Scranton & Ryckman, 1979; Sheare, 1978; Siperstein, Bopp & Bak, 1978). Despite this research, conclusions about the prevalence and severity of such problems, as well as the relationship between a diminished capacity to perceive relevant social cues and academic competence (i.e., the social cognition hypothesis), are equivocal.

Maheady and Sainato (1986) reviewed 22 studies comparing the abilities of learning disabled and non-learning disabled children to comprehend nonverbal communication and to assume the roles of others. The data from these studies were compelling in that approximately 76% of the studies showed significant differences in social skills in favor of the non-learning disabled children, whereas the other 24% showed no significant differences between non-learning disabled and learning disabled children. None of the studies showed an overall significant difference in favor of the learning disabled children.

Research results, however, were obfuscated by a number of methodological issues such as generalization of laboratory tasks and, particularly, subject-selection procedures. For example, in all 22 studies reviewed, participants were included based solely on classification as learning disabled; neither subtyping information nor criteria regarding the psychosocial adjustment status of the participants were considered. Given these methodological problems, Maheady and Sainato (1986) suggested that it probably is inaccurate to assume that all learning disabled individuals, as a heterogeneous group, experience interpersonal adjustment problems.

In support of this interpretation, Perlmutter, Crocker, Cordray, and Garstecki (1983) identified a subtype of learning disabled high school students who were well liked by their classmates as assessed by sociometric ratings. In his review of the social-emotional characteristics of children and adolescents with learning disabilities, Perlmutter (1986) suggested that those learning disabled individuals who were well liked by their peers had a better understanding of how their peers felt about them than those who were not well liked. Moreover, these individuals were better able to perceive and interpret in an efficient manner those subtle social cues that signal changing social expectations or norms of conduct. That particular subtypes of learning disabled children and adolescents are delayed in their ability to use these kinds of discriminative social stimuli now has been supported in a number of studies (Axelrod, 1982; Gerber & Zinkgraf, 1982; Goldman & Hardin, 1982; Pearl & Cosden, 1982). A major implication of this research is that the psychosocial/interpersonal problems of some learning disabled individuals may represent performance deficits rather than acquisition deficits (also see Pearl, 1987), requiring a differentiated treatment approach (Elliott, Gresham, & Heffer, 1987). The amount of within-groups variance in these studies is great, however, begging the question of homogeneity of learning disabilities in terms of the social-emotional features of the disorder.

AFFECTIVE DISTURBANCES

Research in child and adolescent psychopathology clearly indicates that affective disturbances are manifested differentially as, for example, broad-band internalized (i.e., overcontrolled) or externalized (i.e., undercontrolled) disorders (Achenbach, 1985). A number of studies have focused on these dimensions of psychopathology for learning disabled individuals. For instance, Bruck (1986) identified seven separate studies, including the standardization study, in which the Behavior Problem Checklist (Quay & Peterson, 1975) was completed for learning disabled, behavior disordered, and normal children. Average ratings obtained in these studies for the three primary subscales of this instrument (i.e., Conduct Problem, Personality Problem, and Inadequacy-Immaturity) were compared.

Bruck (1986) interpreted these data to suggest that the profiles of the learning disabled children were healthier than the behavior disordered children. Close inspection of the data, however, suggests that alternative intepretations also are feasible, illustrating the equivocal nature of these results. For example, of 12 separate comparisons of learning disabled children with their normal counterparts, six (i.e., 50%) were significantly different, all in favor of the normal children. In constrast, of nine separate comparisons of learning disabled children with behavior disordered children, only three (i.e., 33%) were significantly different, albeit all in favor of the learning disabled children. Moreover, two of these differences were on the Conduct Problem Scale, reflecting externalized psychopathology, whereas only one difference was on the Personality Problem Scale, reflecting internalized psychopathology. Perhaps these data suggest that, across these seven studies, the learning disabled children were rated more like children with behavior disorders, particularly those with internalized psychopathology, than normal children.

Clearly, this suggestion at best represents a hypothesis rather than a conclusion. An evaluation of this hypothesis would be informative, however, particularly if considered in terms of other research that suggests that depression, a major internalized disorder, may be an important feature of some learning disabilities (Goldstein & Dundon, 1987; Goldstein et al., 1985), and that social-emotional problems may co-occur with only particular subtypes of learning disabilities (Bruck, 1986; Perlmutter, 1986).

Summary

In summary, a number of hypotheses have been proposed and evaluated to account for the social-emotional features of learning disabilities as a heterogeneous disorder. For example, some investigators have proposed that psychosocial factors cause learning disabilities through a social discrimination and stereotyping process (e.g., Bartel & Guskin, 1980). Others have suggested that affective conditions, such as depression, cause the neurocognitive, neurolinguistic, and academic characteristics of learning disabilities (e.g., Goldstein & Dundon, 1987). Still others have perceived the psychosocial/interpersonal problems and affective disturbances of many learning disabled individuals as manifestations of the same disorder that underlies its neurocognitive, linguistic, and academic characteristics (e.g., Pearl, 1987). Thus, particular social-emotional variables have been considered as antecedents, consequences, and concomitants of learning disabilities. Although the precise nature of the relationships between these variables and learning disabilities remains equivocal, relationships clearly seem present, at least for some learning disabled individuals. A number of investigators (e.g., Pearl, 1987) recently have begun to question the influence of methodological factors on the equivocal nature of this research. Among the most important of these factors, and especially relevant to this volume, is the homogeneity of samples of learning disabled subjects.

Research with Homogeneous Groups

It was not until the 1980s that investigators began to explore the social-emotional features of homogeneous subtypes of learning disabilities. At this writing, there still are very few studies addressing this issue. Because the history of this research is so brief and the literature is so sparse, definitive conclusions are premature. Some interesting hypotheses, however, already are beginning to emerge. Thus, it would be predicted that this kind of research has great potential to advance the understanding of learning disabilities beyond more traditional foci related to the neurocognitive, neurolinguistic, and academic features of this group of disorders.

To date, studies that have explored social-emotional features of learning disability subtypes generally have assumed one of two major approaches. One approach has been to use either clinical-inferential or empirical methods to identify learning disability subtypes on the basis of traditional variables that are related to learning (e.g., neurocognitive, neurolinguistic, achievement). Subsequently, these identified subtypes have been studied in terms of potentially distinctive social-emotional features. In these instances, therefore, the social-emotional features of predefined, homogeneous subtypes of learning disabilities have been explored. These studies are classified here as "traditional models" for the purpose of organization. Two of these studies are discussed in Chapter 4 (Nussbaum & Bigler, 1986; Satz & Morris, 1981) because the homogeneous subtypes that formed the basis for subsequent social-emotional comparisons were identified through empirical methods using traditional variables related to learning. Additionally, included among these studies is a unique effort in which learning disability subtypes were predefined through a clinical-inferential method that combined traditional variables that are related to learning with social-emotional variables (Goldstein et al., 1985).

In constrast, for the other approach, learning disability subtypes have been identified from a purely empirical perspective. In these instances, investigators have studied heterogeneous groups of learning disabled subjects in attempts to determine if social-emotional variables have contributed to homogeneous subtype identification. Thus, the models on which these studies have been based conceptually are similar to those discussed in Chapter 4. Unlike most of the models discussed in Chapter 4, however, social-emotional features have been emphasized, even though in some instances traditional variables that are related to learning also have contributed to subtype derivation. These studies are classified here as "empirical models," again for the purpose of organization. Table 7.1 presents a description of these studies in terms of this classification scheme.

TABLE 7.1. Studies exploring social-emotional features of learning disability subtypes

Study	Sample	Measures	Analysis	Results
Traditional models				
Wiener (1980)	(1) Conceptual LD (n = 21) (2) Spatial LD (n = 14) (3) Sequential LD (n = 25)	Sociograms Counselor ratings of peer relationships	ANOVA	Subtypes 1 & 2 had poorer peer relationships than Subtype 3 on both measures
Satz & Morris (1981)	Global language deficits (n = 27) Specific language deficits (n = 14) Mixed deficits (n = 10) Visual-perceptual deficits (n = 23) Unexpected (n = 12)	Children's Personality Questionnaire (CPQ)	MANOVA	No differences among subtypes
Weintraub & Mesulam (1983)	Patients with right-hemisphere dysfunction, interpersonal problems, & nondyslexic LD (n = 14)	Interview/history Affective tasks	Frequencies	Eye contact deficit (100%) Shy (93%) Prosody deficit (86%) Gesture deficit (79%) Depressed (57%)
Goldstein, Paul, & Sanfilippo-Cohn (1985)	(1) LD (n = 44) (2) LD/low IQ (n = 11) (3) LD/emotionally disturbed (n = 17) (4) LD/hyperactive (n = 10)	WISC-R Children's Depression Inventory (CDI) Key Math Test Woodcock Reading Test	MANOVA ANOVA Chi-square Correlations	Subtype 1: no correlations Subtype 2: CDI & verbal/ performance IQs Subtype 3: CDI & achievement tests Subtype 4: CDI & IQ/ achievement tests
McConaughty & Ritter (1985)	VIQ > PIQ LD VIQ < PIQ LD VIQ = PIQ LD (total LD n = 123) Nonreferred (n = 300)	Child Behavior Checklist (CBCL)	ANOVA	No differences among subtypes on any subscales LD overall rated as experiencing more problems in social competence and behavior than nonreferred
Ozols & Rourke (1985)	(1) Spatial LD (n = 7) (2) Language LD (n = 7) (3) Normal (n = 7)	Toward Affective Development Kit: (a) Gesture	MANOVA ANOVA ANCOVA	Kit tasks a & b not significant for any subtype Kit tasks c & d: Subtype

Study	Groups	Measures	Analysis	Results
Strang & Rourke (1985)	(1) VIQ > PIQ LD ($n = 7$) (2) VIQ < PIQ LD ($n = 7$) (3) VIQ = PIQ LD ($n = 7$)	(b) Facial expression (c) Feelings (d) Social inferences Personality Inventory for Children (PIC)	Comparison of profiles	2 < Subtype 3 Subtype 1 withdrawn; social-skill problems
Nussbaum & Bigler (1986)	(1) VIQ > PIQ LD ($n = 17$) (2) VIQ < PIQ LD ($n = 35$) (3) Mixed LD ($n = 23$)	PIC CBCL	MANOVA	Psychobehavioral-affective profiles similar across all subtypes; Subtype 2 had higher depression & internalizing scales
Voeller (1986)	Patients with right-hemisphere dysfunction ($n = 15$)	Affect Recognition Test Auditory Affect Recognition Test Interview/history	t tests z tests Frequencies	Scored below normal on both tests Attention deficit disorder (93%) Special education class (87%) Poor peer relations (87%) Atypical prosody (60%) Shy & withdrawn (53%) Insensitive (47%) Gesture deficit (40%)
Glosser & Koppell (1987)	(1) Right-hemisphere/bilateral LD ($n = 11$) (2) Left-hemisphere LD ($n = 18$) (3) Nonlateralized LD ($n = 38$)	Emotional/behavioral categories: (a) Depression/anxiety (b) Aggression (c) Attention disorder (d) Somatization	Kruskal-Wallis ANOVA on ranks	Subtype 1 < Subtypes 2 & 3 for depression & anxiety Subtype 3 > Subtype 1 > Subtype 2 for aggression & attention disorder Subtype 1 > Subtypes 2 & 3 for somatization
Landau, Milich, & McFarland (1987)	(1) VIQ > PIQ LD ($n = 12$) (2) VIQ < PIQ LD ($n = 26$) (3) VIQ = PIQ LD ($n = 27$) (4) Normal ($n = 252$)	Pupil Evaluation Inventory Teacher Rating Scale	MANOVA ANOVA	Subtype 1 had few peer-relationship difficulties Subtypes 2 & 3 less popular than Subtype 4 Subtype 3 more rejected by peers: perceived as more aggessive than Subtypes 1 & 2

TABLE 7.1. Continued

Study	Sample	Measures	Analysis	Results
Empirical models McKinney (1984)	LD (*n* = 59)	WISC-R Peabody Individual Achievement Test (PIAT) Classroom Behavior Inventory (CBI)	Cluster analysis	4 subtypes: (1) independence, task-orientation, spatial, sequencing, & mild achievement problems; verbal skills average (33%); (2) WISC-R scatter; severe achievement & behavior problems across all CBI dimensions (10%); (3) task-orientation & mild achievement problems; inconsiderate, hostile, extroverted; conceptual skills good (47%); (4) cognitive profile like Subtype 1 normal behavior (10%)
Porter & Rourke (1985)	LD (*n* = 100)	WISC Wide Range Achievement Test PIC	Q-type factor analysis MANOVA	77 subjects assigned to 4 subtypes: (1) well adjusted (44%); (2) serious internalizing disorder (26%); (3) somatic concern (13%); (4) conduct disorder (17%) No cognitive/academic differences among subtypes

Speece, McKinney, & Appelbaum (1985)	LD (n = 63), Normal (n = 66)	Cluster analysis MANOVA	WISC, PIAT, CBI, Schedule of Classroom Activity Norms	7 subtypes: (1) attention deficit (29%); (2) normal behavior (25%); (3) conduct problems, all male (14%); (4) withdrawn behavior, mostly female (11%); (5) normal behavior, slightly hostile (10%); (6) global behavior problems (5%); (7) low positive behavior (6%). No cognitive/academic differences among subtypes
Strawser & Weller (1985)	LD resource room (n = 74), LD self contained (n = 38)	Cluster analysis ANOVA	WISC-R, PIAT, Development Test of Visual-Motor Integration, Clinical Evaluation of Language Functions, Illinois Test of Psycholinguistic Abilities, Weller-Strawser Scales of Adaptive Behavior	3 subtypes: (1) average IQ; mild-to-moderate adaptive behavior deficits; achievement discrepancy (38%); (2) average IQ; moderate-to-severe adaptive behavior deficits; greater achievement discrepancy than Subtype 1 (33%); (3) borderline to low-average IQ; variable adaptive behavior; no achievement or processing discrepancy (29%)
Del Dotto, Fisk, & Rourke (1988)	Neurological, learning, language, & behavioral disturbances (primarily LD) (n = 96)	Cluster analysis ANOVA	Vineland Adaptive Behavior Scales	3 subtypes: (1) low communication (45%); (2) low Socialization (26%); (3) low Daily Living (29%)

Note. ANCOVA, analysis of covariance; ANOVA, analysis of variance; MANOVA, multivariate analysis of variance. Measures for traditional models only include social-emotional tasks; measures for empirical models include all tasks analyzed in the clustering methods.

Traditional Models

SINGLE SUBTYPE FOCUS

Among the traditional models, several investigators have explored the social-emotional features of predefined learning disability subtypes by limiting their focus to one particular subtype. Here, the subtype has been defined on the basis of a priori criteria. The social-emotional features associated with the subtype then have been described. Three examples are studies conducted by Weintraub and Mesulam (1983), by Voeller (1986), and by Strang and Rourke (1985).

Weintraub and Mesulam (1983) described 14 cases of nondyslexic learning disabilities that ranged in age from 12 to 42 years. All cases had average intellectual abilities but experienced academic failures in school, particularly in arithmetic. Neurological and neuropsychological examinations generally were consistent with right-hemisphere dysfunctions. For example, although the sample was heterogeneous for classical neurological signs, abnormal features were present in all cases. These features included upper motor neuron signs, asymmetrical posturing during various complex gaits, and abnormally large lateral asymmetries for psychomotor speed tasks. Neuropsychological profiles were characterized by average to superior verbal abilities but poor to severely impaired nonverbal abilities.

Accompanying social-emotional features included a lack of eye contact in interviews; complaints of shyness, social isolation, and chronic depression; exaggerated or absent facial and body gestures; and flat or atypical speech prosody. Given these findings, Weintraub and Mesulam (1983) suggested that there may be a syndrome of early right-hemisphere dysfunction that is associated with chronic emotional difficulties, disturbed interpersonal skills, and poor visuospatial abilities.

Voeller (1986) described a similar but younger sample ranging in age from 5 to 13 years. Subjects were selected based on evidence of a right-hemisphere lesion or dysfunction as documented by computerized tomography or neurological examination. Psychometric profiles revealed significantly better developed verbal than nonverbal abilities and significantly better developed reading than arithmetic skills.

Approximately 87% of these youngsters were in special education classes and the majority presented attention deficits, poor peer relations, atypical speech prosody, and introverted behaviors. Additionally, as a group these youngsters scored below normal on tests designed to assess the ability to perceive the emotional states of others. Based on these results, Voeller (1986) speculated that right-hemisphere dysfunction in children may be characterized by better verbal than visuospatial skills, better reading and spelling than arithmetic performances, and profoundly negative influences on affective development.

Although both of these studies are informative in a descriptive sense, they are seriously limited by their lack of comparison groups. Moreover, these studies also lack reliability and validity evidence for the informal measures of social-emotional functioning used (e.g., interviews, nonstandardized tasks). Finally, the high degree of selectively required to recruit subjects for these studies militates against generalizing results even to specific subtypes of learning disabled individuals. For example, the 14 subjects studied by Weintraub and Mesulam (1983) were selected consecutively over a 4-year period, and the 15 subjects studied by Voeller (1986) were selected from approximately 600 children referred for pediatric neurological evaluations.

A study reported by Strang and Rourke (1985) addressed these criticisms. Although the focus of this report was on the social-emotional characteristics of a learning disability subtype called a "nonverbal perceptual-organization-output disability" (NPOOD), two other subtypes also were included for comparison purposes ($n = 7$ for each subtype, mean age = 10 years). Subtypes were identified based on intelligence, achievement, and neuropsychological test results. The NPOOD subtype was characterized by better developed verbal than nonverbal abilities and depressed arithmetic relative to reading and spelling skills. Thus, in this sense these subjects were similar to those studied by Weintraub and Mesulam (1983) and by Voeller (1986). In contrast to these studies, however, neurological evidence of right-hemisphere lesions or dysfunction was not required.

The subjects were assessed with the Personality Inventory for Children (PIC) (Wirt, Lachar, Klinedinst, & Seat, 1977), a 600-item scale completed by the subjects' mothers. In addition to validity, response-style screening, and supplemental syndromic scales, the PIC includes 12 clinical scales: Achievement, Intellectual Screening, Development, Somatic Concern, Depression, Family Relations, Delinquency, Withdrawal, Anxiety, Psychosis, Hyperactivity, and Social Skills. Results indicated that the NPOOD subtype exhibited a distinct mean PIC profile characterized by an internalized, or overcontrolled, form of psychopathology. Scale elevations were present on the Psychosis, Social Skills, Anxiety, Withdrawal, and Depression scales. Strang and Rourke (1985) described these children as highly dependent and as having social-interaction difficulties. Here, it was suggested that these children do not seem to attend to or to understand nonverbal gestures and communication. Consequently, they may tend to alienate peers and to elicit negative feedback from them. Rourke and Strang speculated that this can result in a secondary anxiety that further can exacerbate the characteristic social interaction problems. More recently, as noted in Chapter 2, Rourke (1987) proposed a neuroanatomical substrate for nonverbal learning disabilities (e.g., NPOOD). Further research with larger samples will be useful in validating associated hypotheses.

MULTIPLE SUBTYPE FOCUS

Other investigators have explored the social-emotional features of several different predefined learning disability subtypes. Again, subtypes have been defined on the basis of a priori criteria; subsequently, associated social-emotional features have been described. One advantage of these studies is that distinctive social-emotional features can be identified that distinguish among various subtypes. Eight examples are discussed.

In a relatively early attempt to study the social-emotional features of homogeneous groups of learning disabilities, Wiener (1980) identified three subtypes based on Bannatyne's (1971) categorization of WISC score profiles. These were *conceptual disability* ($n = 21$), *spatial disability* ($n = 14$), and *sequential disability* ($n = 25$) subtypes. A comparison group of normal subjects was not included.

Subjects, aged 8 to 12, attended a summer camp for learning disabled children. Sociometry and ratings by camp counselors were used to compare the learning disability subtypes in terms of peer relationships developed during a 5-week period at the camp. Results indicated that children with conceptual and spatial disabilities had more problems developing positive relationships than children with sequential disabilities.

In a subsequent investigation, Ozols and Rourke (1985) studied a *language disorder* subtype and a *spatial disorder* subtype, as well as a group of normal children of a similar age range (8 to 11 years; $n = 7$ in each group). Four tasks were administered from the Toward Affective Development Kit (Dupont, Gardner, & Brody, 1974). These tasks were designed to measure: (a) the ability to select a nonverbal gesture on the basis of a story that was orally delivered by the examiner, (b) the ability to select an appropriate facial expression on the basis of a story that was orally delivered by the examiner in conjunction with a visual illustration of that story, (c) the oral ability to describe feelings portrayed in a visual llustration of a social situation, and (d) the oral ability to describe a social inference about the reasons for feelings that could occur based on a visual illustration of a social situation.

Results indicated that all three of these subtypes performed equally well on tasks requiring nonverbal behavior. Unsurprisingly, however, the language disorder subtype performed significantly worse than the group of normal children on both tasks requiring verbal behavior. Of course, this deficit simply may have reflected an impairment in verbal-expressive skill rather than in social-decoding skill. By definition, the language disorder subtype possessed age-appropriate visual-perceptual organization abilities. Moreover, this subtype performed comparably to normals when asked to select appropriate nonverbal gestures and facial expressions on the basis of verbally presented cues.

Although the spatial disorder subtype did not differ from the normal group in terms of these social-perceptual aptitudes, as previously noted,

Strang and Rourke (1985) found that a comparable subtype presented a number of social-skill deficits such as excessively shy and withdrawn behaviors. Further, despite the putative ability of these subjects to perceive social cues at age-appropriate levels while in a laboratory setting, one wonders if this finding would generalize to less directive and less structured social situations.

For example, one hypothesis discussed previously, on the basis of research with heterogeneous groups, is that the social-skill problems of some learning disabled individuals may represent performance rather than acquisition deficits. Here, Pearl (1987) reviewed the evidence on the abilities of heterogeneous groups of learning disabled children to decode and perceive social cues and interactions. In her review, she showed that the apparent deficits of the learning disabled children were ameliorated when they were highly motivated to attend to relevant cues.

Additionally, on the basis of his independent review of the peer relations of children and adolescents with learning disabilities, Perlmutter (1986) hypothesized that although learning disabled individuals appeared capable of performing appropriate social behaviors, they seemed to lack the ability to understand when it was appropriate for them to perform those behaviors. Again, further research will be useful in evaluating these hypotheses.

In a more comprehensive study, Glosser and Koppell (1987) explored the social-emotional features of 67 learning disabled children aged 7 to 10 years. Subjects were classified according to one of three predetermined subtypes: a *nonlateralized dysfunction* subtype ($n = 38$), a *right-hemisphere/bilateral dysfunction* subtype ($n = 11$), and a *left-hemisphere dysfunction* subtype ($n = 18$). Unfortunately, similar to Wiener (1980), a group of non-learning disabled subjects was not included. Subtypes were predefined primarily based on neurocognitive and academic test results. Social-emotional characteristics of these subtypes were assessed by parent, teacher, and clinician behavioral ratings that were aggregated to form four categories: (a) depression-anxiety, (b) aggression, (c) attention disorder, and (d) somatization.

Results indicated that distinct social-emotional profiles differentiated among the three subtypes. For example, the nonlateralized dysfunction subtype was rated as the most aggressive and most motorically active subtype. This subtype also was rated as especially distractible and likely to manifest attention deficit disorders. Moreover, this subtype was characterized by relatively mild depression and anxiety problems as well. In contrast, the right-hemisphere/bilateral dysfunction subtype was rated as the least depressed and least anxious. This subtype, however, was prone to manifest ill-defined somatic complaints and mild aggression. Finally, the left-hemisphere dysfunction subtype was rated as the least aggressive, but most depressed and anxious subtype.

Further support for differentiated social-emotional subtypes of learning disabilities was provided by Landau, Milich, and McFarland (1987), who studied 65 elementary school, learning disabled males and 252 non-learning disabled male classmates. Learning disabled subjects were classified into three subtypes based on WISC-R IQ scores: $VIQ > PIQ$ ($n = 12$), $VIQ < PIQ$ ($n = 26$), and $VIQ = PIQ$ ($n = 27$). A sociometric device, the Pupil Evaluation Inventory (Pekarik, Prinz, Liebert, Weintraub, & Neale, 1976), which includes measures of Aggression, Likeability, and Withdrawal, and a 39-item Teacher Rating Scale (Conners, 1973), which includes measures of Inattention/Overactivity and Aggression, were administered. Results indicated that not all learning disabled children were at equal risk for peer problems. Specifically, the $VIQ > PIQ$ subtype evidenced relatively intact interpersonal skills, whereas the other two subtypes were perceived as less popular than their non-learning disabled peers. Moreover, the $VIQ = PIQ$ subtype was perceived as the most aggressive.

Nussbaum and Bigler (1986), as noted in Chapter 4, also studied $VIQ > PIQ$, $VIQ < PIQ$, and *mixed* subtypes of disabled learners. Here, social-emotional differences among these subtypes were explored using the PIC and the Child Behavior Checklist (CBCL) (Achenbach & Edelbrock, 1983). The CBCL contains behavior-problem and competency items that are rated by parents about their child. The items are subsumed by two first-order, or broad-band, scales that represent internalizing (i.e., over-controlled) and externalizing (i.e., undercontrolled) dimensions of psychopathology. There also are nine second-order, or narrow-band, scales that are labeled Schizoid (i.e., Anxious), Depressed, Uncommunicative, Obsessive-Compulsive, Somatic Complaints, Social-Withdrawal, Hyperactive, Aggressive, and Delinquent.

Nussbaum and Bigler (1986) found no differences among subtypes on the PIC. The $VIQ < PIQ$ subtype, however, was found to score somewhat higher on the Internalizing and Depressed scales of the CBCL than the other two subtypes. Based on these results, Nussbaum and Bigler speculated that a possible left-hemisphere basis for this learning disability subtype may accentuate its associated social-emotional features.

Despite these differences, Nussbaum and Bigler (1986) were struck with the personality and behavioral similarities among the subtypes. This led them to suggest potential generic effects of learning disabilities on personality and behavior variables regardless of subtype. Although a group of non-learning disabled subjects was not included in this study, comparisons with normative data from the PIC and CBCL suggested that the learning disabled subjects as a heterogeneous group were characterized by a variety of social-emotional maladjustments.

In support of this suggestion of generic effects were the results of studies conducted by Satz and Morris (1981; see Chapter 4) and by McConaughty and Ritter (1985). Neither team of investigators found differences among subtypes on the Children's Personality Questionnaire (Porter & Cattell,

1975), which is a scale designed to measure 14 personality traits of children aged 8 to 12, or on the CBCL, respectively. Clearly, comparisons across studies are complicated by a variety of methodological issues including a lack of congruence of learning disability definitions and subtypes, of diagnostic methods, of samples, and of measures.

A Combined Model

A unique study among those we have classified as traditional was conducted by Goldstein et al. (1985). These investigators examined selective social-emotional features of learning disability subtypes that were predefined through clinical-inferential methods where the basis for those subtypes was a combination of intellectual aptitude with secondary diagnosis.

The sample comprised a total of 85 children, ranging in age from 6 to 12 years, all of whom met general criteria for a primary diagnosis of learning disability. Four subtypes were established on the basis of this clinical-inferential paradigm: (a) learning disabled, single diagnosis (LD); (b) learning disabled with Full-Scale IQ between 70 and 84, single diagnosis (LD/low IQ); (c) learning disabled with social-emotional disturbance, multiple diagnoses (LD/SED); and (d) learning disabled with hyperactivity, multiple diagnoses (LD/H). Goldstein et al. noted that there were insufficient subjects available to form low IQ categories within the multiple diagnoses subtypes.

All subjects were administered the Children's Depression Inventory (CDI) (Kovacs, 1981), which is a scale designed to assess the severity of overt symptoms of depression in children aged 8 to 13 years, in addition to a standard battery of cognitive and academic tests. Results suggested that all four subtypes exhibited comparably elevated levels of depression when compared to the normative sample for the CDI. There was a significant correlation between levels of depression and academic achievement, but not between levels of depression and intelligence over all subtypes combined.

Perhaps more interesting, however, was the finding that even though the LD and LD/SED subtypes showed similar levels of elevated depression, CDI indexes were correlated differentially with achievement test scores for these two subtypes. LD depression was unrelated to achievement, whereas LD/SED depression and achievement showed a strong inverse relationship. Separate analyses for the LD/low IQ and LD/H subtypes were considered unreliable, given the insufficient sample sizes for these two subtypes.

Furthermore, the nature of the depressions in the LD and LD/SED subtypes was found to differ in terms of stability. The LD depression was characterized as transient, whereas the LD/SED depression was characterized as stable. Goldstein et al. (1985) interpreted these differential stabilities in terms of limited capacity interference of the LD/SED subtype in contrast to a reaction to failure for the LD subtype. In this sense it was postulated that, for the LD/SED subtype, stable depression may represent a cause of the learning disability, at least in part, because it diminishes the resources (or capacity) available for effortful processing of tasks such as those involved in most academic activities. In contrast, the transient depression characteristic of the LD subtype more likely represents a reaction to, rather than a cause of, failure given its orthogonality to academic competence.

More extensive research is needed to validate this hypothesis, of course, but this hypothesis may be especially relevant from a neuropsychological perspective. For example, if this hypothesis is true, one might expect to find neuropsychological differences between these two subtypes of learning disabilities. Previous research has focused on the neuropsychology of depression in children (see Tramontana & Hooper, in press) and speculative neuropsychological models of childhood depression have been proposed (Hynd & Willis, 1988). The concepts of endogenous versus exogenous depressions were not addressed by Goldstein et al. (1985), but this seems to present a logical extension of this research, particularly when considered from a neurobiological perspective. For example, it would be informative to determine the relationship between endogeneous depression and the stable depression of the LD/SED subtype as well as between exogeneous depression and the transient depression of the LD subtype. Finally, the information-processing model that provides the foundation for the framework proposed by Goldstein and Dundon (1987) has been considered in terms of potential neural substrates; alternative cognitive neuropsychological models have received empirical support (Friedman & Polson, 1981; Hynd & Willis, 1988; Kinsbourne, 1982; Willis & Hynd, 1987).

Empirical Models

In contrast to these traditional models, several investigators have explored the social-emotional features of learning disability subtypes through multivariate clustering methods. Thus, these empirical models represent attempts to determine if social-emotional variables have contributed to subtype identification. The work of McKinney and colleagues (McKinney, 1984; Speece, McKinney, & Appelbaum, 1985), Rourke and colleagues (Del Dotto, Fisk, & Rourke, 1988; Porter & Rourke, 1985), and Strawser and Weller (1985) is illustrative.

McKinney (1984) described a study in which measures from 59 school-identified learning disabled children were cluster analyzed. Measures were from the WISC-R, Peabody Individual Achievement Test (PIAT), and Classroom Behavior Inventory (CBI). The CBI (Schaefer, Edgerton, & Aronson, 1977) is a teacher rating scale that assesses dimensions of independence versus dependence, task orientation versus distractibility, extroversion versus introversion, and considerateness versus hostility.

Four subtypes were identified. *Subtype 1* comprised 20 subjects. (i.e., 33% of the sample). The cognitive-academic profile of this subtype was characterized by average verbal skills, deficient sequential and spatial skills, and mildly impaired reading recognition and math skills. The behavioral profile of this subtype indicated independence and task-orientation deficits. Subtype 1, however, was rated as the most considerate and least hostile of the subtypes identified.

Subtype 2 comprised 6 subjects (i.e., 10% of the sample). The cognitive-academic profile of this subtype was characterized by unevenly developed cognitive skills and severely impaired achievement. The behavioral profile of this subtype indicated severe impairment on all CBI scales. Subtype 2 was rated as inconsiderate, hostile, academically incompetent, and poorly task oriented.

The largest subtype, *Subtype 3*, comprised 27 subjects (i.e., 47% of the sample) and was almost exclusively male. The cognitive-academic profile of this subtype was characterized by above-average conceptual skills and mildly impaired academic skills. The behavioral profile of this subtype indicated extroversion and low task orientation. Similar to Subtype 2, Subtype 3 was rated as inconsiderate and hostile.

Finally, *Subtype 4* comprised 6 subjects (i.e., 10% of the sample). Similar to Subtype 1, the cognitive-academic profile for Subtype 4 was characterized by average verbal skills, and deficient sequential and spatial skills, but somewhat more impaired reading recognition and math skills. The behavioral profile of this subtype indicated no behavioral deficits. Thus, of four learning disability subtypes identified, three showed evidence of psychobehavioral deficits whereas one did not. Moreover, ratings of task orientation–distractibility, extroversion–introversion, and hostility–considerateness contributed to discriminations among the subtypes. Evidence from behavioral observations supported the external validity of these subtypes. Even so, results were limited by the lack of a comparison group of normal subjects and the use of a school-identified heterogeneous sample of learning disabled subjects.

In support of these results, Del Dotto et al. (1988) cluster analyzed selected Vineland Adaptive Behavior Scale (VABS) scores obtained from a heterogeneous clinical sample primarily (albeit not exclusively) comprised of learning disabled children. The VABS (Sparrow, Balla, & Cicchetti, 1984) is a semistructured interview that assesses Motor, Communication, Daily-Living, and Socialization skills, in addition to maladaptive behaviors. Three subtypes were identified that were characterized by differential patterns of social-adaptive behavior. Further analyses revealed academic achievement and aptitude differences among the subtypes.

In a related study, Strawser and Weller (1985) found that social-adaptive behaviors contributed to discriminations among subtypes of learning disabled children. These investigators cluster analyzed results of a psychoeducational battery in order to identify three learning disability subtypes. The subtypes identified were characterized by: (a) average intellectual ability, low academics, and mild-to-moderate adaptive behavior deficits; (b) average intellectual ability, poor academics and information processing, and moderate-to-severe adaptive behavior deficits; and (c) borderline to low-average intellectual ability, achievement levels and information-processing skills commensurate with demonstrated intellectual functioning, and a nonspecified level of adaptive behavior deficit. Although these subtypes appear similar to those derived from several of the clinical-inferential models based on intellectual tests, this study is important because of its intent to operationalize the issue of severity of learning disability in respective subtypes.

Using a different psychoeducational battery, Speece et al. (1985) reported, result of a study that included a matched comparison group of normal subjects and a well-described sample of learning disabled subjects. This study included 63 newly identified learning disabled children from the first and second grades and 66 normally achieving children matched according to race, gender, and mainstream classroom. Additionally, the study included internal validation (i.e., split sample replication and forecasting) and external validation attempts, which supported results of a cluster analysis.

A cluster analysis of WISC-R, PIAT, and CBI data identified seven learning disability subtypes. Only CBI measures differentiated among subtypes; there were no subtype differences on WISC-R or PIAT subtests. The subtypes were characterized by: (a) good adjustment with mild attention deficits and problems with idependent work in the classroom (28.6% of the sample); (b) two variations of normal classroom behavior (25.4% and 9.5% of the sample); (c) poor socialization, conduct problems, and acting-out behavior in the classroom (14.3% of the sample, exclusively male); (d) social withdrawal and overdependence (11% of the sample, disproportionately female); and (e) serious impairment and somewhat less serious impairment on all CBI dimensions (4.8% and 6.3% of the sample, respectively).

Speece et al. (1985) emphasized that over one third of the children in the learning disabled sample did not exhibit a maladaptive pattern of behavior. Of those who did exhibit a maladaptive behavior pattern relative to non-learning disabled children, most could be classified as having different degrees of attentional problems combined with conduct and personal adjustment problems. Both internalized and externalized dimensions of childhood psychopathology were identified. In a follow-up study, McKinney and Speece (1986) found that even though some subjects who were initially characterized as behaviorally maladjusted improved (i.e., 11%), most were likely to remain maladjusted after 3 years (i.e., 55%).

It also is interesting to not that, in contrast to traditional models, results of the study reported by Speece et al. (1985) suggested that, during the first and second grades, social-emotional and cognitive-academic dimensions were relatively independent, albeit both important, features of learning disabilities. After 3 years, however, particular social-emotional subtypes demonstrated distinct patterns of academic growth (i.e., normal and withdrawn subtypes) and decline (i.e., attention-deficit and problem-behavior subtypes) (McKinney & Speece, 1986).

In support of the independence of social-emotional and cognitive-academic dimensions of learning disabilities, Porter and Rourke (1985) found that a sample of learning disabled children were heterogeneous for personality features, but that particular social-emotional subtypes could not be distinguished on the basis of cognitive or academic measures. Specifically, Porter and Rourke (1985) conducted a Q-type factor analysis on PIC socres of 100 learning disabled children ranging in age from 6 to 15 years. A comparison group of normal children was not included. Four reliable social-emotional subtypes were identified and supported through replication; 77 subjects met criteria (i.e., at least one factor loading of at least .50, and an interval of at least .10 between the highest and next highest loadings) for subtype assignment.

Subtype 1 comprised 37 subjects (i.e., 44% of those assigned). The personality profile of this subtype was characterized by good social-emotional adjustment. *Subtype 2* comprised 20 subjects (i.e., 26% of those assigned). In marked contrast to Subtype 1, the personality profile of Subtype 2 was characterized by serious internalized psychopathology, with abnormal elevations on all PIC scales except the Family Relations scale.

Subtype 3 comprised 10 subjects (i.e., 13% of those assigned). The personality profile of this subtype was characterized by basically normal social-emotional functioning, but considerable focus on physical well-being and maternal distress about the child's health. It was unclear if the somatic complaints that characterized Subtype 3 were functional in origin or associated with a positive medical history of physiological disorders.

Finally, *Subtype 4* comprised 13 subjects (i.e., 17% of those assigned). The personality profile of this subtype was characterized by externalized psychopathology (e.g., Conduct Disorder) manifested by overactivity, distractibility, interpersonal insensitivity, and antisocial behavior. Subtype 4 children were described as restless, impulsive, disobedient, disrespectful, unreliable, and argumentative. They tended to engage in aggressive behaviors, to experience little anxiety or internal discomfort, and to endure unstable home lives.

Summary

In summary, researchers recently have begun to explore possible social-emotional subtypes of learning disabilities, but the literature to date in this area is meager. Research that has been conducted can be considered in terms of traditional or empirical models. Given the preliminary nature of this work, conclusions are not warranted at this time, but a number of questions and testable hypotheses have begun to emerge.

For example, when learning disabled individuals are subtyped in terms of traditional neurocognitive, neurolinguistic, and academic variables, differential profiles of social-emotional adjustment may emerge. Here, one might predict that particular social-emotional profiles may be characteristic of particular traditional subtypes of learning disabilities.

When heterogeneous groups of learning disabled individuals are subtyped via empirical techniques, and social-emotional variables are included, differential profiles also emerge. These profiles can be considered in terms of internalized and externalized psychopathology. From the empirical models, however, another social-emotional profile clearly seems to emerge, that is, a profile that represents appropriate adjustment or a variant of normal psychosocial and affective behavior. Indeed, some research (e.g., Porter & Rourke, 1985; Speece et al., 1985) suggests that this profile may characterize the largest single social-emotional learning disability subtype (i.e., perhaps as large as 50%). It remains to be determined if this finding is age dependent. For example, do younger children show more normal social-emotional profiles than their older, more frustrated counterparts? Although this is a tenable hypothesis, it has yet to be resolved (e.g., Kistner & Osborne, 1987; McKinney & Speece, 1986). Further, given that social-emotional differences have been identified among traditionally classified learning disabled subtypes, it is interesting to note that in some cases these traditional variables (i.e., neurocognitive, neurolinguistic, academic) have not differentiated among empirically identified social-emotional subtypes.

Conclusions

A number of hypotheses about the social-emotional features of learning disabilities have been identified, but few conclusions have been derived given the relative dearth of studies addressing these concerns in specific learning disability subtypes. One reasonable hypothesis is that differential social-emotional profiles may be associated with particular subtypes of learning disabilities. Further, at least one of these subtypes may represent essentially normal psychosocial and emotional adjustment. Clinically, this hypothesis implies that evaluations of learning disabled individuals should include careful and thorough assessment of social-emotional functioning. Many questions remain, however, related to a variety of issues such as the replicability, validity, and longitudinal stability of social-emotional subtypes.

Much of the impetus for the recent trend to identify social-emotional issues that are associated with specific learning disability subtypes has arisen from the equivocal nature of the research conducted with heterogeneous samples. At the same time, this previous research continues to be important because it provides the foundation for well-informed hypotheses about social-emotional functioning of specific subtypes; it also is applicable to individual clients.

Just as previous investigators, who studied heterogeneous samples of disabled learners, were motivated by a dissatifaction with methodological inadequacies in their research, it is hoped that present investigators also will be motivated to refine current methods of studying the social-emotional features or subtypes of learning disabilities. For example, one serious methodological flaw of several of the subtyping studies reviewed in this chapter involves the lack of appropriate comparison groups. Thus, one probably should not be surprised that results of the relatively few studies conducted to date have been convergent in terms of general classifications of social-emotional disturbance. Indeed, internalized, externalized, and generalized forms of psychopathology reliably have been identified in general populations (Achenbach, 1985), begging the question of the specificity of these social-emotional subtypes within the learning disabled population. Moreover, although reliably different personality profiles have emerged for subtypes of learning disabled individuals, the clinical significance of these profiles is difficult to assess without the benefit of comparison groups (e.g., normal groups).

Another methodological issue concerns the generalization of laboratory tasks (cf. Pearl, 1987). For example, evidence from traditional models for subtyping suggests that at least some learning disabled individuals may perform social-perception tasks at age-appropriate levels when in laboratory settings, but fail to do so when in natural environments. Clinically, this suggests that a thorough social-emotional assessment may require a naturalistic approach in order to obtain an accurate estimate of an individual's social-emotional status and interpersonal skills. Issues such as these may be illuminated by studying the psychosocial and affective behavior of learning disabled individuals who have been subtyped according to a combination of traditional variables related to learning as well as social-emotional variables. To date, little of this kind of research has been conducted, but identifying learning disability subtypes using this combination of variables may be an especially productive strategy in this field of study.

Finally, differences between the two models used to examine social-emotional features of learning disability subtypes also deserve mention. For example, reliable social-emotional differences may emerge among subtypes of learning disabilities that have been predefined according to traditional variables related to learning. When social-emotional variables contribute to the empirical identification of subtypes, however, traditional variables related to learning may fail to contribute to discriminations among subtypes. Reasons for this finding are unclear at this juncture, and remain to be addressed.

The study of the social-emotional features of learning disability subtypes is still in an early stage of development. Continued progress in studying the subtyping issues associated with these features and their clinical importance are essential for advancing our understanding of this group of disorders.

8
Treatment

Perhaps one of the most important reasons for determining homogeneous subtypes of learning disabled individuals and, ultimately, developing a classification system is the potential for specific intervention plans to be developed. Conceptually, given the support for specific subtypes, it makes sense that these subtypes would respond differently to selected treatment interventions.

To date, most of the subtyping studies investigating educational parameters have focused on the external validation of their respective models. Here, demonstrated achievement levels of the obtained subtypes have been compared. For example, Lyon et al. (1981) attempted to provide evidence to distinguish their empirically identified subtypes across measures of reading (i.e., recognition and comprehension), spelling, and written-language tasks.

Statistical analyses revealed that particular subtypes differed in terms of these measures in a predictable fashion. Lyon et al. (1981) noted that subtypes characterized by receptive-language deficits showed problems with spelling. Subtypes characterized by visual-perceptual deficits showed problems with written expression and general written output. Subtypes characterized by language deficits showed difficulties with reading. A similar pattern of findings also was noted when the qualitative features of reading and spelling errors for each subtype were explored (e.g., subtypes characterized by visual-perceptual deficits demonstrated poor sight-word vocabularies). These findings were cross-validated with a younger group of children (Lyon et al., 1982).

The Lyon et al. studies illustrate the importance of educational differences to the external validation of a subtyping model. Although this kind of external validation begins to address the specific treatment needs of these subtypes, it only suggests that a specific treatment approach might be useful. For greater assurance, specific treatment plans need to be developed and statistically evaluated in order to determine the effectiveness of a particular approach with a particular subtype in a valid manner. Only in this way can assessment-treatment linkages become more valid and classification models more useful to both clinicians and researchers.

In this chapter, several of the major treatment approaches that have been proffered for learning disabilities are discussed. Several unidimensional approaches with heterogeneous groups of learning disabilities are noted, followed by a more extensive discussion of three neuropsychological approaches to treatment. Conceptual models that propose intervention strategies for specific subtypes of disabled learners and the research completed to date that has attempted to validate these subtype-to-treatment linkages then are presented. The chapter concludes with a discussion of issues important in subtype-to-treatment planning.

Unidimensional Treatment Approaches

As noted, a number of unidimensional approaches have been proffered for treating heterogeneous learning disabilities. Some of these approaches have been well supported by empirical research, others have been less well supported, and still others clearly have been refuted (see e.g., Silver, 1987). Many others have not been subjected to empirical testing. Several of these many diverse treatment interventions are noted as examples. Subsequently, neuropsychologically based approaches are discussed in greater detail.

Pharmacological Interventions

One contemporary unidimensional intervention approach to the treatment of learning disabilities is medical management. The psychopharmacological treatment of learning disabilities typically is accomplished with analepic, or stimulant, medications (e.g., methylphenidate or Ritalin, dextroamphetamine or Dexadrine) that are directed toward the often accompanying attentional inefficiencies or deficits. These medications are the most widely studied psychotropic drugs prescribed to children (Biederman & Jelliner, 1983). Even so, the effects of these drugs on learning and academic achievement are controversial as well as equivocal (Forness & Kavale, 1988; Hutchens & Hynd, 1987; Pelham, 1986). Currently, these medications may change behaviors and, in fact, improve selected components of cognitive functioning (e.g., attention), but their ability to improve academic skills has not been supported. Denckla (1978) noted that psychostimulants represent little more than 25% of a total treatment program and suggested that professionals exercise judicial use of these interventions.

Another class of medications, the nootropics (e.g., Piracetam), have been discussed as potentially having a direct effect on a learning disabled individual's academic skills (Dimond & Brouwers, 1976). In a cursory review of the literature, Wilsher, Atkins, and Manfield (1985) noted that some improvements were observed on learning tasks in normal and patient populations. Based on this review, Wilsher et al. (1985) administered

Piracetam or placebo in a double-blind, parallel experiment to 46 dyslexic males who ranged in age from 8 to 13 years. This medication regimen lasted for total of 8 weeks. Wilsher et al. found no significant differences between the two conditions (i.e., placebo or Piracetam) in reading. When the data were examined intraindividually, however, significant improvements were noted in reading speed and accuracy in individuals treated with Piracetam. Further, when levels of reading performance were considered (i.e., higher versus lower reading levels), Wilsher et al. found that dyslexics with higher reading levels improved significantly when on Piracetam as compared to the placebo condition. Although these data should be viewed as preliminary, they do suggest the possibility of specific pharmacological treatments having a positive influence directly on academic tasks, particularly if medications can be applied in a methodical manner to specific subtypes of learning disabled individuals.

Given the incidence of social-emotional and blatent psychiatric symptoms (e.g., depressed, withdrawn behaviors) characteristic of some subtypes of learning disabilities (see Chapter 7), other pharmacological interventions should be explored. Forness and Kavale (1988), in fact, predicted that the use of tricyclic antidepressants (e.g., imipramine or Tofranil) could be helpful in the psychopharmacological treatment of some learning disabilities. This class of drugs, however, has been studied much less extensively than the analeptics in learning disabled samples (Gadow, 1986; Garfinkel, Wender, Sloman, & O'Neill, 1983).

In general, the pharmacological treatment of learning disabilities may hold promise for particular subtypes, but evidence to date suggests that for those subtypes these medications should be used in conjunction with other kinds of interventions as well. For example, using case-study methodology, Spijer, De Jong, and Bakker (1987) found a selective positive effect of Piracetam on particular aspects of a reading task (i.e., speed and accuracy) for a P-type dyslexic, especially when combined with hemisphere-specific stimulation. For a L-type dyslexic, however, Piracetam was found to have a detrimental effect on reading. As Denckla (1978) noted, medications should represent only one potential component of a total intervention plan for a learning disabled individual.

Cognitive-Behavioral Interventions

Another unidimensional intervention approach that has been applied to learning disabilities is cognitive-behavioral modification (Harter, 1982; Meichenbaum, 1976; Ryan, Weed, & Short, 1986). The approach attempts to involve the individual as an active participant in the learning process and to provide both general and specific strategies for solving problems. A major technique used in this approach is self-instruction, based on Vygotsky's (1978) theory of second-signal-system development (i.e., the use of thought as internalized or covert speech). Here, the learner initially solves problems by imitating a model who self-instructs via overt verbalizations. Through a progressive series of stages, the learner eventually solves problems by covert self-instructions. This approach has been used with learning disabled individuals to reduce impulsive and off-task behaviors as well as to improve academic skills in reading, writing, and arithmetic. To date, however, mixed results have been presented (see Ryan et al. [1986] for a review).

METACOGNITIVE STRATEGIES

One of the most actively studied cognitive-behavioral intervention techniques used with learning disabled individuals is the training of learning strategies. Many learning disabled students are characterized as strategy-deficient or inactive learners. As such, many investigators have advocated teaching various learning strategies to these individuals in order to improve problem-solving skills. To date, there have been at least three major approaches for training strategies to individuals with learning disabilities: (a) Lloyd's (1980) academic strategy training, (b) Torgesen's (1982) strategy training, and (c) Deshler's (Deshler, Alley, & Carlson, 1980) learning strategies model.

Lloyd (1980) emphasized the training of academic strategies in order to teach disabled learners a set of prerequisite skills and an accompanying system for implementing these strategies for a specific academic problem (e.g., letter decoding). Although this model of strategy training is similar to direct educational instructional paradigms, it differs by developing new strategies for each academic problem area. Lloyd described modeling, corrective feedback, and reinforcement as major components of his training program. Self-verbalization and self-instruction were not described as crucial in this model.

In contrast, Torgesen (1982) described a strategy training model that emphasized three different kinds of intervention. The first kind of intervention is founded upon the repertoire of cognitive strategies that are present in a disabled learner's problem-solving repertoire but, for undefined reasons (e.g., motivation), the learner does not access these strategies in an efficient or appropriate manner. Torgesen's first kind of intervention, then, concentrates on providing incentives for individuals to invoke strategies already present. The second kind of intervention involves the use of an orienting task to improve memory, whereas the third kind of intervention pertains to different levels of direct instruction (i.e., teaching specific task strategies, teaching more general problem-solving strategies, and enhancing problem-solving awareness).

The third major model, proposed by Deshler and colleagues (Deshler et al., 1980), was developed primarily for secondary students with learning disabilities. Their approach is to teach students *how* to learn as opposed to specific content areas. Alley and Deshler (1979) define learning strategies as "techniques, principles, or rules that will facilitate the acquisition, manipulation, integration, storage, and retrieval of information across situations and settings" (p. 13). These investigators proposed a 10-step method for developing strategies: (a) test to determine student's current learning habits, (b) describe the learning strategy, (c) model the strategy, (d) verbally rehearse the strategy, (e) practice on controlled materials, (f) feedback, (g) test, (h) practice in grade materials, (i) feedback, and (j) test (Schumaker, Deshler, Alley, Warner, & Denton, 1982).

Although all of these models describe the use of "strategies," the term actually is used in a different manner by each. As can be surmised, the approaches do not refer to a homogeneous group of intervention procedures and they are not used to intervene with similar kinds of learning problems. More research is needed to refine these distinctions to a greater degree, particularly as different kinds of metacognitive strategies may be applied to the learning difficulties of specific subtypes of learning disabilities. Other kinds of cognitive-behavioral interventions have been reported, such as biofeedback muscle relaxation training (Carter & Russell, 1985) and altering the teaching approach and lesson structure (Zigmond, Sansone, Miller, Donahoe, & Kohnke, 1986), but conclusions regarding these kinds of intervention are premature.

Other Unidimensional Approaches

There are a multitude of other unidimensional approaches that have been used in the remediation of heterogeneous groups of learning disabled individuals. Some of these are direct skill training (Lovett, Warren, Ransby, & Borden, 1987), mastery learning (Carnine & Kinder, 1985), direct instruction, an operantly based approach for teaching specific academic skills (Hallahan, Lloyd, Kauffman, & Loper, 1983), modality-specific approaches (e.g., Clark, Deshler, Schumaker, & Alley, 1984; Howe, 1982; Maginnis, 1986), modifications of material presentation, and psychosocial skills training (Ozols & Rourke, 1985; Strang & Rourke, 1985). It is clear, however, that despite the effectiveness of any one treatment approach, none of the strategies is effective in improving the academic performance of all learning disabled individuals.

Finally, this discussion would be uncomplete, at least from a historical perspective, if process training approaches were not acknowledged. These early treatment approaches were based on the premise that academic learning disabilities were due to fundamental perceptual-motor (e.g., Kephart, 1971), visual-perceptual (e.g., Frosting & Horne, 1964), or psycholinguistic (e.g., Kirk & Kirk, 1971) processing deficiencies. Remediation was focused on strengthening these fundamental cognitive processes. Currently, of course, these approaches are notorious for their overwhelming lack of research support (Cook & Welch, 1980; Hallahan & Cruickshank, 1973; Hammill & Larsen, 1974; Hicks, 1980; Liberman &

Shankweiler, 1979; Sowell, Parker, Poplin, & Larsen, 1979; Vellutino, 1979).

Neuropsychologically Based Treatment Approaches

In contrast to these unidimensional approaches to treatment, other approaches have been based on neuropsychological theory. Similar to the unidimensional approaches, however, the neuropsychologically based approaches have received various levels of empirical support. Three of these approaches are described here as examples: (a) a developmental neuropsychological approach, (b) a behavioral-neuropsychological approach, and (c) a neuropsychological strength approach.

Developmental Neuropsychological Approach

Rourke, Fisk, and Strang (1986; see also Rourke et al., 1983) proffered a developmental neuropsychological remediation/habilitation approach that comprises seven stages. This approach, shown in Figure 8.1, is useful for conceptualizing the treatment and management of individuals with learning disabilities because it provides a strong link with the neuropsychological assessment of these disorders. In this sense, it also provides the foundation for conceptualizing treatment strategies for specific learning disability subtypes, particularly when subtypes are identified using neuropsychological methods.

The stages of this approach successively lead from specifying the nature of the relationship between the individual's neuropsychological functioning and neurological deficits to evaluating a realistic treatment intervention. Evaluating the intervention is related closely to the initial stage of this approach. This provides a particularly strong assessment-treatment linkage, and emphasizes that it is the recursive relationship between stages that characterizes effective therapeutic programs. The stages are outlined here with specific reference to learning disabilities and subtypes of this group of disorders.

BRAIN-BEHAVIOR RELATIONSHIPS

As noted throughout this volume, given the marked discontinuities in human development, understanding brain-behavior relationships, particularly in children, is truly a complex matter. It is clear that there is no direct relationship between extent of brain impairment and behavioral deficit. Instead, this relationship is moderated by a variety of factors, some of which are known or suspected, such as the age of the individual and the site of the lesion, and others of which currently are unknown. The first stage of

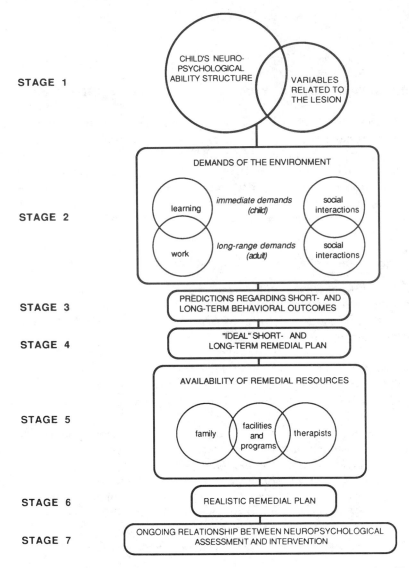

FIGURE 8.1. A developmental neuropsychological treatment approach. (From Rourke, B.P., Fisk, J.L., & Strang, J.D. (1986). *The neuropsychological assessment of children: A treatment-oriented approach* (p. 2). New York: The Guilford Press. With permission.)

this approach involves specifying this relationship. Although research evidence is useful toward this endeavor, individual differences militate against broad generalizations. Each case must be investigated individually and thoroughly. Both the details of the brain impairment (i.e., history) and a comprehensive neuropsychological profile must be considered.

In the case of developmental learning disabilities, of course, there usually are not definitive or classical hard signs of brain impairment. Other cases of acquired learning disabilities, however, may be associated with these signs as documented by various neuroimaging procedures. Regardless of the assumed or documented nature of the lesion, it is useful to consider the consequences of its etiology in terms of prognosis, because prognosis inextricably is connected with treatment. Here, important issues include those associated with anticipated deterioration versus improvement of function; the level, extent, and chronicity of the brain lesion; and any potential secondary effects or sequelae. Particularly important for learning disabilities is the issue of the age at which the brain impairment was sustained. In the case of developmental learning disabilities, for example, the lesion often is assumed to be present at least from birth, perhaps resulting from embryonic neurodevelopmental errors (Galaburda et al., 1985). Again, although the precise effects of the age of impairment on the interaction of brain-behavior relationships is unknown, it is reasonable to suspect differential effects for earlier versus later lesions. For example, individuals with developmental learning disabilities (i.e., present from birth) probably have experienced much different learning histories than individuals who have acquired learning disabilities due to craniocerebral traumata subsequent to the school-age years.

The consideration of a comprehensive neuropsychological function profile involves a thorough evaluation. This is discussed in detail in Chapter 6 but, again, in the case of learning disabilities, this evaluation necessarily includes assessment of more than just academic skills. The subtyping literature to date clearly shows that one also must consider neurocognitive, linguistic, and social-emotional factors in these evaluations. In addition to these functions, Rourke et al. (1983) particularly emphasized assessment of sensory-perceptual and motor functions for pediatric evaluations. This is because serious developmental consequences may accrue in the presence of fundamental sensory-perceptual or sensorimotor impairments. This, of course, is especially cogent for the neuropsychological evaluation of developmental learning disability subtypes that may be present from birth. Similar to any evaluation, when selecting measures of these functions, clinicians need to be concerned with psychometric issues. Of particular relevance to treatment are criterion-related validities that address the developmental demands with which the learning disabled individual is and will be confronted. Given the ultimate treatment goal, it is important to elicit the best possible level of performance from the individual (i.e., as opposed to a typical level). This facilitates an understanding of the conditions that influence the presentation, persistence, and remission of academic as well as other (e.g., psychosocial, metacognitive, adaptive) problems.

ENVIRONMENTAL DEMANDS

In the second stage of the approach, formal and informal environmental demands are considered. For children, of course, the major formal environment is the school. The school presents both general (e.g., conduct, social-interactive) and specific (e.g., academic skills) demands, many of which are particularly challenging for individuals with learning disabilities. Competence in these general and specific school-related demands substantially contributes to self-esteem and the potential for postschool success. It is important, therefore, for interventions to address these demands. Treatment plans, however, should not focus exclusively on the school environment, even for highly academic deficits such as learning disabilities. Instead, clinicians also must recognize the importance of informal environmental demands (i.e., general and specific demands) and the contribution of non-school-related environments toward the development of prosocial and adaptive behaviors. These other environments should neither be excluded from nor transgressed by learning disability interventions. Understanding the beneficial roles of informal as well as formal environments helps the clinician to maintain a balanced perspective between the long- and short-term demands confronted by the learning disabled individual.

PROGNOSIS

The third stage of the approach involves predictions about long-term and short-term behavioral outcomes. These kinds of predicitions, or prognoses, are essential to well-informed treatment planning. In fact, Rourke et al. (1986) asserted that if clinicians are unable to proffer educated predictions about probable outcomes, then they should not presume to develop treatment interventions. Of course, this not meant to suggest that accurate predictions are conceived easily. As noted in Chapter 5, learning disabilities comprise a classification that is characterized by many conceptual problems, thus making their associated prognoses particularly difficult. Progress in studying learning disabilities from subtyping and developmental perspectives, however, has the potential to contribute to more accurate prognoses. For example, as discussed in Chapter 4, preliminary evidence (e.g., Spreen & Haaf, 1986) suggests that particular subtypes of learning disabilities identified during childhood (i.e., linguistic deficient subtype) may develop more global impairments in adulthood. In contrast, other subtypes identified during childhood (e.g., visual-perceptual deficit subtype) may continue to show similar profiles of impairment into adulthood. Other research (discussed in Chapter 5) clearly shows that learning disabilities can be predicted from particular variables during the preschool years and that learning disabilities can be conceptualized multidimensionally even at this young age level (Tramontana et al., 1988). Still other research (discussed in Chapter 7) suggests that particular learning disability subtypes may predispose individuals toward distinctive social-emotional profiles (or perhaps vice versa). These kinds of research should be considered concomitantly with variables that are unique to individual cases when predicting long- and short-term behavioral outcomes for these individuals.

Treatment Intervention Plan

The fourth through sixth stages of the approach involve developing the intervention plan. Here, ideal plans are mitigated by available resources to derive a realistic treatment intervention. In formulating ideal plans, Rourke et al. (1986) emphasized that both long-term and short-term treatment needs should be considered. Particularly when considered from a developmental perspective, these needs may be at variance with one another. Thus, the overall plan should address issues such as foci changes in intervention as well as times when particular strategies should be terminated and others initiated.

Once developed, the ideal intervention plan must be considered in terms of the resources required versus the resources available for effective implementation. The family probably is the most influential resource available, although, unfortunately, this very powerful agent frequently is omitted from consideration in favor of professional efforts. Other resources, of course, include teachers, specialists/therapists, support services (i.e., "related services," as defined by the rules and regulations for P.L. 94-142), various school and community programs, and specialized facilities and equipment, among others. Sometimes these resources are less than ideal, but can be adapted with minimal effort. With some exceptions, public school districts and associated personnel can be remarkably creative and responsive to the unique needs of learning disabled individuals. This creativity and responsiveness can be channeled for the mutual benefit of both the school district and the learning disabled individual through skilled consultation efforts on the part of the clinician. These characteristics also can be thwarted quickly by directive efforts that show little sensitivity to systemic and individualized issues of importance in the school milieu (Idol & West, 1987; West & Idol, 1987).

Evaluation of Effectiveness

The final stage in this approach emphasizes the ongoing, or recursive, relationship between neuropsychological assessment and treatment. Established interventions are evaluated in terms of effectiveness by neuropsychological performance changes. Such evaluations may signal, for example, that minor adjustments or major changes are required in the intervention plan. This kind of follow-up is especially important when considered from a developmental perspective and our currently limited understanding of the ontogeny of brain-behavior relationships in both learning disabled and non-learning disabled individuals.

Behavioral-Neuropsychological Approach

Another treatment approach that has been proposed involves the integration of two major disciplines. At one time, scientific progress required that the disciplines of behavior and neurology be studied separately. For example, in 1938 Skinner emphasized the distinct nature of these two disciplines, suggesting that the science of behavior was independent of neurology, and urged that behavioral science be established as a separate field of study (Skinner, 1938). Now, over 50 years later, many believe that the time has come for a rapprochement of these two disciplines. Indeed, as our knowledge base has expanded, the artificial boundaries once established between neurology and psychology have become increasingly less tenable. The treatment of learning disability subtypes perhaps provides one of the most cogent examples of the importance of such a rapprochement.

Behavioral neuropsychology is a specialty that integrates principles of behavior therapy with neuropsychology (Horton & Puente, 1986). It is based on the ideas that a neuropsychological perspective can (a) contribute to the understanding of the etiology of behavior and (b) facilitate functional analyses of particular behavioral deficits (Horton, 1979). Both of these ideas are useful in formulating learning disability treatment interventions from a behavioral perspective. Toward this goal, it is helpful to conceptualize behavioral-neuropsychological approaches to treatment within the framework of the "S-O-R-K-C" heuristic originally presented by Lindsley (1964) and discussed by others (Goldfried & Sprafkin, 1976; Kanfer & Phillips, 1970; Mash & Terdal, 1984).

S-O-R-K-C Framework

This framework provides a convenient classification of the variables of interest in a functional (i.e., behavioral) analysis of a problem (e.g., a specific learning disability). Within this framework, S designates the antecedent stimuli that signal the occurrence of the behavior, or provide the opportunity for its occurrence. For example, discriminative stimuli are considered in terms of this designation.

Of particular significance to this volume, O designates organismic variables that influence the behavior. These include neuropsychological, genetic, personality, medical, and other variables considered to be intrinsic to the individual. It is through these organismic variables that neuropsychological information is integrated effectively within a more general behavioral treatment paradigm.

The third component of the heuristic, R, designates the response class, that is, those behaviors targeted in the treatment intervention plan. Covert as well as overt behaviors are appropriate targets for these plans and, in the case of learning disabilities, can include a variety of metacognitive, academic, motoric, linguistic, and social-adaptive responses. Response classes typically are defined clearly, often in an operational manner, for behaviorally oriented treatments. Here, aspects to consider include the rates, durations, topographies, and magnitudes of behaviors, as well as the common properties that interrelate behaviors within the response class.

Finally, K designates the contingencies by which the response class is linked to C, the response-controlling consequences. Specification of contingencies involves clarifying the schedule of reinforcement that maintains the response class. Consequences may include positive and negative reinforcers as well as punishment and response-cost stimuli.

TREATMENT IMPLICATIONS

When treatment is considered from the perspective of the S-O-R-K-C heuristic, neuropsychological and behavioral approaches appear quite compatible. As Barkley (1984) identified, behaviorism emphasizes environmental antecedents and consequences in the functional analysis of behavior, whereas neuropsychology emphasizes the role of the central nervous system. Treatment goals of both disciplines, however, are similar, whereas differences primarily are related to variables selected for manipulation. For example, behavioral (i.e., R) change can result from either central nervous system (i.e., O) or environmental (i.e., S, K, C) change. Theoretically, all aspects are important for the thorough understanding and effective management of behavior, particularly the behavior of neurologically compromised learning disabled individuals. Continued empirical efforts are needed to evaluate the effectiveness of behavioral neuropsychology approaches for the treatment of particular subtypes of learning disabilities.

Neuropsychological Strength Approach

The neuropsychological strength approach (Hartlage & Reynolds, 1981; Hartlage & Telzrow, 1983; Kamphaus & Reynolds, 1987; Reynolds, 1981a, 1986) also has been advocated for the treatment of learning disabled and, more generally, learning problem children. This approach is essentially an individualized aptitude-by-treatment paradigm, where direct instruction is directed toward specific problem areas (e.g., reading, social skills). Instructional methods that are congruent with the individual's neuropsychological processing strengths (e.g., simultaneous cognitive processing) are used, whereas those that are more congruent with weaknesses (e.g., sequential cognitive processing) generally are avoided. Rationale for this approach include its intuitive appeal, tenuous neurodevelopmental empirical support, and the circumvention of stress and anxiety often associated with methods that focus on areas of weakness.

APTITUDE-BY-TREATMENT INTERACTIONS (ATI)

ATI paradigms have been prevalent in the field of special education for many years, particularly in learning disabilities. For these paradigms, particular instructional approaches are matched with particular learning styles or profiles. For example, a different teaching approach would be used for an individual with auditory learning problems than for an individual with visual learning problems. Unfortunately, research clearly indicates that treatment approaches based on these kinds of ATI paradigms do not work (Arter & Jenkins, 1979; Forness & Kavale, 1983; Glass, 1983; Kampwirth, 1979; Larivee, 1981; Lewis, 1983; Ysseldyke & Mirkin, 1982). Howell (1986, p. 326) even called ATI "a pervasive . . . affliction in special education," and Lakin (1983, p. 236) identified the continued use of ATI as, "a professional disgrace, given the wealth of [refuting] evidence . . ."

In contrast, others (e.g., Hartlage & Reynolds, 1981; Kamphaus & Reynolds, 1987; Reynolds, 1986) have argued that the neuropsychological strength approach differs from these more traditional ATI paradigms in at least two important ways. First, many traditional ATI paradigms have identified cognitive or perceptual processing deficits and focused instructional efforts on ameliorating these deficits. Second, in focusing on these cognitive/perceptual deficits, these paradigms have circumvented direct instruction of academic skills. For the neuropsychological strength approach, however, identified strengths are used solely to determine how specific subject matter should be taught. Consequently, deficit processing does not become the focus of remediation. Instead, behavioral and psychoeducational approaches are used to analyze academic tasks to determine exactly what should be taught. Thus, in contrast to many traditional ATI paradigms, the neuropsychological strength approach uses identified learner aptitudes to determine *how* to teach, rather than *what* to teach.

There is an additional difference between traditional ATI paradigms and the neuropsychological strength approach. When a neurocognitive function is considered in terms of Guilford's structure-of-intellect model (Guilford, 1985), three facets are conceptualized. These are: (a) content, or characteristics of the input stimulus: (b) operation, or characteristics of the cognitive process; and (c) product, or characteristics of the output response. In terms of the aptitude variable in ATI paradigms, the traditional focus has been on contents and products (e.g., auditory-oral, visual-motor). In contrast, the neuropsychological strength approach tends to focus on operations (e.g., sequential, simultaneous).

RESEARCH EVIDENCE

Of course, the true value of the neuropsychological strength approach will lie in its demonstrated empirical support. There are very few studies that address this issue at the present time, and results of the available preliminary investigations are equivocal (Ayres, Cooley, & Severson, 1988; Kaufman & Kaufman, 1983). Thus, current clinical application of the neuropsychological strength approach in treating subtypes of learning disabilities should be practiced cautiously. Additional research clearly is required. One issue to consider in future research efforts in this area concerns the clear separation of facets of the aptitude variables selected for study. Here, cognitive operations assessed by tasks in many commonly administered assessment instruments (e.g., K-ABC, WISC-R) often are confounded by modality-specific contents and operations (Willis, 1985b). For example, most standardized tasks of simultaneous cognitive processing involve visual contents and motoric products, whereas most standardized tasks of sequential cognitive processing involve auditory contents and oral products. Partitioning effects to distinct aptitude variables may be particularly important given the possibility that interactions among facets (e.g., cognitive processing strategies by stimulus-response modalities) may contribute to differential cerebral organization of functional systems (Willis & Hynd, 1987).

Subtype-to-Treatment Linkages

As already noted, one of the most important aspects of subtyping learning disabilities is the relevance of the classification to treatment planning. From a neuropsychological perspective, some investigators have noted that the power of subtyping models in relation to treatment lies in the clear and reliable delineation of a profile of strengths and weaknesses, the relationship of these cognitive processing variables to specific patterns of recovery, and the direct linkages that can be made from assessment to specific intervention plans (Alfano & Finlayson, 1987; Lyon & Moats, in press; Lyon et al., 1988; Newcomb, 1985).

At the present time, however, few studies exist to confirm these assessment-to-subtype-to-treatment connections. To date, most of the treatment-intervention studies have been attempted with heterogeneous groups of learning disabled children, whereas most of the classification studies have been directed toward subtype identification. Further, as Lyon et al. (in press) noted, most of the evidence about treatment of specific subtypes tends to be of a case study or anecdotal variety (e.g., Boder, 1970; Johnson & Myklebust, 1967; Rourke, 1986). Generally, all of the subtype models presented in Chapters 3 and 4 addressed the importance of treatment and several offered treatment guidelines (e.g., Boder, 1970). Unfortunately, few addressed this issue in an experimental fashion. There have been several conceptual treatment models proposed, however, that have involved specific subtyping models and specific treatment programs (Boder, 1971, 1973; Hynd, 1986; Hynd & Cohen, 1983; Mattis et al., 1975). In addition, there have been several experimental research studies that have addressed this question (Bakker, 1984; Bakker et al., 1981; Bakker & Vinke, 1985; Cohen, Krawiecki, & DuRant, 1987; Flynn, 1987; Lyon, 1983; Lyon, 1985b; Simeon, Waters, Resnick, et al., 1980).

Conceptual Models

HYND AND COHEN'S TREATMENT MODEL

Hynd and Cohen (1983) matched selective unidmensional treatment approaches to the Boder (1970) and Mattis et al. (1975) subtype models. Using information presented from these who models, Hynd and Cohen constructed a table listing specific treatment programs that may prove most useful for each respective subtype. These subtype-to-treatment program matches are reproduced in Table 8.1. Currently, this conceptual model awaits validation efforts.

BODER'S TREATMENT MODEL

Boder (1971, 1973) suggested that the dysphonetic subtype, characterized by primary weaknesses in auditory processing, would learn most efficiently when provided with whole-word approaches to reading as opposed to more phonic-based teaching strategies. Interventions using the tactile-perceptual aspects of learning also were suggested (e.g., Fernald Approach). For this subtype, Boder suggested that a phonetic approach to reading instruction was contraindicated and should not be attempted until an adequate sight-word foundation had been developed.

Similarly, Boder indicated that the dyseidetic subtype, characterized by primary visual processing deficiencies, would benefit most from a remedial phonics program (e.g., Orton-Gillingham). Tactile-kinesthetic strategies also were suggested as possible avenues for initiating the reading process for young disabled learners. This latter group of strategies was deemed by Boder to be the treatment of choice for the mixed or alexic subtype as well. Boder provided no data to validate this subtype-to-treatment model, but one experimental study (discussed subsequently) has provided support for the general conceptualization (Flynn, 1987).

MATTIS ET AL.'S TREATMENT MODEL

In a related fashion, Mattis et al. (1975) also provided specific suggestions for treatment of each of the subtypes in their model. Although the matchings are consistent with those outlined by Boder, Mattis et al. provided considerably more detail with respect to when and how particular interventions should be employed. For the language disorder subtype, for example, characterized by poor verbal retrieval and anomia, Mattis (1981) suggested a graduated program of techniques. Initially, only the sound-blending qualities of a word are taught, with letter labels and sight-word develop-

TABLE 8.1. Hynd and Cohen's conceptual treatment model for learning disability subtypes.

Treatment method	Boder's Dysphonetic	Boder's Dyseidetic	Boder's Alexic	Mattis' Language Disorder Syndrome	Mattis' Graphomotor Syndrome	Mattis' Visual-Perception Syndrome
Orton-Gillingham or other phonics methods such as SRA or Distar	No	Yes	No	After letter recognition is established	No	After letter recognition is established
Fernald-VAKT	In some cases	No	Yes	No	No	No
Doman-Delacato	No	No	No	No	No	No
ITPA Psycholinguistic	No	No	No	No	No	No
Visual-Perceptual Kephart, Frostig	No	No	No	No	Yes	No
Look-Say or Language Experience	Yes	No	No	In later stages	Yes	No
Linguistic Structural Analysis	In later stages	No	No	No	In later stages	No

Adapted from Hynd, G.W., & Cohen, M. (1983). *Dyslexia: Neuropsychological theory, research, and clinical differentiation* (p. 231). New York: Grune & Stratton. With permission.

ment considered secondary. Once these sound qualities of letters and sight words are ingrained, a phonics program is suggested (e.g., SRA Basic Reading Series). As reading skills near a third- or fourth-grade level, a language-based experience approach is implemented in order to strengthen comprehension skills.

A similar graduated program is suggested for the articulation and graphomotor dyscoordination subtype, with the exception that the inital stages of instruction should avoid the use of phonic strategies and, instead, consist of whole-word analysis (e.g., look-say approach). Once these foundation skills are stabilized, a linguistic or structural analysis program is instituted in order to facilitate word decoding by using word parts (e.g., prefix, suffix, root) as opposed to phonetic skills.

For the visual-perceptual subtype, characterized by intact auditory processing skills but deficient visual processing, Mattis recommended the use of verbal mediation strategies (i.e, overt and covert). Verbal mediation would serve to help overcome the interference that may be present from the poor visual-perceptual abilities. As adequate identification of letters, words, and corresponding sounds begins to be demonstrated, the verbal mediation strategies should be faded from overt to covert. Mattis noted that any reading system placing a high emphasis on visual-perceptual aspects would overwhelm these children and care should be taken to avoid this. As with the Boder system, however, Mattis (1981) provided no data to support these claims. Nonetheless, the conceptual presentation by Hynd and Cohen provides a foundation for treatment studies investigating these proposed subtype-to-treatment models.

HYND'S TREATMENT MODEL

Hynd (1986) provided a similar conceptual model using a neurolinguisitic subtyping model, but she reviewed the subtype-to-treatment matches in a more detailed fashion. This treatment conceptualization is presented in Table 8.2. Hynd identified a neurolinguistic model developed by Marshall (1984) (see Chapter 3) and documented clinical teaching strategies in her presentation of potential subtype-to-treatment matchings.

This model is similar to the one presented by Hynd and Cohen (1983) in that subtypes are matched to a particular teaching strategy based on their respective processing strengths. This model, however, presents specific teaching strategies as well as selected instructional programs that have been used for disabled readers. For example, the surface dyslexic shows relative strengths in phonological processing, but deficiencies in comprehension due to an inability to employ visual strategies in whole-word analysis. Consequently, this subtype would probably benefit most from teaching strategies and programs designed to use the phonological strengths. In contrast, the use of visual-search strategies or morphological analysis would prove less efficient and, perhaps, unproductive for this dyslexic subtype. A

TABLE 8.2. Hynd's conceptual model for treatment of subtypes.

Treatment method	Surface dyslexia	Deep dyslexia	Phono-logical dyslexia	Direct dyslexia
Word recognition				
Crossmodal[a]	Yes	Yes	Yes	Yes
VAKT				
Aaron's seven-step method				
Cunningham's method				
Visual-imageable	No	Yes	Yes	Yes[b]
Whole-word				
Fading				
Sight-vocabulary (Edmark)				
Syllabary				
Rebus readers				
Phonetic	Yes	No	No	Yes[b]
Distar				
Orton-Gillingham				
Hegge-Kirk & Kirk				
Letter strings or linguistic				
Linguistic-spelling patterns	Yes	No	Yes	Yes
Morphemic analysis	No	Yes	Yes	Yes
Context clues	No	Yes	Yes	No
Compare-contrast	Yes	No	No	Yes
Comprehension				
Visual	No	Yes	Yes	No
Structured overviews				
Herringbone				
Schema based				
Language experience	Yes	Yes	Yes	No
List-group-label				
Possible sentences				
Anticipation-reaction				
Directed reading-thinking activity (DRTA)				
Visual/Language based				
Auditory discrimination in depth (ADD.)	Yes[b]	Yes[c]	Yes	Yes[b]
Fitzgerald keys	No	Yes	Yes[b]	No
McGinnis	Yes	No	No	Yes[b]
Compensatory				
Glossing	Yes	Yes	Yes	Yes
Slicing	Yes	Yes	Yes	Yes
Guided listening	Yes	No	Yes	Yes
Guide-o-rama	Yes	Yes	Yes	Yes

Adapted from Hynd, C.R. (1986). Educational intervention in children with developmental learning disorders. In J.E. Obrzut & G.W. Hynd (Eds.), *Child neuropsychology: Vol. 2. Clinical practice* (pp. 280–281). New York: Academic Press. With permission.
[a]Depending on modifications, can be adapted to most subtypes.
[b]Not necessary.
[c]Used with difficulty.

similar clinical paradigm is followed for the other three subtypes previously described in Chapter 3.

This conceptual model for treatment based on neurolinguistic subtypes is impressive, but its components still remain to be validated. From a clinical perspective, however, conceptual models such as those provided by Hynd and Cohen (1983) and Hynd (1986) provide clinicians and researchers structured hypotheses for conducting treatment research with subtypes. Further investigation of these conceptual models and the development of others are imperative for the study of learning disability subtypes.

Research Studies

At present there are only ten research studies that have attempted to explore specific subtype-to-treatment connections in an experimental fashion. Eight of the studies have explored this question using clinical-inferential subtype models (Bakker, 1984; Bakker et al., 1981; Bakker & Vinke, 1985; Bouma, Bakker, & Gardien, 1988; Cohen et al., 1987; Flynn, 1987; Simeon et al., 1980; Spijer et al., 1987), whereas the other two used empirical models (Lyon, 1983, 1985b). These studies are described in Table 8.3.

SIMEON ET AL.'S STUDY

Simeon et al. (1980) perhaps provided one of the first subtype-by-treatment studies. Using a clinical-inferential classification model, learning disabled children were subtyped based on their intellectual profiles. Similar to the classification models provided by Rourke et al. (1971) and Smith et al. (1977), Simeon et al. identified one subtype that showed a Verbal IQ (VIQ) greater than Performance IQ (PIQ) pattern, a second subtype that showed a VIQ lower than PIQ pattern, and a VIQ equal to PIQ pattern. All subjects were administered a daily dose of Piracetam (4,800 mg) or placebo in a double-blind crossover fashion. Treatment occurred over a 4-week period. Results revealed significant increases for the VIQ equal to PIQ subtype in EEG power and ratings of memory function by a neuropsychologist; however, no significant differences were noted in reading. Although there were a number of methodological problems with this study (e.g., small sample size), Simeon et al. addressed an important concern in the subtyping treatment literature.

BAKKER ET AL.'S STUDIES

In addition to differential results of pharmacological intervention noted previously (Spijer et al., 1987), other treatment research has been conducted using the subtyping model offered by Bakker (1979a). For example, Bakker et al. (1981) and Bakker (1984) provided preliminary support for treatment methods using hemispheric stimulation to alter event-related

TABLE 8.3. Studies examining subtype- by-treatment linkages.

Study	Subtypes	Intervention	Results
Clinical-inferential models			
Simeon, Waters, Resnick, et al. (1980)	VIQ > PIQ LD ($n = 9$) VIQ < PIQ LD ($n = 10$) VIQ = PIQ LD ($n = 10$)	Daily double-blind crossover administration of Piracetam (480 mg) or placebo over a 4 week period	EEGs showed increased power Improvement rated in memory for some subjects No significant changes in congitive tasks

Bakker, Moerland, & Goekoop-Hoefkens (1981)	L-type dyslexia
	  Treatment ($n = 4$)
	  Control 1 ($n = 3$)
	  Control 2 ($n = 3$)
	P-type dyslexia:
	  Treatment ($n = 3$)
	  Control 1 ($n = 3$)
	  Control 2 ($n = 3$)
		L-types received left visual presentation of words
		P-types received right visual-field presentations
		All treatment subjects received individual training over 16 40-minute sessions twice per week
		Control 1 received remedial training for a similar duration
		Control 2 remained in regular class-rooms
			Both subtypes of dyslexia improved relative to controls, but L-type improved more than P-type
			Altered wave forms of the event-related potentials corresponded to specific hemispheric treatment
			Improved reading performance

Bakker (1984)	L-type dyslexia ($n = 35$) P-type dyslexia ($n = 35$)	Each subtype was divided into 5 treatment groups of 7 subjects L-types received left visual-field presentations of words P-types received right visual-field presentations Subtype controls received central field training or no training Training occurred once a week for 45 minutes over 22 sessions	Altered wave forms of the event-related potentials in the parietal and temporal lobe regions of the stimulated hemi-sphere Hemispheric charges correlated with pretest vs, posttest reading improvement
Bakker & Vinke (1985)	L-type dyslexia ($n = 35$) P-type dyslexia ($n = 35$)	Each subtype was divided randomly into 5 treatment groups of 7 subjects Four groups received direct hemisphere stimulation through right or left visual-field presentation	Significant changes in event-related potentials and reading improvement in both subtypes relative to controls following direct stimulation of the under-used hemisphere

TABLE 8.3. Continued.

Study	Subtypes	Intervention	Results
		Four groups received indirect hemisphere stimulation by modified text formats Two groups received no training Stimulation occurred once a week for 45 minutes over 22 sessions	Within each treatment condition there were some children who showed gains while others with the same profile had less than average gains
Flynn (1987)	Dysphonetic LD ($n = 10$) Dyseidetic LD ($n = 6$)	Children were randomly assigned to a language experience, synthetic phonetics, or multisensory treatment group Each child received 1 year of treatment, 3 times a week	
Cohen, Krawiecki, & DuRant (1987)	Language disorder LD ($n = 14$) Visual-spatial LD ($n = 3$) Mixed LD ($n = 3$)	The subtypes were divided into "Progress" and "No-Progress" groups based on their gains on standardized achievement testing for the previous year A neuropsychological treatment model was used in the child's special education classroom for the entire school year	Children in the "Progress" group had been taught via methods consistent with their cognitive strengths, thus they showed minimal change in reading scores from pre- to postintervention Children in the "No Progress" group showed significant gains in reading recognition from pre- to postintervention due to the improved match between teaching strategies and cognitive abilities
Spijer, De Jong, & Bakker (1987)	L-type dyslexia ($n = 1$) P-type dyslexia ($n = 1$)	Piracetam Piracetam supplemented with hemisphere-specific stimulation	For the L-type dyslexic, Piracetam had a detrimental effect on reading For the P-type dyslexic, hemisphere-specific stimulation improved the effects of Piracetam for speed and accuracy of passage reading but not single-word reading

Bouma, Bakker, & Gardien (1988)	L-type dyslexia: Treatment ($n = 30$) Control ($n = 21$) P-type dyslexia: Treatment ($n = 29$) Control ($n = 22$)	Hemisphere-specific tactile training	For both subtypes, hemisphere-specific tactile training improved reading more for treatment than control groups
Empirical models Lyon (1983)	Significant mixed deficits ($n = 5$) Mild mixed deficits ($n = 5$) Language comprehension, sound-blending deficits ($n = 5$) Language comprehension, auditory memory, sound blending deficits ($n = 5$) Selected visual-motor deficit ($n = 5$) Normal profile, low reading ($n = 5$)	Synthetic phonics program taught to all subtypes for 1 hour per week over 26 weeks; preintervention reading recognition levels were obtained	The normal and visual motor deficit subtypes showed significant gains in reading recognition Other subtypes showed minimal gains
Lyon (1985a)	Auditory receptive and expressive deficits ($n = 10$)	This subtype was divided in half, with 5 children randomly assigned to a synthetic phonics program and 5 to a combined program Both groups received approximately 30 hours of instruction; preintervention reading recognition levels were obtained	Children in the combined group showed significant reading gains when compared to the phonics group and preintervention levels The phonic group showed no gains

potentials and improve reading scores in P- and L-type dyslexics. Bakker speculated that these preliminary data provided support for the relationship between neural mechanisms and specific subtypes of dyslexia.

Bakker and Vinke (1985) found significant differences between the two subtypes on event-related potentials and reading tasks following direct and indirect stimulation of the cerebral hemispheres. As in the previous studies, children were classified as either L- (i.e., linguistic deficits) or P-type dyslexics (i.e., perceptual deficits) on the basis of a dichotic listening task. These investigators presented words to the subjects' left and right visual fields. They also modified test formats to both visual fields; specifically, L-type dyslexics were required to attend to the graphic features of text (e.g., mixed and altered typefaces) and P-type dyslexics were required to attend to letter sequences without the use of pictures or titles. Remediation sessions were scheduled once a week for 22 weeks. These investigators found significant positive changes in reading along with commensurate changes in event-related potentials following the regimented stimulation to the underactive hemisphere for each respective subtype. More recently, Bouma et al. (1988) found that hemisphere-specific tactile training significantly improved reading performance for treatment groups of L- and P-type dyslexics when compared to matched groups of dyslexics.

Although impressive, these results should be viewed only as preliminary. Bakker and Vinke (1985) stated that these data provided evidence for Bakker's balance model of dyslexia. Others (Lyon et al., in press), however, are more cautious, particularly given the study's methodological concerns (e.g., wide IQ range, poor internal validation of subtypes, use of dichotic listening to identify subtypes, no control for classroom reading instruction). Nonetheless, these studies represent initial attempts to address treatment components for specific neuropsychological subtypes.

FLYNN'S STUDY

Flynn (1987) reported another treatment study that used a clinical-inferential classification model in exploring the efficacy of subtype-to-treatment matching. Flynn used a modified version of Boder's model to classify subjects into subtypes. Subjects were 22 first-, second-, and third-grade students, 16 of whom were classified as dysphonetic ($n = 10$) or dyseidetic ($n = 6$). These children were assigned to one of three treatment groups in a random fashion. The three interventions included a language experience, stressing analytic phonetic strategies, a synthetic phonics program (i.e., Distar), and a multisensory approach employing analytic phonetics and regular orthography. Children participated in three treatment sessions per week over the course of a complete school year. Flynn found evidence for improvement for some subjects from subtypes in each of the treatment groups, but results were not overwhelming. More importantly, Flynn noted that a simple match between subtype and specific treatment condition should be only part of a total intervention program. In this regard, Lyon et al. (1988) argued that it is important for more dynamic and interactive models to be developed in an effort to describe how subtypes can be affected by variables other than instructional formats. The Flynn study is noteworthy in that it is one of the first studies to attempt to intervene directly in the classroom.

COHEN ET AL.'S STUDY

Cohen et al. (1987) reported another experimental subtype-by-treatment study that occurred outside of a laboratory school. Initially, these investigators grouped 20 reading disabled children into progress (i.e., greater than 6 months gain per year) and no-progress (i.e., less than 6 months gain per year) groups in accordance with standardized achievement testing during the previous year in the learning disabilities program. During the pretreatment phase of this study (i.e., the 1st year), these children were classified further, using neuropsychological data and clinical-inferential criteria, into three dyslexic subtypes: (a) language disorder/dysphonetic, (b) visual-spatial/dyseidetic, and (c) mixed. Based on the neuropsychological profile of each subtype a specific remedial reading program was developed for each child in accordance with a neuropsychological treatment approach (e.g., instruction for the visual-spatial subtype consisted of a synthetic phonics program, supplemented by high-interest reading materials when a third-grade reading level was attained). These programs were developed without prior knowledge of previous remedial strategies or the placement of a child into the progress or no-progress group. Treatment occurred daily for an entire school year.

Results of this study revealed support for the neuropsychological treatment approach for this specific subtyping model. These investigators noted that, prior to the intervention, children in the no-progress group received instruction that was directed toward improving cognitive weaknesses rather than teaching to the child's relative cognitive strengths. An opposite pattern was noted for the progress group (i.e., these children were being instructed according to their relative cognitive strengths) during the pretreatment phase. As predicted, once reading instruction was matched to a child's relative cognitive strengths, the no-progress group showed significant gains (i.e, in excess of 1 year) in reading recognition, but not reading comprehension. As expected, no significant gains were demonstrated by the progress group, largely because this group of children already was receiving instruction, perhaps by accident, that matched their cognitive strengths.

Although the results of the Cohen et al. study are limited in their generalization due to a small sample size, it is important from several vantage points. First, along with Flynn (1987), it is one of the first studies to investigate subtype-to-treatment effects in a regular classroom setting. This serves to increase the efficacy of the neuropsychological treatment approach from an ecological validity perspective. Second, it is the only study conducted to date that has attempted to control for prior instruction of the subjects (i.e., history), a variable that is difficult to control in treatment studies. Finally, this study presented initial support for the conceptual model outlined by Hynd and Cohen (1983) and, thus, provides an experimental prototype for other investigators.

LYON'S STUDIES

Lyon (1983, 1985a) provided the other two subtype-to-treatment studies completed to date and he was perhaps the first to examine these questions in a systematic and experimental manner. Using his empirically developed neuropsychological subtyping model, Lyon (1983) applied a single treatment condition across six subtype patterns. Children included in this study ($n = 30$; 5 from each subtype) were 12 years old and matched on the basis of age, IQ, gender, socioeconomic status, race, and preintervention reading recognition level. Lyon used a synthetic phonics program (Traub & Bloom, 1975) as the single remedial program. All of the children received 1 hour of remedial reading a week over the course of 26 weeks.

Following the intervention phase, the children were retested with the reading recognition measure. Results indicated that the subtypes showing intact auditory-verbal abilities showed the most significant gains with this instructional program. Conversely, subtypes showing weaknesses in this domain demonstrated minimal, if any, reading recognition gains over the 26-week period.

In a second study, Lyon (1985b) demonstrated a similar pattern of skill remediation with a younger sample of disabled readers. Using a creative experimental design, Lyon selected one subtype and employed multiple treatment interventions. The subtype chosen for study was charaterized by significant language deficits and intact visual-perceptual, motor, and memory abilities. The 10 children in this subtype were divided randomly into two groups. One of the groups received the synthetic phonics program and the other a combined program incorporating sight-word development, contextual and structural analysis, and analytic phonics. No differences were noted between the two groups on a preintervention reading recognition measure. Both groups of children engaged in about 30 hours of individualized instruction with their respective teaching approach (i.e., 3 hours a week for 10 weeks).

After completing their intervention programs, all of the children were reevaluated with the reading recognition test. Results revealed that the group receiving the combined treatment program scored significantly higher than their phonics program counterparts. Similar to Cohen et al.'s conclusions, this study suggested that specific subtype patterns may exhibit a differential response to treatment, particularly if treatment is designed to accommodate cognitive processing strengths.

Summary

Although all of these studies contain methodological flaws (e.g., small sample size, inability to control for teacher characteristics, previous educational experiences), they do represent exciting efforts in subtype-to-treatment investigations. Lyon et al. (in press) noted further that these findings were limited by the subtype models used. Here, specific subtypes identified may not have reflected accurately the wide range of potential cognitive difficulties that might have been present. Consequently, the remedial plans that could have been implemented were limited. Other treatment efforts also have been initiated that have potential application to learning disability subtypes, but these programs have not directly addressed issues related to subtyping per se (Das, Kirby, & Jarman, 1979; Gunnison, 1984).

Issues in Subtype-to-Treatment Planning

Although the literature on subtype-to-treatment models is sparse, it is clear that direct and accurate matching of subtypes to specific treatment regimens has tremendous instructional potential for learning disabled individuals. The few research studies conducted, however, also suggest that this simple matching probably will not account for all of the variability in treatment response. Rather, it is likely that there are other variables that also play important roles in shaping treatment response. In a review of the literature related to learning disability treatment, Lyon and Moats (in press) noted several additional variables that should be considered. These include (a) using theory-based instruction based on the "goodness-of-fit" between student needs and choice of instructional approach, (b) accounting for nonspecific intervening factors (e.g., those related to teacher, student, and classroom environment), and (c) understanding processes by which instructional decisions are made in the classroom.

Conceptually, it seems that if learning problems are multidimensional, then instituted treatment also should be multidimensional. The subtype-to-treatment match actually may represent one of many components of a comprehensive treatment intervention for an individual with learning disabilities. Other issues that should be considered in developing a comprehensive treatment intervention include the contribution of related variables, specific assessment-to-treatment linkages, and prognosis.

Related Variables

As already noted, the few treatment studies that have been reported with specific subtypes suggest that the use of the aptitude-by-treatment intervention model accounts for only part of the variability in treatment response. Other variables are necessarily involved given the interactional complexities of teaching and learning processes.

SOCIAL-EMOTIONAL VARIABLES

As discussed in Chapter 7, the behavior of some learning disability sub-types is characterized by particular patterns of social-emotional malad-justment. Further, the influence of these features actually may become more confounding as age increases (Kistner & Osborne, 1987; Tramon-tana, Hooper, & Nardolillo, in press). Thus, by adolescence or, even ear-lier, during the latency-age period, the child may have developed an aver-sion to school-related activities, and treatment response may be influenced as much by those features (e.g., lack of motivation and interest, behavioral difficulties) as by neurocognitive or neurolinguistic ones. Although this emphasizes the utility of early identification and intervention (Hooper, 1988), the actual impact on specific subtypes remains to be explored. Nor-mal variations in social-emotional functioning (e.g., learning style) also will require exploration with respect to their impact on treatment interven-tion.

SCHOOL VARIABLES

School-related variables also are important in this regard. In addition to the specific treatment intervention plan, there are a number of variables that can influence functioning in, as yet, unknown ways. For example, how a child interacts with the teacher, the instructional style of the teacher (e.g., directive, nondirective), the specific curriculum and materials em-ployed, previous learning experiences, and the situation in which treat-ment is delivered, all are likely to influence potential gains that a child may show. Further, the interactions among these variables also are likely to be important, particularly with respect to specific subtype patterns.

FAMILY VARIABLES

Finally, there are many family-related variables that should be addressed. The child's family functioning and the importance of education to the fami-ly both are likely to influence how the child approaches a task. The struc-ture provided by the child's family on such issues as homework and the use of leisure time also seem important. These latter issues may be particularly important to learning disabled children because characteristics of specific subtypes may hinder or facilitate different kinds of structured activities (e.g., learning a musical instrument, becoming involved in team sports, homework strategies). Appropriate involvement of these children in selected activities may improve self-esteem and interpersonal skills.

Assessment-Treatment Linkages

Linking the diagnostic components of an evaluation to specific treatment needs in a reliable and valid manner is one of the major goals of classification research with learning disabilities. Many current assessment strategies were not designed with treatment in mind (Lyon et al., 1988), and the need for different kinds of assessment strategies is apparent. For example, it is important for diagnostic techniques to gauge the developmental parameters surrounding the evolution of specific cognitive or academic skills. Here, the development of assessment strategies with strong theoretical underpinnings is necessary.

Lyon et al. (1988) also called for greater use of dynamic assessment strategies. Not only are these assessment strategies useful for accurate diagnosis of level and pattern of function, but they also allow for the flexibility needed to test possible treatment interventions during the assessment process. Here, these approaches begin to relate a profile of abilities to functional aspects of an individual's daily functioning. This contributes to the validity of the obtained results.

Prognosis

The classification of disabled learners in a reliable and valid fashion potentially provides greater predictive accuracy with respect to treatment outcome. By identifying specific prognoses of specific learning disability subtypes, clinicians and researchers will be able to develop more appropriate treatment intervention plans. For example, Sweeney and Rourke (1978) noted specific outcomes associated with children with spelling deficits. Children showing phonetic deficiencies in spelling had a poorer academic outcome than children showing similar numbers of spelling errors, but good phonetic attempts.

Boder (1970) also speculated about the potential prognostic outcomes for dyslexic subtypes. She asserted that dysphonetic children would have the best potential for positive academic outcomes. Given that these children tend to acquire adequate sight-word vocabularies, they can develop nearly age-appropriate contextual reading skills. However, because of their phonetic difficulties, they show chronic deficiencies in spelling and word analysis. In contrast, dyseidetic children have the potential to develop adequate spelling skills but, because of poor development of sight-word skills, reading remains labored with a tendency for overuse of phonetic strategies. Boder noted that alexic children maintained severe reading deficits and, that without intensive intervention, remain nonreaders. Knowledge of the underlying dimensions of learning disabilities will facilitate a greater understanding of prognostic courses with and without treatment.

Continued Research Efforts

The intervention components of learning disability subtyping are only beginning to be explored. For example, the efforts of Lyon (1983, 1985b),

Bakker and colleagues (Bakker, 1984; Bakker & Vinke, 1985; Bakker et al., 1981), Flynn (1987), and Cohen et al. (1987) are noteworthy in beginning to tackle the seemingly endless number of variables that may be related to subtype-to-treatment paradigms. The conceptual models offered to date (e.g., Hynd, 1986) also merit exploration with respect to their utility. This kind of research, however, is extraordinarily difficult to conduct. The difficulties principally lie in the pragmatic and ethical aspects of conducting these in vivo studies. Although methodological strategies have been outlined (e.g., Hynd & Cohen, 1983; Lyon, 1985a), none of these strategies can ameliorate the problems presented by this kind of research.

It is absolutely essential to validation efforts, however, that this kind of research be pursued. Creative strategies, such as those used by Lyon, offer important contributions in this regard. Further, it is important for future studies to direct some effort toward arithmetic and spelling disability subtypes. To date, all of the subtype-to-treatment studies have addressed reading problems. Research also should continue to focus on developing reliable and valid classification models for learning disabilities because these models form the foundation for subtype-to-treatment studies.

Summary

The overview of treatment issues relevant to the subtyping literature presents several unifactor approaches and three neuropsychologically based treatment approaches that have been advanced. The few studies that have been conducted to date exploring the subtype-to-treatment interaction are discussed. In addition to showing promising results in their own right, these studies highlight the importance of other variables on treatment response. The influence of developmental factors, prognosis, and dynamic assessment strategies for planning treatment interventions, however, requires further delineation.

Section IV Epilogue

9
Summary and Future Directions

The overall intent of this volume is to provide a relatively comprehensive compendium of the literature dealing with learning disability subtyping. As such, the text focuses on providing an overview of most of the subtype classification models presented to date. In conjunction with this fundamental goal, additional discussion is directed toward particular issues relevant to subtyping efforts.

In particular, the first section of the text provides a foundation for subtype analysis. Here, one chapter is devoted to the historical antecedents and definitional issues surrounding learning disabilities. This chapter discusses case-study methodology, past and present, as well as information about the multitude of single-factor theories proposed to account for learning problems. Definitional issues also are presented with respect to the numerous attempts to operationalize the learning disability concept. In the next chapter, specific neuropsychological foundations are presented. Here, the importance of theories and research dealing with issues related to nervous system development, functional brain organization, and functional systems are emphasized with respect to conceptualizing multiple subtypes of learning disabilities. A subsequent section of this text is concerned with the various subtyping models presented to date and accompanying issues relevant to subtype derivation. Specifically, clinical-inferential and empirical subtype models are reviewed in detail. In addition, this section addresses methodological and theoretical issues, and concerns specific to subtype derivation. Related to these classification models, another section of the text provides an overview of important clinical issues directly impinging on classification research in the learning disability domain. The clinical components of assessment, social-emotional features, and treatment are inextricably tied to specific classification efforts.

Despite the progress made in understanding this heterogeneous group of disorders in terms of its neuropsychological foundations, conceptual models, and clinical differentiation, however, much remains to be learned. For example, in a metaanalysis of 1,077 studies investigating achievement, neurocognitive, neurolinguistic, and social-emotional features of learning disabilities (i.e., variables and combinations thereof used to derive many of the subtyping models reviewed in this volume), Kavale and Nye (1985/1986) were able to account for only about 40% of the variance between learning disabled and normal samples of subjects. Clearly, such results pose both research and clinical challenges for the field of learning disabilities and demand careful consideration of the future direction in which this field will progress. This chapter reviews some of the advances noted in the subtyping domain over the past several years and discusses further directions for clinicians and researchers.

Advances in Learning Disability Subtyping

Hopefully, it is clear from the preceding chapters that the conceptualization of learning disabilities as a multisyndrome group of disorders is much more tenable than the unidimensional thinking that once was prevalent in this area. Since the early 1960s there have been rapid advances with respect to the development of a learning disability classification model. These efforts at classification are only in the beginning stages of development, but several of the more prominent advances in this domain are noteworthy.

Definition

One of the most significant advances has occurred in the definition of learning disabilities. Since the coining of the term *learning disability* by Kirk in 1963, this term has been revised a number of times. Nonetheless, all of these revisions have fallen prey to criticism largely because of their vague qualities, lack of operational guidelines, and exclusionary natures. Definitional issues have interfered with nearly every aspect of the subtyping literature and have contributed to difficulties in the cross-comparison of studies. The difficulties also have hindered the accurate calculation of incidence and prevalence rates, although it is clear that males do tend to outnumber females regardless of the specific classification model employed or specific subtype membership.

Although arguments about definitional constraints are likely to continue, more current definitions of learning disabilities proposed by the Interagency Committee on Learning Disabilities (ICLD) and National Joint Committee for Learning Disabilities (NJCLD) represent significant improvements over previous attempts. This is partially the result of input from a variety of disciplines, although some might argue that it is precisely this multidisciplinary involvement that contributes to definitional confusion. Learning disabilities traditionally have been recognized as falling under the rubric of educational disorders; however, it is clear that they no longer exclusively fall within this domain.

Moreover, operational criteria also remain elusive (Epps, Ysseldyke, & Algozzine, 1985). Here, the newer definitions provide a framework for viewing learning disabilities as a heterogeneous group of disorders. These definitions also recognize the possible coexistence of psychopathology and acknowledge the neurological foundation of learning disabilities. This latter point is important in nurturing a theoretical basis for the field. Clearly, future efforts must be directed toward developing acceptable operational criteria for this group of disorders and advancing the diagnosis of learning disability from a descriptive to a prognostic level of refinement. Progress in this direction is represented by the increasing emphasis on subtyping.

Theoretical/Conceptual Basis

A second major thrust that has occurred with respect to subtype derivation has been the evolution of a theoretical/conceptual basis for this field. The current definition places a heavy emphasis on underlying neurological dysfunction as a major contributor to learning disabilities, a position supported by much of the evolving research as well as early case reports. Neuropsychological theory provides a strong foundation from which to understand learning disabilities and, in fact, is consistent with a multidimensional conceptualization of these disorders. This theoretical orientation also facilitates the conceptualization of learning disabilities within developmental parameters. Thus, the qualitative and quantitative differences in learning patterns of younger and older children are acknowledged. It also provides a foundation for the early prediction of learning disabilities. Further, it suggests reasons why some children seem to develop learning difficulties as they grow older and helps to explain the emergence of a learning disability during the adolescent years, a phenomenon that has not been extensively studied.

Rourke's (1987) first approximation of a developmental neuropsychological theory of nonverbal learning disabilities (see chapter 2) is exemplary because it addresses these issues. Rourke's theory may prove to be seminal because it provides a basis for guiding future research efforts in learning disability subtyping. Although continued refinement of the theoretical foundation is required, it is clear that there is a direct relationship between neurological deficits and dysfunctions, and potential learning disabilities.

Methodology

A third major advance that has been observed in the learning disability subtyping research is the improvement in the application of empirical classification methods (e.g., hierarchical cluster analysis) to this heterogeneous group of disorders. Currently, models based on these methods are much more prevalent than clincal-inferential models of classification. These methods also allow for greater distinction to be posited among different kinds of disorders (e.g., mental retardation versus learning disabilities) and different subtypes of learning disabilities.

The application of these methods has been aided by the availability of high-speed data management systems and computers. Consequently, the field has witnessed a rapid increase in the number of subtyping models proffered. These methods have contributed to greater homogeneity of specific subtypes and have allowed for increased complexity in the number and kind of variables included in analyses. Additionally, the empirical clustering has permitted investigators to address subtyping issues such as continuity, reliability, and validity in systematic, unbiased fashions.

Many of the studies conducted using these methods, however, have been atheoretical in nature. Further, because these methods are not probability-based, great care must be invested in the selection of assessment variables, decisions about cluster retention versus deletion, and how the reliability and validity of the final subtyping model will be addressed. Nonetheless, it is clear that the empirical classification models do allow the researcher greater power and flexibility in exploring potential classification schemes.

Directly related to the advances noted from the application of classification technology is the large number of subtyping models that have been proffered during the past decade. Given that the field is in the beginning stages of classification endeavors, all of these efforts are noteworthy. There have been several exemplary studies completed to date, however, that should serve as a foundation for future investigations. Specifically, the subtyping models presented by Rourke (1985), Lyon and Watson (1981), Satz and colleagues (Morris, Blashfield, & Satz, 1986; Satz & Morris, 1981), and Spreen and Haaf (1986) provide excellent guidelines for future research. Their contributions lie not so much in the subtypes identified as in the solid empirical technology and methodology used.

For example, Satz and colleagues avoided the definitional issues inherent in learning disabilities and statistically determined a disabled group of learners. Morris et al. (1986) and Spreen and Haaf (1986) addressed the complex issue of subtype continuity, and the latter investigators extended findings into the young adult years, a population that has received an increased amount of attention over the past several years. Finally, all of these studies have strengthened the neuropsychological foundations that have been proposed for this group of disorders.

Other Advances

Related to the quest for an acceptable and clinically feasible subtyping model has been the development of other relevant concerns. In particular, the assessment methods employed in determining the various profiles have been quite varied. Methods have ranged from isolated foci on academic-achievement, neurolinguistic, neuropsychological, and social-emotional variables, to a multidimensional focus involving a combination of variables. All of these efforts are important. For example, studies that have used academic achievement variables in the subtype identification may help to establish ecological validity because they begin classification according to the identified academic problem. Further, neurolinguistic models, used primarily in the clinical-inferential domain, hold promise for describing in detail one of the major components (i.e., language) involved in the learning process. It remains, however, for these descriptive strategies to be applied to other academic areas and across other processing domains. The application of empirical classification methods to these descriptive data also awaits study.

Advances in the assessment of specific subtypes also have been suggested. Here, researchers have advocated using more developmentally appropriate, dynamic tasks. Similarly, other researchers have advocated the use of fewer modality-specific measures and more measures evaluating the interactive components of learning (e.g., strategies, metacognition). These kinds of assessment strategies not only will be more appropriate to the developmental changes that occur in the learning process, but their dynamic nature will contribute to suggestions for treatment interventions. The direct application of assessment data to treatment planning is of extraordinary importance if the classification of learning disabilities is to be successful. Homogeneous and reliable subtypes of individuals with learning disabilities have limited clinical utility if they cannot be validated with respect to differential treatment interventions. Including a standard set of variables (e.g., marker variables) in assessments also will permit improved comparison efforts and, perhaps, a better integration of data. It is clear that the degree of detail of variables included in the classification model is directly related to the degree of detail of the identified subtypes.

Although the search for learning disability subtypes is in an early stage of development, the examination of their associated social-emotional features and treatment interventions is of even more recent origin. Results are far from conclusive, but it does appear that differential social-emotional profiles may be associated with particular subtypes of learning disabilities. Despite preliminary estimates that many, perhaps as many as half, of learning disabled individuals evidence a relatively normal personality profile, it seems that particular patterns of social-emotional disturbance may characterize particular subtypes of learning disabilities. Obviously, this area requires further study, particularly as classification models change and research sophistication improves. The literature reported to date, however, clearly suggests that social-emotional factors are an important aspect of the assessment of learning disability subtypes.

Further, preliminary evidence from the treatment domain supports the efficacy of subtype-to-treatment matches that contribute, at least in part, to maximizing the learning potential of a learning disabled individual. It is clear from the few studies that have been conducted, however, that such matches do not account for all of the variance associated with learning. The importance of other variables (e.g., characteristics of teacher, learner, environment, and task) in the conceptualization of treatment models needs to be given weighted consideration (Lyon & Toomey, 1985). Consistent with the multidimensional nature of learning disabilities, comprehensive treatment interventions also should be approached in multidimensional fashions in order to address the diverse needs of learning disabled individuals (e.g., social-emotional as well as academic concerns).

Future Directions

Advances in the area of learning disability subtyping have continued to emerge, but the area still has far to go before a particular subtyping model will be accepted routinely by researchers and clinicians. Many critical issues remain unresolved, not the least of which are definitional in nature.

Perhaps one primary question that remains is, "How many different subtypes are there?" It would be presumptuous at this time to say with any certainty how many subtypes exist. The answer remains elusive; however, it probably is safe to say that the number of subtypes exceeds the numbers initially suggested by many of the clinical-inferential models. Although consistent with neurodevelopmental theory, this question requires continued exploration. Findings from the Task Force on Nosology (David, 1988) and other such multidisciplinary efforts are anxiously awaited.

It remains important, however, for such explorations to be pursued in a logical, theoretical manner. One approach is for all relevant variables to be included in proposed classification model. This will ensure that all major functional domains are addressed in classifying learning disabled individuals. Another approach advocates a more selective inclusion of variables, perhaps from a single functional domain (e.g., language) and, thus, has the potential to classify learning disabled individuals in a more refined manner. With respect to the latter approach, it seems that the neurolinguistic variables may prove especially productive by providing detailed behavioral data to identify subtypes. The application of these approaches to other academic areas besides reading, however, must be pursued in order to be useful to broader domains of learning.

The data presented to date suggest that the empirical classification models provide the most power and flexibility for establishing classification models. Researchers using these techniques, however, should move toward providing guidelines for their appropriate use for learning disability classification. At present, multiple solutions can be obtained from the same data depending on the strategies used. Therefore, it is important that guidelines suggested for their use be based on well-considered and objective clinical judgment. This will promote improved comparisons among studies and various classification models.

Another important area that requires further effort concerns the continuity of learning disability subtypes. Although this volume concentrated largely on learning disabilities in children and adolescents, there is a rapidly advancing literature dealing with adult learning disabilities (e.g., Miles, 1986). To date, few longitudinal studies have been completed that investigated the issue of subtype continuity, and even fewer of these have followed subjects into the adult years. It is important for additional studies to investigate this concern, particularly in terms of prognostic issues that are germane to treatment.

The efficacy of subtype-to-treatment paradigms also requires further development. In addition, the general utility of cognitive-behavioral (Horton & Puente, 1986) and cognitive-developmental principles (Lyon & Toomey, 1985) in the treatment of learning disabilities remains to be determined, particularly with respect to selected subtypes. It is important for research endeavors directed at treatment to attempt to adhere to methodological constraints and to move away from anecdotal reports and case study claims of improvement. Success in the treatment arena for a specific subtype model may be among the best tests for determining the ecological validity of that classification model.

In addition, the ICLD (1987) has advanced several other initiatives, some of which have implications for policy research. For example, the ICLD concluded that further study is warranted with respect to accurate prevalence estimates of learning disabilities and their underlying etiologies, particularly as applied to specific subtypes. Moreover, the ICLD advocated increasing multidisciplinary efforts in the study of this group of disorders and establishing actions to improve the dissemination of research findings. Specific priorities delineated by the ICLD included those related to: (a) etiology, particularly as it relates to neurobiological mechanisms; (b) diagnosis; (c) treatment; and (d) prevention.

McKinney (1988) noted similar directions for future research. In contrast to the ICLD's focus on etiology, however, McKinney argued for more process-oriented research. Here, such research would emphasize the processes by which individuals within particular subtypes learn information as opposed to describing deficits or focusing on etiology. Most studies to date have addressed deficit aspects of learning; that is, how individuals fail to learn rather than how they succeed in learning situations. Perhaps the latter may provide useful classification parameters as well. Finally, given persistent concerns of misclassification, McKinney called for comparative studies of different diagnostic groups to improve clinical differentiation.

This volume has attempted to provide a compendium of the literature of the learning disability subtyping area. As the literature presented in this volume attests, however, the classification of learning disabilities is only at a beginning stage of clarification, with related areas, such as social-emotional functioning and treatment, only now emerging. Given the information generated at the present time, it is recommended that investigators heed the advice of Kavale and Nye (1985/86), Lyon (1985b), and McKinney (1988) who urged that measurement and methodology be directed toward the development of a single nosology that has merit from theoretical, developmental, and treatment perspectives.

References

Aaron, P.G. (1978). Dyslexia, an imbalance in cerebral information processing strategies. *Perceptual and Motor Skills*, *47*, 699–706.

Aaron, P.G. (1981). Diagnosis and remediation of learning disabilities in children: A neuropsychological key approach. In G.W. Hynd & J.E. Obrzut (Eds.), *Neuropsychological assessment and the school-age child: Issues and procedures* (pp. 303–334). New York: Grune & Stratton.

Accardo, P.J. (1980). *A neurodevelopmental perspective on specific learning disabilities*. Baltimore: University Park Press.

Achenbach, T.M. (1985). *Assessment and taxonomy of child and adolescent psychopathology*. Beverly Hills, CA: Sage.

Achenbach, T.M., & Edelbrock, C.S. (1983). *Manual for the Child Behavior Checklist and Revised Child Behavior Profile*. Burlington: University of Vermont.

ACLD (1985). CLD offers new definition. *Special Education Today*, *2*, 19.

Adams, K.M. (1985). Theoretical, methodological, and statistical issues. In B.P. Rourke (Ed.), *Neuropsychology of learning disabilities: Essentials of subtype analysis* (pp. 17–39). New York: Guilford Press.

Adelman, H.S. (1979a). Diagnostic classification of LD: A practical necessity and a procedural problem. *Learning Disability Quarterly*, *2*, 56–62.

Adelman, H.S. (1979b). Diagnostic classification of LD: Research and ethical perspectives as related to practice. *Learning Disability Quarterly*, *2*, 5–16.

Adelman H.S., & Taylor, L. (1986). The problems of definition and differentiation and the need for a classification schema. *Journal of Learning Disabilities*, *19*, 514–520.

Alexander, P.A. (1984). Enlarging the gap between theory and practice: A review of the Boder Test of Reading-Spelling Patterns. *School Psychology Review*, *13*, 529–533.

Alfano, D.P., & Finlayson, M.A.J. (1987). Clinical neuropsychology in rehabilitation. *The Clinical Neuropsychologist*, *1*, 105–123.

Algozzine, B., & Ysseldyke, J.E. (1986). The future of the LD field: Screening and diagnosis. *Journal of Learning Disabilities*, *19*, 394–398.

Alley, G.R., & Deshler, D.D. (1979). *Teaching the learning disabled adolescent: Strategies and methods*. Denver: Love Publishing Co.

Aram, D.M., & Nation J.E. (1975). Patterns of language behavior in children with developmental language disorders. *Journal of Speech and Hearing Research*, *18*, 229–241.

Arter, J.A., & Jenkins, J.R. (1979). Differential diagnostic-prescriptive teaching: A critical appraisal. *Review of Educational Research*, *49*, 517–555.

Axelrod, L. (1982). Social perception in learning disabled adolescents. *Journal of Learning Disabilities*, *15*, 610–613.

Aylward, E.H. (1984). Lateral asymmetry in subgroups of dyslexic children. *Brain and Language*, *22*, 221–231.

Ayres, A.A., Cooley, E.J., & Severson, H.H. (1988). Educational translation of the Kaufman Assessment Battery for Children: A construct validity study. *School Psychology Review*, *17*, 113–124.

Badian, N.A. (1983). Dyscalculia and nonverbal disorders of learning. In H.R. Myklebust (Ed.), *Progress in learning disabilities* (Vol. 5, pp. 235–264). New York: Grune & Stratton.

Bakker, D.J. (1967). Temporal order, meaningfulness, and reading ability. *Perceptual and Motor Skills*, *24*, 1027–1030.

Bakker, D.J. (1972). *Temporal order in disturbed reading*. Rotterdam: Univesity Press.

Bakker, D.J. (1973). Hemispheric specialization and stages in the learning to read process. *Bulletin of the Orton Society*, *23*, 15–27.

Bakker, D.J. (1979a). Perceptual asymmetries and reading proficiency. In M. Bortner (Ed.), *Cognitive growth and development* (pp. 134–152). New York: Brunner/Mazel.

Bakker, D.J. (1979b). Hemispheric differences and reading strategies: Two dyslexias? *Bulletin of the Orton Society*, *29*, 84–100.

Bakker, D.J. (1981). Cognitive deficits and cerebral asymmetry. *Journal of Research and Development in Education*, *15*, 48–54.

Bakker, D.J. (1984). The brain as a dependent variable. *Journal of Clinical and Experimental Neuropsychology*, *6*, 1–16.

Bakker, D.J., Licht, R., Kok, A., & Bouma, A. (1980). Cortical responses to word reading by right- and left-eared normal and reading-disturbed children. *Journal of Clinical Neuropsychology*, *2*, 1–12.

Bakker, D.J., Moerland, R., & Goekoop-Hoefkens, M. (1981). Effects of hemisphere-specific stimulation on the reading performance of dyslexic boys: A pilot study. *Journal of Clinical and Experimental Neuropsychology*, *3*, 155–159.

Bakker, D., & Vinke, J. (1985). Effects of hemisphere-specific stimulation on brain activity and reading in dyslexics. *Journal of Clinical and Experimental Neuropsychology*, *7*, 505–525.

Bandura, R. (1977). *Social learning theory*. Englewood Cliffs, NJ: Prentice-Hall.

Bannatyne, A. (1966). The etiology of dyslexia and the colorphonics system. In J. Money (Ed.), *The disabled reader: Education of the dyslexic child*. Baltimore: Johns Hopkins Press.

Bannatyne, A. (1971). *Language, reading, and learning disabilities: Psychology, neuropsychology, diagnosis and remediation*. Springfield, IL: Charles C Thomas.

Barkley, R.A. (1984). Learning disabilities. In E.J. Mash & L.G. Terdal (Eds)., *Behavioral assessment of childhood disorders* (pp. 441–482). New York: Guilford Press.

Bartel, N.R., & Guskin, S.L. (1980). A handicap as a social phenomenon. In W.M. Cruickshank (Ed.), *Psychology of exceptional children and youth* (4th ed.) (pp. 45–73). Englewood Cliffs, NJ: Prentice-Hall.

Bateman, B.D. (1966). Learning disorders. *Journal of Educational Research*, *5*, 36.

Bateman, B. (1968). *Interpretation of the 1961 Illinois Test of Psycholinguistic*

Abilities. Seattle: Special Child Publications.

Bauserman, D.N., & Obrzut, J.E. (1981). Spatial and the temporal matching ability among subgroups of disabled readers. *Contemporary Educational Psychology*, *6*, 306–313.

Bayliss, J., & Liversey, P.J. (1985). Cognitive strategies of children with reading disabilities and normal readers in visual sequential memory. *Journal of Learning Disabilities*, *13*, 326–332.

Beauvois, M.F., & Derouesne, J. (1979). Phonological alexia: Three dissociations. *Journal of Neurology, Neurosurgery, and Psychiatry*, *42*, 1115–1124.

Becker, M.G., Isaac, W., & Hynd, G.W. (1987). Neuropsychological development of nonverbal behaviors attributed to "frontal lobe" functioning. *Developmental Neuropsychology*, *3*, 275–298.

Bender, L.A. (1956). *Psychology of children with organic brain disorders*. Springfield, IL: Charles C Thomas.

Bender, L.A. (1957). Specific reading disabilities as a maturational lag. *Bulletin of the Orton Society*, *7*, 9–18.

Bender, W.M. (1987). Secondary personality and behavioral problems in adolescents with learning disabilities. *Journal of Learning Disabilities*, *20*, 208–285.

Benton, A.L. (1975). Developmental dyslexia: Neurological aspects. In W.J. Friedlander (Ed.), *Advances in neurology* (Vol. 7, pp. 1–47). New York: Raven Press.

Benton, A.L. (1977). Reflections on the Gerstmann syndrome. *Brain and Language*, *4*, 45–62.

Benton, A.L. (1987). Mathematical disability and the Gerstmann syndrome. In G. Deloche & X. Seron (Eds.), *Mathematical disabilities: A cognitive neuropsychological perspective* (pp. 111–120). Hillsdale, NJ: Lawrence Erlbaum.

Benton, A.L., Hamsher, K., Varney, N.R., & Spreen, O. (1983). *Contributions to neuropsychological assessment: A clinical manual*. New York: Oxford University Press.

Biederman, J., & Jelliner, M.S. (1983). Current concepts: Psychopharmacology in children. *New England Journal of Medicine*, *308*, 968–972.

Bing, S.B. (1985). A review of the Boder Test of Reading-Spelling Patterns: A diagnostic screening test for subtypes of reading disability. *Psychology in the Schools*, *22*, 488–489.

Birch, H.G. (1962). Dyslexia and the maturation of visual function. In J. Money (Ed.), *Reading disabilities: Progress and research needs in dyslexia* (pp. 161–169). Baltimore: Johns Hopkins Press.

Birch, H.G., & Belmont, S. (1964). Auditory-visual integration in normal and retarded readers. *American Journal of Orthopsychiatry*, *34*, 852–861.

Birch, H.G., & Belmont, L. (1965). Auditory-visual integration, intelligence, and reading ability in school children. *Perceptual and Motor Skills*, *20*, 295–305.

Blank, M., & Bridger, W.H. (1964). Cross-modal transfer in nursery school children. *Journal of Comparative and Physiological Psychology*, *58*, 227–282.

Blank, M., & Bridger, W. (1966). Deficiencies in verbal labeling in retarded readers. *American Journal of Orthopsychiatry*, *36*, 840–847.

Blank, M., Weider, S., & Bridger, W. (1968). Verbal deficiencies in abstract thinking in early reading retardation. *American Journal of Orthopsychiatry*, *38*, 823–834.

Blashfield, R.K. (1980). Propositions regarding the use of cluster analysis in clinical research. *Journal of Consulting and Clinical Psychology*, *3*, 456–459.

Board of Trustees of the Council for Learning Disabilities. (1987). The CLD position statements. *Journal of Learning Disabilities*, *20*, 349–350.

Boder, E. (1970). Developmental dyslexia: A new diagnostic approach based on the identification of three subtypes. *The Journal of School Health*, *40*, 289–290.

Boder, E. (1971). Developmental dyslexia: A diagnostic screening procedure based on three characteristic patterns of reading and spelling. In B. Bateman (Ed.), *Learning disorders, Vol. 1.* Washington: Special Child Publications.

Boder, E. (1973). Developmental dyslexia: A diagnostic approach based on three atypical reading-spelling patterns. *Developmental Medicine and Child Neurology*, *15*, 663–687.

Boder, E., & Jarrico, S. (1982). *The Boder Test of Reading-Spelling Patterns.* New York: Grune & Stratton.

Boll, T.J. (1974). Behavioral correlates of cerebral damage in children aged 9–14. In R.M. Reitan & L.A. Davison (Eds.), *Clinical neuropsychology: Current status and applications* (pp. 91–102). New York: John Wiley.

Bouma, A., Bakker, D.J., & Gardien, C.J. (1988). Hemisphere-specific stimulation through tactile modality in dyslexics [Abstract]. *Journal of Clinical and Experimental Neuropsychology*, *10*, 323.

Bouma, H., & Legein, C.P. (1977). Foveal and parafoveal recognition of letters and words by dyslexics and average readers. *Neuropsychologia*, *15*, 69–80.

Boyan, C. (1985). California's new eligibility criteria: Legal and program implications. *Exceptional Children*, *52*, 131–141.

Brainerd, C.J., Kingma, J., & Howe, M.L. (1986). Long-term memory development and learning disability: Storage and retrieval loci of disabled/nondisabled differences. In S.J. Ceci (Ed.), *Handbook of cognitive, social, and neuropsychological aspects of learning disabilities* (pp. 161–184). Hillsdale, NJ: Lawrence Erlbaum.

Breen, M.J. (1986). Cognitive patterns of learning disability subtypes as measured by the Woodcock-Johnson Psychoeducational Battery. *Journal of Learning Disabilities*, *19*, 86–90.

Brodal, A. (1981). *Neurological anatomy in relation to clinical medicine* (3rd ed.). New York: Oxford University Press.

Bruck, M. (1986). Social and emotional adjustments of learning-disabled children: A review of the issues. In S.J. Cecil (Ed.), *Handbook of cognitive, social, and neuropsychological aspects of learning disabilities* (Vol. 1, pp. 361–380). Hillsdale, NJ: Lawrence Erlbaum.

Bryan, T. (1974a). An observational analysis of learning disabled children. *Journal of Learning Disabilities*, *7*, 199–206.

Bryan, T.H. (1974b). Peer popularity of learning disabled children. *Journal of Learning Disabilities*, *7*, 621–625.

Bryan, T.H. (1976). Peer popularity of learning disabled children: A replication. *Journal of Learning Disabilities*, *9*, 307–311.

Bryan, T., Bay, M., & Donahue, M. (1988). Implications of the learning disabilities definition for the regular education initiative. *Journal of Learning Disabilities*, *21*, 23–28.

Byring, R., & Jarvilehto, T. (1985). Auditory and visual evoked potentials of school boys with spelling disabilities. *Developmental Medicine and Child Neurology*, *27*, 141–148.

Cambell, S. (1974). Cognitive styles and behavior problems of clinic boys. *Journal of Abnormal Child Psychology*, *2*, 307–312.

Camp, B., & McCabe, L. (1977). *The Denver reading and spelling test, research manual.* Denver: University of Colorado Medical Center.

Carnine, D., & Kinder, D. (1985). Teaching low performing students to apply generative and schema strategies to narrative and expository material. *Remedial and Special Education (RASE)*, *6*, 20–30.

Carter, J.L., & Russell, H.L. (1985). Use of EMG biofeedback procedures with learning disabled children in a clinical and an educational setting. *Journal of Learning Disabilities*, *18*, 213–216.

Cattell, R.B., Coulter, M.A., & Tsujioka, B. (1966). The taxonomic recognition of types and functional emergents. In R.B. Cattell (Ed.), *Handbook of multivariate experimental psychology* (pp. 288–329). Chicago: Rand-McNally.

Cawley, J.F., & Webster, R.E. (1981). Reading and behavior disorders. In G. Brown, R.L. McDowell, & J. Smith (Eds.), *Educating adolescents with behavior disorders* (pp. 294–325). Columbus, OH: Charles E. Merrill.

Chapman, R.B., Larsen, S.C., & Parker, R.M. (1979). Interactions of first grade classroom teachers with learning disabled student. *Journal of Learning Disabilities*, *12*, 225–230.

Child Neurology Society, Task Force on Nosology of Disorders of Higher Cerebral Function in Children. (1981). *Proposed nosology of disorders of higher cerebral function in children.* Washington, DC: Author.

Childs, B., & Finucci, J.M. (1983). Genetics, epidemiology, and specific reading disability. In M. Rutter (Ed.), *Developmental neuropsychiatry* (pp. 507–519). New York: Guilford Press.

Christensen, A.L. (1975). *Luria's neuropsychological investigation.* Copenhagen: Munksgaard.

Clairborne, J.H. (1906). Types of congenital symbol amblyopia. *Journal of the American Medical Association*, *47*, 1813–1816.

Clark, F.L., Deshler, D.D., Schumaker, J.B., & Alley, G.R. (1984). Visual imagery and self-questioning strategies to improve comprehension of written materials. *Journal of Learning Disabilities*, *17*, 145–149.

Clark, M.M. (1970). *Reading difficulties in school.* Harmondsworth: Penguin Press.

Cohen, J., & Breslin, P.W. (1984). Visual evoked responses in dyslexic children. *Annals of the New York Academy of Sciences*, *425*, 338–343.

Cohen, M., Krawiecki, N., & DuRant, R.H. (1987). The neuropsychological approach to the remediation of dyslexia. *Archives of Clinical Neuropsychology*, *2*, 163–173.

Cohen, R.L., & Netley, C. (1978). Cognitive deficits, learning disabilities and WISC-performance consistency. *Developmental Psychiatry*, *14*, 6.

Cohen, R.L., & Netley, C. (1981). Short term memory deficits in reading disabled children in the absence of opportunity for rehearsal strategies. *Intelligence*, *5*, 69–76.

Coltheart, M. (1980). Deep dyslexia: A review of the syndrome. In M. Coltheart, K. Patterson, & J.C. Marshall (Eds.), *Deep dyslexia* (pp. 22–47). Boston: Routledge & Kegan Paul.

Conners, C.K. (1973). Rating scales for use in drug studies with children. *Psychopharmacology Bulletin Special Issue: Pharmacotherapy with Children*, *9*, 24–60.

Cook, J.M., & Welch, M.W. (1980). Reading as a function of visual and auditory process training. *Learning Disability Quarterly*, *3*, 76–87.

Craig, D.L. (1979). Neuropsychological assessment in public psychiatric hospitals: The current state of practice. *Clinical Neuropsychology*, *1*, 107.

Cromwell, R.L., Blashfield, R.K., & Strauss, J.S. (1975). Criteria for classification systems. In N. Hobbs (Ed.), *Issues in the classification of children* (Vol. 1, pp. 4–25). San Francisco: Jossey-Bass.

Cruickshank, W.M. (1972). Some issues facing the field of learning disability. *Journal of Learning Disabilities*, *5*, 380–388.

Cullinan, D., Epstein, M., & Dembinski, R. (1979). Behavior problems of educationally handicapped and normal pupils. *Journal of Abnormal Child Psychology*, *7*, 495–502.

Curtiss, S., & Tallal, P. (1988). Neurolinguistic correlates of specific developmental language impairment [Abstract]. *Journal of Clinical and Experimental Neuropsychology*, *10*, 18–19.

Dahmen, W., Hartje, W., Büssing, A., & Sturm, W. (1982). Disorders of calculation in aphasic patients: Spatial versus verbal components. *Neuropsychologia*, *20*, 145–153.

Dalby, J., & Gibson, D. (1981). Functional cerebral lateralization in subtypes of disabled readers. *Brain and Language*, *14*, 35–48.

D'Amato, R.C., Gray, J.W., & Dean, R.S. (in press). A comparison between intelligence and neuropsychological functioning. *Journal of School Psychology*.

Das, J.P., Kirby, J.R., & Jarman, R.F. (1979). *Simultaneous and successive cognitive processes*. New York: Academic Press.

David, R. (1988). History and overview of the project [Abstract]. *Journal of Clinical and Experimental Neuropsychology*, *10*, 80.

Davidoff, J.B. (1982). Studies with non-verbal stimuli. In J.G. Beaumont (Eds.), *Divided visual field studies of cerebral organization* (pp. 30–55). New York: Academic Press.

de Ajuriaguerra, J. (1966). Speech disorders in childhood. In E.C. Carterette (Ed.), *Brain function: Speech, language, and communication* (Vol. 3, pp. 117–140). Los Angeles: University of California Press.

Decker, S.N., & DeFries, J.C. (1981). Cognitive ability profiles in families of reading-disabled children. *Developmental Medicine and Child Neurology*, *23*, 217–227.

de Hirsch, K., Jansky, J., & Langford, W. (1966). *Predicting reading failure*. New York: Harper & Row.

Del Dotto, J.E., Fisk, J.L., & Rourke, B.P. (1988). Differential subtypes of adaptive impairment in a neuropsychologic service population [Abstract]. *Journal of Experimental and Clinical Neuropsychology*, *10*, 57.

Del Dotto, J.E., & Rourke, B.P. (1985). Subtypes of left-handed learning-disabled children. In B.P. Rourke (Ed.), *Neuropsychology of learning disabilities. Essentials of subtypes analysis* (pp. 89–103). New York: Guilford Press.

Delis, D.C., Kramer, J.H., Kaplan, E., & Ober, B.A. (1986). *The California Verbal Learning Test: Children's Version*. New York: Psychological Corp.

Deloche, G., Andreewsky, E., & Desi, M. (1982). Surface dyslexia: A case report and some theoretical implications to reading models. *Brain and Language*, *15*, 12–31.

Deloche, G., & Seron, K. (1982). From three to 3: A differential analysis of skills in transcoding quantities between patients with Broca's and Wernicke's aphasia. *Brain, 105,* 719–733.

Deloche, G., & Seron, K. (Eds.). (1987). *Mathematical disabilities: A cognitive neuropsychological perspective.* Hillsdale, NJ: Lawrence Erlbaum.

DeLuca, J., Del Dotto, J., & Rourke, B. (1987). Subtypes of arithmetic disabled children: A neuropsychological taxonomic approach [Abstract]. *Journal of Clinical and Experimental Neuropsychology, 9,* 26.

Denckla, M.B. (1972). Clinical syndromes in learning disabilities: The case for "splitting" vs. "lumping." *Journal of Learning Disabilities, 5,* 401–406.

Denckla, M.B. (1978). Minimal brain dysfunction. In J. Chall & A. Mirsky (Eds.), *Education and the brain.* Chicago: University of Chicago Press.

Denckla, M.B. (1981). Minimal brain dysfunction and dyslexia: Beyond diagnosis by exclusion. In M.E. Blair, I. Rapin, & M. Kinsbourne (Eds.), *Child neurology.* New York: Spectrum.

Denckla, M.B., LeMay, M., & Chapman, C.A. (1985). Few CT scan abnormalities found even in neurologically impaired learning disabled children. *Journal of Learning Disabilities, 18,* 132–135.

Denckla, M.B., & Rudel, R. (1976a). Naming of pictured objects by dyslexic and other learning disabled children. *Brain and Language, 3,* 1–15.

Denckla, M.B., & Rudel, R. (1976b). Rapid "automatized" naming (RAN): Dyslexia differentiated from other learning disabilities. *Neuropsychologia, 14,* 471–479.

Deshler, D.D., Alley, G.R., & Carlson, S.C. (1980). Learning strategies: An approach to mainstreaming secondary students with learning disabilities. *Education Unlimited, 2,* 6–11.

Dimond, S.J., & Brouwers, E.Y.M. (1976). Improvement of human memory through the use of drugs. *Psychopharmacology, 49,* 307–309.

Doehring, D.G. (1985). Reading disability subtypes: Interactions of reading and nonreading deficits. In B.P. Rourke (Ed.), *Neuropsychology of learning disabilities. Essentials of subtype analysis* (pp. 133–146). New York: Guilford Press.

Doehring, D.G., & Hoshko, I.M. (1977). Classification of reading problems by the Q-technique of factor analysis. *Cortex, 13,* 281–294.

Doehring, D.G., Hoshko, I.M., & Bryans, B.N. (1979). Statistical classification of children with reading problems. *Journal of Clinical Neuropsychology, 1,* 5–16.

Doehring, D.G., Trites, R.L., Patel, P.G. & Fiedorowicz, A.M. (1981). *Reading disabilities: The interaction of reading, language, and neuropsychological deficits.* New York: Academic Press.

Dooling, E.C., Chi, J.G., & Gilles, F.H. (1983). Telencephalic development: Changing gyral patterns. In F.H. Gilles, A. Leviton, & E.C. Dooling (Eds.), *The developing human brain: Growth and epidemiologic neuropathology* (pp. 94–104). Boston: John Wright.

Doris, J. (1986). Learning disabilities. In S.J. Ceci (Ed.), *Handbook of cognitive, social, and neuropsychological aspects of learning disabilities* (pp. 3–54). Hillsdale, NJ: Lawrence Erlbaum.

Dorval, B., McKinney, J.D., & Feagans, L. (1982). Teacher interaction with learning disabled children and average achievers. *Journal of Pediatric Psychology, 17,* 317–330.

Drake, W.E. (1968). Clinical and pathological findings in a child with a developmental learning disability. *Journal of Learning Disabilities, 1*, 486–502.

Duane, D.D. (1979). Toward a definition of dyslexia: A summary of views. *Bulletin of the Orton Society, 29*, 56–64.

Duffy, F.H., Burchfiel, J.L., & Lombroso, C.T. (1979). Brain electrical activity mapping (BEAM): A method for extending the clinical utility of EEG and evoked potential data. *Annals of Neurology, 5*, 309–321.

Duffy, F.H., Denckla, M.B., Bartels, P.H., & Sandini, G. (1980). Dyslexia: Regional differences in brain electrical activity by topographic mapping. *Annals of Neurology, 7*, 412–420.

Duffy, F.H., Denckla, M.B., Bartels, P.H., Sandini, G., & Kiessling, L.S. (1980). Dyslexia: Automated diagnosis by computerized classification of brain electrical activity. *Annals of Neurology, 7*, 421–428.

Dupont, H., Gardner, O.S., & Brody, D.S. (1974). *Toward affective development.* Circle Pines, MN: American Guidance Service.

Dykman, R.A., Ackerman, P.T., Clements, S.D., & Peters, J.E. (1971). Specific learning disabilities: An Attentional deficit syndrome. In H.R. Myklebust (Ed.), *Progress in learning disabilities* (Vol. 2, pp. 56–93). New York: Grune & Stratton.

Elliott, S.N., Gresham, F.M., & Heffer, R.W. (1987). Social-skills interventions: Research findings and training techniques. In C.A. Maher & J.E. Zins (Eds.), *Psychoeducational interventions in the schools* (pp. 141–159). New York: Pergamon Press.

Ellis, N. (1981). Visual and name coding in dyslexic children. *Psychological Research, 43*, 201–219.

Ellis, N.C., & Miles, T.R. (1981). A lexical encoding deficiency 1: Experimental evidence. In G. Th. Pavlidis & T.R. Miles (Eds.), *Dyslexia research and its applications to education.* (pp. 177–215). New York: Wiley.

Elterman, R.D., Abel, L.A., Daroff, R.B., Dell'Osso, S.F., & Bornstein, J.J. (1980). Eye movement patterns in dyslexic children. *Journal of Learning Disabilities, 13*, 16–21.

Epps, S., Ysseldyke, J.E., & Algozzine, B. (1983). Impact of different definitions of learning disabilities on the number of students identified. *Journal of Psychoeducational Assessment, 1*, 341–352.

Epps, S., Ysseldyke, J.E., & Algozzine, B. (1985). An analysis of the conceptual framework underlying definitions of learning disabilities. *Journal of School Psychology, 23*, 133–144.

Everitt, B. (1980). *Cluster analysis* (2nd ed.). New York: Halsted Press.

Eysenck, H. (1952). *The scientific study of personality.* London: Routledge & Kegan Paul.

Farnham-Diggory, S. (1986). Commentary: Time, now, for a little serious complexity. In S.J. Cecil (Ed.), *Handbook of cognitive, social, and neuropsychological aspects of learning disabilities* (Vol. 1, pp. 123–158). Hillsdale, NJ: Lawrence Erlbaum.

Feagans, L., & Appelbaum, M.I. (1986). Language subtypes and their validation in learning disabled children. *Journal of Educational Psychology, 78*, 358–364.

Fein, D., Allen, D., & Waterhouse, L. (1988). Subtypes within pervasive developmental disorders [Abstract]. *Journal of Clinical and Experimental Neuropsychology, 10*, 80.

Fein, G., Galin, D., Johnstone, J., Yingling, C.D., Marcus, M., & Kiersch, M.E.

(1983). Electroencephalogram power spectra in normal and dyslexic children: 1. Reliability during passive conditions. *Electroencephalography and Clinical Neurophysiology, 55*, 399–405.

Fisher, J.H. (1905). Case of cogenital word-blindness (inability to learn to read). *Ophthalmic Review, 24*, 315–318.

Fisk, J.L., & Rourke, B.P. (1979). Identification of subtypes of learning disabled children at three age levels: A neuropsychological multivariate approach. *Journal of Clinical Neuropsychology, 1*, 289–310.

Fisk, J.L., & Rourke, B.P. (1983). Neuropsychological subtyping of learning-disabled children: History, methods, implications. *Journal of Learning Disabilities, 16*, 529–531.

Fleiss, J.L., Lawlor, W., Platman, S.R., & Fieve, R.R. (1971). On the use of inverted factor analysis for generating typologies. *Journal of Abnormal Psychology, 77*, 127–132.

Fletcher, J.M. (1985). Memory for verbal and nonverbal stimuli in learning disability subgroups: Analysis by selective reminding. *Journal of Experimental Child Psychology, 40*, 244–259.

Fletcher, J.M., & Morris, R. (1986). Classification of disabled learners: Beyond exclusionary definitions. In S.J. Ceci (Ed.), *Handbook of cognitive, social, and neuropsychological aspects of learning disabilities* (Vol. 1, pp. 55–80). Hillsdale, NJ: Lawrence Erlbaum.

Fletcher, J.M., & Satz, P. (1985). Cluster analysis and the search for learning disability subtypes. In B.P. Rourke (Ed.), *Neuropsychology of learning disabilities: Essentials of subtype analysis* (pp. 40–64). New York: Guilford Press.

Flynn, J. (1987). *Neurophysiologic characteristics of dyslexic subtypes and response to remediation.* Grant awarded by the Initial Teaching Alphabet Foundation. Roslyn, New York.

Flynn, J., & Deering, W. (in press). Subtypes of dyslexia: Investigation of Boder's system using quantitative neurophysiology. *Developmental Medicine and Child Neurology.*

Forness, S.R., & Kavale, K.A. (1983). Remediation of learning disabilities: Part one. Issues and concepts. *Learning Disabilities, 11*, 141–152.

Forness, S.R., & Kavale, K.A. (1988). Psychopharmacologic treatment: A note on classroom effects. *Journal of Learning Disabilities, 21*, 144–147.

Fox, B., & Routh, D.K. (1980). Phonemic analysis and severe reading disability in children. *Journal of Psycholinguistic Research, 9*, 115–119.

Fried, I. (1979). Cerebral dominance and subtypes of developmental dyslexia. *Bulletin of the Orton Society, 29*, 101–112.

Fried, I., Tanguay, P.E., Boder, E., Doubleday, C., & Greensite, M. (1981). Developmental dyslexia: Electrophysiological evidence of clinical subgroups. *Brain and Language, 12*, 14–22.

Friedman, A., & Polson, M.C. (1981). Hemispheres as independent resource systems: Limited-capacity processing and cerebral specialization. *Journal of Experimental Psychology: Human Perception and Performance, 7*, 1031–1058.

Frith, U. (1983). The similarities and differences between reading and spelling problems. In M. Rutter (Ed.), *Developmental neuropsychiatry* (pp. 453–472). New York: Guilford Press.

Frostig, M. (1964). *Frostig Developmental Test of Visual Perception.* Palo Alto, CA: Consulting Psychologists Press.

Frostig, M., & Horne, D. (1964). *The Frostig Program for the Development of Visual Perception. Teacher's Guide.* Chicago: Follett.

Funnell, E. (1983). Phonological processes in reading: New evidence from acquired dyslexia. *British Journal of Psychology*, 2, 159–180.

Gaddes, W.H. (1985). *Learning disabilities and brain function: A neuropsychological approach (2nd ed.).* New York: Springer-Verlag.

Gadow, K.D. (1986). *Children on medication.* San Diego, CA: College-Hill.

Gajar, A. (1979). Educable mentally retarded, learning disabled, emotionally disturbed: Similarities and differences. *Exceptional Children*, 45, 471–472.

Galaburda, A.M., & Kemper, T.C. (1979). Cytoarchitectonic abnormalities in developmental dyslexia: A case study. *Annals of Neurology*, 6, 94–100.

Galaburda, A.M., Sherman, G.F., Rosen, G.D., Aboitiz, F., & Geschwind, N. (1985). Developmental dyslexia: Four consecutive patients with cortical anomalies. *Annals of Neurology*, 18, 222–233.

Garfinkel, B.D., Wender, P., Sloman, L., & O'Neill, I. (1983). Tricyclic antidepressant and methylphenidate treatment of attention deficit disorder in children. *Journal of Child Psychiatry*, 22, 343–348.

Garrett, M.K., & Crump, W.D. (1980). Peer acceptance, teacher references, and self-appraisal of social status among learning-disabled students. *Learning Disability Quarterly*, 3, 42–48.

Geary, D.C., & Gilger, J.W. (1984). The Luria-Nebraska Neuropsychological Battery–Children's Revision: Comparison of learning disabled and normal children matched on Full Scale IQ. *Perceptual and Motor Skills*, 58, 115–118.

Geary, D.C., & Gilger, J.W. (1985). The Luria-Nebraska Neuropsychological Battery–Children's Revision: An instrument for school psychologists? *School Psychology Review*, 14, 383–384.

Geary, D.C., Jennings, S.M., Schultz, D.D., & Alper, T.G. (1984). The diagnostic accuracy of the Luria-Nebraska Neuropsychological Battery–Children's Revision for 9 to 12 year old learning disabled children. *School Psychology Review*, 13, 375–380.

Gerber, P.J., & Zinkgraf, S.A. (1982). A comparative study of social-perceptual ability in learning disabled and nonhandicapped students. *Learning Disability Quarterly*, 5, 374–378.

Geschwind, N. (1986). Dyslexia, cerebral dominance, autoimmunity, and sex hormones. In G. Th. Pavlidis & D.F. Fisher (Eds.), *Dyslexia. Its neuropsychology and treatment* (pp. 51–63). New York: John Wiley.

Geschwind, N., & Behan, P.O. (1982). Left handedness: Association with immune disease, migraine, and developmental learning disorders. *Proceedings of the National Academy of Sciences*, 79, 5097–5100.

Gilger, J.W., & Geary, D.C. (1985). Performance on the Luria-Nebraska Neuropsychological Test Battery–Children's Revision: A comparison of children with and without significant WISC-R VIQ-PIQ discrepancies. *Journal of Clinical Psychology*, 41, 806–811.

Ginn, R. (1979). *An analysis of various psychometric typologies of primary reading disability.* Unpublished doctoral dissertation, University of California, Los Angeles.

Glass, G.V. (1983). Effectiveness of special education. *Policy Studies Review*, 2, 65–78.

Glavin, J.P., & Annesley, F.R. (1971). Reading and arithmetic correlates of conduct-problem and withdrawn children. *Journal of Special Education*, 5, 213–291.

Glosser, G., & Koppell, S. (1987). Emotional-behavioral patterns in children with learning disabilities: Lateralized hemispheric differences. *Journal of Learning Disabilities*, 20, 365–368.

Goldberg, E., & Costa, L.D. (1981). Hemisphere differences in the acquisition and use of descriptive systems. *Brain and Language*, 14, 144–173.

Goldberg, H., & Schiffman, G. (1972). *Dyslexia: Problems of reading disabilities*. New York: Grune & Stratton.

Golden, C.J. (1981). The Luria-Nebraska Children's Battery: Theory and formulation. In G.W. Hynd & J.E. Obrzut (Eds.), *Neuropsychological assessment and the school-age child: Issues and procedures* (pp. 277–302). New York: Grune & Stratton.

Golden, C.J., Hammeke, T.A., & Purisch, A.D. (1980). *Manual for the Luria-Nebraska Neuropsychological Battery*. Los Angeles: Western Psychological Services.

Goldfried, M.R., & Sprafkin, J.N. (1976). Behavioral personality assessment. In J.T. Spence, R.C. Carson, & J.W. Thiabaut (Eds.), *Behavioral approaches to therapy* (pp. 295–321). Morristown, NJ: General Learning Press.

Goldman, R., Fristoe, M., & Woodcock, R.W. (1974). *Manual for the Goldman-Fristoe-Woodcock Auditory Skills Test Battery*. Circle Pines, MN: American Guidance Service.

Goldman, R.L., & Hardin, V.B. (1982). The social perception of learning disabled and non-learning disabled children. *Exceptional Children*, 49, 57–63.

Goldstein, D., & Dundon, W.D. (1987). Affect and cognition in learning disabilities. In S.J. Ceci (Ed.), *Handbook of cognitive, social, and neuropsychological aspects of learning disabilities* (Vol. 2, pp. 233–249). Hillsdale, NJ: Lawrence Erlbaum.

Goldstein, D., Paul, G.G., & Sanfilippo-Cohn, S. (1985). Depression and achievement in subgroups of children with learning disabilities. *Journal of Applied Developmental Psychology*, 6, 263–275.

Grafman, J., Passafiume, D., Faglioni, P., & Boller, F. (1982). Calculation disturbances in adults with focal hemispheric damage. *Cortex*, 18, 37–50.

Groenendaal, H.A., & Bakker, D.J. (1971). The part played by mediation processes in the retention of temporal sequences by two reading groups. *Human Development*, 14, 62–70.

Gross-Glenn, K., Duara, R., Yoshii, F., Barker, W., Chen, J.Y., Apicella, A., Boothe, T., & Lubs, H.A. (1988). PET-Scan reading studies of familial dyslexics [Abstract]. *Journal of Clinical and Experimental Neuropsychology*, 10, 34–35.

Guilford, J.P. (1985). The structure-of-intellect model. In B.B. Wolman (Ed.), *Handbook of intelligence: Theories, measurements and applications* (pp. 225–266). New York: John Wiley.

Gunnison, J.A. (1984). Developing educational intervention from assessments involving the K-ABC. *Journal of Special Education*, 18, 325–344.

Guskin, S.L. (1978). Theoretical and empirical strategies for the study of the labeling of mentally retarded persons. In N. Ellis (Ed.), *International review of research in mental retardation* (Vol. 9, pp. 127–158). New York: Academic Press.

Gustavson, J.L., Golden, C.J., Wilkening, G.N., Hermann, B.P., Plaisted, J.R., MacInnes, W.D., & Leark, R.A. (1984). The Luria-Nebraska Neuropsychological Battery–Children's Revision: Validation with brain-damaged and normal children. *Journal of Psychological Assessment, 2,* 199–208.

Hale, R.L., & Saxe, J.E. (1983). Profile analysis of the Wechsler Intelligence Scale for Children–Revised. *Journal of Psychoeducational Assessment, 1,* 155–162.

Hallahan, D.P., & Cruickshank, W.M. (1973). *Psychoeducational foundations of learning disabilities.* Englewood Cliffs, NJ: Prentice-Hall.

Hallahan, D.P., & Kauffman, J.M. (1977). Labels, categories, behaviors: ED, LD, and EMR reconsidered. *Journal of Special Education, 11,* 139–149.

Hallahan, D.P., Lloyd, J.W., Kauffman, J.M., & Loper, A.B. (1983). Academic problems. In R.J. Morris & T.R. Kratochwill (Eds.), *Practice of child therapy: A textbook of methods* (pp. 113–141). New York: Pergamon Press.

Halstead, W.C. (1947). *Brain and intelligence: A quantitative study of the frontal lobes.* Chicago: University of Chicago Press.

Hammill, D.D., & Larsen, S.C. (1974). The effectiveness of psycholinguistic training. *Exceptional Children, 41,* 5–15.

Hammill, D.D., Leigh, J.E., McNutt, G., & Larsen, S.C. (1981). A new definition of learning disabilities. *Learning Disability Quarterly, 4,* 336–342.

Harter, S. (1982). A developmental perspective on some parameters of self-regulation in children. In P. Karoly & F.H. Kanfer (Eds.), *Self-management and behavior change: From theory to practice.* New York: Pergamon Press.

Hartlage, L.C., & Reynolds, C.R. (1981). Neuropsychological assessment and the individualization of instruction. In G.W. Hynd & J.E. Obrzut (Eds.), *Neuropsychological assessment and the school-age child: Issues and procedures* (pp. 355–378). New York: Grune & Stratton.

Hartlage, L.C., & Telzrow, C.F. (1983). The neuropsychological basis of educational intervention. *Journal of Learning Disabilities, 16,* 521–528.

Hasher, L., & Zacks, R.T. (1979). Automatic and effortful processes in memory. *Journal of Experimental Psychology, 108,* 356–388.

Haslam, R.H., Dalby, J.T., Johns, R.D., & Rademaker, A.W. (1981). Cerebral asymmetry in developmental dyslexia. *Archives of Neurology, 38,* 679–682.

Heaton, R.K. (1981). *Manual for the Wisconsin Card Sorting Test.* Odessa, FL: Psychological Assessment Resources.

Hécaen, H., Angelergues, R., & Houillier, S. (1961). Les varietes cliniques de acalculies au cours des lesions retrorolandiques: Approche statistique du problem. *Revue Neurologique, 105,* 85–103.

Henderson, J.G. (1983). *An assessment of the effects of depression upon effortful and automatic processes in reading.* Unpublished doctoral dissertation, Temple University, Philadelphia.

Henry, A. (1975). Specific difficulties in reading. *Remedial Education, 10,* 81–85.

Hermann, K. (1959). *Reading disability: A medical study of word-blindness and related handicaps.* Copenhagen: Munksgaard.

Heverly, L.L., Isaac, W., & Hynd, G.W. (1986). Neurodevelopmental and racial differences in tactual-visual (cross-modal) discrimination in normal black and white children. *Archives of Clinical Neuropsychology, 1,* 139–145.

Hicks, C. (1980). The ITPA Visual Sequential Memory task: An alternative interpretation and the implications for good and poor readers. *British Journal of Educational Psychology, 50,* 16–25.

Hier, D.B., LeMay, M., Rosenberger, P.B., & Perlo, V.P. (1978). Developmental dyslexia: Evidence for a subgroup with a reversal of cerebral asymmetry.

214   References

Archives of Neurology, *35*, 90–92.
Hinshelwood, J. (1895). Word-blindness and visual memory. *Lancet*, *1*, 1506–1508.
Hinshelwood, J. (1900). Congenital word-blindness. *Lancet*, *2*, 1564–1570.
Hinshelwood, J. (1902). Congenital word-blindness with reports of two cases. *Opthalmic Review*, *21*, 91–99.
Hinshelwood, J. (1909). Four cases of congenital word-blindness occurring in the same family. *British Medical Journal*, *2*, 1229–1232.
Holcomb, P., Ackerman, P.T., & Dykman, R.A. (1985). ERPs: Attention and reading deficits. *Psychophysiology*, *22*, 656–667.
Holmes, C.L., & Peper, R.J. (1977). An evaluation of the use of spelling error analysis in the diagnosis of reading disabilities. *Child Development*, *48*, 1708–1711.
Hooper, S.R. (1988). Relationship between the clinical components of the Boder Test of Reading-Spelling Patterns and the Stanford Achievement Test: Validity of the Boder. *Journal of School Psychology*, *26*, 91–96.
Hooper, S.R. (1988). The prediction of learning disabilities in the preschool child: A neuropsychological perspective. In M.G. Tramontana & S.R. Hooper (Eds.), *Assessment issues in child neuropsychology* (pp. 313–335). (New York: Plenum Publishing Corp.
Hooper, S.R., Boyd, T.A., Hynd, G.W., Stahl, V., & Rubin, J. (1988). *Current definitional issues and neurobiological foundations in neurodevelopmental learning disorders.* Manuscript submitted for publication.
Hooper, S.R., & Hynd, G.W. (1985). Differential diagnosis of developmental dyslexia with the Kaufman Assessment Battery for Children (K-ABC). *Journal of Clinical Child Psychology*, *14*, 145–152.
Hooper, S.R., & Hynd, G.W. (1986). A comparison between normal and dyslexic readers on the Kaufman Assessment Battery for Children: A discriminant analysis. *Journal of Learning Disabilities*, *19*, 206–210.
Hooper, S.R., & Hynd, G.W. (1988). *Multivariate classification of disabled readers with the Kaufman Assessment Battery for Children.* Manuscript submitted for publication.
Hooper, S.R., Hynd, G.W., & Tramontana, M.G. (1988). *Visual-spatial dyslexia: A neuropsychological case report.* Manuscript submitted for publication.
Horton, A.M., Jr. (1979). Behavioral neuropsychology: Rationale and research. *Clinical Neuropsychology*, *1*, 20–23.
Horton, A.M., & Puente, A.E. (1986). Behavioral neuropsychology with children. In J.E. Obrzut & G.W. Hynd (Eds.), *Child neuropsychology: Vol. 2. Clinical practice* (pp. 299–316). Orlando, FL: Academic Press.
Howe, B. (1982). A language skills program for secondary LD students. *Journal of Learning Disabilities*, *15*, 541–544.
Howell, K.W. (1986). Direct assessment of academic performance. *School Psychology Review*, *15*, 324–335.
Hutchens, T.A., & Hynd, G.W. (1987). Medications and the school-age child and adolescent: A review. *School Psychology Review*, *16*, 527–542.
Hyman, L.M. (1983). *An investigation of the neuropsychological characteristics of learning disabled children as measured by the Luria-Nebraska (Children).* Doctoral dissertation, University of Southern California, Los Angeles.
Hynd, C.R. (1986). Educational intervention in children with developmental learning disorders. In J.E. Obrzut & G.W. Hynd (Eds.), *Child neuropsychology:*

Vol. 2. Clinical practice (pp. 265–297). Orlando FL: Academic Press.

Hynd, G.W. (1984). A review of Boder and Jarrico's Boder Test of Reading-Spelling Patterns: A diagnostic test for subtypes of reading disability. *Journal of Learning Disabilities, 17,* 512.

Hynd, G.W., & Cohen, M. (1983). *Dyslexia: Neuropsychological theory, research, and clinical differentiation.* New York: Grune & Stratton.

Hynd, G.W., Connor, R.T., & Nieves, N. (1988). Learning disability subtypes: Perspectives and methodological issues in clinical assessment. In M.G. Tramontana & S.R. Hooper (Eds.), *Assessment issues in child neuropsychology* (pp. 281–312). New York: Plenum Publishing Corp.

Hynd, G.W., & Hynd, C.R. (1984). Dyslexia: Neuroanatomical/neurolinguistic perspectives. *Reading Research Quarterly, 19,* 482–498.

Hynd, G.W., Hynd, C.R., Sullivan, H.G., & Kingsbury, T.B. (1987). Regional cerebral blood flow (rCBF) in developmental dyslexia: Activation during reading in a surface and deep dyslexic. *Journal of Learning Disabilities, 20,* 294–300.

Hynd, G.W., & Obrzut, J.E. (Eds.). (1981). *Neuropsychological assessment and the school-age child: Issues and procedures.* New York: Grune & Stratton.

Hynd, G.W., Obrzut, J.E., Hayes, F., & Becker, M.G. (1986). Neuropsychology of childhood learning disabilities. In D. Wedding, A.M. Horton, & J. Webster (Eds.), *The neuropsychology handbook: Behavioral and clinical perspectives* (pp. 456–485). New York: Springer.

Hynd, G.W., Obrzut, J.E., Hynd, C.R., & Connor, R. (1978). Attentional deficits and work attributes preferred by learning disabled children in grades 2, 4, and 6. *Perceptual and Motor Skills, 47,* 643–652.

Hynd, G.W., & Semrud-Clikeman, M. (1988). *Dyslexia and brain morphology.* Manuscript submitted for publication.

Hynd G.W., Snow, J., & Becker, M.G. (1986). Neuropsychological assessment in clinical child psychology. In B. Lahey & A. Kazdin (Eds.), *Advances in clinical child psychology.* New York: Plenum Publishing Corp.

Hynd, G.W., & Willis, W.G. (1988). *Pediatric neuropsychology.* Orlando, FL: Grune & Stratton.

Idol, L., & West J.F. (1987). Consultation in special education: Part II. Training and practice. *Journal of Learning Disabilities, 20,* 474–494.

Ingram, T.S., Mason, A.W., & Blackburn, I. (1970). A retrospective study of 82 children with reading disability. *Developmental Medicine and Child Neurology, 12,* 271–281.

Interagency Committee on Learning Disabilities. (1987). *Learning disabilities: A report to the U.S. Congress.* Washington, DC: Author.

Jackson, E. (1906). Developmental alexia (congenital word-blindness). *American Journal of Medical Science, 131,* 843–849.

Jernigan, T.J., Tallal, P., & Bellugi, U. (1988). Cerebral morphology on magnetic resonance (MR) in developmental cognitive disorders [Abstract]. *Journal of Clinical and Experimental Neuropsychology, 10,* 19.

Johnson, D.J., & Myklebust, H.R. (1967). *Learning disabilities. Educational principles and practices.* New York: Grune & Stratton.

Johnston, C.S., Fennell, E.B., & Satz, P. (1987). Learning disability subtypes: A cross-validation [Abstract]. *Journal of Clinical and Experimental Neuropsychology, 9,* 28.

Jorm, A.F. (1979a). The cognitive and neurological basis of developmental dyslexia: A theoretical framework and review. *Cognition*, 7, 19–33.

Jorm, A.F. (1979b). The nature of reading deficit in developmental dyslexia: A reply to Ellis. *Cognition*, 7, 421–433.

Joschko, M., & Rourke, B.P. (1985). Neuropsychological subtypes of learning-disabled children who exhibit the ACID pattern on the WISC. In B.P. Rourke (Ed.), *Neuropsychology of learning disabilities: Essentials of subtype analysis* (pp. 65–88). New York: Guilford Press.

Kahneman, D. (1973). *Attention and effort*. Englewood Cliffs, NJ: Prentice-Hall.

Kamphaus, R.W., & Reynolds, C.R. (1987). *Clinical and research applications of the K-ABC*. Circle Pines, MN: American Guidance Service.

Kampwirth, T.J. (1979). Teaching to preferred modalities: Is it worth it? *Claremont Reading Conference*, 163–176.

Kanfer, F.H., & Phillips, J.S. (1970). *Learning foundations of behavior therapy*. New York: John Wiley.

Kauffman, J.M. (1981). *Characteristics of children's behavior disorders* (2nd ed.). Columbus, OH: Charles E. Merrill.

Kaufman, A.S., & Kaufman, N.S. (1983). *Kaufman Assessment Battery for Children: Interpretive manual*. Circle Pines, MN: American Guidance Service.

Kavale, K.A. (1988). Epistemological relativity in learning disabilities. *Journal of Learning Disabilities*, 21, 215–218.

Kavale, K.A., & Nye, C. (1985/1986). Parameters of learning disabilities in achievement, linguistic, neuropsychological, and social/behavioral domains. *Journal of Special Education*, 19, 443–458.

Keefe, B., & Swinney, D. (1979). On the relationship of hemispheric specialization and developmental dyslexia. *Cortex*, 15, 471–481.

Keogh, B.K. (1983). Classification, compliance, and confusion. *Journal of Learning Disabilities*, 16, 25.

Keogh, B.K. (1986). A marker system for describing learning disability samples. In S.J. Ceci (Ed.), *Handbook of cognitive, social, and neuropsychological aspects of learning disabilities* (Vol. 1, pp. 81–94). Hillsdale, NJ: Lawrence Erlbaum.

Keogh, B.K., Major-Kingsley, S., Omori-Gordon, H., & Reid, H.P. (1982). *A system of marker variables for the field of learning disabilities*. Syracuse, NY: Syracuse University Prsss.

Kephart, N.C. (1971). *The slow learner in the classroom* (2nd ed.). Columbus, OH: Charles E. Merrill.

Kimberling, W.J., Pennington, B.F., & Lubs, H.A. (1983). Specific reading disability: Identification of an inherited form through linkage analysis. *Science*, 219, 1345–1347.

Kinsbourne, M. (1982). Hemispheric specialization and the growth of human understanding. *American Psychologist*, 37, 411–420.

Kinsbourne, M. (1986). Models of dyslexia and its subtypes. In G.T. Pavlidis & D.F. Fisher (Eds.), *Dyslexia: Its neuropsychology and treatment* (pp. 165–180). New York: Wiley.

Kinsbourne, M., & Caplan, P.J. (1979). *Children's learning and attentional problems*. Boston: Little, Brown.

Kinsbourne, M., & Hiscock, M. (1981). Cerebral lateralization and cognitive development: Conceptual and methodological issues. In G.W. Hynd & J.E. Obrzut (Eds.), *Neuropsychological assessment and the school-age child: Issues and procedures* (pp. 125–166). New York: Grune & Stratton.

Kinsbourne, M., & Warrington, E.K. (1963). Developmental factors in reading and writing backwardness. *British Journal of Psychology, 54*, 145–146.

Kirk, S.A. (1963). Behavioral diagnosis and remediation of learning disabilities. In *Proceedings of the Conference on Exploration into the Problems of the Perceptually Handicapped Child.* Chicago: Perceptually Handicapped Children.

Kirk, S.A., & Kirk, W.D. (1971). *Psycholinguistic learning disabilities: Diagnosis and remediation.* Urbana: University of Illinois.

Kistner, J., & Osborne, M. (1987). A longitudinal study of LD children's self-evaluations. *Learning Disability Quarterly, 10*, 258–266.

Klonoff, H., Robinson, G.C., & Thompson, G. (1969). Acute and chronic brain syndromes in children. *Developmental Medicine and Child Neurology, 11*, 198–213.

Knights, R.M. (1966). Normative data on tests for evaluating brain damage in children from 5 to 14 years of age. *Research Bulletin No. 20.* University of Western Ontario, London, Ontario.

Korhonen, T. (1985). Statistical subgrouping of learning disabled children (Abstract). *Journal of Clinical and Experimental Neuropsychology, 7*, 150–151.

Korhonen, T. (1986). A 3-year follow-up study of neuropsychologically different subtypes of learning disabled children [Abstract]. *Journal of Clinical and Experimental Neuropsychology, 8*, 119.

Korhonen, T. (1987). Stability of neuropsychological profiles in different subgroups of learning disabled children: A 3-year follow-up [Abstract]. *Journal of Clinical and Experimental Neuropsychology, 9*, 275.

Korhonen, T. (1988). External validity of subgroups of Finnish learning disabled children [Abstract]. *Journal of Clinical and Experimental Neuropsychology, 10*, 56.

Korkman, M. (1988). *NEPSY. A proposed neuropsychological test battery for young developmentally disabled children: Theory and evaluation.* Unpublished doctoral dissertation, University of Helsinki, Helsinki, Finland.

Kovacs, M. (1981). Rating scales to assess depression in school-aged children. *Acta Paedopsychiatrica, 46*, 305–315.

Krupski, A. (1986). Attention problems in youngsters with learning handicaps. In J.K. Torgeson & B.Y.L. Wong (Eds.), *Psychological and educational perspectives on learning disabilities* (pp. 161 192). Orlando, FL: Academic Press.

Kussmaul, A. (1877). Disturbance of speech. *Cyclopedia of Practical Medicine, 14*, 581.

Lakin, K.C. (1983). A response to Gene V. Glass. *Policy Studies Review, 2*, 233–239.

Landau, S., Milich, R., & McFarland, M. (1987). Social status differences among subgroups of LD boys. *Learning Disability Quarterly, 10*, 277–282.

Languis, M., & Wittrock, M.C. (1986). Integrating neuropsychological and cognitive research: A perspective for bridging brain-behavior relationships. In J.E. Obrzut & G.W. Hynd (Eds.), *Child neuropsychology: Vol. 1. Theory and research* (pp. 209–239). Orlando, FL: Academic Press.

Larivee, B. (1981). Modality preference as a model for differentiating beginning reading instruction: A review of the issues. *Learning Disability Quarterly, 4*, 180–188.

Leisman, G., & Ashkenazi, M. (1980). Aetiological factors in dyslexia: IV. Cerebral hemispheres are functionally equivalent. *Neuroscience, 11*, 157–164.

LeMay, M. (1981). Are there radiological changes in the brains of individuals with dyslexia? *Bulletin of the Orton Society, 31*, 135–141.

Lenneberg, E.H. (1967). *Biological foundations of language*. New York: Wiley.

Lennox, C., & Siegel, L. (1988). Visual and phonetic spelling errors in subtypes of children with learning disabilities [Abstract]. *Journal of Clinical and Experimental Neuropsychology*, *10*, 91.

Leton, D.A., Miyamoto, L.K., & Ryckman, D.B. (1987). Psychometric classifications of learning disabled students. *Psychology in the Schools*, *24*, 201–209.

Levine, M.D. (1987). *Developmental variation and learning disorders*. Cambridge, MA: Educators Publishing Service.

Lewis, R.B. (1983). Learning disabilities and reading: Instructional recommendations from current research. *Exceptional Children*, *50*, 230–241.

Lewis, R.D., & Lorion, R.P. (1988). Discriminative effectiveness of the Luria-Nebraska Neuropsychological Battery for LD Adolescents. *Learning Disability Quarterly*, *11*, 62–70.

Liberman, I.Y., & Shankweiler, O. (1979). Speech, the alphabet, and teaching to read. In L. Resnick & P. Weaver (Eds.), *Theory and practice of early reading* (Vol. 1, pp. 109–132). Hillsdale, NJ: Lawrence Erlbaum.

Lindsley, O.R. (1964). Direct measurement and prosthesis of retarded behavior. *Journal of Education*, *147*, 62–81.

Lloyd, J. (1980). Academic instruction and cognitive behavior modification: The need for attack strategy training. *Exceptional Education Quarterly*, *1*, 53–63.

Lou, H.C., Henriksen, L., & Bruhn, D. (1984). Focal cerebral hypoperfusion in children with dysphasia and/or attention deficit disorder. *Archives of Neurology*, *41*, 825–829.

Lovett, M.W. (1984). A developmental perspective on reading dysfunction: Accuracy and rate criteria in the subtyping of dyslexic children. *Brain and Language*, *22*, 67–91.

Lovett, M.W., Warren, P.M., Ransby, M.J., & Borden, S.L. (1987). Training the word recognition skills of dyslexic children: Treatment and transfer effects [Abstract]. *Journal of Clinical and Experimental Neuropsychology*, *9*, 53.

Lubar, J.F., Bianchini, K.J., Calhoun, W.H., Lambert, E.W., Brody, Z.H., & Shabsin, H.S. (1985). Spectral analysis of EEG differences between children with and without learning disabilities. *Journal of Learning Disabilities*, *18*, 403–408.

Lund, P.E., Yingling, C.D., Galin, D., Marcus, M., & Simons, H. (1984, February). *Validity studies of the Boder Test of Reading-Spelling Patterns*. Paper presented at the Twelfth Annual Meeting of the International Neuropsychological Society, Houston, TX.

Luria, A.R. (1966). *Human brain and psychological process*. New York: Harper & Row.

Luria, A.R. (1970). Functional organization of the brain. *Scientific American*, *222*, 66–78.

Luria, A.R. (1973). *The working brain: An introduction to neuropsychology*. New York: Basic Books.

Luria, A.R. (1980). *Higher cortical functions in man*. New York: Basic Books.

Lyle, J.G. (1969). Reading retardation and reversal tendency: A factorial study. *Child Development*, *40*, 833–843.

Lyle, J.G., & Goyen, J. (1968). Visual recognition development lag and strephosymbolia in reading retardation. *Journal of Abnormal Psychology*, *73*, 25–29.

Lyle, J.G., & Goyen, J. (1975). Effects of speed of exposure and difficulty of discrimination on visual recognition of retarded readers. *Journal of Abnormal*

Psychology, 84, 673–676.

Lyon, G.R. (1983). Learning disabled readers: Identification of subgroups. In H.R. Myklebust (Ed.), *Progress in learning disabilities* (Vol. 5, pp. 103–133). New York: Grune & Stratton.

Lyon, G.R. (1985a). Educational validation of learning disability subtypes. In B.P. Rourke (Ed.), *Neuropsychology of learning disabilities: Essentials of subtype analysis* (pp. 228–256). New York: Guilford Press.

Lyon, G.R. (1985b). Identification and remediation of learning disability subtypes: Preliminary findings. *Learning Disabilities Focus, 1*, 21–35.

Lyon, G.R., & Moats, L.C. (in press). Critical issues in the instruction of the learning disabled. *Journal of Consulting and Clinical Psychology*.

Lyon, G.R., Moats, L., & Flynn, J.M. (1988). From assessment to treatment: Linkage to interventions with children. In M.G. Tramontana & S.R. Hooper (Eds.), *Assessment issues in child neuropsychology* (pp. 113–142). New York: Plenum Publishing Corp.

Lyon, G.R., Rietta, S., Watson, B., Porch, B., & Rhodes, J. (1981). Selected linguistic and perceptual abilities of empirically derived subgroups of learning disabled readers. *Journal of School Psychology, 19*, 152–166.

Lyon, G.R., & Risucci, D. (1988). Classification of learning disabilities. In K. Kavale (Ed.), *Learning disabilities: State of the art and practice* (pp. 44–70). San Diego, CA: College-Hill Press.

Lyon, G.R., Stewart, N., & Freedman, D. (1982). Neuropsychological characteristics of empirically derived subgroups of learning disabled readers. *Journal of Clinical Neuropsychology, 4*, 343–365.

Lyon, G.R., & Toomey, F. (1985). Neurological, neuropsychological, and cognitive-developmental approaches to learning disabilities. *Topics in Learning Disabilities, 2*, 1–15.

Lyon, G.R., & Watson, B. (1981). Empirically derived subgroups of learning disabled readers: Diagnostic characteristics. *Journal of Learning Disabilities, 14*, 256–261.

Lyytinen, H., & Ahonen, T. (1988). Developmental motor problems in children: A 6-year longitudinal study [Abstract]. *Journal of Clinical and Experimental Neuropsychology, 10*, 57.

MacMillan, D.L., Meyers, C.E., & Morrison, G.M. (1980). System identification of mildly retarded children: Implications for interpreting and conducting research. *American Journal of Mental Deficiency, 85*, 109–115.

Maginnis, G.H. (1986). An evaluation of a non-visual method. *Journal of Learning Disabilities, 19*, 215–217.

Maheady, L., Maitland, G., & Sainato, D. (1984). The interpretation of social interactions of learning disabled, socially/emotionally disturbed, educable mentally retarded, and nondisabled children. *Journal of Special Education, 18*, 151–159.

Maheady, L., & Sainato, D.M. (1986). Learning-disabled students' perceptions of social events. In S.J. Cecil (Ed.), *Handbook of cognitive, social, and neuropsychological aspects of learning disabilities* (Vol. 1, pp. 381–402). Hillsdale, NJ: Lawrence Erlbaum.

Malatesha, R.N., & Dougan, D.R. (1982). Clinical subtypes of developmental dyslexia: Resolution of an irresolute problem. In R.N. Malatesha & P.G. Aaron (Eds.), *Reading disorders: Varieties and treatment* (pp. 69–89). New York: Academic Press.

Marge, M. (1972). The general problem of language disabilities in children. In J.V. Irwin & M. Marge (Eds.), *Principles of childhood language disabilities* (pp. 75–98). Englewood Cliffs, NJ: Prentice-Hall.

Marshall, J.C. (1984). Toward a rational taxonomy of the developmental dyslexias. In R.N. Malatesha & H.A. Whitaker (Eds.), *Dyslexia: A global issue* (pp. 45–58). The Hague: Nijhoff.

Marshall, J.C., & Newcombe, F. (1973). Patterns of paralexia: A psycholinguistic approach. *Journal of Psycholinguistic Research, 2*, 175–197.

Mash, E.J., & Terdal, L.G. (1984). Behavioral assessment of childhood disturbance. In E.J. Mash & L.G. Terdal (Eds.), *Behavioral assessment of childhood disorders* (pp. 3–76). New York: Guilford Press.

Matthews, B.A., & Seymour, C.M. (1981). The performance of learning disabled children on tests of auditory discrimination. *Journal of Learning Disabilities, 14*, 9–11.

Mattis, S. (1981). Dyslexia syndromes in children: Toward the development of syndrome-specific treatment programs. In F.J. Pirozzolo & M.C. Wittrock (Eds.), *Neuropsychological and cognitive processes in reading* (pp. 93–107). New York: Academic Press.

Mattis, S., Erenberg, G., & French, J.H. (1978, February). *Dyslexia syndromes: A cross validation study.* Paper presented at the Sixth Annual Meeting of the International Neuropsychological Society, Minneapolis, MN.

Mattis, S., French, J.H., & Rapin, I. (1975). Dyslexia in children and young adults: Three independent neuropsychological syndromes. *Developmental Medicine and Child Neurology, 17*, 150–163.

Mayeux, R., & Kandel, E.R. (1985). Natural language, disorders of language, and other localizable disorders of cognitive functioning. In E.R. Kandel & J.H. Schwartz (Eds.), *Principles of neural science* (2nd ed.) (pp. 688–703). New York: Elsevier.

McCarthy, J.M. (1975). Children with learning disabilities. In J.J. Gallagher (Ed.), *The application of child development research to exceptional children* (pp. 299–317). Reston, VA: The Council for Exceptional Children.

McClure, P., & Hynd, G.W. (1983). Is hyperlexia a severe reading disorder or a symptom of psychiatric disturbance? *Clinical Neuropsychology, 5*, 145–149.

McConaughty, S.H., & Ritter, D.R. (1985). Social competence and behavioral problems of learning disabled boys aged 6–11. *Journal of Learning Disabilities, 18*, 547–553.

McDermott, P.A. (1981). Sources of error in the psychoeducational diagnosis of children. *Journal of School Psychology, 19*, 31–44.

McKeever, W.F., & Van Deventer, A.D. (1975). Dyslexic adolescents: Evidence of impaired visual and auditory language processing. *Cortex, 11*, 361–378.

McKinney, J.D. (1984). The search for subtypes of specific learning disability. *Journal of Learning Disabilities, 17*, 43–50.

McKinney, J.D. (1988). Research on conceptually and empirically derived subtypes of specific learning disabilities. In M.C. Wang, H.J. Walberg, & M.C. Reynolds (Eds.), *The handbook of special education: Research and practice* (pp. 253–281). Oxford, England: Pergamon Press.

McKinney, J.D., & Feagans, L. (1984). Academic and behavioral characteristics: Longitudinal studies of learning disabled children and average achievers. *Learning Disabilities Quarterly, 7*, 251–265.

McKinney, J.D., Short, E.J., & Feagans, L. (1985). Academic consequences of perceptual-linguistic subtypes of learning disabled children. *Learning Disabilities Research, 1*, 6–17.

McKinney, J.D., & Speece, D.L. (1986). Longitudinal stability and academic consequences of behavioral subtypes of learning disabled children. *Journal of Educational Psychology, 78*, 365–372.

Meacham, M.L., & Fisher, G.L. (1984). The identification and stability of subtypes of disabled readers. *The International Journal of Clinical Neuropsychology, 4*, 269–274.

Meehl, P.E. (1973). *Psychodiagnosis: Selected papers.* Minneapolis: University of Minnesota Press.

Meichenbaum, D. (1976). Cognitive factors as determinants of learning disabilities: A cognitive functional approach. In R. Knights & D. Bakker (Eds.), *The neuropsychology of learning disorders: Theoretical approaches* (pp. 423–422). Baltimore, MD: University Park Press.

Menken, G.A. (1981). *A comparison of auditory disabled and non-auditory disabled children on a time/speech compression task.* Unpublished doctoral dissertation, University of Southern California, Los Angeles.

Merola, J.M., & Liederman, J. (1985). Developmental changes in hemispheric independence. *Child Development, 56*, 1184–1194.

Milberg, W.P., Hebben, N., & Kaplan, E. (1986). The Boston process approach to neuropsychological assessment. In I. Grant & K.M. Adams (Eds.), *Neuropsychological assessment of neuropsychiatric disorders* (pp. 65–86). New York: Oxford University Press.

Miles, T.R. (1986). On the persistence of dyslexic difficulties into adulthood. In G.Th. Pavlidis & D.F. Fisher (Eds.), *Dyslexia: Its neuropsychology and treatment* (pp. 149–163). New York: Wiley.

Mitterer, J.O. (1982). There are at least two kinds of poor readers: Whole word readers and recoding poor readers. *Canadian Journal of Psychology, 36*, 445–461.

Montgomery, D. (1981). Do dyslexics have difficulty accessing articulatory information? *Psychological Research, 43*, 235–245.

Morency, A., Wepman, J., & Hass, S.K. (1970). Developmental speech inaccuracy and speech therapy in the early school years. *Elementary School Journal, 70*, 219–224.

Morgan, W.P. (1896). A case of congenital word-blindness. *British Medical Journal, 2*, 1978.

Morgan, S.B., & Brown, T.L. (1988). Luria-Nebraska Neuropsychological Battery—Children's Revision: Concurrent validity with three learning disability subtypes. *Journal of Consulting and Clinical Psychology, 56*, 463–466.

Morris, G.L., Levy, J., & Pirozzolo, F.J. (1988). Electrophysiological assessment in learning disabilities. In M.G. Tramontana & S.R. Hooper (Eds.), *Assessment issues in child neuropsychology* (pp. 337–366). New York: Plenum Publishing Corp.

Morris, R. (1988). Differentiating developmental language disorders from pervasive developmental disorders in young children [Abstract]. *Journal of Clinical and Experimental Neuropsychology, 10*, 80.

Morris, R., & Blashfield, R. (1983). *Monte Carlo comparative studies of Q-analysis and cluster analysis.* Unpublished manuscript.

Morris, R., Blashfield, R., & Satz, P. (1986). Developmental classification of reading-disabled children. *Journal of Clinical and Experimental Neuropsychology*, *8*, 371–392.

Morris, R., Blashfield, R., & Satz, P. (1981). Neuropsychology and cluster analysis: Potential and problems. *Journal of Clinical Neuropsychology*, *3*, 79–99.

Moscovitch, M. (1979). Information processing and the cerebral hemispheres. In M.S. Gazzaniga (Ed.), *Handbook of behavioral neurobiology: Vol. 2. Neuropsychology* (pp. 379–446). New York: Plenum Publishing Corp.

Myklebust, H.R. (Ed.) (1968). *Progress in learning disabilities* (Vol. 1). New York: Grune & Stratton.

Myklebust, H.R. (1978). Toward a science of dyslexiology. In H. R. Myklebust (Ed.), *Progress in learning disabilities* (Vol. 4, pp. 1–39). New York: Grune & Stratton.

Myklebust, H.R., & Johnson, D.J. (1962). Dyslexia in children. *Exceptional Children*, *29*, 14–25.

Naidoo, S. (1972). *Specific dyslexia*. New York: Wiley.

Nathan, P.E. (1967). *Cures, decisions, and diagnoses: A systems-analytic approach to the diagnosis of psychopathology*. New York: Academic Press.

Nelson, H.E., & Warrington, E.K. (1974). Developmental spelling retardation and its relation to other cognitive abilities. *British Journal of Psychology*, *65*, 265–274.

Nelson, H.E., & Warrington, E.K. (1980). An investigation of memory functions in dyslexic children. *British Journal of Psychology*, *71*, 487–503.

Newcomb, A. (1985). Neuropsychological qua interface. *Journal of Clinical and Experimental Neuropsychology*, *7*, 663–681.

Nielsen, H.H., & Ringe, K. (1969). Visuo-perceptive and visuo-motor performance of children with reading disabilities. *Scandinavian Journal of Psychology*, *10*, 225–231.

Nockleby, D.M., & Galbraith, G.G. (1984). Developmental dyslexia subtypes and the Boder Test of Reading-Spelling Patterns. *Journal of Psychoeducational Assessment*, *2*, 91–100.

Nolan, D.R., Hammeke, T.A., & Barkley, R.A. (1983). A comparison of the patterns of the neuropsychological performance in two groups of learning disabled children. *Journal of Clinical Child Psychology*, *12*, 13–21.

Nussbaum, N.L., & Bigler, E.D. (1986). Neuropsychological and behavioral profiles of empirically derived subgroups of learning disabled children. *International Journal of Clinical Neuropsychology*, *8*, 82–89.

Obrzut, A. (1982). A neuropsychological case report of a child with auditory-linguistic dyslexia. *School Psychology Review*, *10*, 356–361.

Obrzut, J.E. (1979). Dichotic listening and bisensory memory skills in qualitatively diverse dyslexic readers. *Journal of Learning Disabilities*, *12*, 24–33.

Obrzut, J.E. (1981). Neuropsychological assessment in the schools. *School Psychology Review*, *10*, 331–342.

Obrzut, J.E., & Hynd, G.W. (Eds.) (1986a). *Child neuropsychology: Vol. 1. Theory and research*. Orlando, FL: Academic Press.

Obrzut, J.E., & Hynd, G.W. (Eds.) (1986b). *Child neuropsychology: vol. 2. Clinical practice*. Orlando, FL: Academic Press.

Oehler-Stinnett, J., Stinnett, T.A., Wesley, A.L., & Anderson, H.N. (1988). The Luria-Nebraska Neuropsychological Battery–Children's Revision: Discrimination between learning-disabled and slow-learner children. *Journal of Psycho-educational Assessment*, 6, 24–34.

Olson, R.K., Kliegl, R., & Davidson, B.J. (1983). Dyslexic and normal readers' eye movements. *Journal of Experimental Psychology: Human Perception and Performance*, 9, 816–825.

Olson, R.K., Kliegl, R., Davidson, B.J., & Foltz, G. (1985). Individual and developmental differences in reading disability. In T.E. Mackinnon, & G.E. Waller (Eds.), *Reading research: Advances in theory and practice* (Vol. 4, pp. 2–64). New York: Academic Press.

Omenn, G.S., & Weber, B.A. (1978). Dyslexia: Search for phenotypic and genetic heterogeneity. *American Journal of Medical Genetics*, 1, 333–342.

Orton, S.T. (1928). Specific reading disability-strephosymbolia. *Journal of the American Medical Association*, 90, 1095–1009.

Orton, S.T. (1937). *Reading, writing, and speech problems in children*. New York: Norton.

Ozols, E.J., & Rourke, B.P. (1985). Dimensions of social sensitivity in two types of learning-disabled children. In B.P. Rourke (Ed.), *Neuropsychology of learning disabilities: Essentials of subtype analysis* (pp. 281–301). New York: Guilford Press.

Parkins, R., Roberts, R.J., Reinarz, S.J., & Varney, N.R. (1987). CT asymmetries in adult developmental dyslexics [Abstract]. *Journal of Clinical and Experimental Neuropsychology*, 9, 41.

Passler, M.A., Isaac, W., & Hynd, G.W. (1985). Neuropsychological development of behaviors attributed to frontal lobe functioning in children. *Developmental Neuropsychology*, 1, 349–370.

Pavlidis, G. Th. (1978). The dyslexic's erratic eye movements: Case studies. *Dyslexia Review*, 1, 22–28.

Pearl, R. (1987). Social cognitive factors in learning-disabled children's social problems. In S.J. Cecil (Ed.), *Handbook of cognitive, social, and neuropsychological aspects of learning disabilities* (Vol. 2, pp. 273–294). Hillsdale, NJ: Lawrence Erlbaum.

Pearl, R., & Cosden, M. (1982). Sizing up a situation: LD children's understanding of social interactions. *Learning Disability Quarterly*, 5, 371–373.

Pekarik, E.G., Prinz, R.J., Liebert, D.E., Weintraub, S., & Neale, J.M. (1976). The Pupil Evaluation Inventory: A sociometric technique for assessing children's social behavior. *Journal of Abnormal Child Psychology*, 4, 83–97.

Pelham, W.E., Jr. (1986). The effects of psychostimulant drugs on the learning and academic achievement in children with attention-deficit disorders and learning disabilities. In J.K. Torgeson & B.Y.L. Wong (Eds.), *Psychological and educational perspectives on learning disabilities* (pp. 259–295). Orlando, FL: Academic Press.

Pennington, B.F., Smith, S.D., McCabe, L.L., Kimberling, W.J., & Lubs, H.A. (1984). Developmental continuities and discontinuities in a form of familial dyslexia. In R.N. Emde & R.J. Harmon (Eds.), *Continuities and discontinuities in development* (pp. 123–151). New York: Plenum Publishing Corp.

Perlmutter, B.F. (1986). Personality variables and peer relations of children and adolescents with learning disabilities. In S.J. Ceci (Ed.), *Handbook of cognitive, social, and neuropsychological aspects of learning disabilities* (Vol. 1, pp. 339–359). Hillsdale, NJ: Lawrence Erlbaum.

Perlmutter, B.F., Crocker, J., Cordray, D., & Garstecki, D. (1983). Sociometric status and related personality characteristics of mainstreamed learning disabled adolescents. *Learning Disability Quarterly*, *6*, 31–39.

Perlmutter, B.F., & Parus, M.V. (1983). Identifying children with learning disabilities: A comparison of diagnostic procedures across school districts. *Learning Disability Quarterly*, *6*, 321–328.

Petrauskas, R., & Rourke, B. (1979). Identification of subgroups of retarded readers: A neuropsychological multivariate approach. *Journal of Clinical Neuropsychology*, *1*, 17–37.

Pirozzolo, F.J. (1979). *The neuropsychology of developmental reading disorders*. New York: Praeger Press.

Pirozzolo, F.J. (1981). Language and brain: Neuropsychological aspects of developmental reading disability. *School Psychology Review*, *10*, 350–355.

Pirozzolo, F.J., & Rayner, K. (1978). The neural control of EM in acquired and developmental reading disorder. In G. Avakian-Whitaker & H.A. Whitaker (Eds.), *Advances in neurolinguistics and psycholinguistics*. New York: Academic Press.

Porter, R.B., & Cattell, R.B. (1975). *Children's Personality Questionnaire*. Champaign, IL: Institute for Personality and Ability Testing.

Porter, J.E., & Rourke, B.P. (1985). Socioemotional functioning of learning-disabled children: A subtypal analysis of personality patterns. In B.P. Rourke (Ed.), *Neuropsychology of learning disabilities: Essentials of subtype analysis* (pp. 257–280). New York: Guilford Press.

Quay, H.C., & Peterson, D.R. (1975). *Manual for the Behavior Problem Checklist*. Unpublished manuscript.

Quiros, J.B. (1964). Dysphasia and dyslexia in school children. *Folia Phoniatrica*, *16*, 201.

Raim, J., & Adams, R. (1982). The case study approach to understanding learning disabilities. *Journal of Learning Disabilities*, *15*, 116–118.

Rapin, I., & Allen, D.A. (1983). Developmental language disorders: Nosologic considerations. In U. Kirk (Ed.), *Neuropsychology of language, reading, and spelling* (pp. 213–219). New York: Academic Press.

Reed, H.B.C., Reitan, R.M., & Klove, H. (1965). Influence of cerebral lesions on psychological test performance of older children. *Journal of Consulting Psychology*, *29*, 247–251.

Reitan, R.M. (1974). Psychological effects of cerebral lesions in children of early school age. In R.M. Reitan & L.A. Davison (Eds.), *Clinical neuropsychology: Current status and applications* (pp. 53–89). New York: Wiley.

Reitan, R.M., & Wolfson, D. (1985). *The Halstead-Reitan Neuropsychological Test Battery*. Tucson, AZ: Neuropsychology Press.

Reynolds, C.R. (1981a). Neuropsychological assessment and the habilitation of learning: Considerations in the search for aptitude X treatment interactions. *School Psychology Review*, *10*, 343–349.

Reynolds. C.R. (1981b). The neuropsychological basis of intelligence. In G.W. Hynd & J.E. Obrzut (Eds.), *Neuropsychological assessment and the school-age child: Issues and procedures* (pp. 87–124). New York: Grune & Stratton.

Reynolds, C.R. (1984). Psychometric characteristics of the Boder Test of Reading-Spelling Patterns: Take one giant step backwards. *School Psychology Review*, *13*, 526–529.

Reynolds, C.R. (1986). Transactional models of intellectual development, yes. Deficit models of process remediation, no. *School Psychology Review, 15,* 256–260.

Richardson, E., Di Benedetton, B., & Bradley, C.M. (1977). The relationship of sound blending to reading achievement. *Review of Educational Research, 47,* 319–334.

Roeltgen, D. (1985). Agraphia. In K.M. Heilman & E. Valenstein (Eds.), *Clinical neuropsychology* (2nd ed.) (pp. 75–96). New York: Oxford University Press.

Rosenberger, P.B., & Hier, D.B. (1980). Cerebral asymmetry and verbal intellectual deficits. *Annals of Neurology, 8,* 300–304.

Rosenthal, J.H. (1982). EEG-event-related potentials in dyslexia and its subgroups. In D.A.B. Lindberg, M.F. Collen, & E.E. Van Brunt (Eds.), *Computer applications in medical care: AMIA Congress, 82* (pp. 41–47). New York: Masson Publishing.

Rosenthal, J.H. (1980). *Neuropsychological studies of developmental dyslexia.* Unpublished doctoral dissertation, University of California, San Francisco.

Ross, A.O. (1976). *Psychological aspects of learning disabilities and reading disorders.* New York: McGraw-Hill.

Rourke, B.P. (1983). Outstanding issues in research on learning disabilities. In M. Rutter (Ed.), *Developmental neuropsychiatry* (pp. 564–574). New York: Guilford Press.

Rourke, B.P. (Ed.). (1985). *Neuropsychology of learning disabilities: Essentials of subtype analysis.* New York: Guilford Press.

Rourke, B.P. (1987). Syndrome of nonverbal learning disabilities: The final common pathway of white-matter disease/dysfunction. *The Clinical Neuropsychologist, 1,* 209–234.

Rourke, B.P., & Adams, K.M. (1984). Quantitative approaches to the neuropsychological assessment of children. In R.E. Tarter & G. Goldstein (Eds.), *Advances in clinical neuropsychology* (Vol. 2, pp. 79–108). New York: Plenum Publishing Corp.

Rourke, B.P., Bakker, D.J., Fisk, J.L., & Strang, J.D. (1983). *Child neuropsychology: An introduction to theory, research, and clinical practice.* New York: Guilford Press.

Rourke, B.P., & Finlayson, M.A.J. (1978). Neuropsychological significance of variations in patterns of academic performance: Verbal and visual-spatial abilities. *Journal of Abnormal Child Psychology, 6,* 121–133.

Rourke, B.P., Fisk, T.L., & Strang, J.D. (1986). *The neuropsychological assessment of children: A treatment-oriented approach.* New York: Guilford Press.

Rourke, B.P., & Orr, R.R. (1977). Prediction of the reading and spelling performance of normal and retarded readers: A four-year follow-up. *Journal of Abnormal Child Psychology, 5,* 9–20.

Rourke, B.P., & Strang, J.D. (1978). Neuropsychological significance of variations in patterns of academic performance: Motor, psychomotor, and tactile-perceptual abilities. *Journal of Pediatric Psychology, 3,* 62–66.

Rourke, B.P., & Telegdy, G.A. (1971). Lateralizing significance of WISC verbal-performance discrepancies for older children with learning disabilities. *Perceptual and Motor Skills, 33,* 875–883.

Rourke, B.P., Young, G.C., & Flewelling, R.W. (1971). The relationship between

WISC verbal-performance discrepancies and selected verbal, auditory-perceptual, visual-perceptual, and problem-solving abilities in children with learning disabilities. *Journal of Clinical Psychology*, 27, 475–479.

Rumsey, J.M., Berman, K.F., Horwitz, B., Denckla, M., & Weinberger, D.R. (1988). Cerebral blood flow patterns of dyslexic adults [Abstract]. *Journal of Clinical and Experimental Neuropsychology*, 10, 35.

Rumsey, J.M., Dorwart, R., Vermess, M., Denckla, M.B., Kruesi, M.J., & Rapoport, J.L. (1986). Magnetic resonance imaging of brain anatomy in severe developmental dyslexia. *Archives of Neurology*, 43, 1045–1046.

Rutter, M. (1981). Psychological sequelae of brain damage in children. *American Journal of Psychiatry*, 139, 21–33.

Ryan, E.B., Weed, K.A., & Short, E.J. (1986). Cognitive behavior modification: Promoting active, self-regulatory learning styles. In J.K. Torgeson & B.Y.L. Wong (Eds.), *Psychological and educational perspectives on learning disabilities* (pp. 367–397). Orlando, FL: Academic Press.

Saffran, E.M., Bogyo, L.C., Schwartz, M.F., & Martin, O.S.M. (1980). Does deep dyslexia reflect right hemisphere reading? In M. Coltheart, K. Patterson, & J.C. Marshall (Eds.), *Deep dyslexia* (pp. 381–406). Boston: Routledge & Kegan Paul.

Salvia, J., & Ysseldyke, J.E. (1981). *Assessment in special and remedial education* (2nd ed.). Boston: Houghton Mifflin.

Sattler, J.M. (1988). *Assessment of children* (3rd ed.), San Diego, CA: Author.

Satz, P., & Flectcher, J.M. (1982). *Florida Kindergarten Screening Battery*. Odessa, FL: Psychological Assessment Resources.

Satz, P., & Morris, R. (1981). Learning disabilities subtypes: A review. In F.J. Pirozzolo & M.C. Wittrock (Eds.), *Neuropsychological and cognitive processes in reading* (pp. 109–141). New York: Academic Press.

Satz, P., Rardin, D., & Ross, J. (1971). An evaluation of a theory of specific developmental dyslexia. *Child Development*, 42, 2009–2021.

Satz, P., & Soper, H.V. (1986). Left-handedness, dyslexia, and autoimmune disorder: A critique. *Journal of Clinical and Experimental Neuropsychology*, 8, 453–458.

Satz, P., Taylor, H.G., Friel, J., & Fletcher, J.M. (1978). Some developmental and predictive precursors of reading disabilities: A six year follow-up. In A.L. Benton & D. Pearl (Eds.), *Dyslexia: An appraisal of current knowledge* (pp. 315–347). New York: Oxford University Press.

Sawicki, R.F., Leark, R., Golden, C.J., & Karras, D. (1984). The development of the pathognomonic, left sensorimotor, and right sensorimotor scales for the Luria-Nebraska Neuropsychological Battery–Children's Revision. *Journal of Clinical Child Psychology*, 13, 165–169.

Schaefer, E.S., Edgerton, M., & Aronson, M. (1977). *Classroom Behavior Inventory*. Chapel Hill, NC: Frank Porter Graham Child Development Center.

Schonhaut, S., & Satz, P. (1983). Prognosis of children with learning disabilities: A review of follow-up studies. In M. Rutter (Ed.), *Development neuropsychiatry* (pp. 542–563). New York: Guilford Press.

Schumaker, J., Deshler, D., Alley, G., Warner, M., & Denton, P. (1982). Multipass: A learning strategy for improving reading comprehension. *Learning Disabilities Quarterly*, 5, 295–304.

Scranton, T., & Rychman, D. (1979). Sociometric status of learning disabled children in an integrative program. *Journal of Learning Disabilities*, 12, 402–407.

Seidenberg, M., Giordani, B., Berent, S., & Boll, T.J. (1983). IQ level and performance on the Halstead-Reitan Neuropsychological Test Battery for Older Children. *Journal of Consulting and Clinical Psychology*, *51*, 406–413.

Selz, M., & Reitan, R.M. (1979). Rules for neuropsychological diagnosis: Classification of brain function in older children. *Journal of Consulting and Clinical Psychology*, *47*, 258–264.

Senf, G.M. (1969). Development of immediate memory of bisensory stimuli in normal children and children with learning disabilities. *Developmental Psychology*, *6*, 28.

Senf, G.M. (1986). LD research in sociological and scientific perspective. In J.K. Torgeson & B.Y.L. Wong (Eds.), *Psychological and educational perspectives on learning disabilities* (pp. 27–53). Orlando, FL: Academic Press.

Senf, G.M., & Feshback, S. (1970). Development of bisensory memory in culturally deprived dyslexic and normal readers. *Journal of Educational Psychology*, *61*, 461–470.

Senf, G.M., & Freundl, P.C. (1971). Memory and attention factors in specific learning disabilities. *Journal of Learning Disabilities*, *4*, 94–106.

Sevush, S. (1983, February). *The neurolinguistics of reading: Anatomic and neurologic correlates*. Paper presented at the Twelfth Annual Meeting of the International Neuropsychological Society, Mexico City, Mexico.

Shankweiler, D., & Liberman, I.Y. (1972). Misreading: A search for causes. In J.F. Kavanagh & I.G. Mattingly (Eds.), *Language by ear and by eye. The relationship between speech and reading* (pp. 293–317). Cambridge, MA: MIT Press.

Sheare, J.B. (1978). The impact of resource programs upon the social competence and peer acceptance of learning disabled children. *Psychology in the Schools*, *15*, 406–412.

Shepard, L. (1980). An evaluation of the regression discrepancy method for identifying children with learning disabilities. *Journal of Special Education*, *14*, 79–91.

Shepard, L. (1983). The role of measurement in educational policy: Lessons from the identification of learning disabilities. *Educational Measurement: Issues and Practice*, *2*, 4–8.

Shepard, L.A., Smith, M.L., & Vojir, C.P. (1983). Characteristics of pupils identified as learning disabled. *American Educational Research Journal*, *20*, 309–331.

Shinn-Strieker, T. (1986). Patterns of cognitive style in normal and handicapped children. *Journal of Learning Disabilities*, *19*, 572–576.

Short, E.J., Feagans, L., McKinney, J.D., & Appelbaum, M.I. (1986). Longitudinal stability of LD subtypes based on age- and IQ-achievement discrepancies. *Learning Disability Quarterly*, *9*, 214–224.

Siegel, L.S. (1985). Deep dyslexia in childhood? *Brain and Language*, *26*, 16–27.

Siegel, L.S., & Linder, A. (1984). Short-term memory processes in children with reading and arithmetic disabilities. *Developmental Psychology*, *20*, 200–207.

Siegel, L.S., & Ryan, E. (1988) Working memory in subtypes of learning disabled children [Abstract]. *Journal of Clinical and Experimental Neuropsychology*, *10*, 55.

Silver, A.A. (1968). Diagnostic considerations in children with reading disability. In G. Natchez (Ed.), *Children with reading problems: Classic and contemporary issues in reading disability* (pp. 240–250). New York: Basic Books.

Silver, L.B. (1987). The "magic cure": A review of the current controversial approaches for treating learning disabilities. *Journal of Learning Disabilities*, *20*, 498–504.

Simeon, J., Waters, B., & Resnick, M., et. al. (1980). Effects of Piracetam in children with learning disorders. *Psychopharmacology Bulletin*, *16*, 65–66.

Siperstein, G.N., Bopp, M.J., & Bak, J.J. (1978). Social status of learning disabled children. *Journal of Learning Disabilities*, *11*, 98–102.

Skinner, B.F. (1938). *The behavior of organisms.* New York: Appleton-Century.

Skinner, H.A. (1978). Differentiating the contribution of elevation, scatter, and shape in profile similarity. *Educational and Psychological Measurement*, *38*, 297–308.

Skinner, H.A. (1981). Toward the integration of classification theory and methods. *Journal of Abnormal Psychology*, *90*, 68–87.

Skinner, H.A. (1986). Construct validation approach to psychiatric classification. In T. Millon & G.L. Klerman (Eds.), *Contemporary directions in psychopathology* (pp. 307–330). New York: Guilford Press.

Sklar, B., Hanley, J., & Simmons, W.W. (1973). A computer analysis of EEG spectral signatures from normal and dyslexic children. *IEEE Transactions on Bio-Medical Engineering*, *20*, 20–26.

Smith, D.E.P., & Carrigan, P.M. (1959). *The nature of reading disability.* New York: Harcourt, Brace.

Smith, M.D., Coleman, J.M., Dokecki, P.R., & Davis, E.E. (1977). Recategorized WISC-R scores of learning disabled children. *Journal of Learning Disabilities*, *10*, 444–449.

Smith, M.M. (1970). *Patterns of intellectual abilities in educationally handicapped children.* Unpublished doctoral dissertation, Claremont College, Claremont, CA.

Smith, S.D., Goldgar, D.E., Pennington, B.F., Kimberling, W.J., & Lubs, H.A. (1986). Analysis of subtypes of specific reading disability: Genetic and cluster analytic approaches. In G. Th. Pavlidis & D.F Fisher (Eds.), *Dyslexia: Its neuropsychology and treatment* (pp. 181–202). New York: Wiley.

Smith, S.D., Pennington, B.F., Kimberling, W.J., & Lubs, H.A. (1983). A genetic analysis of specific reading disability. In C.L. Ludlow & J.A. Cooper (Eds.), *Genetic aspects of speech and language disorders* (pp. 169–178). New York: Academic Press.

Sneath, P.H.E., & Sokal, R.R. (1973). *Numerical taxonomy.* San Francisco: W.H. Freeman.

Snow, J.H., Cohen, M., & Holliman, W.B. (1985). Learning disability subgroups using cluster analysis of the WISC-R. *Journal of Psychoeducational Assessment*, *4*, 391–397.

Snow, J.H., & Desch, L.W. (1988). Learning disorder subgroups based on medical, developmental, and growth variables [Abstract]. *Journal of Clinical and Experimental Neuropsychology*, *10*, 55–56.

Snow, J.H., Hartlage, L.C., Hynd, G.W., & Grant, D.H. (1983). The relationship between the Luria-Nebraska Neuropsychological Battery–Children's Revision and the Minnesota Percepto-Diagnostic Test with learning disabled students. *Psychology in the Schools*, *20*, 415–419.

Snow, J.H., & Hynd, G.W. (1985a). Factor structure of the Luria-Nebraska Neuropsychological Battery–Children's Revision. *Journal of School Psychology*, *23*, 271–276.

Snow, J.H., & Hynd, G.W. (1985b). A multivariate investigation of the Luria-Nebraska Neuropsychological Battery–Children's Revision with learning disabled children. *Journal of Psychoeducational Assessment, 3*, 101–109.

Snow, J.H., Hynd, G.W., & Hartlage, L.C. (1984). Difference between mildly and more severely learning-disabled children on the Luria-Nebraska Neuropsychological Battery–Children's Revision. *Journal of Psychoeducational Assessment, 2*, 23–28.

Snow, J.H., Koller, J.R., & Roberts, C.D. (1987). Adolescent and adult learning disability subgroups based on WAIS-R performance. *Journal of Psychoeducational Assessment, 5*, 7–14.

Snyder, T.J., Leark, R.A., Golden, C.J., Allison, B., & Grove, T.K. (1983). K-ABC validity study number 39. In A.S. Kaufman & N.L. Kaufman (Eds.), *Kaufman Assessment Battery for Children: Interpretive manual* (p. 98). Circle Pines, MN: American Guidance Service.

Sowell, V., Parker, R., Poplin, M., & Larsen, S. (1979). The effects of psycholinguistic training on improving psycholinguistic skills. *Learning Disability Quarterly, 2*, 69–77.

Sparrow, S.S., Balla, D.A., & Cicchetti, D.V. (1984). *Vineland Adaptive Behavior Scales.* Circle Pines, MN: American Guidance Service.

Speece, D.L. (1987). Information processing subtypes of learning disabled readers. *Learning Disability Research, 2*, 91–102.

Speece, D.L., McKinney, J.D., & Appelbaum, M.I. (1985). Classification and validation of behavioral subtypes of learning disabled children. *Journal of Educational Psychology, 77*, 67–77.

Speer, J. (1971). Behavior Problem Checklist (Peterson-Quay): Baseline-data from parents of child guidance and nonclinic children. *Journal of Consulting and Clinical Psychology, 36*, 221–228.

Spiers, P.A. (1987). Acalculia revisited: Current issues. In G. Deloche & X. Seron (Eds.), *Mathematical disabilities: A cognitive neuropsychological perspective* (pp. 1–25). Hillsdale, NJ: Lawrence Erlbaum.

Spijer, G., De Jong, A., & Bakker, D.J. (1987). Piracetam and Piracetam plus hemisphere-specific stimulation: Effects on the reading performance of two subtyped dyslexic boys [Abstract]. *Journal of Clinical and Experimental Neuropsychology, 9*, 275–276.

Sporn, E. (1981). *Is dyslexia a middle-class disability? A critique of some definitions.* Unpublished doctoral dissertation, Yeshiva University, New York.

Spreen, O. (1978). The dyslexias: A discussion of neurobehavioral research. In A. Benton & D. Pearl (Eds.), *Dyslexia: An appraisal of current knowledge* (pp. 173–194). New York: Oxford University Press.

Spreen, O.J., & Gaddes, W.H. (1969). Developmental norms for 15 neuropsychological tests age 6–15. *Cortex, 5*, 171–191.

Spreen, O., & Haaf, R.G. (1986). Empirically derived learning disability subtypes: A replication attempt and longitudinal patterns over 15 years. *Journal of Learning Disabilities, 19*, 170–180.

Stanovich, K.E. (1988). Science and learning disabilities. *Journal of Learning Disabilities, 21*, 210–214.

Stephenson, S. (1905). Six cases of congenital word-blindness affecting three generations of one family. *Ophthalmoscope, 5*, 482–484.

Sterritt, G.M., & Rudnick, M. (1966). Auditory and visual rhythm perception in relation to reading ability in fourth grade boys. *Perceptual and Motor Skills*, *22*, 859–864.

Stokman, C.J., Shafer, S.Q., Shaffer, D., Ng, S.K.C., O'Connor, P.A., & Wolff, R.R. (1986). Assessment of neurological "soft signs" in adolescents: Reliability studies. *Developmental Medicine and Child Neurology*, *28*, 428–439.

Strang, J.D., & Rourke, B.P. (1983). Concept-formation/non-verbal reasoning abilities of children who exhibit specific academic problems with arithmetic. *Journal of Clinical Child Psychology* , *12*, 33–39.

Strang, J.D., & Rourke, B.P. (1985). Adaptive behavior of children who exhibit specific arithmetic disabilities and associated neuropsychological abilities and deficits. In B.P. Rourke (Ed.), *Neuropsychology of learning disabilities: Essentials of subtype analysis* (pp. 302–328). New York: Guilford Press.

Strawser, S., & Weller, C. (1985). Use of adaptive behavior and discrepancy criteria to determine learning disabilities severity subtypes. *Journal of Learning Disabilities*, *18*, 205–212.

Strom, D.A., Gray, J.W., Dean, R.S., Fischer, W.E. (1987). The incremental validity of the Halstead-Reitan Neuropsychological Battery in predicting achievement for learning-disabled children. *Journal of Psychoeducational Assessment*, *2*, 157–165.

Sutter, E.G., & Battin, R. (1983). Using traditional psychological tests to obtain neuropsychological information on children. *International Journal of Clinical Neuropsychology*, *6*, 115–119.

Sutter, E.G., Bishop, P.C., & Battin, R.R. (1986). Factor similarities between traditional psychoeducational and neuropsychological test batteries. *Journal of Psychoeducational Assessment*, *4*, 73–82.

Swanson, H.L. (1987). Information processing theory and learning disabilities: A commentary and future perspectives. *Journal of Learning Disabilities*, *20*, 155–166.

Swanson, H.L. (1988). Toward a metatheory of learning disabilities. *Journal of Learning Disabilities*, *21*, 196–209.

Sweeney, J.E., & Rourke, B.P. (1978). Neuropsychological significance of phonetically accurate and phonetically inaccurate spelling errors of younger and older retarded spellers. *Brain and Language*, *6*, 212–225.

Szekeres, S.F., Ylvisaker, M., & Cohen, S.B. (1987). A framework for cognitive rehabilitation therapy. In M. Ylvisaker & E.M.R. Gobble (Eds.), *Community re-entry for head-injured adults* (pp. 87–136). Boston: Little, Brown.

Tarver, S.G., & Hallahan, D.P. (1974). Attention deficits in children with learning disabilities: A review. *Journal of Learning Disabilities*, *7*, 560–569.

Tarver, S.G., Hallahan, D.P., Cohen, S.B., & Kauffman, J.M. (1977). The development of visual selective attention and verbal rehearsal in learning disabled boys. *Journal of Learning Disabilities*, *10*, 491–500.

Tarver, S.G., Hallahan, D.P., Kauffman, J.M., & Ball, D.W. (1976). Verbal rehearsal and selective attention in children with learning disabilities: a developmental lag. *Journal of Experimental Child Psychology*, *22*, 375–385.

Taylor, H.G. (1987). The meaning and value of soft signs in the behavioral sciences. In D.E. Tupper (Ed.), *Soft neurological signs* (pp. 297–335). Orlando, FL: Grune & Stratton.

Taylor, H.G., & Fletcher, J.M. (1983). Biological foundations of "specific developmental disorders": Methods, findings, and future directions. *Journal of Clinical Child Psychology*, *12*, 46–65.

Taylor, H.G., Satz, P., & Friel, J. (1979). Developmental dyslexia in relationship to other childhood disorders: Significance and utility. *Reading Research Quarterly*, *15*, 84–101.

Teeter, P.A., Boliek, C.A., Obrzut, J.E., & Malsch, K. (1986). Diagnostic utility of the critical level formula and clinical scales of the Luria-Nebraska Neuropsychological Battery–Children's Revision with learning disabled children. *Developmental Neuropsychology*, *2*, 125–135.

Telzrow, C.F., Century, E., Redmond, C., Whitaker, B., & Zimmerman, B. (1983). The Boder Test: Neuropsychological and demographic features of dyslexic subtypes. *Psychology in the Schools*, *20*, 427–432.

Temple, C.M., & Marshall, J.C. (1983). A case study of developmental phonological dyslexia. *British Journal of Psychology*, *74*, 517–533.

Thomson, M.E. (1982). The assessment of children with specific reading difficulties (dyslexia) using the British Ability Scales. *British Journal of Psychology*, *73*, 461–478.

Thomson, M.E. (1984). *Developmental dyslexia: Its nature, assessment, and remediation*. London: Edward Arnold.

Thomson, M.E., Hicks, C., &Wilsher, C. (1980). *Specific written language difficulty in children: A clinical and factorial description*. Unpublished paper, University of Aston.

Thomson, M.E., & Wilsher, C. (1978). Some aspects of memory in dyslexics and controls. In M.M. Gruneberg, P.E. Morris, & R.N. Sykes (Eds.), *Practical aspects of memory* (pp. 545–560). New York: Academic Press.

Tittemore, J.A., Lawson, J.S., & Inglis, J. (1985). Validation of a learning disability index (LDI) derived from a principal components analysis of the WISC-R. *Journal of Learning Disabilities*, *18*, 449–454.

Tomlinson-Keasey, C., & Kelly, R.R. (1979a). Is hemispheric specialization important to scholastic achievement? *Cortex*, *15*, 97–107.

Tomlinson-Keasey, C., & Kelly, R.R. (1979b). A task analysis of hemispheric functioning. *Neuropsychologia*, *17*, 345–351.

Torgesen, J.K. (1982). The learning disabled child as an inactive learner: Educational implications. *Topics in Learning and Learning Disabilities*, *2*, 45–52.

Town, P.A., Buff, A., & Cohen, M. (1988). Dichotic listening performance in subtypes of developmental dyslexia and a left-temporal-lobe brain-damaged control group [Abstract]. *Journal of Clinical and Experimental Neuropsychology*, *10*, 311.

Tramontana, M.G. (1988). Problems and prospects in child neuropsychological assessment. In M.G. Tramontana & S.R. Hooper (Eds.), *Assessment issues in child neuropsychology* (pp. 369–376). New York: Plenum Publishing Corp.

Tramontana, M.G., & Boyd, T.A. (1986). Psychometric screening of neuropsychological abnormality in older children. *International Journal of Clinical Neuropsychology*, *8*, 53–59.

Tramontana, M.G., & Hooper, S.R. (Eds.) (1988). *Assessment issues in child neuropsychology*. New York: Plenum Publishing Corp.

Tramontana, M.G., & Hooper, S.R. (in press). Neuropsychology of child psychopathology. In C.R. Reynolds & E. Fletcher-Janzen (Eds.), *Handbook of clinical child neuropsychology*. New York: Plenum Publishing Corp.

Tramontana, M.G., Hooper, S.R., & Nardolillo, E. (in press). Behavioral manifestations of neuropsychological impairment in children with psychiatric disorders. *Archives of Clinical Neuropsychology*.

Tramontana, M.G., Hooper, S.R., & Selzer, C.S. (1988). Research on the preschool prediction of later academic achievement. *Developmental Review*, *8*, 89–146.

Tramontana, M.G., Klee, S.H., & Boyd, T.A. (1984). WISC-R interrelationships with the Halstead-Reitan and Children's Luria Neuropsychological Batteries. *International Journal of Clinical Neuropsychology*, *6*, 1–8.

Traub, M., & Bloom, F. (1975). *Recipe for reading*. Cambridge, MA: Educator's Publishing Service.

Trauner, D.A. (1982). Neurological examination of infants and children. In W.C. Wiederholt (Eds.), *Neurology for Nonneurologists* (pp. 47–62). New York: Academic Press.

U.S. Department of Education, Division of Educational Services. (1984). *Sixth annual report to Congress on the implementation of Public Law 94–142: the Education for All Handicapped Children Act*. Washington, DC: Author.

U.S. Office of Education. (1968). *First annual report of the National Committee on Handicapped Children*. Washington, DC: U.S. Department of Health, Education, & Welfare.

U.S. Office of Education. (1977). Assistance to states for education of handicapped children: Procedures for evaluating specific learning disabilities. *Federal Register*, *42* (250), 65082–65085.

Valsiner, J. (1983). Hemispheric specialization and integration in child development. In S.J. Segalowitz (Ed.), *Language functions and brain organization* (pp. 321–343). New York: Academic Press.

Valtin, R. (1973). *Report of research on dyslexia in children*. Paper presented at the Annual Meeting of the International Reading Association, Denver, CO.

Vance, H., Wallbrown, F.H., & Blaha, J. (1978). Determining WISC-R profiles for reading disabled children. *Journal of Learning Disabilities*, *11*, 657–661.

Van der Vlugt, H., & Satz, P. (1985). Subgroups and subtypes of learning-disabled and normal children: A cross-cultural replication. In B.P. Rourke (Ed.), *Neuropsychology of learning disabilities: Essentials of subtype analysis* (pp. 212–227). New York: Guilford Press.

Van Strien, J.W., Bakker, D.J., Bouma, A., & Koops, W. (1988). Familial antecedents of P- and L-type dyslexia [Abstract]. *Journal of Clinical and Experimental Neuropsychology*, *10*, 323.

Vaughan, R.W., & Hodges, L.A. (1973). A statistical survey into a definition of learning disabilities. *Journal of Learning Disabilities*, *6*, 658–664.

Vellutino, F.R. (1978). Toward an understanding of dyslexia: Psychological factors in specific reading disabilities. In A.L. Benton & D. Pearl (Eds.), *Dyslexia: An appraisal of current knowledge* (pp. 61–111). New York: Oxford University Press.

Vellutino, F.R. (1979). *Dyslexia: Theory and research*. Cambridge, MA: MIT Press.

Vellutino, F.R., Steger, J.A., Desetto, L., & Phillips, F. (1975). Immediate and delayed recognition of visual stimuli in poor and normal readers. *Journal of Experimental Child Psychology*, *19*, 223–232.

Vellutino, F.R., Steger, J.A., Kaman, M., & DeSetto, L. (1975). Visual form perception in deficient and normal readers. *Cortex*, *11*, 22–30.

Vernon, M.D. (1977). Varieties of deficiency in the reading process. *Harvard Educational Review*, *37*, 396–410.

Vernon, M.D. (1979). Variability in reading retardation. *British Journal of Psychology*, *70*, 7–16.

Voeller, K.K.S. (1986). Right hemisphere deficit syndrome in children. *American Journal of Psychiatry*, *143*, 1004–1009.

Vygotsky, L.S. (1960). *Development of the higher mental functions*. Moscow: Izd. Akad. Ped. Nauk ASFSR.

Vygotsky, L.S. (1978). *Mind in society: The development of higher psychology processes*. Cambridge, MA: Harvard University.

Waller, T.G. (1976). Children's recognition memory for written sentences: A comparison of good and poor readers. *Child Development*, *47*, 90–95.

Warrington, E.K. (1981). Concrete word dyslexia. *British Journal of Psychology*, *72*, 175–196.

Warrington, E.K. (1982). The fractionation of arithmetic skills: A single case study. *Quarterly Journal of Experimental Psychology*, *34*, 31–51.

Waterman, J.M., Sobesky, W.E., Silvern, L., Aoki, B., & McCaufay, M. (1981). Social perspective-taking adjustment in emotionally disturbed, learning disabled and normal children. *Journal of Abnormal Child Psychology*, *9*, 133–148.

Watson, B.U., & Goldgar, D.E. (1988). Evaluation of a typology of reading disability. *Journal of Clinical and Experimental Neuropsychology*, *10*, 432–450.

Watson, B.U., Goldgar, D.E., & Ryschon, K.L. (1983). Subtypes of reading disability. *Journal of Clinical Neuropsychology*, *5*, 377–399.

Weingartner, H., Cohen, R.M., Murphy, D.L., Martello, J., & Gerdt, C. (1981). Cognitive processes in depression. *Archives of General Psychiatry*, *38*, 42–67.

Weintraub, S., & Mesulam, M.M. (1983). Developmental learning disabilities of the right hemisphere: Emotional, interpersonal, and cognitive components. *Archives of Neurology*, *40*, 463–468.

Weller, C., & Strawser, S. (1987). Adaptive behavior of subtypes of learning disabled individuals. *Journal of Special Education*, *21*, 101–115.

Wepman, J.M. (1960). Auditory discrimination, speech, and reading. *Elementary School Journal*, *9*, 325–333.

West, J.F., & Idol, L. (1987). School consultation: Part I. An interdisciplinary perspective on theory, models, and research. *Journal of Learning Disabilities*, *20*, 388–408.

Wiener, J. (1980). A theoretical model of the acquisition of peer relationships of learning disabled children. *Journal of Learning Disabilities*, *13*, 42–47.

Wiener, J. (1986). Alternatives in the assessment of the learning disabled adolescent: A learning strategies approach. *Learning Disabilities Focus*, *1*, 97–107.

Wiig, E.H., Semel, M.S., & Crouse, M.B. (1973). The use of English morphology by high-risk and learning disabled children. *Journal of Learning Disabilities*, *6*, 457–465.

Wilkening, G.N., Golden, C.J., MacInnes, W.D., Plaisted, J.R., & Hermann, B.P. (1981, August). *The Luria-Nebraska Neuropsychology Battery–Children's Revision: A preliminary report*. Paper presented at the Eighty-Ninth annual meeting of the American Psychological Association, Los Angeles, CA.

Willis, W.G. (1985a). Auditory-successive selective attention for learning disabled and normal boys. *Perceptual and Motor Skills*, *61*, 496–498.

Willis, W.G. (1985b). Successive and simultaneous processing: A note on interpretation. *Journal of Psychoeducational Assessment*, *4*, 343–346.

Willis, W.G. (1988). Neuropsychological diagnosis with children: Actuarial and clinical models. In M.G. Tramontana & S.R. Hooper (Eds.), Assessment issues in child neuropsychology (pp. 93–111). New York: Plenum Publishing Corp.

Willis, W.G., & Hynd, G.W. (1987). Lateralized interference effects: Evidence for a processing style by modality interaction. *Brain and Cognition*, *6*, 112–126.

Willis, W.G., & Widerstrom, A.H. (1986). Structure and function in prenatal and postnatal neuropsychological development: A dynamic interaction. In J.E. Obrzut & G.W. Hynd (Eds.), *Child neuropsychology: Vol. 1. Theory and research* (pp. 13–53). Orlando, FL: Academic Press.

Wilsher, C., Atkins, G., & Manfield, P. (1985). Effect of Piracetam on dyslexic's reading ability. *Journal of Learning Disabilities*, *18*, 19–25.

Wilson, B.C. (1986). An approach to the neuropsychological assessment of the preschool child with developmental deficits. In S.B. Filskov & T. J. Boll (Eds.), *Handbook of clinical neuropsychology* (Vol. 2, pp. 121–171). New York: Wiley.

Wilson, B.C., Aram, D.H., Rapin, I., & Allen, D. (1988). Subtypes within developmental language disorders [Abstract]. *Journal of Clinical and Experimental Neuropsychology*, *10*, 80.

Wilson, B., & Baddeley, A. (1986). Single case methodology and the remediation of dyslexia. In G.T. Pavlidis & D. F. Fisher (Eds.), *Dyslexia: Its neuropsychology and treatment* (pp. 263–277). New York: Wiley.

Wilson, B.C., & Risucci, D.A. (1986). A model for clinical-quantitative classification. Generation I: Application to language-disordered preschool children. *Brain and Language*, *27*, 281–309.

Wilson, L.R. (1985). Large-scale learning disability identification: The reprieve of a concept. *Exceptional Children*, *52*, 44–51.

Wirt, R.D., Lachar, D., Klinedinst, J.K., & Seat, P.D. (1977). *Multidimensional description of child personality: A manual for the Personality Inventory for Children*. Los Angeles: Western Psychological Services.

Witelson, S.F. (1976). Abnormal right hemisphere specialization in developmental dyslexia. In R.M. Knights & D.J. Bakker (Eds.), *The neuropsychology of learning disorders: Theoretical approaches* (pp. 233–255). Baltimore, MD: University Park Press.

Witelson, S.F., & Rabinovitch, M.S. (1972). Hemispheric speech lateralization in children with auditory-linguistic deficits. *Cortex*, *8*, 412–426.

Wolfus, B., Moscovitch, M., & Kinsbourne, M. (1980). Subgroups of developmental language impairment. *Brain and Language*, *10*, 152–171.

Wong, B.Y.L., Wong, R., Perry, N., & Sawatsky, D. (1986). The efficacy of a self-questioning summarization strategy for use by underachievers and learning disabled adolescents in social studies. *Learning Disabilities Focus*, *2*, 20–35.

Yeni-Komshian, G.H., Isenberg, P., & Goldstein, H. (1975). Cerebral dominance and reading disability: Left visual-field deficit in poor readers. *Neuropsychologia*, *8*, 83–94.

Ysseldyke, J.E., & Algozzine, B. (1983). LD or not LD: That's not the question! *Journal of Learning Disabilities*, *16*, 29–31.

Ysseldyke, J.E., Algozzine, B., Shinn, M., & McGue, M. (1982). Similarities and differences between underachievers and students labeled learning disabled. *Journal of Special Education*, *16*, 73–85.

Ysseldyke, J.E., & Mirkin, P.K. (1982). The use of assessment information to plan instructional interventions: A review of the research. In C.R. Reynolds & T.B. Gutkin (Eds.), *Handbook of school psychology* (pp. 395–409). New York: Wiley.

Ysseldyke, J.E., Thurlow, M.L., Graden, J.L., Wesson, C., Deno, S.L., & Algozzine, B. (1983). Generalization from five years of research on assessment and decision making. *Exceptional Education Quarterly, 4*, 75–93.

Zametkin, A.J., & Rapoport, J.L. (1986). The pathophysiology of attention deficit disorder with hyperactivity: A review. In B.B. Lahey & A. Kazdin (Eds.), *Advances in clinical child psychology* (Vol. 9, pp. 177–216). New York: Plenum Publishing Corp.

Zigmond, N., Sansone, J., Miller, S.E., Donahoe, K.A., & Kohnke, R. (1986). Teaching learning disabled students at the secondary school level: What research says to teachers. *Learning Disabilities Focus, 1*, 108–115.

Author Index

Aaron, P.G., 46, 124, 128
Abel, L.A., 9, 209
Aboitiz, F., 20, 211
Accardo, P.J., 202
Achenbach, T.M., 145, 156, 163, 202
Ackerman, P.T., 11, 136, 209, 214
ACLD, 14, 202
Adams, K.M., 63, 69, 70, 97, 101–103, 202, 225
Adams, R., 13, 224
Adelman, H.S., 3, 93–95, 202
Ahonen, T., 66, 80, 219
Alexander, P.A., 46, 132, 202
Alfano, D.P., 177, 202
Algozzine, B., 4, 16, 17, 93, 98, 197, 202, 209, 234
Allen, D.A., 43, 56, 94, 209, 224, 234
Alley, G.R., 167, 168, 202, 206, 208, 226
Allison, B., 116, 229
Alper, T.G., 116, 117, 211
Anderson, H.N., 117, 222
Andreewsky, E., 43, 57, 207
Angelergues, R., 32, 213
Annesley, F.R., 142, 211
Aoki, B., 144, 233
Apicella, A., 212
Appelbaum, M.I., 66, 67, 82, 86, 90, 98, 150, 158, 209, 227, 229
Aram, D.M., 66, 82, 94, 104, 202, 234
Aronson, M., 158, 226
Arter, J.A., 176, 203
Ashkenazi, M., 35, 46, 217
Atkins, G., 165, 233
Axelrod, L., 145, 203

Aylward, E.H., 47, 203
Ayres, A.A., 177, 203

Baddeley, A., 13, 234
Badian, N.A., 12, 19, 203
Bak, J.J., 144, 227
Bakker, D.J., 7, 11, 43, 51–53, 61, 129, 166, 178, 182–186, 191, 203, 205, 212, 225, 229, 232
Balla, D.A., 159, 229
Ball, D.W., 11, 230
Bandura, R., 140, 203
Bannatyne, A., 42, 50, 154, 203
Barker, W., 212
Barkley, R.A., 50, 175, 203, 222
Bartel, N.R., 141, 146, 203
Bartels, P.H., 35, 209
Bateman, B.D., 17, 42, 50, 53, 203
Battin, R.R., 123, 230
Bauserman, D.N., 46, 204
Bayliss, J., 46, 204
Bay, M., 3, 205
Beauvois, M.F., 43, 58, 204
Becker, M.G., 4, 28, 109, 204, 215
Behan, P.O., 36, 211
Bellugi, U., 20, 215
Belmont, S., 7, 10, 204
Bender, L.A., 8, 204
Bender, W.M., 143, 204
Benton, A.L., 7, 9, 31, 32, 129, 204
Berent, S., 114, 226
Berman, K.F., 20, 225
Bianchini, K.J., 218
Biederman, J., 165, 204

Bigler, E.D., 67, 86, 90, 147, 149, 156, 222
Bing, S.B., 46, 132, 204
Birch, H.G., 7, 10, 204
Bishop, P.C., 123, 230
Blackburn, I., 42, 47, 215
Blaha, J., 64, 73, 232
Blank, M., 9, 10, 204
Blashfield, R.K., 16, 63, 66, 71, 75, 97, 198, 204, 207, 221
Bloom, F., 188, 231
Board of Trustees of the Council for Learning Disabilities, 205
Boder, E., 20, 42, 44–46, 60, 79, 97, 103, 104, 129, 130–134, 177–180, 186, 191, 205, 210
Bogyo, L.C., 58, 226
Boliek, C.A., 117, 230
Boller, F., 30, 32, 212
Boll, T.J., 114, 205, 226
Bopp, M.J., 144, 227
Borden, S.L., 168, 218
Bornstein, J.L., 9, 209
Bouma, A., 8, 53, 185, 186, 203, 205, 232
Boyan, C., 18, 205
Boyd, T.A., 114, 116, 214, 231
Bradley, C.M., 9, 224
Brainerd, C.J., 12, 205
Breen, M.J., 50, 205
Breslin, P.W., 20, 136, 206
Bridger, W.H., 9, 10, 204
Brodal, A., 24, 205
Brody, D.S., 154, 209
Brody, Z.H., 218
Brouwers, E.Y.M., 165, 208
Brown, T.L., 118, 221
Bruck, M., 140, 143–146, 205
Bruhn, D., 27, 218
Bryans, B.N., 67, 71, 85, 208
Bryan, T.H., 3, 140, 144, 205
Buff, A., 46, 231
Burchfiel, J.L., 35, 209
Büssling, A., 31, 207
Byring, R., 20, 205

Calhoun, W.H., 218
Camp, B., 47, 133, 206

Campbell, S., 144, 206
Caplan, P.J., 142, 143, 216
Carlson, S.C., 167, 208
Carnine, D., 168, 206
Carrigan, P.M., 67, 83, 84, 90, 91, 228
Carter, J.L., 168, 206
Cattell, R.B., 63, 156, 206, 224
Cawley, J.F., 142, 206
Century, E., 132, 231
Chapman, C.A., 20, 208
Chapman, R.B., 140, 206
Chen, J.Y., 212
Chi, J.G., 25, 208
Child Neurology Society, Task Force on Nosology of Disorders of Higher Cerebral Function in Children, 125, 206
Childs, B., 4, 206
Christensen, A.L., 134, 206
Cicchetti, D.V., 159, 229
Clairborne, J.H., 6, 206
Clark, F.L., 168, 206
Clark, M.M., 9, 206
Clements, S.D., 11, 209
Cohen, J., 20, 136, 206
Cohen, M., 6, 7, 11, 45, 46, 52, 65, 73, 126, 177–182, 184, 187, 188, 191, 192, 206, 215, 228, 231
Cohen, R.L., 11, 206
Cohen, R.M., 142, 233
Cohen, S.B., 137, 230
Coleman, J.M., 43, 51, 228
Coltheart, M., 58, 206
Conners, C.K., 156, 206
Connor, R.T., 11, 12, 126, 127, 215
Cook, J.M., 168, 207
Cooley, E.J., 177, 203
Cordray, D., 145, 223
Cosden, M., 145, 223
Costa, L.D., 28, 212
Coulter, M.A., 63, 206
Craig, D.L., 121, 207
Crocker, J., 145, 223
Cromwell, R.L., 16, 207
Crouse, M.B., 10, 233
Cruickshank, W.M., 168, 207, 213
Crump, W.D., 144, 211
Cullinan, D., 144, 207
Curtiss, S., 44, 56, 207

Dahmen, W., 31, 207
Dalby, J.T., 20, 46, 207, 213
D'Amato, R.C., 114, 207
Daroff, R.B., 9, 209
Das, J.P., 27, 189, 207
Davidoff, J.B., 25, 207
David, R., 93, 105, 200, 207
Davidson, B.J., 12, 222
Davis, E.E., 43, 51, 228
de Ajuriaguerra, J., 43, 56, 207
Dean, R.S., 114, 207, 230
Decker, S.N., 44, 58, 59, 207
Deering, W., 46, 210
DeFries, J.C., 44, 59, 207
de Hirsch, K., 7, 207
De Jong, A., 166, 184, 229
DelDotto, J.E., 64, 65, 71, 75, 77, 90,
    105, 115, 151, 158, 159, 207, 208
Delis, D.C., 129, 207
Dell'Osso, S.F., 9, 209
Deloche, G., 30, 32, 43, 57, 207, 208
DeLuca, J., 64, 71–73, 115, 208
Dembinski, R., 144, 207
Denckla, M.B., 10, 20, 35, 43, 54, 56,
    135, 165, 166, 208, 209, 225, 226
Deno, S.L., 234
Denton, P., 168, 226
Derouesne, J., 43, 58, 204
Desch, L.W., 68, 87, 228
DeSetto, L., 9, 232
Deshler, D.D., 167, 168, 202, 206, 208,
    226
Desi, M., 43, 57, 207
DiBenedetton, B., 9, 224
Dimond, S.J., 165, 208
Doehring, D.G., 67, 71, 84, 85
Dokecki, P.R., 43, 51, 228
Donahue, K.A., 168, 234
Donahue, M., 3, 205
Dooling, E.C., 25, 208
Doris, J., 4, 208
Dorval, B., 140, 208
Dorwart, R., 226
Doubleday, C., 20, 210
Dougan, D.R., 46, 219
Drake, W.E., 36, 135, 208
Duane, D.D., 4, 209
Duara, R., 212
Duffy, F.H., 35, 209

Dundon, W.D., 141, 142, 146, 158, 212
Dupont, H., 154, 209
DuRant, R.H., 178, 184, 206
Dykman, R.A., 11, 136, 209, 214

Edelbrock, C.S., 156, 202
Edgerton, M., 158, 226
Elliot, S.N., 145, 209
Ellis, N.C., 10, 209
Elterman, R.D., 9, 209
Epps, S., 4, 13, 17, 98, 99, 197, 209
Epstein, M., 144, 207
Erenberg, G., 43, 55, 220
Everitt, B., 69, 71, 209
Eysenck, H., 101, 209

Faglioni, P., 30, 32, 212
Farnham-Diggory, S., 18, 209
Feagans, L., 65–67, 81, 82, 86, 98, 140,
    208, 209, 220, 227
Fein, D., 94, 209
Fein, G., 136, 209
Fennell, E.B., 64, 72, 215
Feshback, S., 11, 227
Fiedorowicz, A.M., 67, 85, 208
Fieve, R.R., 71, 210
Finlayson, M.A.J., 42, 49, 61, 99, 115,
    177, 202, 225
Finucci, J.M., 4, 206
Fischer, W.E., 114, 230
Fisher, G.L., 67, 221
Fisher, J.H., 6, 89, 210
Fisk, J.L., 64, 75, 76, 90, 102, 115,
    151, 158, 169, 170, 207, 210, 225
Fleiss, J.L., 71, 210
Fletcher, J.M., 8, 17, 35, 50, 63, 97,
    104, 129, 210, 225, 226, 230
Flewelling, R.W., 42, 53, 121, 225
Flynn, J., 46, 79, 178, 182, 184, 186,
    187, 191, 210
Foltz, G., 12, 222
Forness, S.R., 165, 166, 176, 210
Fox, B., 10, 210
Freedman, D., 64, 76, 219
French, J.H., 43, 54, 55, 125, 220
Freundl, P.C., 11, 227
Fried, I., 20, 35, 46, 136, 210

Friedman, A., 158, 210
Friel, J., 8, 17, 226, 230
Fristoe, M., 129, 212
Frith, U., 42, 48, 103, 210
Frostig, M., 7, 8, 168, 210, 211
Funnell, E., 58, 211

Gaddes, W.H., 109, 114, 138, 211, 229
Gadow, K.D., 166, 211
Gajar, A., 144, 211
Galaburda, A.M., 20, 21, 36, 135, 171, 211
Galbraith, G.G., 46, 133, 222
Galin, D., 133, 209, 218
Gardien, C.J., 185, 186, 205
Gardner, O.S., 154, 209
Garfinkel, B.D., 166, 211
Garrett, M.K., 144, 211
Garstecki, D., 145, 223
Geary, D.C., 116–118, 211
Gerber, P.J., 145, 211
Gerdt, C., 142, 233
Geschwind, N., 20, 36, 101, 211
Gibson, D., 46, 207
Gilger, J.W., 117, 118, 211
Gilles, F.H., 25, 208
Ginn, R., 47, 211
Giordani, B., 114, 226
Glass, G.V., 176, 211
Glavin, J.P., 142, 211
Glosser, G., 149, 155, 212
Goekoop-Hoefkens, M., 53, 183, 203
Goldberg, E., 28, 211
Goldberg, H., 9, 212
Golden, C.J., 115, 116, 212, 226, 229, 233
Goldfried, M.R., 174, 212
Goldgar, D.E., 67, 68, 85–87, 228, 233
Goldman, R., 129, 212
Goldman, R.L., 145, 212
Goldstein, D., 90, 141, 142, 146, 157, 158, 212
Goldstein, H., 8, 147, 148, 234
Goyen, J., 7, 8, 12, 218, 219
Graden, J.L., 234
Grafman, J., 30, 32, 212
Grant, D.H., 117, 228
Gray, J.W., 114, 207, 230

Greensite, M., 20, 210
Gresham, F.M., 145, 209
Groenendaal, H.A., 11, 212
Gross-Glenn, K., 212
Grove, T.K., 116, 229
Guilford, J.P., 176, 212
Gunnison, J.A., 189, 212
Guskin, S.L., 140, 141, 146, 203, 212
Gustavson, J.L., 116, 212

Haaf, R.G., 12, 68, 88, 91, 103, 137, 172, 198, 229
Hale, R.L., 65, 73, 74, 99, 121, 213
Hallahan, D.P., 11, 142, 168, 213, 230
Halstead, W.C., 11, 213
Hammeke, T.A., 50, 115, 212, 222
Hammill, D.D., 9, 14, 15, 142, 168, 213
Hamsher, K., 129, 204
Hanley, J., 136, 228
Hardin, V.B., 145, 212
Harter, S., 166, 213
Hartje, W., 31, 207
Hartladge, L.C., 117, 118, 175, 176, 213, 228
Hasher, L., 142, 213
Haslam, R.H., 20, 35, 213
Hass, S.K., 9, 221
Hayes, F., 4, 215
Heaton, R.K., 129, 213
Hebben, N., 134, 221
Hécaen, H., 32, 213
Heffer, R.W., 145, 209
Henderson, J.G., 142, 213
Henriksen, L., 27, 218
Henry, A., 9, 213
Hermann, B.P., 116, 212, 233
Hermann, K., 8, 213
Heverly, L.L., 28, 213
Hicks, C., 67, 89, 168, 213, 231
Hier, D.B., 20, 35, 135, 213, 225
Hinshelwood, J., 4–6, 214
Hiscock, M., 7, 216
Hodges, L.A., 13, 232
Holcomb, P., 136, 214
Holliman, W.B., 65, 75, 228
Holmes, C.L., 214
Hooper, S.R., 7, 27, 47, 52, 66, 75, 79, 104, 109, 110, 121, 123, 124, 127, 130, 133, 158, 190, 214, 231

Horne, D., 168, 211
Horton, A.M., Jr., 174, 214
Horwitz, B., 20, 225
Hoshko, I.M., 67, 71, 84, 85, 208
Houillier, S., 32, 213
Howe, B., 168, 214
Howell, K.W., 176, 214
Howe, M.L., 12, 205
Hutchens, T.A., 165, 214
Hyman, L.M., 117, 214
Hynd, C.R., 11, 12, 20, 34, 58, 180–
   182, 191, 214, 215
Hynd, G.W., 4, 6, 7, 11, 12, 20, 22,
   24, 25, 27, 28, 33–36, 45–47, 52,
   58, 66, 67, 75, 79, 89, 109–111,
   117, 118, 121, 123, 124, 126, 127,
   130, 132, 134–136, 158, 165, 177–
   182, 187, 191, 192

Idol, L., 172, 215, 233
Inglis, J., 18, 231
Ingram, T.S., 42, 47, 215
Interagency Committee on Learning Disa-
   bilities, 14, 15, 196, 201, 215
Isaac, W., 28, 204, 213, 223
Isenberg, P., 8, 234

Jackson, F., 6, 215
Jansky, J., 7, 207
Jarman, R.F., 27, 189, 207
Jarrico, S., 46, 129–132, 205
Jarvilehto, T., 20, 205
Jelliner, M.S., 165, 204
Jenkins, J.R., 176, 203
Jennings, S.M., 116, 117, 211
Jernigan, T.J., 20, 215
Johnson, D.J., 42, 50, 51, 55, 126, 177,
   215, 222
Johns, R.D., 20, 213
Johnston, C.S., 64, 66, 72, 75, 77, 78,
   99, 215
Johnstone, J., 209
Jorm, A.F., 11, 215, 216
Joschko, M., 65, 75, 77, 115, 216

Kahneman, D., 142, 216
Kaman, M., 9, 232

Kamphaus, R.W., 121, 175, 176, 216
Kampwirth, T.J., 176, 216
Kandel, E.R., 34, 220
Kanfer, F.H., 174, 216
Kaplan, E., 129, 134, 207, 221
Karras, D., 116, 226
Kauffman, J.M., 11, 142, 168, 213, 216,
   230
Kaufman, A.S., 27, 47, 177, 216
Kaufman, N.L., 27, 47, 177, 216
Kavale, K.A., 135, 165, 166, 176, 196,
   201, 216
Keefe, B., 53, 216
Kelly, R.R., 53, 231
Kemper, T.C., 36, 135, 211
Keogh, B.K., 94, 99, 100, 216
Kephart, N.C., 7, 8, 168, 216
Kiersch, M.E., 209
Kiessling, L.S., 35, 209
Kimberling, W.J., 55, 68, 87, 101, 216,
   223, 228
Kinder, D., 168, 206
Kingma, J., 12, 205
Kingsbury, T.B., 20, 215
Kinsbourne, M., 7, 10, 42, 43, 50, 101,
   142, 143, 158, 216, 217, 234
Kirby, J.R., 27, 189, 207
Kirk, S.A., 4, 168, 196, 217
Kirk, W.D., 168, 217
Kistner, J., 143, 162, 190, 217
Klee, S.H., 114, 231
Klerman, G.L., 96, 228
Kliegl, R., 12, 222
Klinedinst, J.K., 153, 234
Klonoff, H., 114, 217
Klove, H., 114, 224
Knights, R.M., 114, 217
Kohnke, R., 168, 234
Kok, A., 53, 203
Koller, J.R., 66, 73, 229
Koops, W., 53, 232
Koppell, S., 149, 155, 212
Korhonen, T., 65, 80, 217
Korkman, M., 118–120, 217
Kovacs, M., 157, 217
Kramer, J.H., 129, 207
Krawiecki, N., 178, 184, 206
Kreusi, M.J., 226
Krupski, A., 11, 217
Kussmaul, A., 4, 217

Lachar, D., 153, 234
Lakin, K.C., 176, 217
Lambert, E.W., 218
Landau, S., 148, 156, 217
Langford, W., 7, 207
Languis, M., 35, 217
Larivee, B., 176, 217
Larsen, S.C., 9, 15, 140, 169, 206, 213, 229
Lawlor, W., 71, 210
Lawson, J.S., 18, 231
Leark, R.A., 116, 212, 226, 229
Legein, C.P., 8, 205
Leigh, J.E., 15, 213
Leisman, G., 35, 46, 217
LeMay, M., 20, 35, 208, 213, 218
Lenneberg, E.H., 25, 218
Lennox, C., 42, 50, 218
Leton, D.A., 66, 80, 218
Levine, M.D., 16, 218
Levy, J., 135, 221
Lewis, R.B., 117, 176, 218
Lewis, R.D., 218
Liberman, I.Y., 10, 169, 218, 227
Licht, R., 53, 203
Liebert, D.E., 156, 223
Liederman, J., 30, 221
Linder, A., 50, 227
Lindsley, O.R., 174, 218
Liversey, P.J., 46, 204
Lloyd, J.W., 167, 168, 213, 218
Lombroso, C.T., 35, 209
Loper, A.B., 168, 213
Lorion, R.P., 117, 218
Lou, H.C., 27, 218
Lovett, M.W., 42, 48, 168, 218
Lubar, J.F., 136, 218
Lubs, H.A., 55, 68, 87, 101, 216, 223, 228
Lund, P.E., 133, 218
Luria, A.R., 23–32, 34, 37, 116, 119, 134, 218
Lyle, J.G., 7, 12, 218, 219
Lyon, G.R., 64, 76, 78, 79, 81, 89, 96–99, 103, 105, 106, 125, 134, 137, 164, 177, 178, 182, 185, 186, 188–192, 198, 201, 219
Lyytinen, H., 66, 80, 219

MacInnes, W.D., 116, 212, 233
MacMillan, D.L., 98, 219
Maginnis, G.H., 168, 219
Maheady, L., 144, 145, 219
Maitland, G., 144, 219
Major-Kingsley, S., 99, 100, 216
Malatesha, R.N., 46, 219
Malsch, K., 117, 230
Manfield, P., 165, 233
Marcus, M., 133, 209, 218
Marge, M., 219
Marshall, J.C., 34, 43, 44, 57, 58, 180, 220, 231
Martello, J., 142, 233
Martin, O.S.M., 58, 226
Mash, E.J., 174, 220
Mason, A.W., 42, 47, 215
Matthews, B.A., 9, 220
Mattis, S., 43, 54, 55, 60, 79, 96–99, 103, 104, 124, 125, 128, 177–180, 220
Mayeux, R., 34, 220
McCabe, L.L., 47, 55, 133, 206, 223
McCarthy, J.M., 17, 220
McCaufay, M., 144, 233
McClure, P., 58, 220
McConaughty, S.H., 148, 156, 220
McDermott, P.A., 16, 220
McFarland, M., 148, 156, 217
McGue, M., 16, 234
McKeever, W.F., 8, 220
McKinney, J.D., 65, 67, 80, 86, 90, 98, 140, 150, 151, 158, 160–162, 201, 208, 220, 221, 227, 229
McNutt, G., 15, 213
Meacham, M.L., 67, 89, 221
Meehl, P.E., 105, 221
Meichenbaum, D., 166, 221
Menken, G.A., 46, 221
Merola, J.M., 30, 221
Mesulam, M.M., 91, 148, 152, 153, 233
Meyers, C.E., 98, 219
Milberg, W.P., 134, 221
Miles, T.R., 10, 201, 209, 221
Milich, R., 148, 156, 217
Miller, S.E., 168, 234
Millon, T., 96, 228
Mirkin, P.K., 176, 234
Mitterer, J.O., 42, 48, 221

Miyamoto, L.K., 66, 80, 218
Moats, L.C., 79, 177, 189, 219
Moerland, R., 53, 183, 203
Montgomery, D., 10, 221
Morency, A., 9, 221
Morgan, S.B., 118, 221
Morgan, W.P., 5, 221
Morris, G.L., 135, 221
Morrison, G.M., 98, 219
Morris, R., 17, 63, 64, 66, 69–72, 75–
    81, 88–91, 94, 96–99, 103, 129,
    147, 148, 156, 198, 210, 221, 226
Moscovitch, M., 10, 25, 43, 221, 234
Murphy, D.L., 142, 233
Myklebust, H.R., 42, 43, 50, 51, 55,
    126, 132, 177, 215, 222

Naidoo, S., 67, 83, 84, 90, 222
Nardolillo, E., 190, 231
Nathan, P.E., 16, 222
Nation, J.E., 66, 82, 104, 202
Neale, J.M., 156, 223
Nelson, H.E., 11, 44, 59, 222
Netley, C., 11, 206
Newcomb, A., 177, 222
Newcombe, F., 43, 58, 220
Ng, S K C , 229
Nielson, H.H., 9, 222
Nieves, N., 12, 126, 127, 215
Nockleby, D.M., 46, 133, 222
Nolan, D.R., 50, 117, 222
Nussbaum, N.L., 67, 86, 90, 147, 149,
    156, 222
Nye, C., 196, 201, 216

Ober, B.A., 129, 207
Obrzut, A., 52, 222
Obrzut, J.E., 4, 11, 46, 109, 117, 124,
    126, 128, 181, 204, 215, 222, 230
O'Connor, P.A., 229
Oehler-Stinnett, J., 117, 222
Olson, R.K., 12, 222
Omenn, G.S., 44, 59, 222
Omori-Gordon, H., 99, 100, 216
O'Neill, I., 166, 211
Orr, R.R., 88, 89, 102, 103, 225
Orton, S.T., 7, 223

Osborne, M., 143, 162, 190, 217
Ozols, E.J., 90, 148, 154, 168, 223

Parker, R.M., 140, 169, 206, 229
Parkins, R., 35, 223
Parus, M.V., 16, 223
Passafiume, D., 30, 32, 212
Passler, M.A., 28, 223
Patel, P.G., 67, 85, 208
Paul, G.G., 90, 148, 212
Pavlidis, G.Th., 9, 223
Pearl, R., 143, 145, 146, 155, 163, 223
Pekarik, E.G., 156, 223
Pelham, W.E. Jr., 165, 223
Pennington, B.F., 55, 68, 87, 101, 133,
    216, 223, 228
Peper, R.J., 47, 214
Perlmutter, B.F., 16, 145, 146, 155, 223
Perlo, V.P., 20, 213
Perry, N., 129, 234
Peters, J.E., 11, 209
Peterson, D.R., 145, 224
Petrauskas, R., 64, 75, 76, 99, 115, 224
Phillips, F., 9, 232
Phillips, J.S., 174, 217
Pirozzolo, F.J., 6, 9, 43, 51, 52, 60,
    135, 221, 224
Plaisted, J.R., 116, 212, 233
Platman, S.R., 71, 210
Polson, M.C., 158, 210
Poplin, M., 169, 229
Porch, B., 78, 219
Porter, J.E., 90, 150, 158, 161, 162,
    224
Porter, R.B., 156, 224
Prinz, R.J., 156, 223
Puente, A.E., 174, 214
Purisch, A.D., 115, 212

Quay, H.C., 145, 224
Quiros, J.B., 42, 50, 224

Rabinovitch, M.S., 8, 234
Rademaker, A.W., 20, 213
Raim, J., 13, 224
Ransby, M.J., 168, 218

Rapin, I., 43, 54, 56, 94, 125, 220, 224, 234
Rapoport, J.L., 25, 226, 234
Rardin, D., 7, 226
Rayner, K., 9, 224
Redmond, C., 132, 231
Reed, H.B.C., 114, 224
Reid, H.P., 99, 100, 216
Reinarz, S.J., 35, 223
Reitan, R.M., 76, 111, 114, 124, 126, 224, 226
Resnick, M., 178, 183, 227
Reynolds, C.R., 7, 46, 121, 132, 133, 175, 176, 213, 216, 224
Rhodes, J., 28, 219
Richardson, E., 9, 224
Rietta, S., 78, 219
Ringe, K., 9, 222
Risucci, D.A., 43, 54, 61, 96, 104, 124, 128, 234
Ritter, D.R., 148, 156, 220
Roberts, C.D., 66, 73, 229
Roberts, R.J., 35, 223
Robinson, G.C., 114, 217
Roeltgen, D., 47, 225
Rosenberger, P.B., 20, 35, 213, 225
Rosen, G.D., 20, 211
Rosenthal, J.H., 35, 46, 225
Ross, A.O., 11, 17, 225
Ross, J., 7, 226
Rourke, B.P., 3, 28, 42, 48–50, 53, 60, 61, 64, 65, 69–72, 75, 76, 88–92, 99, 102–105, 115, 121, 148–150, 152–155, 158, 161, 162, 168–173, 177, 182, 191, 197, 198, 207, 208, 210, 217, 223–225, 230
Routh, D.K., 10, 210
Rubin, J., 214
Rudel, R., 10, 208
Rudnick, M., 10, 229
Rumsey, J.M., 20, 35, 225, 226
Russell, H.L., 168, 206
Rutter, M., 30, 226
Ryan, E., 42, 50, 227
Ryan, E.B., 166, 167, 226
Ryckman, D.B., 66, 80, 144, 218, 226
Ryschon, K.L., 67, 85, 233

Saffran, E.M., 58, 226
Sainato, D.M., 144, 145, 219
Salvia, J., 13, 226
Sandini, G., 35, 209
Sanfilippo-Cohen, S., 90, 148, 212
Sansone, J., 168, 234
Sattler, J.M., 121, 226
Satz, P., 7, 8, 16, 17, 36, 60, 63–65, 72, 75–78, 80, 88, 89, 91, 96–99, 102–104, 129, 137, 147, 148, 156, 198, 210, 215, 221, 226, 230, 232
Sawatsky, D., 129, 234
Sawicki, R.F., 116, 226
Saxe, J.E., 73, 74, 99, 121, 213
Schaefer, E.S., 158, 226
Schiffman, G., 9, 212
Schonhaut, S., 16, 80, 137, 226
Schultz, D.D., 116, 117, 211
Schumaker, J.B., 168, 226
Schwartz, M.F., 58, 226
Scranton, T., 144, 226
Seat, P.D., 153, 234
Seidenberg, M., 114, 226
Selzer, C.S., 104, 231
Selz, M., 114, 226
Semel, M.S., 10, 233
Semrud-Clikeman, M., 33, 35, 36, 136, 215
Senf, G.M., 7, 11, 93, 227
Seron, K., 30, 32, 208
Severson, H.H., 177, 203
Sevush, S., 44, 58, 227
Seymour, C.M., 9, 220
Shabsin, H.S., 218
Shafer, S.A., 229
Shankweiler, D., 10, 169, 218, 227
Sheare, J.B., 144, 227
Shepard, L.A., 18, 98, 99, 227
Sherman, G.F., 20, 211
Shinn, M., 16, 234
Shinn-Strieker, T., 66, 79, 227
Short, E.J., 65, 67, 81, 86, 87, 98, 166, 220, 226, 227
Siegal, L., 42, 50, 58, 218, 227
Silver, A.A., 9, 227
Silver, L.B., 165, 227
Silvern, L., 144, 233
Simeon, J., 178, 182, 183, 227
Simmons, W.W., 136, 228

Simons, H., 133, 218
Siperstein, G.N., 144, 227
Skinner, B.F., 172, 228
Skinner, H.A., 69, 93, 96–98, 228
Sklar, B., 136, 228
Sloman, L., 166, 211
Smith, D.E.P., 67, 83, 84, 87, 90, 91, 228
Smith, M.D., 43, 51, 121, 182, 228
Smith, M.L., 98, 227
Smith, M.M., 42, 51, 53, 55, 228
Smith, S.D., 68, 223, 228
Sneath, P.H.E., 71, 228
Snow, J.H., 65–68, 73–75, 79, 87, 89, 109, 117, 118, 215, 228, 229
Snyder, T.J., 116, 229
Sobesky, W.E., 144, 233
Sokal, R.R., 71, 228
Soper, H.V., 36, 226
Sowell, V., 169, 229
Sparrow, S.S., 159, 229
Speece, D.L., 68, 89, 90, 96, 98, 150, 158, 160–162, 220, 229
Spiers, P.A., 31, 32, 229
Spijer, G., 166, 182, 184, 229
Sporn, E., 47, 229
Sprafkin, J.N., 174, 212
Spreen, O., 10, 12, 68, 88, 91, 103, 114, 129, 137, 172, 198, 204, 229
Stahl, V., 214
Stanovich, K.E., 135, 137, 229
Steger, J.A., 9, 232
Stephenson, S., 5, 229
Sterritt, G.M., 10, 229
Stewart, N., 64, 76, 219
Stinnett, T.A., 117, 222
Stokman, C.J., 229
Strang, J.D., 49, 50, 91, 102, 149, 152, 153, 155, 168–170, 225, 230
Strauss, J.S., 16, 207
Strawser, S., 44, 60, 91, 150, 158, 159, 230, 233
Strom, D.A., 114, 230
Sturm, W., 31, 207
Sullivan, H.G., 20, 215
Sutter, E.G., 123, 230
Swanson, H.L., 69, 93, 96, 105, 135, 230
Sweeney, J.E., 42, 48, 115, 191, 230

Swinney, D., 53, 216
Szekeres, S.F., 137, 230

Tallal, P., 9, 20, 44, 56, 207, 215
Tanguay, P.E., 20, 210
Tarver, S.G., 11, 230
Taylor, H.G., 8, 17, 35, 226, 230
Taylor, L., 3, 93–95, 202
Teeter, P.A., 117, 230
Telegdy, G.A., 115, 225
Telzrow, C.F., 132, 175, 213, 231
Temple, C.M., 58, 231
Terdal, L.G., 174, 220
Thompson, G., 114, 217
Thomson, M.E., 7, 8, 42, 47, 89, 231
Thurlow, M.L., 234
Tittemore, J.A., 18, 231
Tomlinson-Keasey, C., 53, 231
Toomey, F., 201, 219
Torgesen, J.K., 167, 231
Town, P.A., 46, 231
Tramontana, M.G., 7, 52, 104, 109, 110, 114, 116, 123, 124, 127, 130, 158, 172, 190, 214, 231
Traub, M., 188, 231
Trauner, D.A., 232
Trites, R.L., 67, 85, 208
Tsujioka, B., 63, 206

U.S. Department of Education, Division of Educational Services, 4, 232
U.S. Office of Education, 14, 109, 142, 232

Valsiner, J., 30, 232
Valtin, R., 9, 232
Van der Vlugt, H., 60, 64, 65, 72, 76–78, 99, 232
Van Deventer, A.D., 8, 220
Vance, H., 64, 73, 74, 121, 232
Van Strien, J.W., 53, 232
Varney, N.R., 35, 129, 204, 223
Vaughan, R.W., 13, 232
Vellutino, F.R., 9, 60, 103, 169, 232
Vermess, M., 226
Vernon, M.D., 44, 59, 89, 232

Vinke, J., 178, 182, 183, 186, 191, 203
Voeller, K.K.S., 149, 152, 153, 232
Vojir, C.P., 98, 227
Vygotsky, L.S., 29, 166, 232

Wallbrown, F.H., 64, 73, 232
Waller, T.G., 10, 233
Warner, M., 168, 226
Warren, P.M., 168, 218
Warrington, E.K., 11, 30, 32, 42–44,
    50, 59, 217, 222, 233
Waterhouse, L., 94, 209
Waterman, J.M., 144, 233
Waters, B., 178, 183, 227
Watson, B., 64, 67, 68, 76, 78, 79, 85,
    86, 97, 98, 125, 198, 219, 233
Weber, B.A., 44, 59, 222
Webster, R.B., 142, 206
Weed, K.A., 166, 226
Weider, S., 10, 204
Weinberger, D.R., 20, 225
Weingartner, H., 142, 233
Weintraub, S., 91, 148, 152, 153, 156,
    223, 233
Weller, C., 59, 60, 91, 151, 158, 159,
    230, 233
Welsh, M.W., 168, 207
Wender, P., 166, 211
Wepman, J.M., 9, 221, 233
Wesley, A.L., 117, 222
Wesson, C., 234
West, J.F., 117, 215, 233
Whitaker, B., 132, 231
Widerstrom, A.H., 23, 233

Wiener, J., 129, 148, 154, 155, 233
Wiig, E.H., 10, 233
Wilkening, G.N.., 116, 212, 233
Willis, W.G., 11, 22–25, 35, 105, 110,
    135, 158, 177, 215, 233
Wilsher, C., 7, 67, 89, 165, 166, 231,
    233
Wilson, B.C., 4, 11, 43, 54, 61, 94,
    104, 124, 128, 129, 134, 234
Wilson, L.R., 234
Wirt, R.D., 153, 234
Witelson, S.F., 8, 234
Wittrock, M.C., 35, 217
Wolff, R.R., 229
Wolfson, D., 111, 224
Wolfus, B., 10, 43, 56, 234
Wong, B.Y.L., 129, 234
Wong, R., 129, 234
Woodcock, R.W., 129, 212

Yeni-Komshian, G.H., 8, 234
Yingling, C.D., 133, 209, 218
Ylvisaker, M., 137, 230
Yoshii, F., 212
Young, G.C., 42, 53, 121, 225
Ysseldyke, J.E., 4, 13, 16–18, 93, 98,
    176, 197, 202, 209, 226, 234

Zacks, R.T., 142, 213
Zametkin, A.J., 25, 234
Zigmond, N., 168, 234
Zimmerman, B., 132, 231
Zinkgraf, S.A., 145, 211

Subject Index

Accuracy disabled readers, 48
Achievement classification models
  clinical–inferential, 41, 42, 49–50
  empirical, 64, 71–73
Achievement scale, 153
Adjustment problems, interpersonal, 144–145
Affective antecedents, 141–142
Affective disturbances, 145–146
Aggression scales, 156
Alexia, 45, 46
Alexia and agraphia for numbers, 49
American Speech-Language-Hearing Association, 15
Amnesia visualis verbalis, 6
Anarithmetic dyscalculia, 49
Anomic disorders, 56
Anterior cortical unit, 27
Anxiety scales, 153, 156
Aphasia Screening Test, 111
Aptitude-treatment interactions (ATI), 176
Arithmetic
  ability in, and brain functioning, 30–33
  functional system for, 31–32
Arithmetic scales, 76, 115, 117
Arithmetic subtype, 89
Articulatory and graphomotor dyscoordination syndrome, 54
Assessment-treatment linkages, 137–138, 190–191
Association for Children and Adults with Learning Disabilities (ACLD), 14, 15

Attentional-sequential dyscalculia, 49
Attention-deficit Hyperactivity Disorder, 3, 15
Attention/memory deficits, 11–12
Audio-phonic dyslexia, 47, 51
Auditory dyslexia, 59
Auditory-linguistic subtype, 51
Auditory-perceptual deficits, 9–10
Auditory Skills Battery, 129
Autistic syndrome with echolalia, 57

Background markers, 100
Bakker's studies, on subtype-to-treatment linkages, 182–183, 184, 185, 186, 191
Balance model, 53
Behavioral classification models, 90–91
Behavioral-neuropsychological approach, to treatment, 174–175
Benton's Motor Impersistence Battery, 129
Benton Test of Visual Retention, 54, 124
Boder's reading subtype model, 42, 44–47
Boder's treatment model, 178, 180
Boder Test of Reading–Spelling Patterns, 46, 129, 130–133, 134
Bradylexia, 6
Brain
  differentiation of, 21, 22
  functional organization of, 23–29
Brain–behavior relationships, 169, 170–172

California Verbal Learning Test, 129
Carolina Longitudinal Learning Disabilities Project, 81
Case studies, early, 4–6
Case study methodology revisited, 12–13
Category Test, 111
Cattell Profile Pattern Coefficient, 63
Cause, of learning disability, 94, 95
Central auditory processing dyslexia, 51
Central nervous system (CNS), role of, 20
Child Behavior Checklist (CBCL), 156, 157
Child Neurology Society, 125
Children's Depression Inventory, 157
Children's Personality Questionnaire, 156–157
Children with Specific Learning Disability Act of 1969 (P.L. 91-380), 13
Chronicity, 94, 95
Classification, issues in, 92–106
    social-emotional, 140–141
Classification methods, empirical, 63, 69–71, 104–105
Classification models
    achievement, 41, 42, 49–50, 64, 71–73
    behavioral, 90–91
    clinical-inferential, 41–61
    combined, 44, 58–60, 67, 68, 83–90, 157–158
    empirical, 62–91, 150–151, 158–162
    neurocognitive, 42–43, 50–55, 64–66, 73–81
    neurolinguistic, 43–44, 56–58, 66–67, 81–83
    traditional, 148–149, 152–158
Classroom Behavior Inventory (CBI), 158, 160
Clinical-inferential classification methods, empirical methods versus, 104–105
Clinical-inferential classification models, 41–61
Clinical utility, of diagnostic process, 16
Cluster analysis, 69–70
Coding subtest, 76
Cognitive-behavioral interventions, 166–168

Cohen et al.'s study, on subtype-to-treatment linkages, 184, 187, 191
Colorado LD study, 98–99
Color Form Test, 111
Combined classification models
    clinical-inferential, 44, 58–60
    empirical, 67–68, 83–90
    social-emotional features and, 157–158
Communication skills scale, 159
Computerized tomography (CT), 135
Conceptual basis of subtype derivation, summary of advances in, 197
Conceptual disability, 154
Conceptual issues, 92–98
Conceptualizations, single-factor, 6–12
Conceptual models, of subtype-to-treatment linkages, 178–182
Conduct Disorder, 161
Congenital word blindness, 6
Cortical units, 25–29
    anterior, 27
    posterior, 26–27
Council for Learning Disabilities, 15, 18

Daily-Living skills scale, 159
Deep dyslexia, 57
Definitional issues, in learning disabilities, 13–19, 92–98
    summary of advances in, 196–197
Delayed cerebral dominance, 7–8
Delinquency scales, 153, 156
Denver Reading and Spelling Test, 47
Depression scales, 153, 156
Descriptive markers, 100
Developmental alexia, 6
Developmental considerations
    in classification and subtype derivation, 103–104
    functional brain organization and, 27–29
    in neuropsychological assessment, 136–137
Developmental Language Disorder, 93
Developmental neuropsychological approach, to treatment, 169–174
Developmental Test of Visual-Motor Integration, 119, 124
Development scale, 153

Digit Span subtest, 76, 128
Direct dyslexia, 58
Disabled achievers, 87
Distance measure, 63
Division for Children with Communication Disorders, 15
Doehring and colleagues empirical classification model, 84–85
Dual-subtype models, in neurocognitive classification, 50–53
Durrell Analysis of Reading Difficulty, 128
Durrell Oral Reading, 128
Dyscalculia, 49
Dyseidetic dyslexia, 45
Dyslexia
    audio-phonic, 47, 51
    auditory, 59
    central auditory processing, 51
    deep, 57
    direct, 58
    dyseidetic, 45
    dysphonetic, 45, 46
    genetic, 51
    L-type, 53
    minimal neurological, 51
    phonological, 58
    P-type, 53
    surface, 57
    visual, 58, 59
    visual-perceptual, 51
    visuo-spatial, 47, 51, 52, 123–124
    word, 58
Dyslexic patterns, 45–46
Dysphonemic sequencing disorders, 56
Dysphonetic dyslexia, 45, 46

Early case studies, 4–6
Eclectic test batteries, 122–129
Education for All Handicapped Children Act of 1975 (P.L. 94-142), 13, 14, 109
Electroencephalography (EEG), 46, 136
Embedded Figures Test, 78
Empirical classification methods, 63, 69–71
    versus clinical-inferential, 104–105

Empirical classification models, 62–91
    social-emotional features and, 150–151, 158–162
Environmental demands, 172
Exclusionary criteria, issues with, 16–17
Expressive language subtype, 54
Expressive speech scale, 115, 117, 118

Failure explanation, 143
Family Relations scale, 153, 161
Family variables, in treatment studies, 190
Finger Oscillation Test, 111
Fingertip Number Writing, 111
Fixed battery approach, 110–122
Florida Kindergarten Screening Battery, 129
Florida Longitudinal Project, 8, 102, 103
Flynn's study, on subtype-to-treatment linkages, 184, 186, 191
Full-Scale IQ, 117–118, 157
Functional brain organization, 23–29
Functional system(s), 29–37
    for arithmetic, 31–32
    for reading, 34
Future directions, 200–201

General deficiency subtype, 80
General language deficit subtype, 80
Genetic dyslexia, 51
Gerstmann group, 51
Globally deficient language subtype, 54
Grip Strength Test, 111
Group M, 84
Group R, 84, 85

Halstead–Reitan Neuropsychological Battery (HRNB), 86, 110, 111, 114–115, 116, 119, 121, 122, 124
Halstead–Reitan Neuropsychological Test Battery for Children, 111, 112–113
Health Research Extension Act of 1985 (P. L. 99-158), 15
Hemispheric lateralization, 25–26

Heterogeneous groups, research on so-
cial-emotional features with, 140–
147
Hierarchical agglomerative clustering, 70
High IQ subtype, 51
Historical foundations, and definitional
issues, 3–19
Homogenous groups, research on social-
emotional features with, 147–162
Hynd and Cohen's treatment model, 178,
179, 180, 182, 187, 191, 192
Hynd's treatment model, 180–182, 191
Hyperactivity scales, 153, 156

Illinois Test of Psycholinguistic Abilities
(ITPA), 53, 54, 124
Inattention/Overactivity scale, 156
Individual Performance Test, 111
Information subtest, 76
Intellectual batteries, 120–122
Intellectual Processes scale, 115, 117
Intellectual screening scale, 153
Intelligence scale models, 74–75
Interagency Committee on Learning Disa-
bilities (ICLD), 15, 196, 201
International Reading Association, 15
Interpersonal adjustment problems, 144–
145
Intersensory integration deficits, 10–11
IQ
Full-Scale, 117–118, 157
high, subtype of, 51
low, subtype of, 51
Performance, 51, 52, 53, 74, 118, 156
Verbal, 51, 52, 53, 59, 74, 118, 156
IQ-achievement discrepancies, 86
Iterative partitioning, 70

Kaufman Assessment Battery for Children (K-ABC), 47, 75, 116–117,
121, 122, 177

Labeling, social-emotional issues and,
140–141
Language-based subtype models, 56–57
Language disorder subtype, 54, 154

Language disorder syndrome, 54
Language retarded subtype, 51
Lateral Dominance Examination, 111
Learning disabled single diagnosis (LD),
157–158
Learning disabled with social-emotional
disturbance, multiple diagnoses
(LD/SED), 157–158
Learning disability, coining of term, 4
Learning disability subtyping
advances in, summary of, 196–200
definitional issues in, 13–19, 92–98,
196–197
Learning Quotient, 132
Left and Right Sensimotor Scales, 115–
116
Left-hemisphere dysfunction subtype, 155
Lesions, effects of, on arithmetical abil-
ity, 30–31
Likeability scale, 156
Linguistic models, reading-based, 57–58
Linguistic subtype, 89
Low IQ subtype, 51
L-type dyslexia, 53
Luria–Nebraska Neuropsychological Bat-
tery, 50
Luria–Nebraska Neuropsychological Bat-
tery—Children's Revision
(LNNB-C), 89, 113, 115–118,
119, 122
Lyon and colleagues empirical classifica-
tion model, 78–79
Lyon's studies, on subtype-to-treatment
linkages, 185, 186, 188, 191, 192

Manual-Dexterity Test, 128
Marching Test, 111
Matching Familiar Figures Test, 128
Matching Pictures Test, 111
Mattis et al.'s assessment model, 54,
124–125
Mattis et al.'s treatment model, 178, 180
McCarthy Scales of Children's Abilities,
121
Memory and retrieval problems subtype,
54
Memory deficits, 11–12
Memory for Faces Test, 128

Memory scale, 115, 117
Mental Retardation, 3, 93
Metacognitive strategies, 167–168
Methodology, case study
    revisitation of, 12–13
    summary of advances in, 197 198
Minimal neurological dyslexia, 51
Minimal severity, 88
Minnesota Percepto-Diagnostic Test, 117
Mixed pattern subtype, neurolinguistic,
    59
Mixed subtype, of language-based disor-
    ders, 56
Models, classification, see Classification
    models
Motor dyscontrol subtype, 55
Motor-Free Visual Perception Test, 119
Motor scales, 115, 116, 117, 159
Multiple-neurocognitive-subtype models,
    53–55
Multiple subtype focus, social-emotional
    features and, 154 157
Myklebust Learning Quotient, 132

Naming deficits subtype, 80
National Advisory Committee on the
    Handicapped (NACH), 13, 14
National Joint Committee for Learning
    Disabilities (NJCLD), 13, 14, 15,
    196
Nervous system development, 21 23
Neurocognitive classification models
    clinical-inferential, 42–43, 50–55
    empirical, 64–66, 73–81
Neurodiagnostic measures, 135–136
Neurolinguistic classification models
    clinical-inferential, 43–44, 56–58
    empirical, 66–67, 81–83
Neuropsychological approach(es)
    to assessment, 110–134
        elements of, 134–135
        issues in, 134–138
    to treatment, 169–177
        evaluation of effectiveness in, 173–
        177
        prognosis in, 172–173
        treatment intervention plan in, 173
Neuropsycholocial battery models, 75–81

Neuropsychological foundations, 20–37
Neuropsychological Investigation for
    Children (NEPSY), 113, 119–
    120, 122
Neuropsychological key approach, 128
Neuropsychological strength approach, to
    treatment, 175–177
No deficits, 54
Nonlateralized dysfunction subtype, 155
Nonspecific learning disability subtype,
    72
Nonverbal perceptual-organization-output
    disability (NPOOD), 153
Normal learner subtype, 79, 80
Normal pattern with low reading achieve-
    ment subtype, 59
Northwestern Syntax Screening Test, 128
Nosology on Disorders of Cortical Func-
    tion in Children, 125

Obrzut assessment model, 126–128
Obsessive-Compulsive scale, 156
Orton Dyslexia Society, 15

Pathognomonic scale, 115
Peabody Individual Achievement Test
    (PIAT), 158, 160
Peabody Picture Vocabulary Test
    (PPVT), 72
Peabody Picture Vocabulary Test-Revised
    (PPVT-R), 121
Performance IQ (PIQ), on WISC, 51, 52,
    53, 74, 118, 156
Personality Inventory for Children (PIC),
    153, 161
Pervasiveness of problem manifestations,
    94, 95
Pervasive severity, 88
Pharmacological interventions, 165–166
Phonological dyslexia, 58
Phonologic-syntactic subtype, 56
Pirozzolo clinical-inferential classification
    model, 51–52
Posterior cortical unit, 26–27
Prognosis
    classification and, 191
    and treatment, 172–173

Progressive Figures Test, 111
Psychosis scale, 153
P-type dyslexia, 53
Purdue Pegboard, 54, 124

Q-type factor analysis, 70–71, 74–75,
    76, 84, 85, 89, 120, 161

Rate disabled readers, 48
Raven's Coloured or Standard Progres-
    sive Matrices, 51, 54, 121, 124
Reading
    ability in, and brain functioning,
        33–37
    functional system for, 34–36
Reading-based linguistic models, 57–58
Reading scales, 72, 73, 76, 115, 117,
    118
Reading-Spelling-Arithmetic-deficient
    subtype, 50
Reading subtype models, 42, 44–50, 89
Receptive language subtype, 54
Receptive Speech scale, 115, 117
Recoding readers, 48
Reitan–Indiana Neuropsychological Test
    Battery for Children, 111, 112
Research
    on Boder's reading subtype model, 46–
        47
    conceptual framework for subtyping,
        95–98
    on neuropsychological strength ap-
        proach to treatment, 176–177
    on social-emotional features
        with heterogeneous groups, 140–147
        140–147
        with homogeneous groups, 147–162
    on subtype-to-treatment linkages, 182–
        189
    in treatment, continued, 191–192
Rhythm scale, 115, 117
Right-hemisphere/bilateral dysfunction
    subtype, 155
Right hemisyndrome with mixed lan-
    guage disorder, 56
Rourke and colleagues empirical classifi-
    cation model, 76–77

Sampling issues, 98–101
Satz and colleagues empirical classifica-
    tion model, 77–78
Schizoid scale, 156
School variables, in treatment studies,
    190
Seashore Rhythm Test, 111
Sensory Perceptual Examination, 111
Sentence Repetition Subtests, 125
Sequential disability, 154
Sequential Memory Test, 128
Severe autism with mutism, 57
Severity of problem manifestations, 94,
    95
Simeon et al.'s study, on subtype-to-
    treatment linkages, 182, 183
Similarity measure, 63
Simultaneous and Sequential Processing
    Scales, 47
Single-factor conceptualizations, 6–12
Single subtype focus, social-emotional
    features and, 152–153
Slow learners, 86–87
Social-emotional features, 139–163
    antecedents and consequences of, 140–
        143
    manifestations of, 143–146
Social-emotional variables, in treatment
    studies, 189–190
Social Skills scales, 153, 159
Social-Withdrawal scale, 156
Somatic Complaints scale, 156
Somatic Conern scale, 153
S-O-R-K-C framework, 174–175
Sound Blending Subtest, 54, 124
Spatial disability, 154
Spatial disorder subtype, 154
Spatial dyscalculia, 49
Special-purpose measures, 129–134
Specific language disturbance subtype, 55
Speech–Sounds Perception Test, 111
Spelling-Arithmetic deficient subtype, 50
Spelling percentiles,72, 73, 76
Spelling subtype models, 47–50
Spreen–Benton Token Test, 119, 124, 128
SRA Basic Reading Series, 180
Stanford–Binet Intelligence Scale, Fourth
    Edition, 121
Statistical criteria, issues with, 17–18

Subcortical unit, 23–25
Substantive markers, 100
Subtype derivation, issues in, 92–106
Subtype-to-treatment linkages, 177–189
Subtype-to-treatment planning, issues in, 189–192
Summary, 195–200
Surface dyslexia, 57
Syntactic-pragmatic subtype, 56

Tactile Finger Recognition, 111
Tactile Form Recognition, 111
Tactile scale, 115, 116, 117
Tactual Performance Test, 111
Target achievers, 86
Target Test, 111
Task Force on Nosology, 93, 94
Teacher Rating Scale, 156
Theoretical/conceptual basis, of subtype derivation, summary of advances in, 197
Token Test, 119, 124
Token Test for Children, 128
Topical markers, 101
Toward Affective Development Kit, 154
Traditional models, social-emotional features and, 148–149, 152–158
Trail-making Test, 111
Treatment, 164–192
    neuropsychologically based, 169–177
    unidimensional, 165–169
Type A, 85
Type O, 85
Type S, 85

UCLA Marker Variable System, 99–101, 104
Uncommunicative scale, 156
Underachievers, 87
Unidimensional treatment approaches, 165–169

Variables
    in classification and subtype derivation, selection of, 101–102

in subtype-to-treatment planning, 189–190
Verbal auditory agnosia, 57
Verbal IQ (VIQ), of WISC, 51, 52, 53, 59, 74, 118, 156
Verbal memory disorder, 56
Vineland Adaptive Behavior Scale (VABS), 159
Visual dyslexia, 58, 59
Visual-perceptual deficits, 8–9
Visual-perceptual disorder syndrome, 54
Visual-perceptual dyslexia, 51
Visual-perceptual subtype, 89
Visual scale, 115, 117
Visuo-motor deficits subtype, 80
Visuo-spatial disability subtype, 55
Visuo-spatial dyslexia, 47, 51, 52, 123–124

Wechsler Adult Intelligence Scale (WAIS), 51, 54, 124
Wechsler Adult Intelligence Scale—Revised (WAIS-R), 74–75
Wechsler Intelligence Scale for Children (WISC), 51, 53, 54, 59, 73, 76, 77, 114, 124, 154
Wechsler Intelligence Scale for Children—Revised (WISC-R), 51, 74–75, 86, 111, 114, 117, 118, 121, 124, 128, 156, 158, 160, 177
Wechsler Preschool and Primary Scale of Intelligence (WPPSI), 111
Whole-word subtype, 48
Wide Range Achievement Test (WRAT), 48, 49, 50, 54, 72–73, 76, 86, 111, 115, 117, 118, 125
Wilson and Risucci assessment model, 54, 128–129
Wisconsin Card Sorting Test, 129
Withdrawal scales, 153, 156
Woodcock–Johnson Psycho-Educational Battery, 50, 124
Woodcock–Johnson Tests of Cognitive Ability, 121
Word amblyopia, 6
Word blindness, 4
Word dyslexia, 58
Writing scale, 115, 117, 118